# Saving Your
# American
# Dream

## How to Secure a Safe Mortgage,
## Protect Your Home,
## and Improve Your Financial Future

## JASON BIRO

BENBELLA BOOKS, INC.

Dallas, Texas

BENBELLA

BenBella Books, Inc.
6440 N. Central Expressway, Suite 503
Dallas, TX 75206
www.benbellabooks.com
Send feedback to feedback@benbellabooks.com

Printed in the United States of America
10 9 8 7 6 5 4 3 2 1

Library of Congress Cataloging-in-Publication Data is available for this title.

Proofreading by Erica Lovett and Gregory Teague
Printed by Bang Printing

Distributed by Perseus Distribution
perseusdistribution.com

To place orders through Perseus Distribution:
Tel: 800-343-4499
Fax: 800-351-5073
E-mail: orderentry@perseusbooks.com

Significant discounts for bulk sales are available.
Please contact Glenn Yeffeth at glenn@benbellabooks.com or 214-750-3628.

A campaign to restore hope . . .
one home at a time

# Contents

# Acknowledgments

This book is the result of the efforts of so many. To my wife and business partner Carolyn, who has the ability to creatively and organizationally complete everything that's been on our plate. Over the years we've refined our strengths and weaknesses in order to complement each other's work. Our journey together with this book is a testament not only to our partnership, but to our goal to get out there and make a difference.

It's been so important to have the complete support of our families—and we've had it tenfold. To our family and part-time focus group: my parents, John and Regina Biro, and Carolyn's sister, Christine Walker, who has put in countless hours behind the scenes. We also want to thank Christine's husband, Brent, for supporting her total involvement and many late nights working with us on our campaign. To Julia Archer and G. Glen Friedman: thank you for working together with us as if this project were your own. We wouldn't have been able to do it without you. And to all of our friends, who haven't really seen us for a full year: thanks for not forgetting about us.

We'd also like to thank Glenn Yeffeth, our publisher; Leah Wilson, our editor; and the entire BenBella Books crew. You've allowed us so much hands-on involvement and have overwhelmingly supported our needs in order to make this book a reality. You all have been true partners throughout the process, and, for this, we can't express our gratitude enough.

# Introduction

This book is dedicated to you. But who are you?

You are one of the millions of homeowners who are struggling to make their mortgage payments, month after month. You may be one of millions more who are in the process of losing their homes, and don't know where to turn. You are the parent who has invested in the American Dream of homeownership, and you want to protect your family and your home. You are the couple who is buying a home for the first time and are looking to make all the right choices, including the right loan. Or you may be someone who wants to own a home, but, in today's economy, you just don't know where to start.

Maybe you have already suffered through a foreclosure, have lost your home, and would one day like to own again. Maybe you were a victim of predatory lending, but never knew it. Or maybe you just need some help in picking up the pieces.

You could be one of the many people who are simply perplexed by home finance and anything to do with mortgages in general. You could be anyone, really, who wants to protect their biggest investment and who wants to protect their finances overall.

You are a person who is ready to make some positive change in your life. And you are ready to make a new start.

You, like so many other people, are someone who needs help with one of the most important parts of life: homeownership and financing the American Dream.

Since 1996, I have helped over 2,000 individuals and families fulfill the dream of owning a home. As both a mortgage consultant and partner of my own mortgage firm, I've helped homeowners of all kinds not only to secure financing, but also to make some sense of the confusing home finance process.

Throughout my career, I've also managed and worked side-by-side with over 100 mortgage consultants and brokers. I've heard their stories and have seen what their clients have experienced. And I've often had to step in to make things right. It's pretty fair to say that I have been confronted with every type of transaction and situation imaginable. I've also realized one important fact: the majority of people are downright afraid of financing.

When asked about buying a home, mortgages, or lending, most people seem to have a basic knowledge of the subject, but also have a horror story or two. Or three. Maybe it was their own experience with a broker or bank (or maybe it was a story about their sister, their friend, or their neighbor) but at the end of the day, most people are very reluctant to trust anyone in the business of mortgage finance. It's my goal to change that perception and ease that fear.

Over the past two years, as the lending markets collapsed and the economy has declined, I've spent time and resources to help people stay in their homes, manage their debt, and make a plan for the future. I am out there, working one-on-one with people just like you. I've seen the effects of the housing bubble firsthand; I see what's out there, and it's not pretty. I know what you are faced with, and have written this book and dedicated my time and effort to making a difference for you.

Why am I doing this? Well, that's a good question.

## Belief and Purpose

It's so important to wholeheartedly believe in what you are doing, and I share this sense of purpose with my wife Carolyn. Our personal mission for *Saving Your American Dream* began in 2007, when the crisis in real estate and home finance was becoming transparent, and it hit us very close to home—literally. Right in our own neighborhood, we saw the desperation and despair a family was faced with from losing a job, their home, and their security, and it was too much for us to take. Around this same time, I started to get calls from people by the dozens weekly, all looking for advice: What's going on with the markets? My mortgage? My home?

So many individuals in real estate, lending, and home building all contributed to this giant mess and then bailed out, leaving homeowners behind. As a professional, I felt I needed to share my knowledge, think outside the box, and contribute in any way I could. My wife and I decided to focus on how we could take our experience and professional strengths and utilize them to help other families and educate anyone who wished to learn. But we also wanted to provide assistance and resources in a way that would impact as many people as possible. And that was how this book, and our campaign, was born.

After months of intensive research, planning, and focus, we began to realize our collaboration would result in something so meaningful, educational, and positive that we had only one choice . . . Full steam ahead!

## What's so Special About Saving Your American Dream?

*Saving Your American Dream* is a part of a much bigger campaign, a campaign to help anyone who's been impacted by the housing and lending crisis. It's a philanthropic solution for some, and a life-changing event for others. While I don't have all the answers, and I certainly don't have a sweeping economic solution for the entire country, I do have many years of experience and sound common sense that I can share with you. I am also giving you a commitment that goes beyond the written word.

This book comes with my personal invitation to make a difference in your life: I want you to tell me your story. Tell me about yourself, your life, your home, and why you need help. I've established a national fund to provide direct financial assistance to many individuals and families throughout the country who are in genuine need. And just by reading and registering this book at my website, www.savingyouramericandream.com, you'll have the opportunity to receive this assistance. I'll be helping readers with their mortgage payments, providing advice and funding to help save homes from foreclosure, and working with readers one-on-one to develop the tools and strategies to one day own a home again. At the end of this book, you'll find a chapter devoted to giving you more information about the campaign, including how you can register your book and get started right away.

My website also provides other resources that can help you. With this book, you'll receive access to an entire online community: expanded book content and updates, financial tools, special partnerships, and more. As the lending industry changes further, I'll keep you updated through the website. You can even log in online to ask me questions, join in the discussion, network with others, share resources, and maybe even help others yourself.

## What Will You Be Able to Take Away from This Book?

• *A sense that you are not alone.* I've worked with and counseled many people, and I've learned a lot from their lives and situations. By sharing their stories with you, it's easy to see just how common and stressful issues in real estate and finance can be—and what lessons we can learn from them. I've changed the names and a few of the places, but the facts and advice remain true.

• *A refresher on the basics.* I'll cover some basic principles from the worlds of lending and real estate, and I'll help you to see how you can make these basics, from homeowners insurance to credit ratings, work for you.

• *An insider's take on the finance industry.* Many industry terms can be pretty baffling and downright confusing, but they don't have to be. In each chapter, I'll explain how the finance industry works as if I were consulting with you one-on-one. Understanding how lending, mortgages, and finance work will help you to make better decisions, now and in the future, regarding your home and your personal finances.

• *Solid advice and explanations.* Over the years I've had so many clients ask about easy tips, but, honestly, I see a red flag anytime anyone talks about a "hot tip." Instead, I'll provide solid advice with sound explanations that will save you money and help you to protect your home.

• *Ways you can protect yourself.* I'll take some time to deconstruct what happened in the mortgage, lending, and credit collapse, and how things have changed. I'll also talk about some of the perils in the industry, and, most important, I will outline a plan for how you can protect yourself from becoming a victim, and how you can protect your home.

• *Relevant studies and facts.* As boring as they can sometimes seem, studies and facts provide important insight. So I've taken the most important facts and statistics and have compiled them for you here. I'll discuss why they are important and what you can learn from them.

• *A plan of action.* Information is great, but you have to know what to do with it. I'll provide you with the action steps you need to make immediate changes, as well as long-term plans to guide you through larger issues.

## It Starts Now

I've dedicated this book to helping you. Now it's your turn. Make the commitment to yourself to read through the entire book. Sure, you could skip to the end and miss all of the great stories, explanations, advice, and plans, but trust me, the end of the book will always be there. Stay the course, read on, and take the time to really think about what I am telling you and how it can help you. Start taking steps now to improve your situation. I know for a fact you will find something valuable and helpful within these pages.

I know it's not always easy to find a starting point. Let this book be the starting point for you.

# PART I

# Securing a Safe Mortgage

. . .

## How to Understand Lending, Find the Right Loan, and Secure a Safe Mortgage

No matter what's happening with the economy, most people will need financing to purchase a home. And while some homeowners have a general idea of how home finance and lending works, the truth is, the majority of people don't have the information they need to secure a safe, stable mortgage. Are you in this majority?

To begin to understand home finance—and how to make it work for you—we first need to take a look at the new realities in lending. A lot has happened in the past five years. We all know we have experienced a turbulent market. But what exactly happened, and how does this affect how lending works? How does this impact the loan you have now, or the loan you may want to apply for in the future? Who are the players associated with finance, and more importantly, how do you know who you can turn to and trust?

In the following chapters, I'll explain the basics behind lending, loans, and the mortgage process in general. In particular, I'll focus on what's changed in the industry, where the money for your loan comes from and where it goes, and who decides how this money is loaned to you. I'll give you a great foundation for understanding the loans you can choose from, and advice on who can help guide you through the process.

You'll be able to apply this knowledge either to your current loan or the next time you're considering financing. You'll even be able to use this information to help you keep or protect your home. To keep your American Dream alive, this is where we need to start.

# 1

# Then and Now

## Why the Real Estate and Lending Industries Collapsed…and What We All Can Learn

t's safe to say that if you are reading this book, owning a home is important to you. Despite the instability of the housing and lending markets, homeownership is still important to many of us, myself included.

But let's take a step back. What should we really expect when we own a home? With the last few years of incredible profits and unprecedented losses, it's easy to forget how homeownership *should* work. We need to remember that for years, decades even, homeownership was very safe and secure.

Why are we drawn to owning a home? Purchasing a home is the largest investment most families will ever make, with good reason. In theory, owning a home comes down to two basic principles: savings and stability.

Let's start with savings. When you rent a home, the money you spend is no longer yours; the money you pay in rent is gone forever. Owning, on the other hand, builds *equity*: while part of your mortgage payment goes to paying your lender, the rest goes to building ownership in your property. For example, let's say your home is worth $200,000. The balance on your mortgage is $150,000. This difference of $50,000 is your equity. Once you sell your home (and after you pay back your lender for what's left on your loan), the money that is left over is yours to keep. In this respect, your home becomes a long-term savings account, and each month as you pay your mortgage, you are actually adding to your savings.

In addition to the amount you build in equity every month, many homes also appreciate in value each year. For decades, homes steadily appreciated at a national rate of 5 to 6 percent per year. Generations of Americans have invested in their homes, and benefited as their homes maintained or grew in value, adding to their overall net worth and personal wealth. In fact, a large percentage of the average American's total wealth is in their home's equity.

When you own a home, you also save on your income taxes. Both your home's mortgage interest and property taxes are deducted from your income taxes. Own a home, and you owe less to the government. Not a bad deal.

Second, a home provides for stability. In your own home, you—not a landlord—are master of your domain: you can paint, remodel, customize, and repair as you see fit. For many, a home provides a stable foundation for raising a family, and the general peace of mind that comes from knowing you have roots in your community and a place of your own to come home to.

Unfortunately today, in many ways, homeownership is far from this ideal. Homeowners are faced with a decline in home value and equity, a loss of appreciation, and a feeling of general instability, which is a stark contrast to the "boom" years and to the history of homeownership in general.

## The Beginning of the Boom

I've called Florida my home for quite some time now, and have lived in both Broward and Palm Beach counties. So I witnessed it firsthand when Florida, especially southeast Florida, led the country in the housing boom. Starting in 2001, and for five to six years after, it seemed like there was no end in sight: the real estate market grew rapidly, with home values appreciating at more than 50 percent in many areas. This same pattern of wildfire growth was seen nation-wide, from states including California, Florida, and New York to entire regions throughout the Northeast and Southwest. What had started in a few states quickly spread throughout the nation.

For several years, it appeared that everyone was happily reaping the rewards of the housing boom. Just think about how many industries are directly attached to real estate in some way: the finance industry, retail home improvement, utilities, telecommunications and cable, roofing, home repair and restoration, home furnishings, storage . . . The list goes on and on. Even restaurants and entertainment venues are affected; happy homeowners mean healthy consumer spending and financially healthy communities. Shopping centers, plazas, and new businesses all sprung up during the boom, often at alarming rates. Homeowners and businesses alike began to *expect* this level of growth. These unrealistic expectations took on a life of their own—for everyone.

Unfortunately, this same relationship between homeowners and businesses holds true in bad times as well, which is why the real estate crisis is having such a big effect on the rest of the economy. The real estate industry is in such a decimated state today that it has crippled real estate firms, lenders, insurance agencies, appraisers, builders and general contractors, retailers, the credit market, and even the government.

As consumers, we should all expect that industries will have their highs and their lows—these peaks and valleys are what make industries and businesses stronger. During the peaks, businesses thrive. During the valleys, only the strongest companies prevail, providing a stronger foundation as the industry rebuilds. And even though things will eventually get better, we all need to learn from our mistakes, and learn fast, so we don't repeat them. I am not saying to never take a chance, invest, or purchase again, or to proceed with so much caution that you paralyze yourself. I'm also not saying that things will necessarily go back to the way they used to be—but honestly, going back to the unrealistic homeownership expectations from the boom is a not good thing anyway. What I *am* saying is that knowledge is power. Don't give up. The markets will eventually recover. Until then, I will show you what you *can* do, and what you *can* control.

To truly be able to understand not only what happened, but how it all started—and how it will impact our future—we need to start at the beginning. From carefully examining what happened during the boom years, who was involved, and why the housing market crashed, there are a few things we all can learn.

## The Main Players

During the boom, people from all walks of life tried to supplement their incomes by jumping aboard the bandwagon of investing in real estate for quick returns. Many self-proclaimed real estate gurus added "investor" to their resumés, feeding off the frenzy created by builders, lenders, real estate agents, and mortgage brokers.

Builder after builder purchased any available land, and these once-vacant parcels were fitted with residential plans, creating acres of development after development. No matter who the builder was— or where the land was, for that matter—nothing stood in the way of the real estate boom, which funneled all the way down to the pre-existing home market. Any home was a hot commodity, and the more homes you owned or could get your hands on, the better. Even first-time homeowners dove in, buying as many homes as possible.

The real estate frenzy had long arms and soon pulled in the finance industry. New loans were quickly created to accommodate the growing demand for real estate, turning mortgage finance into a cut-throat industry overnight. With so many buyers needing financing, lenders found themselves in heavy competition with one another to win the business of new borrowers. New borrowers meant new profit, and banks and lenders bid against themselves by lowering interest rates and developing new loan programs to entice home buyers. As the demand for loans grew, financing expanded even further, and eventually the massive subprime lending market was born.

Most of the boom's new potential borrowers couldn't qualify for standard financing; they just didn't have the income, savings, or credit needed to purchase a home. Lenders considered these borrowers to be *subprime*—below their usual lending standards. But instead of turning these borrowers away, lenders created new risky loan programs to fit the buyers' needs, introducing new waves of 100 percent financing, 1 percent teaser interest rates, and "no money down" programs. Borrowers were thrilled! Now they could purchase with very little up-front cost, very low interest rates, and no down payments. This fact alone made it possible for millions of people to purchase homes who could not have before, making the expansion of subprime lending a defining turning point within the mortgage industry.

With the growing need for home financing, more and more people became mortgage brokers, and the number of active brokers literally quadrupled in a year's time. This created an extremely unstable pool of brokers who were simply too inexperienced to properly advise their clients. Worse still, many of these brokers entered into the finance industry with the intention of making a quick profit themselves. These brokers didn't understand loans or lending, and they often placed borrowers into questionable or risky loans solely to increase their own profit.

The real estate "buzz" was so powerful—and all parties were so blinded by the potential profit—that new real estate and lending practices were never questioned. It was too fast, and too much. From lenders to finance professionals, to investors, to buyers, the driving force was the almighty dollar. Greed was king.

Here's an in-depth look at the key players, and how they contributed to the lending implosion:

▸ **Lenders**—Lenders created risky loans that resulted in a lending free-for-all. These new loans lacked many of the characteristics that had kept lending stable for decades. Essentially anyone who was interested was quickly ushered into the world of homeownership—including those with bad credit, no employment, and no purchase history. These new groups of homeowners meant more profit for lenders, so who was complaining? Certainly not the lenders. As the demand for homes increased, so did the number of lenders offering new loan programs. For five years straight, more and more lenders opened their doors, ready for business.

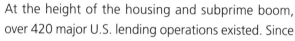

**The Lending Implosion**

At the height of the housing and subprime boom, over 420 major U.S. lending operations existed. Since early 2006, over 300 lenders have shut down completely. In 2009, less than 100 remain.

▸ **Wall Street**—Wall Street tempted investors and offered great returns by packaging loans into mortgage-backed securities, known as CMOs (Collateralized Mortgage Obligations) or CDOs (Collateralized Debt Obligations). The concept was simple and sounded great: investors purchased large groups of mortgages, borrowers made their mortgage payments, and investors were paid back nicely with interest. But many investors didn't know that newly created, risky *subprime* mortgages were being quietly grouped with safe, secure mortgages into CMOs and CDOs. As more people purchased homes and home prices rose, so did the value of these securities, and investors reaped the rewards.

With rising profits, investors clamored to buy more and more mortgage-backed securities . . . and so more and more risky and exotic loans were developed by lenders to meet the insatiable demands of Wall Street. Soon, entire sectors of the economy were directly or indirectly investing in CMOs and CDOs. When the housing bubble burst and homeowners defaulted on their mortgages, the value of these securities burst too, and many of the businesses and industries that had invested heavily in CMOs and CDOs lost millions, sending the economy into a tailspin. Today, these loan securities have lost billions of dollars in value.

▸ **Mortgage Brokers**—With the promise of fast money, a career as a mortgage broker became the "hot" new trend. And the mortgage industry made it easy; even today, a professional license is not required to broker loans. Because lenders offered brokers incentives and large commissions for promoting and placing loans (especially the riskiest loans, which offered the most profit to the lender), brokers often looked the other way or even bent the rules to get borrowers to sign on the dotted line.

Besides, because brokers weren't lending their *own* money—they were just paid to place the loan—many didn't feel responsible if the loan defaulted later or for making sure the loan was even right for the borrower in the first place. Many lenders had a standard policy that as long as the loan didn't default within the first month, there were no consequences for the broker, and the broker's commissions were safe.

▸ **Real Estate Professionals**—During the boom, the real estate industry also became overly saturated with real estate brokers and agents. Real estate values had risen 10, 20, sometimes even 30 percent in a relatively short period, and this rise, combined with the heavy demand for homes, caused the number of new realtors to soar. The sky seemed to be the limit for home values—and for real estate commissions. Many new, inexperienced realtors inflated property values, creating selling prices based on opinion rather than appraised value.

Real estate appraisers, who usually kept home prices in check, were swayed by the frenzy of the market, by incredible documented jumps in value from recent sales, and by pressure to "close the sale" from both realtors and lenders. With all parties happily agreeing to higher values, rapidly rising home prices created an urgency to purchase before prices rose even higher. And prices did indeed climb higher, creating a false sense of security for many homeowners and, ultimately, creating artificial home values.

**DEFINITION** **What Is Artificial Value?**

How much is a property worth? That's a very important question. A professional and licensed appraiser is solely responsible for determining a property's value. An appraiser evaluates several things, from physical characteristics like lot size, square footage, age, condition, upgrades, and location to how a property compares to recent sales and similar properties in the area. When a third party influences an appraisal, and a property's value is reported *higher* than it should be, this increased value is "artificial." Some common ways to create artificial value include ignoring similar properties in the area which would decrease a property's price, and inflating or overstating a home's features or upgrades. During the boom, artificial value had a snowball effect: a home's value would be artificially increased, the home would sell at a higher price, and this high artificial price would then be used as a benchmark for the next sale.

▸ **Builders**—While the lending industry has been handed the biggest share of the blame for the housing and lending crash, many builders are just as responsible. Simply put, builders overbuilt, overextended, overpriced, and overestimated the need for new homes, causing a glut of housing inventory that will last for years. Driven by profit, builders quickly developed vacant land, built new homes and neighborhoods, and then sent home prices through the roof by setting prices based on demand instead of actual cost or appraised value. Due to a lack of regulation, builders could easily determine their own profit. As homebuyers and investors couldn't get enough of the newly built homes, builders got even greedier, charging inflated prices for upgrades, using shady tactics to lock in sales, and charging home buyers exorbitant and unnecessary builder's fees.

▸ **Borrowers**—During the boom, many people were lured by low payments, creative financing, "cheap money," and rapidly increasing home values. People who previously had been shut out of the dream of homeownership were welcomed with open arms by lenders and mortgage brokers. Many of these borrowers didn't question if they *really* could afford a home; most believed home prices would always rise, so they would always have a comfortable safety net. If money got tight, they reasoned, they could simply refinance and take out a new loan to tap into their home's profits. Many homeowners ended up using their homes as giant ATM machines, and home buying quickly became a get-rich-quick business, attracting flippers, investors, and speculators. With so many people buying houses, homeownership rates skyrocketed. At the height of the boom, national homeowner-ship rates topped 70 percent, a record high.

Eventually, the housing market shifted from a seller's market to a buyer's market as houses became easier to buy, but harder to sell. Too many homes were for sale. Too many people had become investors. Builders had built too much. With so much inventory, sellers could no longer demand high home prices. Homeowners suddenly owned properties they could no longer sell—or afford. As interest rates ad-justed, mortgage payments for many homeowners increased, the number of mortgage defaults grew, and the waves of foreclosures began. Payments to Wall Street investors stopped. Banks stopped lending, and the credit crunch began.

Not surprisingly, the impact of the housing bust was not limited to the United States. Along the way, many foreign countries decided they too wanted a piece of the American pie. Investors in countries from Germany to Japan poured as much as $1.2 trillion into lending investments and mortgage-backed securities in 2005 and 2006. When the bubble burst, the pop was felt around the globe.

## The Rise and Fall of Flipping

For years, ordinary people went about their lives, with little or no in-terest in becoming real estate investors. In fact, investment properties were often seen as being burdensome and time-intensive: you had to fix up homes and then find renters or buyers. But the conditions at the start of the boom were like the perfect storm for investing in real estate: lots of money to lend, relaxed lending guidelines, low real estate inventory, and a brand-new group of buyers. Established real estate investors found they were selling homes with no effort. And like a virus, word started to spread.

During the boom, people who shouldn't have been purchasing even *one* home were purchasing two and three homes to try to amplify their potential profit. Most of these buyers weren't concerned about financing and mortgage costs, and for many buyers, it didn't even matter if they could actually *afford* the homes in the first place. They assumed they would be holding on to the homes just long enough to "flip" them, by selling the home before any payment was due. And for a very short period of time, this was almost true. Before the market spiraled out of control, and before everyone started to invest, many investors and short-term homeowners were able to quickly flip and sell homes, making money hand over fist. Flipping became its own urban legend.

---

**Flipping**

"Flipping" is the practice of purchasing and then quickly selling a property before any mortgage payments are due. In short, flipping involves selling a home by assigning a sales contract (which transfers ownership of the home to a new buyer) or by selling to a new buyer shortly after taking ownership of a home.

---

For many, flipping was an exotic way to be an investor. You could make money fast—an entirely different American dream come true. But in reality, flipping for profit—without ever taking possession of a home—is actually illegal in most states. Yes, *illegal*. To legally make a *profit* on the sale of real estate, an individual must actually own the property or be licensed to receive a commission (like real estate agents are).

So why not just flip a home legally? Well, closing on a home—the legal process to take possession of a home or transfer ownership to another buyer—costs money. To avoid these costs, many investors will claim that simply "assigning" their sales contract to a new buyer is legal and binding. And yes, the investors are correct—assigning a contract is 100 percent legal. But when you assign a contract to another party, the conditions of the original sales contract must remain *exactly* the same, including the original sales price. Once you change the price of the home (for example, by raising it to give yourself a nice profit), assigning a contract is off-limits. During the boom, many investors were able to work out "deals" with builders and brokers: they would sign a sales contract to purchase a home, then change the price on the contract and assign it to a new buyer.

The *legal* way to flip a home for profit is to first close on the home in the name of the buyer on the original sales contract (so the buyer technically owns the home), and then close again shortly afterwards in the name of the *new* buyer (which transfers the ownership to the new buyer). Of course, there are costs and fees associated with both closings, but that's the price you pay for the money you make.

As a mortgage consultant and professional I can't stress enough the importance of partnering with reputable real estate, mortgage, and title agents to properly structure your transaction, no matter what your intentions are in purchasing a home. Handling things on your own, as one investor found out, is not always the best decision.

---

THE TALE OF TEN HOMES

---

In 2005, I started working with a new client who was interested in purchasing investment homes pre-construction. Buying "pre-construction" was a common practice at the time here in Florida; buyers would sign a sales contract with a builder to reserve a home long before the builder had even broken ground. It was a win-win situation: the builder generated a decent cash flow to help finance the construction, and, in return, the buyer received a lower price for the home.

Not surprisingly, pre-construction pricing attracted many new investors—including Scott, who worked for an electric company in middle management and had owned his own home for several years. Scott had heard about the huge profits in real estate and was interested in buying two pre-construction homes per year and flipping them as soon as they were complete. And even though he admitted he really had no experience in investing, he was already thirty days from closing on his first pre-construction home, which he had signed a contract for the year before. Scott mentioned the builder had recommended its own on-site lender to provide financing for the home, but he was extremely disappointed with the lender's rates and terms.

I remember being a bit skeptical at this point. Scott was pretty gutsy for a novice investor, which made me reluctant to work with him, but I agreed to at least put together a few financing options for him. I spent some time working up some figures and presented my terms. Scott was extremely pleased, and we started the process.

After all the details were finalized, Scott called again with great news: he had someone who wanted to purchase the home from him before he even closed on the home himself! (As you will remember, this is illegal.) After giving Scott a quick Legal 101 on selling real estate for profit, I called the builder's title company to see what we might be able to work out. The title company rearranged their closing schedule so Scott and the new buyers could close simultaneously, and legally, on the home: Scott would close on the home first, and then the new buyers would close on the home immediately afterward. It wasn't common to arrange this, and the title company had gone out of its way to make the dual closings possible.

But somehow, this wasn't good enough for Scott. On the day of the closing, Scott meticulously questioned, argued against, and challenged the title company's fees for the two closings, and succeeded in badgering the title company so much that they actually lowered their fees. Scott took possession of the home for one hour, the new buyers closed on the home, and Scott received a check for $28,890. Scott left triumphant. I pulled Scott aside and let him know that his treatment of the title company was unacceptable.

A couple of weeks went by and Scott called again. After apologizing for his behavior at the last closing, he explained that he had yet *another* pre-construction unit that was again thirty days out from closing. This home was with a different builder and because he didn't have anyone interested in purchasing the property, he needed 100 percent financing, and fast. This time, after receiving my quotes on a few different loans, Scott called to let me know he would be going with someone else. It turned out that the builder had an in-house finance company that was offering surprisingly low interest rates that Scott couldn't pass up.

Not only were the interest rates better, but Scott had worked out a "special deal" with the builder to purchase even more homes. The builder was "allowing" Scott to purchase up to two townhomes or condos in each of the builder's five developments (for a total of ten homes), and as long as Scott used the builder's in-house finance company, the builder would require only a $5,000 down payment on each home. The builder would also "allow" Scott to flip the homes by assigning the sales contracts—just as long as he found someone to purchase the homes prior to completion, of course. But if Scott wasn't able to find buyers to flip the homes to in time, he would have to hold on to the homes for twelve full months before selling. If Scott's plans to flip the homes flopped, he could end up owning *all* ten homes.

Ten homes? Was he crazy? But Scott was ecstatic; he couldn't believe the deal the builder had given him. He could only see dollar signs, and had already signed contracts on each and every one of the ten homes. Scott enthusiastically explained that even in the worst-case scenario, he would sell the homes after twelve months and make a huge profit on each. And if he couldn't flip them as planned, he would lease the properties during the twelve-month period, then sell them just as soon as the leases were up. To say the least, I was shocked, and extremely concerned. I tried to talk some sense into him. He had signed up for a disaster, but he didn't want to hear it, especially from me. That call was the last time I heard from Scott . . . until two years later.

Out of the blue, in early 2007, Scott left me several messages, each one more urgent than the last. I was out of town at the time, but called him back from the road. Scott was panicked. He had taken possession of six of the original ten homes over the past two years and was still under contract for the four that were left. He desperately needed to refinance several of the properties so he could afford to pay his monthly debts: the mortgages, utilities, and association fees. Scott had it all worked out: since his homes were now worth more, he would take out new loans based on the homes' *new* values. These new loans would pay off his old loans, and he could use the money that was left over to pay his bills. He also told me that he hadn't paid the property taxes on most of the homes and he would need money to cover this as well.

Wait a minute, I said. What had happened with the builder and their in-house financing? What about the plans to flip, rent, and sell? The following week, after Scott came to my office armed with huge stacks of closing settlement statements, contracts, and paperwork, the picture became clear. After reviewing Scott's closing statements, I was shocked to see all of the fees and costs the builder had charged—and that Scott had paid. Scott shrugged, explaining the builder insisted he had agreed to these charges in the original sales contracts. And the builder was right. I looked at the contracts, and right there in black and white were line after line of miscellaneous fees. Someone had gotten a good deal, but it certainly wasn't Scott.

But why hadn't Scott sold the properties after the twelve months? After a lot of tap-dancing, Scott finally admitted that he hadn't sold because he didn't want to miss out on any profit. For a while, home prices were going up every month. How could he sell when the next month promised an even bigger profit? It was a greedy practice I saw all too often. Scott waited too long, trying to make as much as he could, and now he was having a hard time selling the homes.

In the end, I wasn't able to help Scott for several reasons. From trying to juggle the cost of maintaining the properties, Scott's credit had taken a nosedive. It turned out Scott had many late payments reporting on his credit, a few of which were still past due. After some county research, I discovered even more bad news. Apparently, the builder and its in-house lender had gotten into some financial difficulties of their own, and there were several liens tied to the builder's properties. And a lien— a legal claim to a property until a debt is paid—is a red flag when it comes to lending. As long as these liens existed, I explained to Scott, there really wasn't much any lender would be able to do. No lender would want to refinance or lend their money for a property with liens and the possibility of an impending lawsuit. The writing was on the wall: Scott was stuck with the properties, and his bad financial situation, unless he could find cash buyers.

Sound unbelievable? Unfortunately, Scott's story is all too true and was fairly common for the time. I've encountered several clients over the years who had stories just like this one, although Scott's situation was by far one of the worst. Fueled by nothing other than greed, Scott chose to listen to people who told him what he wanted to hear, and he got in over his head. Months later, Scott was forced to foreclose on most of the homes. In the end, he had depleted his savings and destroyed his credit, and had absolutely nothing to show for it.

As for the builder, I can only imagine how many people were given "deals" just like Scott's. Scott told me about several other homeowners who gladly handed their deposits to the builder only to run into similar issues. I looked up the builder, and discovered that due to its own financial troubles, the company had ended up seeking protection under bankruptcy law. The bankruptcy was eventually granted, but, ironically, the builder was still selling homes under another company name.

Most of us are nothing like Scott. But there are a few lessons we can take from his story that apply to anyone, in any real estate market:

▸ **Always work out both best-case and worst-case scenarios.** During the boom, many buyers were blinded by best-case scenarios. It's easy to see everything that could go right. But it's even more important, as in Scott's case, to consider everything that could go wrong.

When making a purchase, whether it's an investment property or a primary residence, always work out *both* best- and worst-case scenarios. Can you afford to pay for the investment if you are unable to rent it out? Can you afford the home if taxes go up? Is the purchase within your current budget? If you answer "no" to a majority of your worst-case questions, don't ignore the bad news. Take a small step back and reconsider your decision.

 Not sure what should be part of your worst-case scenario? Visit the reader's section of my website for an interactive checklist of what to consider with any real estate purchase.

▸ **If you are buying new construction or are building a home, research the builder.** Bad builders didn't disappear when the housing bubble burst. Be sure to research any builder you are considering, from small local builders to large national companies. Is the builder licensed and insured? Are there any complaints with the state or Better Business Bureau? Has the builder completed other successful communities, and does the builder have a good reputation? Are there any liens, judgments, unpaid taxes, or lawsuits against the builder? Check within your county's public records. You can also contact your local builder's association by visiting www.nahb.org. These associations can provide you with more information on a builder, and they also accept complaints. An hour or two on the internet can save you a lot of headaches later.

▸ **Carefully review any sales contract.** Scott could have saved himself a lot of trouble by carefully reading his sales contracts. Whether you are purchasing a home for yourself or as an investment property, it's important to carefully read—and understand—your contract, as well as all costs and payment schedules. This applies to any purchase you make, whether it's an existing home, a new home, or even vacant land.

If you are building a home, you'll also want to carefully review

---

**CONTRACT FOR SALE AND PURCHASE**
(Seller to Construct Home)

The SELLER and the BUYER hereby agree that the SELLER shall sell and the BUYER shall buy the real property described below (the "Property") upon the following terms and conditions.

**SELLER:**

**BUYER:**

**DESCRIPTION OF PROPERTY TO BEING SOLD:**

LEGAL DESCRIPTION:

PERSONAL PROPERTY:

2. **PURCHASE PRICE:** $ _____

   a.    Initial Deposit        $ _____

   b.    Additional Deposit (to be paid by the Buyer in     $ _____     *ESCROW WAIVER*
         monthly installments of $ _____ each)

   c.    Total Deposit (sum of "a" and "b" above)     $ _____

   d.    Balance to be paid at closing     $ _____

✱ THE BUYER OF A ONE OR TWO FAMILY RESIDENTIAL DWELLING UNIT HAS THE RIGHT TO HAVE ALL DEPOSIT FUNDS (UP TO 10% OF THE PURCHASE PRICE) DEPOSITED IN AN INTEREST BEARING ESCROW ACCOUNT. THIS RIGHT MAY BE WAIVED BY THE BUYER.
THE BUYER, BY SIGNING THIS CONTRACT, HEREBY WAIVES THE PLACING OF DEPOSIT FUNDS IN SUCH AN INTEREST BEARING ESCROW ACCOUNT.

---

**Figure 1.1: A Typical Escrow Waiver** *When you sign a builder's contract that contains an escrow waiver, all payments go directly to the builder. If there is a dispute, or if the builder goes bankrupt, your deposits and payments are not protected.*

your contract to see if it includes an *escrow waiver*. For your protection, deposits or down payments to any builder should always be placed in an escrow account, a special third-party account where your money is held until it's legally released for the construction of your home, or until the completion of your home (depending on your contract). But some builder contracts contain an "escrow waiver," which cancels out a buyer's legal right to reserve their payments in escrow. With a waiver in place, your payments go straight to the builder, and are often spent long before the home is completed. If your builder goes belly up like Scott's, you can expect to kiss your money goodbye.

Escrow waivers can be buried anywhere within a builder's sales contract, and are sometimes hard to spot (I've shown you an example of what to look for in Figure 1.1). Unfortunately, most buyers are unaware they have signed a contract that includes an escrow waiver, so read the fine print of your contract carefully. When in doubt, consult with an attorney.

## Everyone's an Investor

Flippers weren't the only ones buying multiple investment properties. During the boom years, many good people and good families got caught up in the whirlwind of investing. Some purchased multiple homes or took advantage of the free flow of money to move into more expensive homes. Many others had good intentions, but simply made bad choices. This is what happened to the Sawyers, a family from Jupiter, Florida.

---

AN HONEST FAMILY LEARNS THE HARD WAY

---

I met Trish and Melanie Sawyer years ago when I moved into a townhouse in a community where they had just purchased as well. We became friends, and over the years I advised them on several loans and refinances, including a recent refinance for a property they had on the west coast of Florida. The new loan yielded the Sawyers a much lower payment, which allowed them to save some money and decrease their monthly expenses. In the three years since then, I'd moved from the neighborhood, but we still kept in contact every so often.

In October 2007 I received a voice message from Trish, and was shocked to hear the stress in her voice: "We really need your help. We're desperate. Could you please meet with us next week?" Calling back, I was immediately bombarded with bits and pieces of random information: family issues, new investment properties, problems with existing properties, and a lot of sighs and frustration. By the end of the call, it was clear the entire family had become investors during the boom, and they all were barely scraping by. Trish, her daughter Melanie, and her son were all deep in debt. They had no idea what the future held for them. Trish made it clear they needed strategic planning or they would lose everything. Could I meet with all of them at once? How soon could I be there?

Knowing the family as I did, it was apparent that the Sawyers had made several poor decisions, and now they were stuck. For months on end they quietly panicked among themselves, thinking the housing market might turn around. Finally, they asked for help.

Later that week, I met the Sawyers at one of their homes in Jupiter. Everyone huddled around the kitchen table as I slowly read through the stacks of documents for all of the properties the family had purchased. Trish look embarrassed as she explained what happened: they had been offered great discounts on several of the homes—but only if they used the builder's in-house lender. Like so many homebuyers, the Sawyers didn't realize that offers like this are unfortunately too good to be true. While they did save on the sticker price of the properties, they ended up with very expensive mortgages and terms. The Sawyers also hadn't considered all of the costs that come with owning multiple properties, and, as a result, their situation was grim: high-cost mortgages, pre-payment penalties, high taxes and insurance, mistakes when planning for real estate taxes, late fees, real estate listing fees, negative equity, no profits…the list went on and on. It was all much more than I had originally anticipated.

All of the complicated details, which were overlooked or ignored when the properties were purchased, were now a heavy burden—and were rapidly draining the Sawyers' finances. By night's end I faced a family that had seven homes among them, increasing interest rates, decreasing home values, unprotected tax positions, insurance increases, high monthly homeowner's dues, and depleting savings and retirement accounts.

Was it too late for the Sawyers?

I left that night with a heavy heart and troubled mind. I knew that there were things I could do for the Sawyers, but would any type of financing make sense? Would my efforts only be a band-aid for their situation? Would a quick fix, or any fix for that matter, help to dig them out of their hole, or would it ultimately just dig them in deeper? And would they ever be able to truly recover from the debt they had accumulated? The current market conditions had many financial planners and experts reeling from the painful realization that sometimes very little could, or even should, be done.

Shouldn't the Sawyers have known better?

Despite their bad choices, the Sawyers were very good people. I listened as they told me how high their taxes and insurance policies were—and how much these rates had risen in just a few short years. They explained how they had substantial, unexpected expenses from the recent hurricanes, which were obviously costs the Sawyers had no control over. They also described how the builders and brokers had made them feel secure about their investments, and how they had been promised they were being placed into the very best loans. You can blame the Sawyers for not doing their homework and for getting in over their heads with too many properties. But you can't blame them entirely for being duped by the shady techniques builders and brokers used to finalize the sale.

But isn't it a homeowner's or an investor's job to evaluate each investment as a whole and determine, after detailed research, whether the investment is a sound one? Yes, it is. But the Sawyers weren't alone in not doing so. Many families truly did not understand or didn't take the time to research what they were getting into. Just open any newspaper, look at the default and foreclosure rate in any part of the country, or even check the public records from your own city. They all show that many people all made the same mistakes, and quickly became trapped by the boom.

As I have spent time meeting homeowners from across the country, I have heard the Sawyers' story again and again. You may even recognize yourself in their story. Many people can. And even if you can't relate to the decisions that the Sawyers made, there are many important lessons we can all take from their experience:

▸ **If it sounds too good to be true, it generally is.** No doubt about it, if it sounds too good to be true, nine times out of ten it is. In the Sawyers' case, the "use our lender and save" sales technique didn't save them anything at all. In most cases, builders who promise discounts if you use their in-house lender do *not* have your best interest in mind—they are usually compensated in some way by the lender to make up for the difference, which often means higher mortgage costs for you. The same can be said for other sales promotions including free pools, free cars, or other upgrades. You've heard there's no such thing as a free lunch? Well, there's no such thing as a free pool. I promise. You will easily pay for the cost of the pool in builder fees and services, or in financing costs, terms, and fees.

Unfortunately, sales techniques like these are just as popular now as they were during the boom. Never commit to a builder's in-house lender or finance company without obtaining your own second estimate for financing. A second estimate will help you to see what you are really saving (if anything), and what you are paying for in the long run. (I'll talk more about how to compare these costs in Chapter 6, and in Appendix I.)

▸ **Interview your builder's broker or lender.** Even today, many builders still have their own in-house lenders or mortgage brokers. Just because a broker has a builder's seal of approval doesn't mean they should have yours. Thoroughly interview any lender or mortgage broker you work with, especially if you choose to use builder financing. In Chapters 5 and 6, I'll show you why you'll want to receive several estimates for financing, as well as what to look for, and specific questions to ask, when working with any lending professional.

▸ **Make sure you understand your loan, all loan charges, and loan fees.** Part of the fallout from the housing boom and bust was the result of millions of bad consumer loans with high rates and terms. Many homeowners didn't understand their financing, and didn't know if their rates would change or if they really would be able to afford their payments. Take the time to thoroughly understand your loan, and if you are unsure of anything, ask. In Chapters 3, 4, and 5, I'll carefully review and explain every detail of your loan, from how the lending process works, to various loans programs and options, to finding the best mortgage consultant who can answer all of your questions.

▸ **The cost of a home isn't just your mortgage payment.** During the excitement of the boom years, many people simply did not consider what owning a home *really* costs. Whether you're thinking of buying a home, a second home, or a true investment property, make sure you fully understand the debt you are about to take on—because this debt is not just your mortgage payment. Your total debt includes your mortgage payment, taxes, insurance, association fees, utilities, property maintenance, future realtor fees, and much more.

A good mortgage consultant will help you to understand the true cost of any property. To help, I've also included a home cost planning worksheet for you in Appendix III, and you can also visit my website for checklists and calculators to help you determine your true costs—and future costs—*before* you make a purchase.

▸   **Plan for rising costs.** Unfortunately, planning for current costs is just the first step; many of the costs associated with your home will go up due to inflation (as the years go by, things get more expensive). Inflation rates over the last five years have ranged from roughly 2 to 4 percent a year. To get an idea of how you need to plan, let's pretend you have a fixed mortgage rate. This means your basic mortgage costs won't increase. But the remaining costs (taxes, insurance, utilities, etc.) will.

Right now, let's say that you are paying $700 a month for these expenses, for a total of $9,600 a year. What will these same costs be five years from now?

```
              A 5-Year Snapshot:

       At 2% Inflation = $10,599
       At 4% Inflation = $11,680
```

Based on this example, you could be paying $2,080 *more* five years from now. When considering a home purchase or a new loan, be sure to factor in these increasing costs. While it would be great if the value of the dollar also increased with inflation, it doesn't. If you stretch your budget too tight now, it's more likely to snap in the future.

▸ **Consider the true risk that comes with multiple purchases.**
Are you purchasing multiple properties? Are you looking only at the
potential profit? The Sawyers, and many other investors, all learned
the hard way. They were completely caught off guard as the expenses
for their properties quickly added up.

With any purchase—but especially with multiple purchases—you
need to consider your true costs, and your true risk. Your true costs
*multiply* with each additional property; owning two properties is twice
as risky as owning one. You can measure your risk by totaling the
monthly debt and costs for each property. Then add an allowance for
inflation. Then total up all of the costs. How does this number look
to you? What if you had unplanned expenses or an emergency, and
this number was almost twice as much?

With more than one purchase, costs can add up quickly, and,
sometimes, if even just *one* thing doesn't go according to plan, costs
can balloon out of control.

▸ **Is your investment property truly a good investment?** Many
boom investors were so convinced that someone would be there to
quickly buy up their investment homes, they didn't pay attention to
the details that would influence whether anyone would want to buy
the property in the first place. As an investor, you need to evaluate
each property to determine if it's a sound investment and makes financial sense. Will the area appreciate in value? Are there many other
homes for sale in the area? Is there a real need for rental property?
What will your total costs be and what costs might increase? Will you
need to upgrade or remodel to sell or rent the property? You'll want
to ask these questions, plus many more, for any type of real estate
purchase you make, whether you're purchasing as an investment or
for your primary home.

▸ **Don't wait to ask for help.** Don't be ashamed or embarrassed to
ask for help. The longer you wait, the harder it can be to find a solution. And even though the news you get may be bad, an informed decision is usually better than an uninformed one.

If you have waited like the Sawyers and are now facing default or foreclosure, don't give up. In Chapter 7, I outline who can help you, and the steps you can take to be proactive in saving your home. I have also provided many additional assistance and counseling resources for you on my website. There are many ways to get the support you need, but you have to take the first step. One of the best decisions you can make is to ask for help now.

## The Builder Debacle

During the boom, many people made poor decisions. Others felt they could trust the people they were working with, and believed they were in good hands. Even ethical and intelligent people fell victim to the boom's complicated legal jargon, poor lending practices, and shady tactics used by mortgage brokers, lenders, and builders.

My own story of an experience my wife and I had with a local builder illustrates just how predatory and profit-driven the boom era had become, and how you can never be too careful when buying a home.

| A LESSON IN THE O |
| --- |

In 2005, my wife and I had moved to a new area, were looking for a home, and had visited a very large new development known as the O. Although most of the neighborhood was still in the planning phase, the builder had already built an impressive multi-story clubhouse for future residents and ten different model homes. The builder's sales materials, site plans, artist renderings, homes, and clubhouse were all top-notch, and new homes were selling at an unbelievable rate. Every time we visited the O, the sales center was packed.

Although we ended up choosing a different, smaller, and more secluded neighborhood, we kept tabs on the O, and would often walk through the model homes or drive through the neighborhood to check on the builder's progress.

After many visits to the O, with real estate still booming and the O sales steadily increasing, we eventually decided to make an investment purchase there ourselves. After signing the sales contract, we elected to take advantage of our three-day right of rescission period. This period gave us some time, after signing the contract, to reject the contract's terms without being charged a penalty or losing any money. If we didn't like the contract's terms, we'd get our deposit back. Both my wife and I have always been people who evaluate any and all investments, and we used this period to really tear apart the contract, the builder's terms and conditions, and the homeowners association's rules and regulations.

After combing through the documents, we found that some of the details were very different than what was presented in the O's fancy sales literature . . . and many details just didn't make sense. First, there was the builder's decision not to cooperate with licensed real estate agents. I've maintained an active Florida real estate license since 1996, and have always represented myself as my own agent on purchases. For their work, real estate agents usually receive a 3 percent commission from the builder, which is standard and customary. But this builder was withholding *all* commissions. In fact, the builder claimed it had so many potential clients that it didn't need any help from realtors at all. A builder who wouldn't work with professional realtors? That was the first red flag.

There was also a hefty builder's fee based on the purchase price, neatly hidden deep within the sales contract. Now, I had paid very small builder's fees in the past on several homes. Some builder's fees help to offset costs in planning and building a development, but many builder's fees are pure profit. In either case, these fees typically are no more than 1 percent of the purchase price. The big O's fee was over $6,000—almost triple the usual fee. I was shocked. I dealt with contracts daily and had never seen a fee that high. That was red flag number two.

Just by reviewing the contract, we'd already produced a potential loss of $12,000—from the loss of the real estate commission and from the builder's fees—and we weren't even through yet. Further in, the fine print revealed that the builder was passing on all title company fees, survey fees, recording fees, government stamps and taxes, and several homeowner start-up fees to us—how nice! These fees are standard for a purchase, and are normally shared by the seller and the buyer, but not in this case. Simple calculations totaled these miscellaneous costs at $4,000—on top of the $12,000 I had already tallied up. It was very apparent that the builder had created a very one-sided contract in order to make as much per customer as possible. It was downright greedy.

The icing on the cake was a document stating that if the home was sold again within a twelve-month time period, any profit from the sale would revert back to the builder. It didn't matter if you had a job transfer or just didn't like the neighborhood. The wording was very clear: sell in under twelve months and pay up—to the builder.

I had seen some pretty crazy things in the business world before that point, but the resale stipulation was the most ridiculous clause I had ever seen in any agreement—and was the final straw that lead us to cancel our purchase contract.

---

In the months that followed, many builders adopted similar tactics regarding add-on costs and builder's fees. My own lending company became the bearer of bad news on many occasions, often having to show clients the total costs and terms they had already agreed to in their sales contracts.

Some clients didn't understand the contract's language or the consequences of the builder's terms. Others didn't take the time (or the rescission period they had a right to) to thoroughly examine the contract or calculate their costs as a whole. Some hadn't even read the contracts at all. And after the right of rescission period passed, it was too late. Buyers were locked in, and had no choice but to execute the contract or else lose their deposits.

Just a little over two years later, in 2007, the builder responsible for the O had changed its tune and lowered prices substantially. Today, the neighborhood is littered with "for sale" signs and vacant homes, a large percentage of which appear to be abandoned. It turns out the O had attracted many investors who were looking to flip properties for an inflated profit. But the houses never flipped, the investors never saw their returns, and the foreclosures in the neighborhood increased.

As the neighborhood began to deteriorate, many of those who had signed sales contracts walked away from their deposits, saddling the builder with empty home after empty home and many vacant lots. The public records for the community tell a sad story of abandoned and foreclosed homes, and the builder has halted all future construction for the development.

Desperate to sell what has already been constructed, the builder now runs weekly full-page newspaper ads that welcome real estate agents, offering a 3 percent cooperating commission for any realtor assistance in selling the O's glut of existing builder-owned properties. And as the final nail in the coffin, an inside source revealed to me that its parent company was forced to characterize the O as a "profitless development" . . . indefinitely.

---

**The Domino Effect: Builder Bankruptcies**

Florida-based company Tousa, Inc., once the largest home builder by volume, sought bankruptcy protection in 2008. Tousa lost 98 percent of its market value in just one year due to declining real estate markets. The second-largest home builder by volume, Levitt Corporation, also filed for Chapter 11 protection in November 2007, listing over $340 million in debt. Even high-end builders, like the luxury builder WCI Communities, have filed for bankruptcy protection. As of 2009, seventy-two major U.S. builders have closed their doors.

---

From the story of the O, it is easy to see how the fallout from the housing and lending collapse will be with us for a long time. Thousands of communities are just like the O, full of abandoned, over-priced homes waiting to be purchased with no buyers in sight. And although the frenzy of new construction has stopped, even in today's market, you still need to be cautious. My own story provides an important checklist for making yourself a savvier buyer:

▸ **Research.** One of the biggest lessons we all should learn from the housing boom and bust can be summarized in one word: research. Research until you are 100 percent satisfied a property meets your needs, as well as your long- or short-term financial goals and expectations. By now, you know your research should include your true costs (your mortgage, real estate taxes, homeowners insurance, association fees, maintenance and upkeep, and padding for inflation). But you should also consider what the neighborhood may be like years from now when it's time to sell. What might the neighborhood look like in the future? What percentage of buyers are investors? What story do sales in the neighborhood tell? Even if you don't have long-term plans to stay in a particular area, you still need to consider these questions. You don't know what might happen, and you may end up living in a home for longer than you planned to. Leave no stone unturned in making sure your decision is a sound one.

▸ **Never assume a contract is "okay."** Whenever you decide to purchase a home, either to live in or as an investment, make sure to read all of the fine print on your real estate sales contract, whether this contract is from a builder, a real estate agent, or a homeowner. If you need assistance deciphering its terms, consult with an attorney; many real estate attorneys will review your sales contract for a very reasonable flat fee.

 WEBLINK Do you need help in finding a flat-rate attorney? In the reader's section of my website, you'll find a list of screened and reputable attorneys who can provide an affordable contract review.

▸ **Rely on your right of rescission.** When you purchase a home, there are many legal rights that will help protect you as a buyer. The *right of rescission* is one of these. During the boom, high pressure sales tactics were common. Many buyers felt that if they didn't sign a sales contract right then and there, they would miss out: the home would be sold, a lot would become unavailable, or prices would increase.

What many buyers didn't realize—and what many buyers still don't realize—is that even after signing a real estate contract, you often still have time to review and either accept or reject the contract's terms. This is called the "right of rescission."

In most states, if you purchase in a planned unit development (which is a development with a homeowners or condominium association), once you receive the homeowners' and/or condominium documents and regulations, you still have three days (for a single-family home or townhome) or fifteen days (for a condominium) to proceed forward with the sales contract. This applies for both existing homes and new home developments. If you find something you don't like or are unhappy with the terms of the contract, you can exercise your right of rescission and be entitled to a full refund of any deposit. Yes, a *full refund*. Within this time frame, any deposit can be refunded for any reason, period.

If you are purchasing in a neighborhood without a governing association, your right of rescission will be determined by state law. Because state laws vary, if anything is unclear, it's always best to consult with a real estate attorney, if possible, *before* signing any type of sales contract.

Remember, especially for new homes purchased through a builder, it's likely that all of a contract's details have *not* been disclosed to you in advance. Most builders will not allow you to review any homeowners' documents or the fine print until after you've signed a contract. This is a common sales technique used in new home construction, and builders are hoping you do not do your homework. But you can keep builders from deceiving you by taking advantage of your legal right of rescission. Just make sure to review all contracts and homeowners' documents in the time allotted by law.

## The Impulse Purchase

*"A man is rich in proportion to the number of things which he can afford to let alone."* — HENRY DAVID THOREAU

The term impulse purchase has so much relevance for what happened during the real estate boom. For several years, the housing buzz was electric. Many people were excited with thoughts of a new start or with the dream of a new home. The promise of profits from climbing home prices and the pictures painted by real estate sales centers persuaded many people to purchase first homes, bigger homes, or status homes. Buying or upgrading wasn't easy to resist, especially when, everywhere you looked, it seemed like everyone and anyone was buying a home, and both homes and loans were plentiful.

Even those who already owned homes were caught up in the boom's excitement as they watched home values rise dramatically, month after month. Many homeowners took advantage of this new-found equity by refinancing their homes: taking out a loan at their home's new high value, paying off their previous loan, and pocketing the difference to spend like never before.

This is exactly what happened to Ike, whose story serves as a cautionary tale about how easy money and impulse spending can quickly spiral out of control.

| MY HOME, MY ATM MACHINE |
| --- |

Ike is a friend and former colleague of mine who is also an accomplished banking professional. We would meet for lunch or drinks a few times a month, and we would sometimes bounce financial scenarios off of each other. Ike worked for a national lender, and was always on top of what was happening in the industry.

One day, Ike asked me to meet him for dinner. He mentioned he needed to have a serious conversation and suggested we have dinner at his house so we could have some quiet time. We met after work one evening and poured ourselves a few cocktails. After catching up for a few minutes, Ike went right into the topic he had wanted to discuss.

Ike explained how he had made $100,000 dollars a year for the past three years. He had also received a lump sum of $75,000 from a real estate deal he was involved in. As he spoke, I remember thinking his income plus the lump sum was very impressive, but Ike seemed depressed. Something didn't add up. Where could he be going with all of this?

Finally it came out: Ike was broke. His situation got worse with every question I asked: "Do you have any equity in your home?" No, he didn't. "Do you have a 401K or retirement account?" No, he had never gotten around to setting up a retirement account. I paused for a moment in shock. Ike had been in the finance industry just as long as I had, and he clearly should have known how to handle his money. "How is this possible?" I asked.

He looked back at me with an empty stare. "I cannot stop spending; I have no will power when it comes to buying things. I can't even budget my money, because I am so far in debt now." Ike admitted his wife's spending habits were just as bad, so bad that she often made a joke of it, explaining to friends and family that she was a "spender" and couldn't be trusted with money. To keep up with their combined high-powered spending, family trips, and new cars, during the boom Ike had turned his home into one big ATM machine: as his home's value climbed, he had refinanced his home not once but *twice* to cash out enough of his home's equity to maintain his family's lifestyle.

In the last months of juggling money, Ike had tried to refinance again, but by this point, the bubble had burst and home values had started to decline. His request to refinance was denied, and Ike didn't have any options left. He was broke. All that money, and this banking professional's bottom line was a big, fat zero.

During the boom, prices were on the rise and many people viewed the increase in their homes' values as free money. As home values increased by thousands of dollars a month, the money homeowners took out was quickly "replaced" by new, artificial value as home prices climbed even higher. Many homeowners refinanced their homes, cashing out their profit. Other homeowners used their homes' equity to secure home equity lines of credit—large lines of credit from banks that let homeowners borrow against their homes' equity to free up extra cash.

For most people right now, the ATM is dry. Values have plummeted, there is no equity to take out, and even when there is, lenders are cautious about allowing homeowners to do so. But as the country rebounds, more and more areas will start to see positive home values again—and that same opportunity to spend. So what should you do when this happens?

▸ **Always aim to maintain at least 20 percent equity in your home.** I have always preached about maintaining at least 20 percent equity in your home if it's a primary residence. That means that your home needs to be worth at least 20 percent more than what you owe on your mortgage. Following this guideline can help to ensure your survival in any market, up or down. Have a $200,000 home? Always try to keep in at least $40,000 in equity (which means if you were to sell your home you would get about $40,000 as profit, minus any closing costs).

How do you get to a 20 percent equity position? The simplest way is to have at least a 20 percent down payment when you purchase the home. If you are refinancing, you can build or maintain your equity by choosing not to "cash out" any equity you have built up (unlike Ike). If you can't manage a 20 percent down payment, you can always build up your equity slowly by paying down your mortgage. Your equity will also improve each year as your home appreciates in value.

Why is having 20 percent equity so important? Lenders base many costs for a loan on this 20 percent guideline; keeping 20 percent in equity will make financing and refinancing more affordable, and it will also help you to avoid additional costs like mortgage insurance and escrow requirements—which we'll look at more in Chapters 4 and 10.

▸ **Think about what you are taking the money out for.** Using your home's equity to replace a worn, leaking roof is not the same as using your equity to build a $40,000 pool. Boom market or bust, always carefully examine what you are using the money for. You may have heard that consolidating your credit card bills is a good reason to tap your equity. It's not. If you do this once, or if you take out equity for an emergency, it's understandable, but selling or refinancing to access your home equity is not something you should rely on. You are only *putting off* paying your debt, not paying the debt off.

For example, let's say you owe $200,000 on your loan. Your home is worth $235,000, which means you have $35,000 in equity. You also have $15,000 in credit card debt, so you decide to cash out some of your home's equity to pay off your credit cards.

You cash out, and your loan amount increases to $215,000. You haven't really paid off anything—you've only *shifted* your debt from one place to another. You may now be paying a lower interest rate for this debt (it's a safe bet that your mortgage has a lower interest rate than your credit cards do) but the debt is still there. It's a *better* idea to get control of your personal spending, which I'll talk about more in Chapters 8 and 10.

▸ **Understand that taking out money costs money.** Every time you refinance your home it costs at least 1 to 5 percent in closing fees just to take the money out (these fees are based on your final loan amount). Looking at the example I just gave, taking out $15,000 to pay off those credit cards could cost you an additional $2,150 to $10,750! Sure, you can sometimes "roll" these costs into the refinance by using some of your home's equity to pay for these costs at your loan's closing (a relatively easy decision for many), but what if you had to produce the 5 percent fees upfront, with cash out of your pocket? Would it still seem like a smart decision?

Of course, just because your home has increased in value or you have taken out some of your home's equity doesn't mean you are going to be an impulse purchaser. But for many, impulse spending is a habit and a part of everyday life. Do you plan what you spend? Do you find yourself with high credit card bills you cannot pay, for things you really don't need? Impulse and poor spending habits are certainly not limited to the days of the boom. If any of this sounds familiar, you may be more of an impulse purchaser than you realize. And if you are, using your home as an ATM machine to pay for your spending will only make your financial situation worse. But it's not a hopeless situation. I'll talk a little more about ways you can change your relationship with spending—and how you can start saving instead—in Chapter 10.

• • •

The boom is finally behind us, but the fallout is not. In hindsight, it's easy to see how everything went wrong, and how consequences from the decisions made by lenders, Wall Street, mortgage brokers, real estate professionals, builders, and even homeowners will be with us for years to come. Even so, there are many lessons we can take from the boom years, and there are many ways we can make better decisions about buying or refinancing a home today. And by understanding what happened during the boom, we'll also be able to understand how and why lending has dramatically changed for the future, which I'll talk about more in the next chapter.

### COMING UP

We've all lived through the real estate and lending collapse. What's happened to the lending industry? How have the rules for financing changed? And what does this mean for your loan? In the next chapter, I'll explain more about how lending has been impacted, and what this means for you—and your ability to refinance or buy a home.

# 2

# Looking to the Future

## The New Realities in Lending

M ajor events (especially negative ones) usually incite change and reform. History and science have shown us time and time again that Isaac Newton was absolutely right: every action has an equal and opposite *re*action. And this is exactly what's happened "post-boom" in the country's lending and credit markets. In response to mounting defaults and foreclosures and declining home values, lenders' reactions have been just as extreme. Most lenders have completely changed how they evaluate and grant loans, at least compared to how they did business during the boom.

Of course, many of these changes are needed for the long-term— they are the building blocks for a stable and secure marketplace. In fact, most other industry experts believe, as I do, that lending and loan availability will eventually return to how it was *before* the boom, with accountability and realistic expectations between borrowers and lenders. In many ways, lenders are simply flipping a switch and going back to the conservative guidelines and practices they used years ago, in the days when lending was stable.

While some of these changes are good, other changes have been so abrupt and inflexible that today, almost anyone who needs a loan is affected in some way. Lenders have become so strict that many honest consumers are having a hard time obtaining financing, and, without access to loans, they must now fend for themselves. Regardless of whether you currently own a home, would like to own a home, or are trying to sell a home, these new realities apply to you. Since we can't change them, let's look at what we can do to make the best of them and of the situation.

## Impacts on Loans: Lenders Are Lending Less

During the boom years, lenders gambled that the demand for real estate would last forever. There appeared to be a loan for just about everyone, and lenders were looking for any reason *to* lend money. Now, lenders are looking for any reason *not* to lend money. Today, there is no guarantee you will be able to qualify for a loan, even if you were able to obtain financing before or during the boom, or even if you currently have a mortgage. And for borrowers who do qualify for financing, the options may seem limited compared to the heyday of recent years. What has changed?

To start, lenders will lend you less. Lenders describe how much they will loan to a borrower in terms of LTV, which is short for *loan to value*. LTV is a description of your loan amount that is based on a home's appraised value. For example, a 90% LTV loan for a home that has appraised at $150,000 is $135,000.

$$\$150{,}000 \text{ x } 90\% = \$135{,}000 \text{ Loan Amount}$$

Your LTV is also directly related to your down payment. In this same example, at 90% LTV, you would be required to have 10 percent as a down payment, so that 100 percent of the home you are purchasing is covered.

```
$150,000 x 10% = $15,000 Down Payment

$135,000 Loan Amount + $15,000 Down Payment =
        $150,000 Appraised Value
```

The higher the LTV, the more of your home the lender is financing, and the greater the risk for the lender. During the boom, many lenders offered to finance 100 percent of your home, no questions asked. That meant that buyers didn't even have to provide a down payment. Today, it's a different story: 100% LTV financing is only available for veterans and through a few community and specialty loan programs. For most homeowners, the highest LTV you can expect is 97 percent, and these loans are becoming harder and harder to get, even if you have impeccable credit and job security. Overall, most loans will have a maximum of 95% LTV, which means you'll be required to come up with *at least* 5 percent as a down payment when you purchase a home. And if you have less than perfect credit, you can expect that lenders will lend much less.

At first glance, the difference of a few percentage points may not seem like a lot. But look at the dollar amount these percentage points add up to. Take, for example, a $150,000 home. Buyers who were required to come up with $0 just a few years ago are now required to have a significant down payment. Today, if you qualify for a 95% LTV loan, you will be required to have a down payment of $7,500 (a down payment of 5 percent). For a 90% LTV loan, the down payment doubles to $15,000 (since your down payment is now 10 instead of 5 percent). As you can see, the difference of a few percentage points can quickly add up to a large dollar amount.

If you are refinancing a home instead of purchasing, things are different too. During the boom, homeowners could refinance and cash out up to 100 percent of their homes' values. Today, lenders are not willing to take this risk. If you want to take cash out of your home, or if you want to roll your refinancing costs into your loan (which a lender also considers to be a "cash out"), lenders have capped their limits at 90% LTV for even the best borrowers. Again, let's look at a $150,000 home as our example. If you are refinancing, the maximum your loan and any cash you take out can add up to is $135,000. If you don't want to take out any cash (for example, if you just want to refinance to lower your interest rate, keeping your loan amount the same), the most lenders will lend is 95% LTV.

## Proof of Income and Reserves

In addition to lending you less, lenders also want to make sure you can *afford* the amount they decide to loan you. Unless you have 35 percent or more to invest as a down payment and a credit score over 720, if you want to receive a loan, you'll need to prove beyond a shadow of a doubt that you can afford it.

As crazy as it sounds now, during the boom years, a borrower could be approved for a mortgage by simply *saying* they could afford it. A *stated loan* is a loan where a borrower "states" his or her income, and the lender believes it—no proof is needed, and no documentation is required. These stated loans, which once had a specific purpose (I'll cover this more in Chapter 4), ended up quickly becoming known as "liar's loans," as borrowers, mortgage brokers, and lenders all abused the system. Borrowers "stated" they could afford a home when they clearly couldn't, brokers didn't care, and lenders approved the loan anyway.

The current lending market is entirely different. To prove you are a good candidate for a loan, not only will you be expected to provide verification of your income and assets, but your lender will also require proof of several months' worth of separate financial reserves. Basically, to own a home, you'll need to show that you can afford it and that you have enough saved to make your mortgage payments if something were to happen and you had a loss in income.

Using the same $150,000 home as an example, let's say you need a 95% LTV loan. Your mortgage payment for the loan is $1,000. Your lender could easily require four to five months worth of reserves, which could add up to $4,000 to $5,000. This is in *addition* to your down payment of $7,500. Between your down payment and your reserves, a lender who once required $0 could now require a total of $12,500. For most people, this is a big difference.

By having these requirements, a lender knows they are not the only party invested in your loan. By having you include your own money in the deal, the lender is shouldering less risk, and you have shown the lender that you have enough financial stability to save for a down payment and reserves. This also means it's more likely you will continue to make your mortgage payments, which is ultimately the most important consideration for the lender.

These types of requirements were actually standard for most loans before the boom; a down payment of at least 5 percent and an additional amount in reserves is really not an unreasonable thing for a lender to require. But for many families, especially in hard economic times, that difference in requirements is sometimes the difference between being able to afford a home and not being able to.

## Changes in Interpretation

Lenders have also changed how they evaluate and approve loans. Lenders are reviewing loan applications very carefully, and the review and approval process has shifted from relying on a quick, automated checklist of requirements to relying on the interpretation and scrutiny (and the approval or denial) of an underwriter.

 **DEFINITION** **The Underwriter Makes the Decisions**

An underwriter works directly for a lender, and is responsible for determining how risky it is to lend to you—and whether or not you'll receive a loan. An underwriter also acts as a main contact between mortgage brokers and lenders once a loan is submitted for approval. Like lenders, banks also employ underwriters, and if you go to a bank for your loan, it will be the bank's underwriter (not your bank's representative) who makes the final decision about your loan.

Underwriters understand that every loan and borrower are unique, and, in the past, underwriters were willing to be flexible. For example, if a borrower's credit score didn't meet a lender's requirements, a broker would be able to work with the underwriter to prove the borrower's worth in other ways: maybe the borrower had more in savings, or a solid job history with a good income. Many times, an underwriter would be willing to make an exception, and would approve the loan.

But in today's lending environment, lenders do not have much flexibility or room for error. It's harder for underwriters to bend the rules. There's less money to lend, and if a lender is going to front the money for your home, it wants to be sure it's making a good investment. While this sounds fair, some lenders have taken it to the extreme, and what may seem like a solid borrower profile to you may be anything but to an underwriter.

Here's an example: Imagine that you have been employed in the same profession for fifteen years. Just a few months ago you started at a new company, and you have a good salary. You have decent credit, and you've saved enough for a down payment plus reserves. Things are looking good for you and your loan. On paper, you certainly meet all of the lender's requirements. Then you get a call from your mortgage broker and are stunned. The underwriter has denied your loan.

The underwriter views your change in employment as risky. Sure, you've worked in the same profession for fifteen years, but you've only worked for this new *company* for a few months. The underwriter isn't able to determine the stability of your *new* employment; simply being employed is no longer enough. Despite your credit, salary, and savings, you are deemed a risk for the lender.

In today's market, many lenders are looking for a sure bet and the least risk. In addition to looking at your income, assets, and down payment, underwriters are scrutinizing not only your credit score and credit history, but *how* you are using your credit, as well as your employment, your employment history, and your job security.

## Expect an Appraisal Review

To better protect their own interests, lenders are also carefully reviewing the collateral: your home. Because most homes have lost so much value, and because the real estate market doesn't seem to have hit bottom even now, lenders have no choice but to scrutinize every home's appraisal to make sure that it accurately represents a home's *true* value.

- Is the home in an area where it could lose more value?
- Is funding the home a sound investment from the lender's point of view?

From a lender's perspective, these are important questions. A lender doesn't want to lend more than a home is worth, and it definitely doesn't want to make a bad investment.

When you purchase or refinance a home, your broker will order an appraisal of your property through a licensed appraiser, and then supply this appraisal to the lender. But sometimes, the lender may reject it, or not take the appraisal at its full value. In fact, some lenders are so serious about making sure that they lend only what a home is worth that they may even conduct their *own* appraisal of a property, which will usually show a *lower* value.

For example, let's say you are purchasing a home, and the appraisal from your broker comes in at $200,000. The lender decides to get their own appraisal, which states that the property is worth only $170,000! This leaves you to either go back and negotiate the asking price with the seller, or to come up with the difference yourself. If you are refinancing your home, a lower appraisal from the lender means that the lender will lend you less. Borrowers don't have control of the market and a home's loss of value, but they do end up paying the price—literally.

In essence, both you *and* your home need to meet with the approval of the underwriter. And in many ways, these changes in lender interpretation can be very unfair to borrowers. Many individuals and families who should be approved for a loan are denied, often for insignificant reasons, usually with little warning, and sometimes for reasons out of their control. Your loan or refinance could be on its way to being approved one day, and denied the next. You may actually need to wait through the approval process several times with several different lenders to get your loan approved, and even then approval is not guaranteed. This instability is very frustrating for borrowers and often difficult for brokers to explain. Are lenders really this fickle? The short answer: right now, yes.

Unfortunately, in most cases there is only one surefire way to avoid these issues: have as much of your own money in the deal as possible. This means having at least a 20 to 30 percent down payment based on the home's appraised value, or having or building at least 20 percent in equity in your home before refinancing. By increasing your own investment in the loan, you are less of a risk for a lender, and they will be more open to lending to you.

## Rising Fees and Costs

Lenders made a lot during the boom years. But in the aftermath, they have also lost billions. To counter losses from defaults, foreclosures, and the economy in general, many lenders are adding fees to loans across the board. Some lenders have also added "declining market value adjustments," adjustments to a home's appraised value, in metro areas or cities where housing prices have fallen or are falling faster than other areas.

"Declining markets" and "oversupply areas," which are both identified on an appraisal, are based on county and state analysis of home availability, pending sales, and the number of recent sales in a given geographic area. If your appraisal includes these phrases, lenders will expect the value of a home to go down even further—which is *not* what a lender wants to see.

With homes decreasing in value, lenders are afraid that you will walk away from your home if you owe more than a home is worth. So in order to protect themselves, lenders will lower your LTV, usually by at *least* 5 percent. This means they will lend you at least 5 percent less. For example, if you qualify for a 90% LTV loan, the lender may change your loan to 85% LTV. Who makes up this difference? You do, by putting down more of a down payment, renegotiating the home's price with the seller of the home, finding a less expensive home, or refinancing a different loan amount.

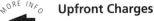

**MORE INFO**  **Upfront Charges**

In 2008, to offset losses from the lending collapse, an additional 0.5 percent upfront charge was added to most mortgages and refinances. This means that for every $100,000 you borrow, you are charged an additional $500. These fees are either paid upfront at your closing or are blended into your interest rate, adding approximately an eighth of a point to the interest rate for your loan.

## On the Positive Side . . .

Even though lending guidelines have changed and costs have increased, that doesn't mean all hope is lost. Lenders will always have an incentive to lend money, thanks to Fannie and Freddie. "Fannie Mae," the Federal National Mortgage Association, and "Freddie Mac," the Federal Home Loan Mortgage Corporation, are government-sponsored enterprises and are the leaders of conventional lending—over half of all home loans are backed by Fannie or Freddie. Fannie and Freddie work with lenders throughout the country, and they set national standards for financing. In short, Fannie and Freddie tell lenders, "If you meet our guidelines, we'll find someone who will buy your loan."

This arrangement is beneficial to both lenders and borrowers. By selling the loan, lenders make a profit, and their original funds are available again to loan to new borrowers. And if Fannie or Freddie cannot find someone to purchase the loan, they are obligated to purchase it themselves. For lenders, this is an incentive to keep writing loans that meet Fannie and Freddie requirements: there is always a guaranteed buyer.

Keep in mind, Fannie and Freddie have strict lending guidelines. In fact, Fannie and Freddie are the ones responsible for setting many of the LTV requirements, qualifying guidelines, and higher fees I described earlier in this chapter. But this is still good for borrowers because having Fannie and Freddie in the equation means that lenders will *continue* to lend money. And the borrowers who do meet Fannie and Freddie's qualification guidelines will receive very good loan rates and terms. (I'll explain more about these loans, and how Fannie and Freddie work with lenders, in Chapters 3 and 4.)

Borrowers also have hope because of loans offered by the federal government. The Federal Housing Administration (FHA), a government agency, also provides special loan programs that are specifically geared to promote homeownership. FHA loans offer lower down payments, lower interest rates, and flexible loan guidelines. These government programs offer stability and relief; they ensure that no matter what happens with the lending market, *affordable* financing will always be available. But you will still need to qualify for the loan. I'll explain much more about the Federal Housing Administration, and how you can apply for FHA loans, in Chapter 4.

## Action You Can Take Now

So what can you do to cope with these changes? And what can you do to make yourself attractive to a lender? Throughout this book, I'll be discussing many of the ways you can get back to the basics, which will improve your ability to obtain or keep financing for your home. A guaranteed way to be approved for almost any type of loan is to have a large down payment or a good amount of equity in your home.

Another way is to have good credit. Even in today's market, this combination can open doors. Together, we'll look at how you can improve your credit, build up your savings, *and* improve your overall financial health.

In the next chapters, I'll also explain more about lending and loans, what lenders require, what loan programs are available, and which loans may be right for you. You'll come away with a solid understanding of what lenders *expect*, what you'll need to do to obtain financing, and how you can use various loan programs to help you achieve your financial goals.

If you are a homeowner who was able to secure financing before or during the boom, but wouldn't be able to in today's market, you'll want to do whatever you can to maintain your current loan. I can't stress this enough. If you lose this loan, you won't be able to get another anytime soon, so you need to be proactive. Anyone can proactively inquire with their lender about improving or modifying their *existing* loan. You do not have to be in financial distress to contact your lender for assistance. If you are in any way nervous about being able to pay, or are struggling to pay, your mortgage, or if you would like to restructure your mortgage to provide for more stability, contact your lender. You really have nothing to lose.

Why would a lender agree to modify an existing loan? Many lenders would rather know they will continue to be paid than face no payments at all. And although each lender is different, many will entertain the following changes:

▸ **A rate and term loan modification.** Your lender may agree to alter your interest rate or the term (the length of your loan) without requiring you to re-qualify or apply for a new loan. This is often referred to as a "rate and term modification." By lowering your interest rate and/or increasing the length of your loan, your monthly payments will decrease and become more affordable.

▸ **Lowering your margins or fixing your rate.** If you have an adjustable rate mortgage (a type of loan where your interest rate and

mortgage payments increase or decrease to adjust to economic conditions), you can ask your lender about two things: 1) lowering your
margins, or 2) modifying your adjustable rate to a fixed interest rate.

Your margin is the portion of your loan's interest rate that represents the lender's cost of doing business and its profit. Some lenders
will agree to lower their margin (and lower their profit), which, for
you, means a lower interest rate and lower payments. (If you are confused about your adjustable rate or your margins, don't worry; just be
sure to read Chapter 4 before contacting your lender.)

You can also ask your lender about modifying your adjustable rate
to a fixed interest rate. With this option, you will not have to worry
about your mortgage payment changing or increasing, which will
provide stability for the remainder of the loan.

▸ **Loan consolidation.** If you have more than one loan (a first mortgage and a second mortgage, or a mortgage and a home equity line
of credit), you can ask if your lender would agree to consolidate your
loans into one loan with one payment. Why will this help? Most
often, the interest rates and terms of home equity lines and second
mortgages are not the greatest. By negotiating both loans into one,
you should receive a more desirable interest rate and terms, which
means lower total payments.

▸ **Deferred payments.** If you need time to catch up or you are fore-
casting a few weak months ahead, you can also ask if your lender
would be willing to defer two or three months of payments. If a borrower has a perfect payment history, it's very common for lenders to
accommodate this request, usually deferring up to a maximum of
three months of mortgage payments.

Keep in mind though, "deferred" does not mean "free." These
payments will be tacked on to the back of your loan, and you will still
have to make them eventually. But by deferring the payments to a
later date, you can gain some time and breathing room to catch up and
get your finances in order. Also, if your real estate taxes and insurance
are included in your mortgage payment (as is required with some

loans, which I'll cover more in Chapter 10), your lender will *not* defer these amounts. They will only defer your mortgage payment.

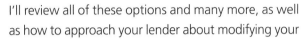

**More Help in Chapter 7**

I'll review all of these options and many more, as well as how to approach your lender about modifying your loan, step by step, in Chapter 7. I've devoted the entire chapter to explain how you can work with your lender to make your mortgage more affordable, what happens if you are facing default and foreclosure, and what options are available to help you save your home.

## Home Equity Loans and Lines of Credit

Home equity loans and lines of credit have also been impacted post-boom. A *home equity loan* is a second mortgage that uses the equity you've built in your home as collateral. You are loaned a one-time lump sum payment, which you pay back in installment payments each month with interest, just like in a regular mortgage. In effect, by taking out a home equity loan (in addition to your mortgage), you'll have two mortgages—and two mortgage payments—for your home.

A *home equity line of credit*, or HELOC, also uses your home's equity as collateral. But with a HELOC, you don't receive the full loan amount at once. A HELOC is very much like a credit card. A lender first determines your total line of credit based on your home's equity. Then, as you borrow against this amount, you are charged only for the money you take out—plus interest. Each month, you can choose to make the minimum monthly payment or pay the full amount back (again, just like a credit card). It's a very flexible and popular loan: you determine how much money you need, and when you need it.

During the boom, when home values were rising, many home-owners took out HELOCs for anticipated future expenses including home improvement, home repair, college tuition, or even medical expenses. They also used HELOCs for personal and luxury items like vacations, cars, and even everyday expenses.

## Some Lenders Are Canceling HELOCs

Today, as home values and home equity have declined, lenders are actively canceling or freezing established HELOCs and blocking borrower access to these funds. This has caused a panic among many homeowners who still have equity in their homes and need to access their HELOCs for planned or emergency expenses.

Why are lenders doing this? Because they're nervous. A lender who holds a HELOC is usually in second position when it comes to recovering money if there's a foreclosure. This is because, after a foreclosure, the lender in first position (usually the lender for the primary mortgage) recovers what is owed to them *first*. The second lender is paid back if (and only if) there is any money left. Remember, even though a HELOC is called a line of credit, it really is the same thing as a *second* mortgage. And second mortgages are never first in line.

As real estate values drop and the equity in a home disappears, there is less and less likelihood there will be any funds left over to repay lenders in this second position. This leaves HELOC lenders scrambling to try to limit their potential losses by preventing borrowers from *continuing* to take out money. From a lender's point of view, the less that is borrowed from a HELOC, the less the lender will have to lose, and the less the lender will have to recover later.

## Keeping Your HELOC Open

How do you know if your HELOC will be affected? Within your HELOC documents, there may be wording that says that your lender reserves the right to cancel, freeze, or reduce your home equity amount.

Lenders can cancel your HELOC for things that you can control, such as suspected fraud, adversely affecting the property's worth, or not making your payments. But lenders can also freeze or reduce the amount of your HELOC for reasons that aren't always under your control, including if the value of your property declines or if your lender has good reason to believe you won't be able to make your payments. In many depressed real estate markets, lenders have watched home values drop. In response, they've reassessed or reappraised home values and notified homeowners that their HELOC has been cancelled. Even if you've made your payments on time, even if you have stellar credit, and even if you haven't used your HELOC funds at all, you still may receive a termination notice from your lender.

Can you protect your HELOC? The good news is that any changes by a lender to a home equity line are governed by federal law and regulations covered in the Truth in Lending Act, the Equal Credit Opportunity Act, and the Fair Housing Act. Your lender *must* have legal cause to modify your HELOC. If they don't have cause, and they modify your HELOC anyway, you do have options as a consumer.

▸ **If your HELOC is still open:** Research the current value of your home, and compare this to your home's value when you opened the HELOC to determine if your credit line is in risk of being frozen. Online sites like www.zillow.com can quickly give you a general idea of your home's value based on sales in your neighborhood. If your home's value has declined and your current equity is *close to* or *less than* your HELOC credit limit, your HELOC is in trouble. If you have an upcoming expense or are depending on having access to the funds in your home equity line, you may want to consider taking the money you need out now, and transferring it to an interest-bearing savings account or CD so you can make sure you'll have access to the funds in the future.

▸ **If you have received a letter stating that your HELOC has been cancelled or frozen:** If the value of your home is not in question but you've still received this letter, you have grounds to appeal to your lender based on your credit score and a six-month history of your home's value. This history needs to show that your home has maintained its value, or that your equity has been consistently *higher* than your HELOC credit limit. Obtaining your own appraisal to document your home's value will also strengthen your case.

If your home's value has decreased significantly, you'll need to work with the lender to see if there is another way to keep your HELOC open. Sometimes, other equity can be used as collateral for the loan; stocks, bonds, cars, or boats may give you some bargaining power. Good credit may also help your cause. And you can also request that your HELOC be reviewed and modified to a lower line of credit rather than it being canceled or frozen altogether. This would enable you to keep the account open, while still reducing the risk for the lender.

• • •

Loans programs have been discontinued, qualifications have increased, and lending overall is more expensive. We really have only one choice: to reset our expectations. We can't change what's happened, but we *can* change how we think about it and how we respond. You can choose to focus on what's been taken away, or you can choose to focus on what you can do to work with the hand you've been dealt. In time, many lending programs and guidelines will stabilize. Banks aren't going to start lending tons of money again overnight. But eventually current conditions will evolve into a stronger and more secure financial environment for everyone.

Is it really possible to pull anything good from this? Believe it or not, absolutely. Eventually, changing the way money is lent will start the lending ball rolling again. Lenders will feel safer about lending their money, and more loans will become available. As this happens, more people will start to buy homes and home values will slowly stabilize. It will be a long process, but we'll get there.

If you are currently looking for a home, it's actually a great time to become a homeowner, especially if you're planning to stay in the home for at least five years. The inventory selection is extensive, and even I don't have to tell you how many great deals are out there. And although it may be harder to obtain financing when you want to make a purchase, take out a loan, or refinance, the financing you do get will be safer for both you and the lender. The boom's biggest professions—real estate, home building, and mortgage lending—have been thinned out considerably. Many inexperienced brokers and agents have left the industry, and only the strongest professionals remain.

## COMING UP

To really understand your lending options, you first need to understand how lending works. In the next chapter, I'll explain the ins and outs of the lending world, from where your loan's money comes from to how it's sold to you, and who might be involved.

# 3

# The Lending Food Chain

## The Main Players Behind Every Loan

You've just put in an offer on a house and now need financing. Or maybe you're thinking about refinancing your home. When you apply for a loan, do you know who is *really* fronting the money for your home? Where does this money come from, and how is it made available to you? Most homeowners don't understand this process because, honestly, the process is pretty complicated. But taking the time to understand more about how lending works and who the main players of lending are is the first step in choosing the right loan.

There are many well-respected professionals in the home finance industry, and as a borrower you have the choice to work with either a bank or a mortgage brokerage firm when you need a loan. Banks have always had a solid reputation; they offer many of today's most common loans, as well as specialty loans for cream-of-the-crop clients. Mortgage brokers and mortgage brokerage firms, in contrast, can cater to a wider group of borrowers because they have access to something banks don't: a much wider selection of loans made avail-

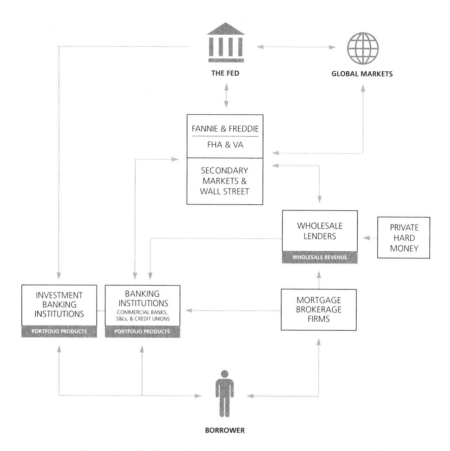

*Figure 3.1: The Main Players: How Your Loan Is Funded and Sold*

- *The Fed determines the overall availability of money and cost to borrow money*
- *Fannie and Freddie determine national lending guidelines for the resale of loans*
- *A Borrower considers a loan from a Banking Institution or a Mortgage Brokerage Firm*
  - *Investment Banking Institutions fund their loans through their own portfolios or through the Federal Reserve*
  - *Commercial Banks, Savings and Loans, and Credit Unions fund their loans through their own portfolios or through secondary market sources*
  - *Wholesale Lenders fund their loans through banking institutions, wholesale revenue, private hard money, or secondary market sources*
  - *Mortgage Brokerage Firms source financing from Wholesale Lenders or Banking Institutions*
- *Loans from Banking Institutions, Wholesale Lenders, and Fannie and Freddie are sold to Secondary Markets as packaged loan portfolios or mortgage-backed securities*
- *Markets from around the world invest in our Secondary Markets*

able by wholesale, commercial, and private lenders.

As a borrower you'll have many people competing for your business, and in many ways, it comes down to a match of Banks vs. Brokers. But no matter who helps you with your loan, in some way, shape or form, all loans lead back to one place: the Fed. To understand your loan, we're going straight to the top.

## The Fed

The Federal Reserve (the Fed) is the Central Bank of the United States and the major regulatory agency for banking institutions. The best way to look at the Federal Reserve is to view it as a bank's bank. In the world of finance, the Fed also makes the rules. Its decisions affect every person and business in the country, as well as many other nations who invest in our economy. When the Fed speaks, the world listens.

The Chairman of the Fed—a role filled by Alan Greenspan for nineteen years before Ben Bernanke took over in 2006—is widely considered to be one of the most powerful presidentially appointed officials in the U.S. government. The Chairman acts as the public face for the Federal Reserve, presiding over the Federal Reserve Board of Governors and twelve regional Federal Reserve banks. The Chairman is the most influential member of the seven-member board, and is responsible for leading the Fed in governing the nation's monetary policies.

The Fed has a big job: it controls the availability of money within our economy as a whole by providing money to (or withdrawing money from) the entire banking system, and by buying and selling government bonds and securities to manage our country's debt. The Fed also sets the price for what it costs to *borrow* money, by setting several key interest rates.

The Fed is directly responsible for setting the *federal funds rate*, which is the interest rate banks charge each other for loans, and for setting the *discount rate*, which is the interest rate banks are charged to borrow money from the Fed. Why are these rates important?

Banks often borrow money from each other or from the Fed to keep enough money in their reserves and to counter the cost of doing business. When the Fed lowers these rates, it's obviously better business for banks because what they borrow costs less. And when banks' costs are lower, this usually translates to better rates for you.

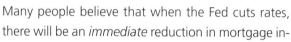

### Where's My Lower Rate?

Many people believe that when the Fed cuts rates, there will be an *immediate* reduction in mortgage interest rates, but that's not always the case. Banks and lenders use a complex combination of indices (financial indicators used to measure inflation) and margins (what the loan costs the bank plus their profit) to set interest rates. So despite moves by the Fed to lower rates, mortgage interest rates could actually go up.

If you want to gauge how mortgage interest rates fluctuate from day to day—and how your loan's own rates might be affected—the easiest thing to do is to start following the Fed's 10-Year Treasury note, also called a T-note. Within the economy, Treasury notes have a dual purpose. For consumers, they are a very secure investment. Consumers can purchase T-notes and earn a small but stable return; the value of a T-note and the note's yield (the amount of interest you will earn on the note as an investment) are both backed by the U.S. government, so they won't change. They are guaranteed, no matter what.

For the government, the T-note, along with other government bills, notes, and bonds (referred to as *treasury securities* or *treasuries*), allows the government to generate money and manage the country's debt. Consumers provide the government with a positive cash flow by investing in treasury securities, and the government utilizes this money until the securities mature and it's time to give the money back. Because of this relationship, T-notes are seen as a good gauge of what

## THE MARKET REPORT

| | | | |
|---|---|---|---|
| ▲ DOW | | 8,017.59 | +39.51 |
| ▲ NASDAQ | | 1,621.87 | +19.24 |
| ▲ S&P 500 | *YIELD* | 842.50 | +8.12 |
| ▲ RUSSELL 2000 | | 456.13 | +5.94 |
| ▲ 10-YR NOTE | *T-NOTE* | 2.90% | +0.14 |

**Figure 3.2:** *The 10-Year Treasury note yield as it may appear in your newspaper.*

is going on with the economy on a bigger scale, as I'll explain next.

While mortgage rates are not *directly* tied to the T-note, the T-note does serve as a good indicator of what's to come. Look online or in your local paper for the Treasury note yield (I've included an example of what this will look like in Figure 3.2). If the yield on the note goes down, it's an indication that the economy is sluggish; the Fed will encourage investment and spending, and as a result, you should expect mortgage rates to stay level or get slightly better. If the yield goes up, the economy is growing too quickly. The Fed will try to control growth, so you can expect mortgage rates to get worse. Other consumer loans including credit cards, car loans, and home equity lines tend to follow the federal funds rate.

```
T-Note Yield Goes Down = Mortgage Rates Go Down
   T-Note Yield Goes Up = Mortgage Rates Go Up
```

While I recommend paying attention to changes in the Fed in a general way, I don't advise becoming too involved in monitoring its daily actions. The system is complex, is far from perfect, and there are many who dispute the Fed's power, purpose, and effectiveness. The Fed has its good days and its bad days, and while the Fed works hard, balancing the economy is obviously far from a simple job.

## Fannie, Freddie, and the Secondary Market

While the Fed determines what happens with money in general, including how much money is available to banks and lenders and how much financing a home costs, your loan is just as influenced by three other players: Fannie Mae, Freddie Mac, and the Secondary Market. In fact, when it comes to mortgages, Fannie and Freddie are just as powerful as the Fed.

As I explained briefly in Chapter 2, Fannie and Freddie make sure loans will always be available. They guarantee that any loans meeting their guidelines can be sold to the secondary market, which generates more cash for banks and lenders, who then can offer even more loans to consumers.

---

DEFINITION **What Is Fannie Mae?**

*Federal National Mortgage Association (FNMA)*
Fannie Mae is a government-sponsored enterprise, or GSE. GSEs are established by the federal government when Congress feels that our country's private business sector is not meeting a public or social need, especially in the areas of agriculture, home finance, and education. Fannie Mae was chartered by Congress back in 1938 with the sole purpose of providing funding for the housing markets during the Great Depression, and thirty years later, in 1968, Fannie was converted to a publicly traded company. And although Fannie Mae is a private company and is *technically* not part of the government, as a GSE, it still performs many duties for the federal government. Fannie Mae sets national lending guidelines, purchases mortgages from banks and lenders, and sells them to the secondary market. Fannie also helps to replenish mortgage funds, allows banks and lenders to lend more, and promotes affordable loan rates and terms. Fannie, along with her brother Freddie Mac, have guaranteed the resale of over half of all loans in the entire U.S. mortgage market.

---

DEFINITION **What Is Freddie Mac?**

*Federal Home Loan Mortgage Corporation (FHLMC)*

Freddie Mac, like his sister Fannie, is also a government-sponsored enterprise (GSE) and is a private, publicly traded company. Fannie and Freddie serve the same purpose; in fact, Freddie was created in 1970 so Fannie wouldn't have a monopoly on the government's secondary market sales. Like Fannie, Freddie sets lending standards and increases the supply of money available for mortgages: Freddie Mac purchases, packages, and guarantees the groups of mortgages that form mortgage-backed securities, which are then sold within the secondary market.

The federal government relies heavily on both Fannie and Freddie to do their jobs. That's why when Fannie and Freddie are in distress (as we've seen in our current lending market) the federal government provides funding—or bailouts—as needed. Without Freddie and Fannie in place, many parts of the economy could simply collapse, even more than they have already.

For many borrowers, selling to the secondary market is a confusing concept. Why would a bank or lender work hard to get my loan, and then sell it? And what is the secondary market?

Many borrowers believe that when they take out a loan with a bank or lender, that's who ultimately owns the loan: take out a loan with Bank Z, Bank Z owns your loan. Makes sense. But sometimes that's not the case. Bank Z may sell your loan to someone else to make a profit, sometimes right away. In fact, the "owner" of a loan may change many times during the loan's life. Your loan could be sold to another bank or lender, or be packaged and sold as a mortgage-backed security to Wall Street, to private investors, or to servicing institutions (who buy and manage loans)—or all of the above.

This resale of your loan is what is referred to as "selling to the secondary market." But don't worry about your loan changing owners.

Your loan will remain exactly the same, even after it is sold. Remember, the secondary market is only a purchaser. Your loan's structure—the loan amount, interest rate, and term—will always remain the same, no matter who legally "owns" your loan.

---

**MORE INFO**    **Is Selling to the Secondary Market Safe?**

Isn't selling mortgages to Wall Street and investors what happened during the boom and bust? Isn't this what got us into this mess in the first place? Shouldn't you be worried?

During the boom, both loans and the secondary market were misused and abused; there were lax standards and regulations for approving, buying, selling, and packaging loans, and most of these loans didn't meet with Fannie or Freddie's approval. But the secondary market has always been a part of modern lending, dating back to the 1930s, and actually benefits the entire lending industry.

Both Fannie and Freddie create national buying guidelines for banks and lenders and arrange for loans to be purchased and sold on the secondary market. Unlike the mortgage-backed securities that caused the mortgage meltdown, Fannie and Freddie enforce strict guidelines to ensure stability. And by selling loans to the secondary market, banks and lenders recycle and generate funding, and all of this buying and selling provides investment vehicles for other parts of the economy. Businesses that invest in the secondary market usually receive a more secure and timely return on their investment, and this security attracts *even more* investors, generating *even more* money to fund new loans. With more money available for loans, more people can purchase homes, and the new loans for these homes may *also* be sold to the secondary market.

As you can see it's a very cyclical process: each part of the process depends on the other. By providing standards for safe loans, which allow for safer *investments*, Fannie and Freddie play an essential role not only in the mortgage industry, but in the economy in general.

---

## What Does "Selling to the Secondary Market" Mean for Your Loan?

After a bank or lender sells a loan to you, they have the choice to keep the loan or to sell it to someone else. But just because a bank or lender would *like* to sell your loan, that doesn't mean there will be a guaranteed buyer—unless the loan meets Fannie or Freddie's guidelines. These guidelines apply to aspects of the loan itself *and* to how a borrower qualifies for the loan.

For you, this means some of your lending options, and whether you *qualify* for these options, may be determined long before you step foot in a bank or meet with a mortgage broker. More often than not, but especially in times when the economy is tough, banks and lenders will want the security of a "guaranteed sale" so they know they will make at least *some* profit on a loan. This means that the lending options that are available today are more or less determined by the team of Fannie and Freddie.

Keep in mind, banks and lenders do not sell all of their loans, and not all loans meet Fannie or Freddie's guidelines (I'll explain more about which loan programs are and are not backed by Fannie and Freddie in Chapter 4). If a bank or lender is planning to hold on to a loan, or if they want to sell it to the secondary market without the help of Fannie or Freddie, banks and lenders will set their own loan qualifications and guidelines. But when they want a guaranteed sale, what Fannie and Freddie say goes.

---

MORE INFO **How Do You Know if Your Loan Has Been Sold?**

If you've received a notice stating that you should now send your payments to a different mortgage servicer, this is a good indication that your loan has been sold to the secondary market. A *mortgage servicer* is a company that collects your mortgage payments on behalf of the bank, lender, or investor who holds your mortgage.

Sometimes, though, your loan is sold and you would never know it, because the company you send your checks to doesn't change. A bank or lender may sell your loan to someone else, but continue to service it themselves. For example, Bank X may package and sell your loan to a group of investors, but agree to continue to service your loan. You continue to make payments to Bank X, not realizing that Bank X is actually forwarding these payments to the investors.

For most borrowers, knowing if your loan has been sold is inconsequential. But if you ever need to modify your mortgage, and you need to contact the company or group that actually owns your loan (as you might need to do if you run into financial difficulty or are facing foreclosure), tracking down the owner of your loan becomes very important, as I'll cover more in Chapter 7.

## The Banks

One of the first places many borrowers look for financing is from a bank. A bank is any institution that provides banking services, including commercial banks, credit unions, and savings and loan associations (to make things easier, in this chapter I'll be referring to all of these institutions as "banks"). When you finance your home through a bank, the money for your loan is backed by one of two sources: the bank's own funds, or one of several government-sponsored or insured programs.

A bank operates just like any other business, providing products and services to make a profit and then leveraging this profit to make even more money. One of the ways they do this is by offering what are known as *portfolio loans*, which are loans that are kept as part of a bank's own investment portfolio. These loans are never sold to the secondary market; portfolio loans are held by the bank, and the bank only, for the entire life of the loan. Because a bank is lending its own money *and* holding on to the loan, it can also decide what kinds of guidelines will be used for qualification and approval.

What does this mean for you? Flexibility. Although most banks use Fannie and Freddie's lending guidelines as a model for their own loans, for portfolio loans banks can bend and change the rules as they see fit. Borrowers who are financially stable but who may not be able to document their income or assets traditionally and borrowers who have unique lending needs are usually good candidates for portfolio loans.

Of course, these loans must make financial sense and be a secure investment for the bank too. Because of this, portfolio loans are reserved largely, but not always, for a bank's own clients (where a bank can gauge a client's stability); for short-term loans of seven years or less (where the loans tie up a bank's funds for less time); or for large loans or loans for multiple properties (where there is a bigger profit for the bank).

Most banks also have the ability to offer government-sponsored loans, which *always* meet Fannie or Freddie's guidelines and can be sold to the secondary market. And many banks also offer government-insured loan programs from the Federal Housing Administration (FHA) and the U.S. Department of Veterans Affairs (VA). FHA loans help provide a source of affordable financing for all homeowners, and VA loans provide affordable financing options for our veterans. Because these loan programs were created to meet various social needs, FHA and VA loans are *insured* by the government. This means that even though a bank is loaning its own funds, the government agrees to pay for a portion of the loan if the homeowner defaults. This obviously offers great protection for a bank, and is an even better incentive for a bank to offer these loans to borrowers.

By offering these government programs, a bank has access to a wide variety of loans, including more affordable loan programs and loans with low down payments, which is great for you. And because banks offer *both* specialty portfolio loans as well as government-sponsored or insured loans, banks are a reliable and efficient way for many homeowners to obtain financing. You can go into a bank for a loan knowing that you will have a good selection of loans to choose from.

DEFINITION

**Government-Sponsored and Government-Insured: What's the Difference?**

These two terms are often confusing. A *government-sponsored loan* passes Fannie or Freddie's guidelines, and in return receives a guarantee that the loan will have a buyer in the secondary market. A *government-insured loan* guarantees that a loan will be "covered" if a borrower defaults. If a homeowner stops making payments, the government steps in, and a government insurance fund—not the bank or lender—makes up part of the loss from the loan. But for both types of loans, whether the loan is sponsored or insured, it's the bank's job to make sure that the loan—*and* the borrower—meets all of the program's guidelines.

As we all know, banks also have local banking locations and other banking products (savings and checking accounts, CDs, credit cards, etc.), and for many homeowners, the convenience of one-stop banking is a big plus. Many borrowers feel more comfortable working with the bank that they have used for years or that is right in their own neighborhood. And if you are already a customer of a bank, many banks will provide you with competitive options for financing because they want to keep your business. Overall, for many borrowers, banks are a great fit.

## The Brokers

When you hear the term *mortgage broker*, you most likely think of a professional who arranges financing. And mortgage brokers do exactly that: they bring borrowers and lenders together, working independently or within a larger mortgage brokerage firm. Mortgage brokerage firms include many different business structures, from simply brokering, or arranging, loans, to being able to lend money from their own funds just like banks. Some of these business structures can lend in all fifty states, and some can only lend in states where they are licensed. It can be confusing, because the individuals and companies who broker loans have so many different legal classifications and names—including mortgage brokers, mortgage consultants, mortgage broker businesses, correspondent mortgage lenders, mortgage lenders, and mortgage bankers. These names can also vary by state, but they all essentially "sell" other institutions' money at a cost to the borrower, the "buyer" of the money.

Like banks, brokers have access to Fannie Mae, Freddie Mac, FHA, and VA programs. And although mortgage brokers are not able to sell banks' in-house portfolio loans, mortgage brokers have access to many other loan sources individual banks do not.

Mortgage brokers, unlike banks, can work with many different wholesale lenders (who sell loans only to brokers) and many commercial banks (who sell loans to both brokers and borrowers directly), as well as private-sector investors (known as hard money lenders) and certain secondary market sources (groups of investors who purchase loans).

The *upside* to this is that brokers fill a *big gap* banks miss. Most banks have strict lending requirements for the loans they offer, so not all borrowers can qualify for bank financing. Brokers, on the other hand, have access to lenders who are more flexible, and even in today's conservative lending market, brokers are able to help many of the borrowers banks turn down. Both the sheer number of funding sources and the variety of loan programs brokers have access to allow brokers to help many of the borrowers banks cannot.

The *downside* to this is that every wholesale lender, bank, and private investor each has its *own* set of procedures, qualifications, and guidelines, and brokers have to keep up with all of them. It's not a job to be taken lightly, so you'll want to work with a professional who understands your needs, has experience, and also has strong lender relationships. In Chapter 5, I'll explain more about the role of a mortgage broker (or what I prefer to call a mortgage consultant), how to find one who is experienced and will put your needs first, and how to

**How Does Wholesale Lending Work?**

The majority of the loan sources and loan programs brokers have access to are not available to you, as a consumer, directly. They are *wholesale lending* sources made available to brokers only, who then make the programs available to you:

**Wholesale Lenders** obtain funds through banking institutions, their own revenue, private investors, and secondary market sources. Funds are packaged into loan products and programs, which are made available to mortgage brokers at a wholesale price determined by availability and demand.

**Mortgage Brokers** act on the wholesale lender's behalf by selling these loans to borrowers according to the lender's terms and guidelines. A mortgage broker determines the retail price for a loan based on the loan's wholesale price, the program availability, the risk factor attached to each borrower, and the difficulty of the loan.

---

tell if he or she is doing his or her job well.

If you decide to borrow directly from a bank, you will have to go from bank to bank to determine if they have a loan for you. A broker, on the other hand, can evaluate your situation and know immediately, based on your borrower profile, which lenders or banks offer loan programs that fit your needs. For many people, a broker will save a lot of time.

Brokers also have a strong working knowledge of how additional documentation can help strengthen your case for a loan, and they have direct access to a lender's underwriter, the gatekeeper for your loan. If your loan runs into trouble, you don't have the option to appeal your case to an underwriter yourself, whereas most brokers can and will. And if worse comes to worst and your loan is denied, your broker can try again with other lenders and funding sources.

To make things even more confusing for borrowers, brokers can also work directly with banks—many times with better results than borrowers will get. Many national banks have both *retail divisions*, selling to you the consumer, and *wholesale divisions*, selling only to brokers. In these cases, a mortgage broker may be able to get better rates, terms, or fees for your loan even if you applied at the same bank yourself. Crazy, isn't it?

## Understanding Profit

Lending, regardless of what parties are involved, is a business, and all businesses need to make a profit to survive. As a borrower, you are ultimately the main source for this profit, so you'll want to pay special attention to how much you are being charged. Banks, lenders, and brokers all make their money any one of four ways—through interest rates, through fees, through selling to the secondary market, or through yield spread premiums—or through a combination of these.

▸ **Banks and lenders are compensated through interest rates, fees, and selling to the secondary market.** Any institution that funds a loan (including banks and lenders), makes its money each month through the loan's interest rate. Even if you are sold a government-sponsored or insured program, banks and lenders still determine their own interest rates and fees for the loan itself. This is what makes the market competitive, and why you'll be quoted many different rates for what appears to be the same loan.

In addition, banks and lenders usually charge underwriting and miscellaneous fees from $595 to $995 to cover the costs of securing your loan. Once your loan closes, banks and lenders can *also* make money by packaging your loan with other loans and selling them to the secondary market.

▸ **Brokers are compensated by the lender and/or the borrower through yield spread premiums (YSP) and origination fees.** A mortgage broker makes their money from the lender, the borrower, or a combination of the two.

Brokers may be paid directly by the lender through a *yield spread premium* (a percentage of the total loan amount) for acting on the lender's behalf and placing the loan. Lenders typically offer to pay brokers a YSP of 0 to 4 percent, depending on the type of loan and the loan's interest rate.

To put this into dollars, for a $150,000 loan your mortgage broker could get paid anywhere from $0 to $6,000 for placing and overseeing your loan, which is then usually split with the mortgage company the broker works for. Within the industry, brokers will refer to yield spread premiums as being paid on the "back" of the loan, because the broker is being paid by the lender, and not the borrower.

---

 CAUTION **How Much Is Fair?**

A yield spread premium of up to 3 percent is very fair to the broker and to you. If a broker is offered more than 3 percent in YSP for your loan, and your loan is not unusual or difficult, a professional broker should pass some of that windfall on to you, usually in the form of a reduced interest rate. It's not required, but it's safe to say that brokers who don't may be greedy, or even predatory, and certainly don't have your best interest at heart.

During the boom, many unethical mortgage brokers purposely placed their clients in higher-rate or otherwise predatory loans because these loans paid a higher YSP. Of course, you don't want this to happen. In Chapter 6, I'll explain more about how yield spread works, how yield spread is directly tied to your loan's interest rate, and how to understand if you are being charged fairly for your loan.

---

If a lender doesn't offer a yield spread premium or offers a very low YSP, a consultant or broker will charge *you* directly for securing

 **The Percentage Point**

In the lending industry, you'll find that many fees are expressed as "points." A broker may say "I'll need to charge you one origination point," or "The lender is paying one point in yield spread premium." A point is just another way of saying "percentage" (taken from the formal phrase "percentage point"). These two terms are interchangeable: 1 point always equals 1 percent of your loan amount, and 1 percent always equals 1 point.

your loan, in the form of an *origination fee*. Like a YSP, an origination fee is a percentage of your total loan amount. If a broker is receiving no YSP, an origination fee of 1 to 2 percent is standard. For example, if you have a $250,000 loan and the lender is not paying the broker *any* YSP, a 1 percent origination fee of $2,500 would be fair.

Does $2,500 sound like a lot? It isn't when you consider most brokers also have to split this fee with the company they work for. Typical splits are fifty/fifty, so in this case your broker would be making $1,250 on your loan. Within the industry, brokers will refer to origination fees as being paid on the "front" of the loan, since the borrower is paying for their profit. If your broker is being paid with a very small YSP and *also* charges you an origination fee, the highest these two rates should add up to is 2 to 3 percent of your loan amount.

You will also be charged a processing fee by the company your broker works for, which should cover the cost of pulling your credit, gathering and submitting documentation as required by a lender's underwriter, ordering appraisals and the title, and overseeing coordination with the title company, the insurance company, any real estate firms, and any other parties involved with your loan. Generally, processing fees should run no more than $375 to $795.

You'll find your yield spread premium, origination fee, processing fee, and lender fees all in your Good Faith Estimate (GFE), which is a detailed estimate of all the fees and charges associated with your loan, listed line by line. As you meet with various banks or brokers to find the *right* loan, you'll receive many different GFEs. A GFE will help you to understand what loans a bank or broker can offer you, what interest rate you will be charged, and your loan's total fees and costs. I'll talk more about the role of a GFE in getting the right loan in Chapters 5 and 6. In the meantime, to see what a GFE will usually look like, and for a description of *all* of the charges you should expect on a GFE (and charges you should look out for), turn to Appendix I.

Both banks and brokers are required by law to provide you with a GFE *before* you commit to a loan. If they don't, go somewhere else. GFEs are also used to document your loan during the lending process: as your loan progresses, if it changes, the broker's fees change, or the interest rate or loan terms change, a redisclosure—a revised GFE—is also required prior to closing.

## Your Good Faith Estimate and Your HUD Settlement Statement

Before your closing, you'll want to compare your final GFE, which details all of your final fees and costs, to your HUD-1 settlement statement (which you should receive at least one day before your closing). Your HUD is basically a legal version of the GFE, as instituted by the U.S. Department of Housing and Urban Development. This statement lists the final costs and charges for all the parties who have been involved in your loan, and how these charges will be paid out. These charges include lender and broker fees, title company fees and title searches, government taxes and recording fees, and appraisal fees, just to name a few.

While you are legally required to receive this statement one day before your closing, in the "real world" this doesn't always happen. Sometimes, you could receive your final HUD just a few hours before your closing, or even at the closing table itself! Lenders are very busy, and they may get information and approvals to the title company (which is responsible for entering the final amounts on the HUD) at

MORE INFO

## When the Yield Spread Premium Is Not on Your Good Faith Estimate

When you work with a mortgage broker, any yield spread premium is legally required to be disclosed on your GFE, along with any origination fees. But if you work with a company that lends its own money, like a bank, direct lender, or mortgage banker, you *won't* see yield spread premiums on your GFE, or any other amount that shows you a bank or lender's profit. This causes an uproar with many mortgage brokers in the home finance industry, who claim this practice is unfair to brokers. Banks don't have to show these amounts, but brokers do?

The easiest way to explain why a bank doesn't have to disclose its yield or profit is to relate lending money to selling a home. If you sell your own home, without the help of a realtor, you determine the price for your home and your own profit. However, if you hire a realtor to sell your home *for* you, you want to know in advance how much they'll be charging you.

The same applies to lending. If you go to a bank directly for your loan, you are getting your money from the source. It's the bank's money to lend, so they can determine their own profit, and they don't have to tell you what that profit is—it's part of how they run their business. However, if you are hiring someone else to find a loan *for* you (like a mortgage broker), you want to understand what they are getting paid to arrange your loan. This is why a broker's yield spread premium is required to be disclosed.

If you work with a bank directly, you won't see a yield spread premium on your GFE, but you *can* expect to see a lender's "front-end" fees, including the same kind of origination fees, processing fees, and lending fees that you would see if your worked with a broker. Banks are required to show these fees, because they are being passed on to you directly.

the last minute. This means the title company may be getting this information to *you* at the *very* last minute.

If you don't receive your settlement statement in advance, make sure you bring your final GFE to the closing table and compare it to your HUD carefully. You'll find a detailed explanation of both a GFE and a HUD (and how to compare the two documents at your closing) in Appendix I. If you run into any issues, or if something on your HUD doesn't make sense, you are *not* required to follow through with the closing. In Chapter 6, I'll explain more about what you can do if you don't receive your HUD statement on time—and what to do if it doesn't match up to your GFE.

 In addition to the GFE and HUD I've shown you in Appendix I, you'll also find additional samples, case studies, and explanations in the reader's section of my website.

By reviewing and completely understanding your GFE long before your closing, you'll be better prepared and will decrease the risk of surprises—or shocks—at the closing table. If your bank or broker has done a good job, your final loan costs should be no more than $100–$200 above your GFE. Period. You may have heard stories (or you may have experienced yourself) how loan fees, rates, or terms suddenly change at the closing table. This should never happen, and when it does, it's usually predatory. For an insider's take of what to do in these situations, and how to avoid these situations overall, be sure to carefully read Chapters 5 and 6, where I cover step by step what to expect from the entire loan approval process, from your initial GFE to your loan's final approval, and how to avoid any issues at the closing table.

· · ·

Lending, the Fed, banks, brokers—it's fair to say I try to explain most subjects associated with the lending industry as simply as possible, and this is especially true for the lending food chain. Following the "money trail" for a loan, or even for a single dollar, is far more complicated than the process I've laid out here. I could have given you the technical details about how banks and lenders filter the majority of their funds through warehouse lines of credit, or how profits are calculated and marginally split among investors. I could have explained the fractional lending guidelines banks once used or how many politicians believe that the Fed has too much unsupervised power and has been deflating the dollar since it was detached from gold standards. And I could have written more about how the Fed is considered the last resort for lending. But what really matters for you, as a borrower, is understanding more about your loan and who can help you with it. I could have given you the intricate details; instead, I've tried to give you the details that you really need.

So in the end, who should you choose to help you with your loan? Being in the business as long as I have, I've discovered there is only one hard and fast rule: every borrower and every loan are truly unique. Your own needs and circumstances should determine who you go to and how you approach financing, not the other way around. You don't want to be the square peg crammed into the round hole. If you find that you have a solid financial background and know exactly what you want, both banks and brokers can easily help you. If you need someone to help you understand your options, or help you with other areas like managing credit or saving for a down payment, a broker is often a better fit. Much of your choice depends on which loan program is the best fit for your specific circumstances, and, in the next chapter, I'll review just what your options are. Let your own lending needs determine who is right for you.

## COMING UP

Getting a feel for how lending works behind the scenes is a great first step. The second step is to understand what loans are available. Do you know what loans you can qualify for? Do you understand your current loan? In the next chapter, I'll take a closer look at lending terms and loan programs, as well as the advantages and disadvantages of many of today's most common loans.

# 4

## Loan Specific

Inside the Programs and the Process

I n the past decade alone, the home finance industry has not only seen its share of banks, brokers, and lenders, it's seen an explosion of new loans and programs, as well as fundamental shifts in how loans are structured. Lending seems like it should be simple: you agree to borrow money, and you agree to pay it back. Simple, right? But in reality, lending is a complicated equation of guidelines, rates, terms, margins, penalties, caps, and more. Even the history of loans and lending is complicated.

Believe it or not, insurance companies, not banks or lenders, offered the very first mortgages. Imagine making mortgage payments on your home, but in three to five years, the balance on your loan is due in full. Yes, that's right, in full. This is how home finance worked for a very long time, and not surprisingly, it was extremely difficult for many people to own homes. These loans required a large down payment (often as much as 50 percent) followed by interest payments every month. At the end of the loan, if the balance wasn't paid in full, a homeowner would lose the home, as well as the down payment they had already paid in.

It wasn't until the Great Depression, when the government was forced to completely revamp the country's entire banking system, that the responsibility of mortgage lending shifted from insurance companies to banks and savings and loan institutions. In 1932 Congress established the Federal Home Loan Bank, which created a source of funding for banks to offer mortgages, and in 1934 Congress created the Federal Housing Administration, which paved the way for loan programs geared toward long-term homeownership. The loans of the Great Depression era were revolutionary—they offered lower stable payments over a period of twenty to twenty-five years, a radical change from the short three- to five-year mortgages borrowers had known before—and these loans soon became the foundation for affordable financing.

With the formation and growth of Fannie Mae and the secondary market in the years to follow, more funding was made available for loans, jumpstarting the creation of many of the loan programs we know today. And as the economy and the needs of homeowners have changed, so have mortgages, as a way to expand homeownership *and* as a way to offer more returns to investors in the secondary market.

During the recent real estate boom, more loan programs were created than ever before, as banks, lenders, and Wall Street finance experts developed new, creative, and risky loans to fuel their own profits and fill investor's pockets. And in the end, when the real estate bubble popped, many of these loans popped as well.

When loans popped and markets crashed, there was a backlash from, well, everyone. People became fearful of anything "creative" or "subprime." Although creative loans have without a doubt contributed to our problems in lending and real estate (as I have mentioned), it doesn't mean that these loans are bad or without a purpose. Having a particular loan does not mean you will lose your home. It's not being able to *afford* your loan or not paying your mortgage that causes the problems.

The thing is, the "bad boys" of lending—Alt-A, subprime, creative loans, and others—were originally created to be temporary band-aids for borrowers with issues like bad credit, low income, or little savings. In theory, once the issues were fixed, borrowers were supposed to refinance into secure, long-term loans with better rates and terms. But because lending fees and interest rates were so profitable to lenders and brokers, and because the loans offered short-term flexibility and lower payments to the borrower, these loans quickly made their way into the general marketplace. They became very popular very fast, and quickly ended up being abused.

If you look back just ten to twelve years, the lending market for the most part consisted of conventional loans (loans that meet Fannie and Freddie lending guidelines), jumbo loans (very large loan amounts), and government-insured loans from the Federal Housing Administration and the Department of Veterans Affairs (loans guaranteed by the government in the case of default). Unless a private lender was willing to take a chance and lend to a borrower, the average person had limited options. Without at least 20 percent to put down, borrowers had no choice but to prove their income and employment history for at least the past two years and show at least two months of assets and financial reserves. Borrowers also needed to have good credit, as well as a perfect rental or mortgage history—no excuses and no exceptions. Sound familiar? We are faced with these same issues right now.

Many borrowers then, just like many borrowers today, couldn't meet these qualifications and were turned down for financing. But loan guidelines have a purpose, and sometimes there is a good reason for being turned down for a loan. If you don't have a stable income or a good financial history, or if you have abused your credit or have problems with debt, homeownership may not be right for you. This is something to give real thought to. Even if you don't have any of these issues, owning a home is not a one-size-fits-all decision. *Not* owning a home could easily be a better decision for you, and, further still, you may not even *want* to own a home. This is perfectly okay. There are a lot of responsibilities that come with homeownership, and, as I've mentioned, financing a home is about much more than your mortgage payment. There are many other costs that come with a home, including taxes, insurance, upkeep, and more—sometimes much more (we'll look at these in Chapter 10). For some people, owning a home is just not worth the trouble, and renting may be a much better choice.

There are also those who technically fall short of a loan's qualifications and guidelines who could easily afford a loan. You might be self-employed with a great accountant who writes everything off for tax purposes, so your taxes make it look like you make less income than you actually do. You may earn enough, but haven't been saving enough and so you don't have decent reserves. Or you may have a solid income and a significant amount of money saved, but at one point damaged your credit. There are many cases where borrowers could easily afford a loan and its payments, but they have a hard time obtaining standard, conventional financing. That's where many nonconforming and creative loans come in as responsible alternatives.

Even with all of the bad press surrounding creative lending, I still feel lenders were doing a service by trying to provide certain borrowers with avenues for financing. Many lenders started with good intentions, but greed took over and they just didn't know when to say enough is enough. Even though the rates were higher and the terms were shorter, even though there were prepayment penalties associated with paying the loan off early, and even though lenders charged more to make up for the risk, these loans meant people who had *always* been turned down for financing were given a chance they'd never had before. Although many of these new borrowers were responsible with their loans, many others were not, and in part, that's what has led us to where we are today.

Once you take the time to dissect and analyze the types of creative loans sold during the boom (as we will in this chapter), some of them actually look quite intelligent—but only *if* you made responsible financial decisions and *if* you also had a responsible broker who didn't take advantage of you or your loan. That's a lot of ifs, and that's why a lot of these programs fell apart. But if everything goes right, as was the case with my client Lisa, these loans can be very beneficial for both the borrower and the lender.

FATHER KNOWS BEST?

In 2006, I met with Lisa, who had been shopping for a refinance and was having a hard time finding an affordable payment. Lisa and her husband Mark had received many different estimates: some were for traditional fixed-rate loans, and others were for new subprime loans that had just started to be offered by banks and brokers. Even though Lisa and Mark had done their research, all of the quotes they received included payments they just couldn't afford on a monthly basis. Lisa had been recovering from some health issues, and the couple was still juggling medical bills and living expenses.

As they explained their situation, I looked over their finances and their bills, as well as their combined income and total debt. Although their debt, when compared to their income, was pretty high, they were still able to qualify for conventional, traditional financing. The payments were just too expensive. Even though it seemed *on paper* that Lisa and Mark could afford the higher payments, they knew they would be stretching their budget too thin. Their single goal was to keep their mortgage payments low and manageable.

After carefully reviewing all of their options, Lisa and Mark decided on an Option ARM (short for "adjustable rate mortgage"), a fairly new creative loan. This loan met their needs: in months when money was tight, they had the option to pay a lower monthly payment. And in any months when they could afford more, or once their medical expenses were no longer an issue, they had the option to pay a higher monthly payment in order to pay down the loan faster. Overall, the loan saved Lisa and Mark $425 a month, which was a welcome relief.

To cover all their bases, I also developed a long-term plan for other costs related to their home, including their real estate taxes and insurance, as well as a plan for their long-term financial goals. After the closing, Lisa and Mark were very happy to be in a more affordable loan *with* a long-term plan. We left on great terms.

About six months later, I received a call from Lisa's father. Now, Lisa was a grown woman, so I have to admit, this call caught me by surprise. Her father immediately bombarded me with questions and accusations about the loan I had arranged for his daughter. According to the father, his own sister (who had just refinanced into a 30-year fixed rate loan herself) told him that any subprime or exotic loan was destined to fail. The newspapers and news shows were all talking about it. The subprime market was tanking and his daughter was part of the subprime mess. She would surely lose her home because it was backed by a subprime lender! The lender would go under and take his daughter along with it. The father went on for a full fifteen minutes, and ended with, "Well, what do you have to say for yourself?"

I took a deep breath. I understood Lisa's father; underneath the insults and the anger, he only wanted to protect his daughter. So I took the time to explain: with each loan, there are many needs and variables to consider, and the most important variable to his daughter was the payment. Lisa could have chosen several other loan programs, but the other programs had higher payments, which she couldn't afford. And he certainly couldn't compare his daughter's loan to his sister's loan; they were two different people with completely different circumstances and needs. His daughter's loan was safe, and she wasn't in jeopardy of losing her home. As long as she made the payments, it didn't matter what lender or group was associated with her loan. And even though the loan was a subprime loan, his daughter also had the option to make higher payments if she wanted to pay down the loan faster, just like with the loans he was used to. Plus, Lisa and her husband had developed a strong long-term plan, both for their mortgage and for their finances overall. It really was a well–thought out decision. The father wasn't convinced. The next day, Lisa called, apologizing profusely.

Lisa's father had been misled by the media, family influences, and those who represent themselves as experts even though they have no real expertise. I couldn't help but realize how many people must be just like Lisa's father—misinformed, confused, weary of the mortgage and finance industry, baffled by all the terms and technical details, and finally just downright afraid of lending.

Taking the time to learn about lending and your loan is one of the most important things you can do to make the right decisions for yourself and your family. Only you know what works for you, and ultimately, only you can decide what type of financing best fits your needs. To be able to make this choice, however, you have to do your homework about loans and the lending process. You may need financing to purchase a home. Or you may need to refinance because you would like to switch loans, you want to save money, or you would like to take money out of your home. Depending on your needs and your financial situation, you may have a lot of choices, and you will have a lot of decisions to make. Understand, though, that even with a solid knowledge of loans and lending, it might still be difficult to make your final decision without some professional guidance. Learn these basics, and then find someone who can help you navigate the waters. In fact, I'll help you to find this person in the very next chapter.

Even in today's post-boom lending market, there are still many different loan options and many different ways to qualify for loans. Let's take a look at some of these differences and confusing terms, and let's also break down some of the loans and their unique characteristics. Although there are so many kinds of loans out there that it would be impossible to list them all, I'll use this chapter to review and explain the core loan programs you'll be most likely to encounter in any market.

 Lending changes all the time, and loans will definitely change more in the years to come. To keep up with the most recent program changes, updates, and new loan options, just check in on my website. The foundation I provide here in this book will help you to understand any loans you may come across, either now or in the future.

## Fannie and Freddie

It's hard to envision loans or lending at all without talking about Fannie Mae and Freddie Mac standards again; their presence and importance in the industry as a whole are undisputed. As we saw in the last chapter, Fannie and Freddie outline national lending guidelines, and lenders create loan programs based on these requirements. If a borrower passes Fannie and Freddie's requirements, they are referred to as a *conforming borrower*. Loans that follow Fannie and Freddie guidelines are called *conforming loans*, and as we know, these loans can be sold through Fannie and Freddie to the secondary market (we'll talk about loans that *don't* follow these guidelines later on).

Fannie and Freddie guidelines are so solid, they're often used as a benchmark for all loans—even loans that aren't sold through Fannie or Freddie. In fact, some of the riskiest loans available during the boom still had qualification requirements that resembled Fannie and Freddie guidelines. Fannie and Freddie spend a lot of time carefully evaluating risk and underwriting practices; they determine what borrower and property characteristics will make for the safest and most stable loans, and they do their job well.

## Conventional Loans

Conventional loans are the heart of lending; they're the traditional loans banks and lenders have used for years. These loans can be written through a bank or a lender, but they *always* conform to Fannie and Freddie guidelines.

If there is one word I can use to describe conventional loan programs, it is "stable." Conventional loans have long been considered the most stable of all loan categories: they attract the most stable borrowers and provide loans that give stability to secondary market portfolios. Even during the height of subprime lending, conventional loans were consistently sold by the millions. And even now, after most creative and subprime products have vanished, conventional loans remain. Today, a homeowner with a conventional loan is secure and in one of the best positions to weather the storm of the economy.

What makes these loans so stable? The structure of the loans themselves is one reason. The majority of conventional loans have a fixed interest rate so no matter what happens with the economy, the

DEFINITION **Conventional and Conforming: One and the Same?**
Within the lending industry, you'll hear the terms "conventional" and "conforming" used almost interchangeably. "Conventional" refers to the loan itself, and describes any loan that's not insured by the government. "Conforming" refers to the borrower, who "conforms" to Fannie and Freddie's strict guidelines. As most conventional loans are also conforming, these two terms often go hand-in-hand. Throughout this book, when a loan is referred to as conventional, you can also assume the loan is conforming.

loan's rates and terms stay the same—an obvious benefit to the borrower. These loans also have requirements that actually seek out stability in borrowers. To qualify for a conventional loan, you usually need a stable job with a stable income and stable credit (which usually translates to stable loan payments to lenders). And because these loans conform to Fannie and Freddie guidelines, which are *also* designed for stability, they are a guaranteed sale to the secondary market, usually within a Wall Street portfolio. This makes them a more stable investment for lenders as well.

## What Are the Guidelines for a Conventional Loan?

What qualifications do you need to meet to be approved for a conventional loan? Every conventional loan starts with the same basic eleven guidelines:

### 1. Verifiable income for two consecutive years
For a conventional loan, you'll need to show your lender that you make what you say you do: you will need to document your income, and your lender will need to be able to verify the information you've provided. Most borrowers are able to document their income by providing thirty days' worth of current pay stubs and two consecutive

years of W-2s. If you are paid through other methods, your lender will ask for your last two years' tax returns and conduct a verification of employment (VOE). With a VOE, a lender contacts your employer to confirm your income, the stability of your position, and the likelihood of your *continued* employment.

If you have other sources of income, including bonuses, child support, rental property income, social security, pensions, or disability payments, lenders might ask for *more* documentation: a history of the income, cancelled checks or check stubs, court records, leases, account statements, award letters, and so on. A lender will look for an explanation of the income, how you expect to continue to receive the income, and proof in your documentation.

## 2.  Verifiable assets

Your lender will also require proof of your assets, including your checking and savings accounts, credit union accounts, money market accounts, CDs, 401Ks, SEPs, IRAs or ROTHs, mutual funds, investment accounts, full-term insurance policies with cash value, and whole insurance policies. A lender will require copies of all of your account statements for the past sixty days.

I've mentioned several types of accounts, but what about cash? Obviously cash is an asset for you, but envelopes of cash won't be considered by a lender. A lender won't know how long you've had the cash, and they may wonder if you borrowed the money (to look like you have *more* money) just for the purpose of the loan. If you have cash and would like for it to count as an asset, you'll need to deposit the cash into your bank account at least sixty days before you close on a loan (see below).

## 3.  Verifiable down payment funds, seasoned for sixty days

If you are purchasing a home, the down payment for your home must be funded from your checking, savings, CD, and/or money market accounts. But you can't deposit the money into these accounts right before you need a loan. A lender will also require that this amount be seasoned, which means the *full* amount has been maintained in your own accounts for a minimum of sixty days. As long as you meet this sixty-day requirement, the lender will accept this money for the down payment.

## 4.  A minimum of two to six months' worth of cash reserves

*Cash reserves* are any funds that can be immediately liquefied without penalty. Depending on your credit and the type of home you are purchasing (whether it's your primary home or an investment), you'll be required to have anywhere from two to six months' worth of reserves to cover mortgage-related expenses, including your mortgage payment, real estate taxes, and homeowners insurance. Add up these amounts for one month, then multiply the total by the number of months your lender will require. This is your required cash reserve. Your lender will require you to have this reserve *in addition* to the money you've set aside for your down payment (if you are making a purchase) and/or your closing costs.

## 5.  A qualifying debt-to-income ratio

What is your total debt compared to your total income? This is what's known in the industry as your DTI, and lenders will put a lot of weight on this equation. In fact, your DTI determines how much a lender will loan to you. To determine your DTI, you'll want to divide your total monthly debt by your total monthly income. Your "debt" is the total of all of your monthly expenses, including your new mortgage, taxes, insurance, homeowner's dues, credit cards, car payments, the child support you pay, student loans, and more. Your monthly income includes your gross salary, overtime, bonuses, commissions, income from interest or dividends, the child support you receive, and any other sources of income.

What magic number are lenders looking for when it comes to your DTI? No more than *38 to 42 percent.* There are exceptions, but this is the preferred range for a purchase or a refinance. DTIs under 38 percent are very good: your total debt is under 38 percent of your total income, which means your lender will feel very comfortable that you can afford all of your long-term expenses, including your mortgage. DTIs over 42 percent are considered to be risky. To a lender you have too much debt, making it more likely that at some point you may not be able to afford, and may default on, your loan.

Lenders will also be looking for one more magic number when they calculate your income and your debt. Lenders will want your total housing expenses (which include your mortgage payment, monthly taxes and insurance, and any homeowners' or condominium association dues) to be *no more* than 28 percent of your total income. To see how much your lender will think you can afford for your housing expenses (and how they will view your total debt), I've included a worksheet for you on the next page.

 Calculating your own debt-to-income can help you to determine how much house you can afford even before you start looking for a home. Use the worksheet in this chapter, or visit the reader's section on my website for interactive worksheets and calculators that will help give you a clear picture of your DTI, how you can improve your DTI, and what home prices will fit into your budget.

### 6.  Qualifying loan to value percentages and loan amounts

As I explained in Chapter 2, if you are purchasing a home, conventional loans are allowed to have a *maximum* loan to value (LTV) of 95 percent, meaning that a lender will not finance more than 95 percent of your home's appraised value (if they will lend you this amount at all). As a borrower, you are responsible for the remaining 5 percent, plus any closing costs, which typically range from 1 to 5 percent of the loan amount.

If you are refinancing to change your loan program or your interest rate, your loan to value can still go up to 95 percent. But if you are *refinancing* to take money out of your home, Fannie and Freddie's maximum loan to value is *90 percent*, based on your home's current appraised value.

Why is there a difference? Fannie and Freddie's conventional

# Quick Debt-to-Income Worksheet

Based on your income, how much of a mortgage payment will your lender think you can afford? How much debt will your lender allow? Fill out this quick debt-to-income worksheet to find out.

**YOUR MONTHLY INCOME**

| | |
|---|---|
| Gross Salary | $ |
| Hourly Wages | $ |
| Overtime | $ |
| Commission | $ |
| Bonuses | $ |
| Interest / Dividends | $ |
| Child Support | $ |
| Alimony | $ |
| Other | $ |
| | |
| **TOTAL MONTHLY INCOME** | $ |
| | X .28 |
| **MAXIMUM HOUSING EXPENSE** | = |

*This amount must cover: your mortgage payment, monthly taxes and insurance, mortgage insurance, and homeowner's or condominium association dues*

| | |
|---|---|
| Total Monthly Income | $ |
| | X .38 |
| **MAXIMUM MONTHLY DEBT** | = |

*This amount must cover: all of the housing expenses listed above, plus credit card payments, car payments, child support, student loans, and other long-term debt* lending guidelines are about promoting responsible, stable home-ownership. By offering 95% LTV loans for purchases, Fannie and Freddie make it possible for more people to buy homes. And by limiting loans to a maximum of 90% LTV for cash-out refinances, Fannie and Freddie force homeowners to view their home as a long-term investment that responsibly builds equity (instead of encouraging them to cash out home equity at a higher LTV loan).

In addition to LTV, conventional loans also set limits for the amount of the loan itself. Although qualifying loan amounts and loan limits vary by county and state, most conforming loans normally do not exceed $417,000, although in specific high-cost areas, this limit may jump to $625,500. When loans are over these limits, they are considered to be "jumbo" loans, and are outside of Fannie and Freddie guidelines; I'll explain more about these a little later in this chapter.

**7.  A credit score of 660 or above, in most cases**
Your credit, and specifically your credit score, is very important to your lender. Your credit score sums up years of how you have used credit, and it will instantly tell your lender how responsible you'll be with their loan. For conventional loans, a minimum credit score of 660 is required to receive affordable financing. In limited cases, Fannie and Freddie guidelines will allow for lower credit scores, ranging from 580 to 659, but if approved, you'll be charged a higher interest rate and higher fees, and your loan will be much more expensive.

If you currently have poor credit and are faced with high lending fees, there *is* something you can do about it. In Chapter 9, I'll explain more about how lenders view credit, how your credit score is determined, and how you can start taking steps immediately to improve your own score.

**8.  A sufficient credit history**
Showing you can manage your credit for twelve to twenty-four months is also important to a lender. Do you pay on time? Do you consistently pay down your debt? A lender will look for a minimum of four active credit accounts, each with an average limit of at least

$1,000, and carefully evaluate the history for each account.

### 9. No open collections, or the ability to bring accounts current

A lender will look in your credit report to see if any of your accounts have ever been turned over to a collection agency. Lenders will be looking for any type of collections, from big accounts including installment loans, credit cards, car loans, student loans, and doctor's bills, to small accounts like cell phone accounts or gym memberships.

If you have any "open" collections that have not been resolved, a lender will want to see if you can "bring the accounts current," which means paying the amount that is owed or working out an agreement with the creditor to have the collection settled or removed from your credit report. At times, lenders will make exceptions for open collections, but usually *only if* at least twenty-four months have passed since the account was turned over to a collection agency and *only if* the amount in question is very small. Most of the time, though, lenders will require that the collection be resolved.

### 10. No late mortgage or rent payments within the last year

Have you been on time paying your previous mortgage or rent? A lender will be happy to hear that you have. Lenders will look back over twelve months for any late or missed payments, whether you currently rent or own.

### 11. No foreclosures or bankruptcies in the past five years

Regardless of *why* you experienced a foreclosure or a bankruptcy, in order to be approved for a conventional loan, conforming guidelines require that your foreclosure or bankruptcy must have happened more than five years ago.

Although these eleven guidelines and requirements are fairly standard for all conventional loans, an individual lender or an underwriter may grant an exception on a case-by-case basis. Remember, no two loans or borrowers are ever alike. You may have a lower credit score, but can afford a larger down payment. Or you may not show much income on your tax returns, but you have more than enough money in the bank for reserves and a down payment, plus you have excellent credit. Many times, lenders will consider these compensating factors when reviewing your loan, and will sometimes grant exceptions.

Why wouldn't lenders just make *more* exceptions? Even though lenders made many exceptions in the past, especially during the boom years, today an exception may come with big consequences for the lender. When a lender makes an exception, the loan may no longer meet conforming guidelines, which means that the lender may lose out on the option of having Fannie or Freddie buy and sell the loan. Rarely, if all of the stars align, Fannie or Freddie *may* approve an exception, allowing the lender to sell the loan to the secondary market as a conforming loan. But most times, if a lender makes an exception, Fannie and Freddie will turn down the loan, and a lender will have to find another buyer or hold on to the loan themselves.

Today, with fewer investors purchasing loans, exceptions are becoming less common, but they still can happen. If lenders are presented with a borrower who does not meet all of the qualifying guidelines but is still a strong candidate, with strong collateral *and* a strong down payment, an exception is certainly not out of the question. In these cases, a lender may consider the borrower for a portfolio loan or a nonconforming loan, which I'll explain in depth later in this chapter.

## Individual Guidelines May Get in the Way

So all conventional loans follow these guidelines and these guidelines alone, right? Well, no. Fannie and Freddie guidelines are quite extensive, and there are even *more* guidelines than the base conventional guidelines I have listed here, including additional guidelines about your loan, your home itself, and even the neighborhood your home is in.

In addition, some lenders have their own individual guidelines and rules *on top* of Fannie and Freddie's guidelines. A lender might require a higher credit score, more in reserves, or less total borrower debt. Lenders do this for several reasons. For one, sometimes Fannie and Freddie guidelines are so complex that a lender doesn't want to take any chance that their loan will be rejected. So lenders will tighten restrictions to make a loan even *more* attractive to Fannie and Freddie and to the secondary market.

Other times, a lender has plans to sell the loan to someone *other* than Fannie and Freddie, and they will adjust their individual guidelines to match that investor's needs. And it's also possible that a lender may *not* have plans to sell the loan; they may plan to keep your loan in their own portfolio, and in this case lenders may want to decrease their risk by adding their own strict requirements.

Individual lender guidelines are unimportant to other lenders, but these additional guidelines can be very important to you as a borrower. Even though you meet Fannie and Freddie's requirements, your loan could still be denied—all because of a lender's individual guidelines. If all these differences have you confused, you are not alone! I often refer to this entire dynamic as "deliberate industry confusion."

Each and every lender has a thick, dusty lending manual devoted entirely to its own standards for conventional and conforming loans. Unfortunately, these manuals are for a lender's eyes only and are rarely shared with the consumer, so you can never really know if you will qualify for a loan. In our ever-changing market, lenders are defaulting to these individual, sometimes obscure guidelines in efforts to lessen their own risk. And sometimes these individual lending guidelines may make it difficult for you to obtain financing, through no fault of your own.

Here are a few examples of how individual lender guidelines could easily get in between you and your new loan:

▸ **Does your appraisal indicate you are in a declining market?** As I covered in Chapter 2, declining market adjustments are a sad new reality in lending. In a declining market, a lender assumes your home's value will decrease further. Depending on what is happening in the housing market in your area, a lender may decrease your total loan amount by at least 5 percent to compensate for this anticipated drop in value. And even though Fannie and Freddie guidelines allow for declining markets, and do *not* require an adjustment to the loan amount, individual lenders may still adjust how much they will lend to you.

▸ **Is your lender conducting a formal appraisal review?** An appraisal is an important tool for the lending process. A professional, licensed appraiser will visit a property and the surrounding area and evaluate a home's value based on physical characteristics and similar properties in the area. That sounds fair, and it usually is. But as I mentioned in Chapter 2, so many lenders are weary of artificial and declining value that most, if not all, lenders will require an appraisal review, which essentially is an *additional* appraisal performed by a lender-appointed appraiser.

In most cases, the lender's appraiser will only review recorded sales, looking for a neighborhood's lowest sales and lowest home values, without viewing the actual home or neighborhood in person. What might this mean for you? Your home's value will most likely be lowered to match the *lowest* comparable sale in your neighborhood, and usually this value is reduced unjustly.

While Fannie or Freddie guidelines don't require lenders to obtain their own appraisals, most lenders have made this a standard practice for most loans.

▸ **Is your homeowners insurance coverage worded correctly?** What's correct wording? Well, that's for the individual lender to decide. All lenders will require you to insure your home to receive a loan. But some lenders take it one step further, and will also require particular language within the actual insurance policy. If the policy has the wrong language, it could result in the denial of a loan. Most of the time this will require flexibility on the part of the insurance company, which will need to modify its policy language to meet with the lender's approval.

▸ **Are there too many rental or investment properties in the neighborhood?** If you live in a Planned Unit Development (PUD), which is a neighborhood with a homeowners association and shared common areas (including clubhouses, roads, pools, or playgrounds), or if you live in a townhome or condominium community, Fannie and Freddie guidelines dictate how many rental or investment properties are allowed in the neighborhood for a loan to be considered conforming. This is based on the theory that owner-occupied properties make for stable neighborhoods and stable home values.

If your neighborhood has too many homes for rent, or too many homes that are not primary residences (including homes that are investment properties, rented, or second homes), you may be turned down for a conventional loan. Some individual lenders will also *lower* these allowed numbers to reduce their own risk. For example, Fannie and Freddie's guidelines may say eight rental or investment homes are allowed, and a lender's guidelines may decrease that number to four.

▸ **What does your homeowners association questionnaire say about your home?** If a property is part of a homeowners or condominium association, Fannie and Freddie lending guidelines will require the association to complete a condominium questionnaire, which usually includes questions about association insurance, any impending neighborhood lawsuits, the number of homes that are rentals, and association guidelines and bylaws.

While these questionnaires have always been standard for conventional loans, many are now being scrutinized by individual lenders for everything from common area ownership to—believe it or not—child age and pet requirements. If lenders are at all uncomfortable with what they see, they may deny your loan. Maybe the lender doesn't want to lend in a community where a homeowner has shared ownership of common areas (like a playground or clubhouse). Or maybe the lender doesn't want to lend in a retirement or active-adult community. Lenders often have strange ways of evaluating a home's future value, and often there is not a valid reason for these types of restrictions. Can a lender do this? Yes, and they can do it without giving a good reason. It's their money to lend, and they can make their own rules.

▸ **Does your loan's approval rely on alternative documents?** Within standard conforming guidelines, there are several ways you can provide documentation to a lender to show you can qualify for a loan. For example, let's say you need to show what you have in your checking and savings accounts. To document these funds, lenders usually require the last two months of bank statements. However, Fannie and Freddie's guidelines also allow for a VOD, a verification of deposit by a bank representative, in lieu of actual statements. Although conforming guidelines allow for substitutions like this, the lender's individual guidelines may not—it happens all too often.

These are just a few ways where cautious lenders and individual lender guidelines can make financing extremely difficult. More and more, it seems that lenders' denials are made on a case-by-case basis instead of following consistent guidelines. And although there probably is a dusty manual somewhere that lays out these guidelines, I have often wondered how "real" these manuals really are.

Situations like these are where a good mortgage consultant or broker comes in handy. A proactive consultant will be able to look at a property and evaluate it from the perspective of a conservative lender, and will be able to red flag anything you should be prepared for. Maybe there are issues with the property that will make it difficult to work with a particular lender. Or maybe there's additional documentation that you'll need to get a loan approved. Most times, a good consultant will be able to let you know what to expect in advance. And because additional, individual guidelines vary from lender to lender, a consultant will also be able to take your loan from one lender to the next to find the lender who says your loan is "just right."

If you are approved for a conventional loan, you should celebrate. Being approved for conventional financing means you meet the highest qualification guidelines within the lending industry. You will be able to choose from any of the loan programs I cover in this chapter. By proving your worth as a conforming borrower, you can easily prove your worth for any loan.

## Fixed-Rate Loans

The most common conventional loan is a *fixed rate loan*. A fixed rate loan is just what it sounds like: your interest rate is fixed, so your payments will never change for the entire life of the loan. Nice, right? Each month, your mortgage payment is applied toward paying down your principal (the actual loan amount) and paying down the interest (what you have been charged to finance the loan). This paying down of your loan in lending terms is called *amortization*. A loan's *amortization schedule* shows exactly how your loan will be paid back each month, as well as the loan's term, which is how many years you have to pay back the loan in full.

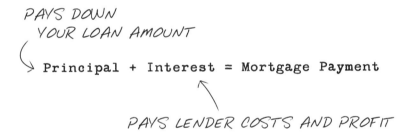

PAYS DOWN
YOUR LOAN AMOUNT

Principal + Interest = Mortgage Payment

PAYS LENDER COSTS AND PROFIT

At the beginning of any loan, the majority of your payment goes toward paying interest, so you're essentially paying the lender back first (a great deal for the lender). As you get further into your loan, more and more of your payment goes toward paying down the loan's principal. I've included a sample amortization chart in Appendix I, and have also included other examples and an amortization calculator on my website, so you can see how the principal and interest amounts change over the years for your own loan.

The most common fixed rate loans are a 15- or 30-year fixed. Fixed rate loans are a great option if you want to stay in your home for ten-plus years, or if you feel more comfortable knowing your mortgage payment will never change. Deciding between fixed rate loan programs comes down to payment and payoff. A 30-year fixed offers lower payments, but it will take longer to pay down and you'll be paying more in interest. A 15-year fixed has a higher payment (as you're paying down the same debt in less time), but you'll not only pay your home off much faster, you will save much more in interest.

Let's say your loan is $200,000, and your interest rate is fixed at 6 percent. At the end of each fixed rate loan, how much interest will you have paid?

```
15-Year: Interest Paid = $103,788
30-Year: Interest Paid = $231,676
```

For most people, these numbers are shocking. Will I really pay this much in interest? Unfortunately, yes. When purchasing or refinancing a home, many borrowers tend to focus on their monthly payment instead of on the total interest amount. If you are concerned about the total interest you will pay, and if you can afford a higher payment and know you want to stay in your home for a longer period of time, a 15-year fixed is a smart choice. If you don't plan on staying in your home for long, and if lower payments are more important, opt for a 30-year fixed. Fixed rate loans are also available for longer terms, including forty and even fifty years. While that may sound tempting because your payments will be even lower, look at Figure 4.1. You will be paying *much* more for the same loan amount in interest alone.

| LOAN TERM | NUMEBER OF PAYMENTS | MONTHLY PAYMENT | TOTAL INTEREST PAID | TOTAL LOAN COST |
|---|---|---|---|---|
| 15 Years | 180 | $1,687.71 | $103,788.46 | $303,788.46 |
| 30 Years | 360 | $1,199.10 | $231,676.38 | $431,676.38 |
| 40 Years | 480 | $1,100.43 | $328,205.09 | $528,205.09 |
| 50 Years | 600 | $1,052.81 | $431,685.75 | $631,685.75 |

**Figure 4.1: Comparing Fixed Rate Loans** *A $200,000 mortgage at 6 percent interest.*

## Adjustable Rate Loans

In contrast to the structure of a fixed rate loan, an *adjustable rate mortgage*, called an ARM for short, is a mortgage where the interest rate changes at some point to reflect changes in the economy and in the costs of financing overall.

Lenders like ARMs because more risk is transferred from the lender to the borrower. For fixed rate loans, a lender agrees to honor a rate no matter what happens with market conditions. For example, if a lender agrees to a fixed rate loan of 5.5 percent and the cost of lending money increases, the lender bears the difference. This is great for the borrower, but it's not ideal for the lender. But with an adjustable rate loan, a loan's interest rate adjusts to *reflect* changes in the market, so the borrower shoulders more of the burden if costs increase. If rates rise, your mortgage payments can as well. But it's not a lopsided arrangement; ARMs can also benefit borrowers. If interest rates fall, your mortgage payments could decrease too.

So how often will payments change to reflect what's going on in the market? It depends on the individual loan. For some ARMs, the interest rate may adjust every month, or every three, six, or twelve months. For other ARMs, the interest rate remains fixed for a set period (just like a fixed rate loan) and adjusts afterward; typical ARMs in this category are 3/1, 5/1, and 7/1 loans. The first number—the 3, 5, or 7—indicates how long the interest rate is fixed. The second number indicates how *often* the loan adjusts after the fixed period, which is based on either month or year increments (again, depending on the loan program). For example, in a 5/1 ARM, the interest rate is fixed for five years, then adjusts once a year, every year, for the remaining life of the loan.

How long does it usually take to pay off an ARM? Well, most ARMs are amortized over thirty years. Going back to our 5/1 example, this means this loan would have a fixed rate (and a fixed payment) for five years, and adjustable rates (with increases or decreases in payments) for twenty-five years. During the entire loan, your payments are applied toward both your principal and your interest, and after the thirty years you own the home free and clear.

## HOW ARM RATES ARE DETERMINED

How does your lender determine your loan's interest rate each time your rate adjusts? Although there are many different ARM programs, their rates are all based on the same equation:

```
Index + Margin = Total Interest Rate
```

*ADJUSTS*          *FIXED*

▶ **Index.** An *index* is a published table of interest rates used to monitor the economy and measure inflation. The index determines how your loan adjusts: if an index goes up, it means it costs a lender more to fund your loan, so your interest rate increases as well. If the index goes down, so does your rate. Where it gets confusing is that there is more than one index. Financial institutions and lenders use a wide variety of indices as the base for their ARM programs, including the London Inter Bank Offered Rate (LIBOR), the 12-Month Treasury Average (MTA), the Costs of Funds Index (COFI), Treasury Bills (TCM), and the prime rate set by the U.S. government.

Although you can't tell your lender which of these indices you would like to use for your loan (that's the lender's decision; lenders use different indices for different loans), you *can* shop for loans based on a particular index and your own needs. Prior to finalizing your loan, always ask about and read up on the index your loan is attached to.

Lenders will also be able to show you the history of an index, which will help you see how stable or volatile that index is over time. Generally speaking, gradual fluctuations within an index are fine; you can expect your payments to remain fairly consistent, or increase or decrease slowly over time. Sharp or frequent spikes or declines are bad; the more volatile the index, the greater the chances that your payments will range wildly, and the more unpredictable your loan will be. While an index's history can't predict the future, it can give you a relatively good idea of what *might* happen with your loan and your interest rates.

Want to learn more about your loan's index? Would you like to research other indices? On my website, you'll find direct links to all of the available indices, including information on each index's history, stability, and reliability.

▸ **Margin.** A *margin* is a fixed percentage that is added to your index rate to determine your loan's *total* interest rate. A margin represents the lender's cost of doing business plus their profit, and usually ranges from 1.75 to 4 percent. This part of your rate will never change, so as a borrower, you'll want the lowest margin possible (for a lower total interest rate). Lenders, on the other hand, may push for a higher margin, so they can make more profit.

Let's say your lender is charging you a margin of 2.5 percent, and your index right now is at 4.35 percent. Your final interest rate would be 6.85 percent. If the index adjusts to 4.5 percent, your final interest rate becomes 7.0 percent.

```
          Your original rate:
   4.35 Index + 2.5 Margin = 6.85%

        When your rate adjusts:
   4.5 Index + 2.5 Margin = 7.0%
```

Your index and margin aren't the only important numbers that influence your ARM's rate. ARMs also come with resets and adjustment periods, teaser rates, and rate caps:

▸ **Resets and Adjustment Periods.** A *reset* tells you when you will have your *first* rate adjustment. To determine your reset, look at the first number used in an ARM's name. For example, in a 7/1 adjustable rate mortgage, "7" is your official reset. Your interest rate will be fixed for seven years, and after the seven years are up, the loan resets and will start to adjust.

Your *adjustment period* describes how *often* your loan will adjust. This is the second number in an ARM's name. In a 7/1 ARM, your adjustment is "1," meaning the loan adjusts every year. Most ARMs adjust once a year, but adjustments could be as frequent as once a month, or as infrequent as once every five years, depending on the lender and the loan.

Both resets and adjustment periods impact the total cost of your loan. The less your loan adjusts, the more risk your lender is taking on, so the more your lender will charge you, either in the form of a higher margin or a higher initial interest rate.

▸ **Initial Interest Rate.** Even though an ARM's interest rate will adjust, most ARMs start with a fixed *initial interest rate*. This rate is usually low and may be fixed for several years. For example, let's say you have an initial interest rate of 5.25 percent. In the 7/1 ARM above, your loan will have a 5.25 percent interest rate for seven years.

But with other ARMs, your initial interest rate could be fixed for a very short period, sometimes as little as a month, before your loan starts to adjust. In this case, you could have the initial rate of 5.25 percent for the first month, and a 5.50 rate the next.

▸ **Teaser Rate.** In addition to your initial interest rate, some loans offer an extremely low (and very enticing) starting rate known as a *teaser rate*. These rates are often very tempting for borrowers because very low rates mean very low payments.

But you need to be careful. These rates are temporary and only last for a short period of time, usually just a few months. When the teaser rate expires, either your rate will change to your initial interest rate, or it will be determined by your index and margin. Either way, after the teaser rate period is over, your interest rate will usually increase significantly—right along with your mortgage payment.

As a rule of thumb, loans with low teaser rates often do more damage than good for you as a borrower. Sure, you'll be saving money during the teaser period, but will you really *save* the money? During this period, most people enjoy the lower rates and lower payments, but don't save their money as they should, and when the teaser period is over, they're usually not prepared for the *higher* rates and payments.

▶   **Rate Caps.** *Rate caps* set limits for how much your interest rate can fluctuate. They let you know how far up or down your rate can adjust, and in turn how expensive or inexpensive your mortgage can ever be. Each adjustable rate mortgage has three basic types of caps: an initial cap, a periodic cap, and a lifetime cap.

DEFINITION   **An initial cap** is the limit for how much an interest rate can increase or decrease the very *first* time your loan adjusts. Generally, an initial cap allows for a large, one-time increase to your interest rate, as a way for lenders to generate more profit, and this can be expensive for borrowers.

For example, if your loan's initial cap is 5 percent, this means your interest rate could increase by as much as 5 percent with your loan's very first adjustment. If your index rose by 5 percent, your interest rate would increase by 5 percent too. The good news is that many lenders have stopped using initial caps, and today, most ARMs use a periodic cap for your loan's first adjustment instead.

**A periodic cap** is the limit for how much an interest rate can increase or decrease at *each* adjustment period. Most adjustable rate mortgages have a periodic cap ranging from 1 to 3 percent. For instance, if your periodic cap is 2 percent, then each time your loan adjusts, your interest rate cannot go up or down more than 2 percentage points, *even if* your index has fluctuated more.

**A lifetime cap** is the maximum interest rate you can *ever* be charged during the life of the loan. Most adjustable rate mortgages have lifetime caps ranging from 5 to 7 percentage points above your initial interest rate (excluding teaser rates). So if your ARM starts with a rate of 4 percent, and has a lifetime cap of 6 percent, the highest interest rate you can ever be charged is 10 percent.

Your loan's caps can certainly be confusing, but understanding the "facts of caps" can be very important for your loan and your mortgage payments.

For example, let's say you have an initial interest rate of 5 percent, and a lifetime cap of 7 percent. On a $150,000 loan this is the difference between a $805.23 payment (at 5 percent interest) and a $1,542.92 payment (at 12 percent interest), which is a huge increase, and almost doubles your payment.

## WHEN ARMS ARE A GOOD CHOICE

With all of these confusing rate changes, why are ARMs so popular? ARMs rival fixed rate loans for one important reason: the majority of the time, they offer lower rates and lower payments. This makes adjustable rate mortgages a great alternative for many homeowners, especially if you know you only want to stay in your home for a relatively short period of time. Many homeowners choose ARMs with an initial fixed interest rate (which can be fixed for up to ten years), with the intention of selling the home before the rate adjusts. During this fixed period, an ARM's lower rates and payments give you a chance to save money or get your finances back on track. You can also use an ARM to afford "more home" than you normally would be able to—since the money you are borrowing costs less, you can afford more.

On the lender's side, ARMs generate profit just like fixed rate loans: more interest is paid to lenders at the beginning of the loan, and lenders continue to earn interest throughout the life of the loan. If a borrower stays in an ARM for the full 30-year term, it's also a good deal for lenders: a borrower's payments adjust and allow for inflation, a lender's costs are covered, and the lender continues to receive a predetermined amount in profit. ARMs can also conform to Fannie and Freddie guidelines, giving lenders an opportunity to also make money from selling the loan to the secondary market.

Is there a downside to ARMs? Yes, for the borrower. Adjusting interest rates usually adjust upward, right along with your payments.

And if there is anything we've learned from the housing crash it is this: if you are considering an ARM, paying attention to an initial low fixed rate is not enough. You need to pay just as much attention to how much you *could* end up paying in the future.

Many homeowners have found that when their ARM begins to adjust, they can't afford their payments—and depending on the market, they may not be able to refinance or sell. They become stuck in a house they can no longer pay for. If you are considering an ARM, you need to look at your worst-case scenarios. Would you still be able to afford the loan if the interest rate was near the lifetime cap? How long could you afford to pay the mortgage at these higher rates? Could you afford to pay the higher interest rate right now?

## The Strong ARM Checklist

How do you know if an ARM is right for you? Start by asking yourself the following questions. I also offer an interactive version of this checklist on my website, to help you see how rate adjustments will affect your monthly mortgage payments.

- ☐ What is your index?
- ☐ What is the history of your index?
- ☐ What is your margin?
- ☐ When does your rate reset?
- ☐ How often does your rate adjust?
- ☐ How long does your initial interest rate last?
- ☐ How much could your rate increase when it adjusts?
- ☐ What is the highest your rate can ever be?
- ☐ How high could your mortgage payment ever be?
- ☐ Can I afford this loan at the highest rates?
- ☐ How long can I afford this loan at the highest rates?

## Balloon Loans

At first glance, a balloon loan looks very much like the country's first mortgages from insurance companies. A balloon loan is a short-term loan with a low fixed interest rate, and just like an ARM's rate, a balloon loan's rate is consistently lower than a "regular" 30-year fixed rate loan. But there's a catch. After a predetermined period, the payment blows up like a balloon: the loan is due, in full. A balloon loan's monthly payments are calculated as if you were going to pay the loan off over thirty years (even though you are not), creating low stable payments. But after just a few years—usually three, five, or seven—you are required to pay the balance of the loan.

 **Planning Ahead**

Balloon loans require you to have a definite game plan for your home: at the end of the loan, you'll need to have an exit strategy, usually involving selling or refinancing your home to be able to pay off the loan in full. If you don't have a strategy . . . well, you might as well be trying to outrun a train—on foot.

Balloon loans allow lenders to make a profit and have an exit strategy of their own. By offering you a low interest rate, not only does the lender receive a substantial profit from your interest-heavy initial mortgage payments, but at the end of the loan, the lender will either receive their investment *in full*, or have the ability to renegotiate terms with a refinance. And if you refinance, the lender will be able to make *even more* profit from the new, refinanced loan. In addition, balloons are usually conforming loans; for the lender, this ensures a stable borrower, and also gives the lender the additional option of selling the loan on the secondary market. With balloon loans, lenders certainly have all of their bases covered.

Many borrowers consider both ARMs and balloons due to their

low interest rates. If you are considering a balloon loan, you need to be especially careful. It may not be as easy as you think to sell or refinance your home when the loan comes due, and you may be left with only one option: renegotiating with your lender. If you are currently in a balloon mortgage and haven't figured out your exit strategy, speak with your lender now about the possibility of modifying your loan, even if it is still some time before your lump sum payment is due.

## Interest-Only Loans

Interest-only (I/O) loans are just as simple as they sound: for a set period of time, your monthly mortgage payments pay back only the interest on your loan, which means you have a lower payment. An interest-only period can last anywhere from one to ten years; after this period is up (depending on the loan program) your loan will convert to either a fixed rate or adjustable rate mortgage for the remaining life of the loan.

With an interest-only loan, just because you are paying the interest doesn't mean the lender is going to forget about the principal you still owe. Once your interest-only period ends, you still have the same loan amount you started with, and your payments adjust to start paying the balance down immediately.

Here's an example: Let's say you have a $240,000 interest-only loan. At the end of your interest-only period, you still owe $240,000 and the loan is *recast*. With a recast, your loan's payments are recalculated so that the full amount is paid back over the years that are left in your loan. Most interest-only loans have a term of thirty years, so this means if your interest-only period was three years, you now have twenty-seven years to pay back the loan; if the interest-only period was ten years, you have twenty years to pay the loan. All of your payments are adjusted to meet this goal.

When your loan is recast, it affects the size of your monthly mortgage payments—the longer your interest-only period, the less time you'll have to pay the principal back, and the higher your payments will be. As I've mentioned, some interest-only loans also *turn into*

ARMs when the interest-only period is up (you'll know whether your loan converts to a fixed or an adjustable rate before you agree to the loan). Between paying back the original loan amount and your loan's new adjusting interest rates, you could easily find yourself facing higher payments than you anticipated.

Lenders like interest-only loans because they receive their profit for the entire interest-only period, and then *continue* to receive profit once the loan converts to a fixed or adjustable rate loan. Lenders also like interest-only loans because Fannie and Freddie require these loans to be at 90% LTV, which makes the loan less risky for the lender. But even though interest-only loans are great for lenders, they can end up being very risky for borrowers if they aren't used correctly.

I've seen many brokers place clients into interest-only loans for all the wrong reasons. Interest-only loans, with their lower payments, can make it *appear* that a borrower can afford a home when, in reality, they cannot. In these cases, brokers focus on saving a borrower money each month for the short term, but ignore the fact that the borrower can't really afford the home over the long-term. This can easily set a homeowner up for foreclosure. If the homeowner isn't able to save money during the interest-only period (as many cannot), when the period ends and the loan adjusts to a higher monthly payment, the homeowner is often unprepared and usually defaults on the loan.

Interest-only loans should *only* be used when a borrower can commit to saving for the future higher payments, and in these cases, a 10-year interest-only term can be the best option. Let's look at an example to understand how interest-only loans should work, and how they can be used responsibly to save money.

## A 3-YEAR INTEREST-ONLY LOAN

Let's say you are buying a house for $268,000 and have put down a little over 10 percent. You have borrowed $240,000, and you have a 30-year fixed rate loan at 5 percent. For this loan, your total monthly payment is $1,288.37, which breaks down to $288.37 toward the principal amount and $1,000 in interest to the lender. (In reality, how your

payment is divided to pay your principal and interest fluctuates a little each month, as shown in Appendix I. I've simplified things for the
purposes of this example.)

```
            Payment on a fixed rate loan:
$288.37 Principal + $1,000 Interest = $1,288.37
```

If you borrowed the same $240,000 at the same interest rate of 5 per-
cent, but with a three-year interest-only period, your payment for
those three years would only be $1,000 a month.

```
           Payment on a interest-only loan:
    $0 Principal + $1,000 Interest = $1,000
```

So now you have to pick your poison: Do you limit the amount you
pay each month and save $288.37 a month, or do you pay *more* each
month to start building equity in your home, so you have a lower loan
balance to pay off if you decide to sell or refinance the home?

Will putting off paying the principal help you financially in the
long run? Let's find out. You've decided to save the $288.37 every
month, and you've also decided to invest it into a money market savings account earning 1 percent interest. Where would you be after
three years?

```
    $10,381.32 (saved principal)
   + $161.61 (earned interest)
   _____
    $10,542.93 (total saved)
```

You've saved $10,542.93, and the amount you have left to pay off on
your loan is $240,000—your original loan amount. Is this good or

bad? Well, there are a few more things to consider. Your loan has been recast at the same fixed rate of 5 percent, and your monthly payment is now $1,351.29. Can you afford this amount? If so, fantastic. If not, and you need to sell or refinance, realtor fees or closing costs will quickly eat up a large portion of the $10,542 you've saved. If your home has appreciated significantly during the last three years, you may very well come out ahead—but not by much. And if the housing market has been flat and your home *hasn't* appreciated, it's a wash. You haven't gained or lost anything.

Here's another, less pleasant scenario. Let's say that at the end of the three years, your loan turns into an adjustable rate mortgage with an interest rate of 7.5 percent. Your monthly payment jumps to $1,729.76 a month. That's an enormous increase from the initial payments of $1,288.37, and will be much harder to afford, whether you have saved money or not. You now have the same choices: pay the higher payment, or pay the costs associated with refinancing or selling. Needless to say, if you're in this position and also haven't saved money as you should have, you may very well be in trouble.

## A 10-YEAR INTEREST-ONLY LOAN

Now let's compare these same numbers with a 10-year interest-only period. You've decided that instead of three years, you are going to stay in your home for ten years. You are in the same 5 percent fixed rate loan with a 10-year interest-only period. What will you save in ten years from not paying the monthly principal?

```
  $34,604.40 (saved principal)
+ $1,803.75 (earned interest)
─────────────────────────────
  $36,408.15 (total saved)
```

Even if your home has only appreciated at an average of 1 percent a year, after ten years your home has gained approximately $28,000 in value. (It's much more likely your home will appreciate at least some amount over ten years than over three years, even with recent market conditions.) Add this to the $36,408.15 you have saved—not bad:

$$\$36{,}408.15 + \$28{,}000 = \$64{,}408.15$$

If you invest what you've saved in a higher-yield account, or if your house is in a strong appreciating real estate market, you will have saved even more. When an interest-only loan is utilized this way, it can put you in a better financial position to afford future higher monthly payments, to refinance, or to purchase a new home. And if you need to refinance to use your home's equity, you'll have enough money to cover the closing costs. It's a good game plan, but only if you have saved the principal amount diligently each month. Would you be able to save this money, or would you need it for monthly expenses? Would you spend it? If you would, an interest-only loan is not for you.

## Combination Loans and Mortgage Insurance

A combination loan is one loan amount that is purposely broken into two loans, known as a "first" and a "second." During the boom, the most common combination loans were 80/20s and 70/30s. The larger number represents the loan to value percentage of the first loan (or first position loan), while the smaller number represents the loan to value percentage of the loan in the second position. So for example, in an 80/20 loan, the first loan has a loan to value of 80 percent, and the second loan has a loan to value of 20 percent. With a combination loan, you make payments on both loans each month to pay off your home.

Combination loans were originally developed for one reason only: to avoid mortgage insurance (MI), also referred to as private mortgage insurance (PMI). Mortgage insurance is required by a lender if your loan to value is *above* 80 percent. This means that if you have less than 20 percent equity in your home, or are putting down less than 20 percent as your down payment, you'll be required to pay for mortgage insurance, no matter what kind of loan you have, be it fixed, adjustable, interest-only, or any other type of loan. Over time, as you pay down your loan's balance and your home's value increases through appreciation, your loan will reach 80% LTV, and you'll no longer have to pay for the premium.

Why do lenders even require mortgage insurance? For a lender, it's all about managing their risk. The less of your own money you have in your own home, the greater the possibility that you might default on your loan. To protect lenders from this risk, they use mortgage insurance as a safety net—if you miss payments, mortgage insurance helps to cover the lender's loss until you start making payments again, or until the lender takes ownership of the home. This lowered risk also assists lenders in selling the riskier higher-LTV loans to the secondary market, because with mortgage insurance in place, a loan is also less risky for an investor.

If you are required to pay mortgage insurance, it will usually be added as a separate charge to your mortgage payment. Your actual premium depends on several different variables (including the loan program, your credit score, and the loan amount), but usually, you can expect to pay a total of 0.5 to 2 percent of your loan amount *each year*. It's certainly not cheap: on a $200,000 loan, you're looking at a yearly bill of $1,000 to $4,000, which means you'll be paying $83 to $333 each month on top of your mortgage payment. And although you are paying for the insurance premiums yourself, because the policy protects the lender, lenders will shop for insurance (with mortgage insurance companies who work directly with lenders) and take out a policy on your behalf, whether you want them to or not.

During the boom, combination loans were frequently used to avoid mortgage insurance because they divided one loan into two or more loans that, individually, were under 80% LTV. Combinations loans also took advantage of a loophole within lending and allowed borrowers to finance 100 percent of a home while saving money: when broken up into two loans, a combination loan is often less expensive than a single loan that includes a mortgage insurance premium.

**Removing Mortgage Insurance From Your Loan**

Lenders like having mortgage insurance in place, no matter what the LTV is for your home. So don't expect your lender to be in any hurry to remove your mortgage insurance premium, even after your loan has dipped below the 80% LTV mark. It will be up to you to request that the premium be removed, and you will also need to provide documentation that it *should* be removed. Your lender will review what you've paid toward your loan's principal, and if you have reached 80% LTV from increases in your home's value, you will need to provide your lender with an appraisal. Once the appraisal has been reviewed (and approved), the mortgage insurance requirement will be removed from your loan.

Here's a comparison to show just how this would work. In this example, both first loans are based on a 7 percent fixed interest rate, an average premium has been applied for the mortgage insurance (1.35 percent of the loan amount), and the second loan carries an average interest rate of 4.75 percent.

| Option 1: Loan with MI | | Option 2: Combination Loan | |
|---|---|---|---|
| $200,000 | LOAN AMOUNT | $200,000 | LOAN AMOUNT |
| $1,330.60 | MONTHLY PAYMENT | $1,064.48 | 80% 1ST LOAN |
| $225.00 | MI PREMIUM | $208.66 | 20% 2ND LOAN |
| $1,555.60 | TOTAL PAYMENT | $1,273.14 | TOTAL PAYMENT |

You are the borrower. Your options are a loan with mortgage insurance for $1,555.60 or two loans for $1,273.14. Which would you choose? This payment comparison alone sold combination loans 100 percent of the time—borrowers just couldn't resist the lower payment. But by focusing on the payment and the payment *only*, it's easy to miss potential problems. *Why* is the payment lower? Is it because that second loan is an interest-only loan that's not paying down your principal? A balloon loan that will be due in full in a few years? An ARM with high margins and caps where your payments may increase later? Many borrowers don't take the time to ask these questions, and that's a problem.

During the boom, many brokers used this payment comparison to sell a loan, but glossed over the loan details. Combination loans flourished due to an excess of risky loan programs, 100 percent financing, and the ease and availability of second mortgages and home equity lines, and were used frequently for a home's primary financing. Lenders now view combination loans very differently, and the combination loans of yesterday are obsolete.

## COMBINATION LOANS TODAY

Today, combination loans come into play only when you need a second mortgage or home equity line. Unlike in the past, if you already have one loan and need the financial leverage of a second or home equity loan, your combined loan to value amounts (referred to as CLTV) usually cannot exceed 70 percent of a home's appraised value. This means that if a home is worth $200,000, the maximum loan amount you can get, in any combination of loans, is $140,000. So if your current loan is $100,000, then a *maximum* of $40,000 may be available as a second loan or home equity line. Who decides this? The lenders who offer second mortgages and home equity lines. They don't want to take the risk, and have set the 70 percent guideline.

If you are purchasing a home and need financing, this 70 percent CLTV limit is what makes the post-boom's combination loans pointless. Why would you only finance 70 percent of a home with two loans when an individual loan may allow for up to 95 percent financing? You wouldn't. There just wouldn't be any benefit to you. But like anything else, lending is cyclical, and you never know if or when loan programs and restrictions may change, or when new or improved combination loans may appear. In the future, combination loans may once again become a good option for borrowers.

### DEFINITION

### A Last Word: Who Does Mortgage Insurance Really Help?

Mortgage insurance is designed to offset a lender's loss in the event of a default or foreclosure. If a claim is granted, mortgage insurance may cover up to 17 to 25 percent of the unpaid loan amount. For instance, on a $200,000 loan balance, mortgage insurance could cover anywhere from $34,000 to $50,000, depending on the insurance and the claim.

Couldn't lenders use some of this money to *help* a borrower stay in their home after a default, instead of proceeding forward with a foreclosure? That's a good question. It all depends on the individual lender and mortgage insurance company.

Some mortgage insurance companies will provide a cash advance to borrowers, so they can make up their missed payments with the lender and become current on their loan. For these companies, paying out a small amount to help a borrower catch up is less expensive than paying out for the policy in full.

So in theory, mortgage insurance *should* make it easier for all borrowers to work out an alternative to foreclosure with their lenders. But today, even with rising defaults, many lenders and insurance companies won't consider using this insurance to assist borrowers (even though the borrower has been paying for the policy on the lender's behalf). How mortgage insurance is used by lenders and insurance companies, and mortgage insurance's true purpose, remains inconsistent.

If you are required by your lender to have mortgage insurance, be sure to request the contact and policy information for the mortgage insurance company. In the event that you run into trouble and are unable to make your mortgage payments, this insurance might be used to help you stay in your home. There's no guarantee you will receive help, but it's worth the effort to find out.

## Nonconforming Loans

What if you are one of the many borrowers who don't meet Fannie and Freddie's requirements and are turned down for a conventional loan? What if you meet the requirements, but your property doesn't? As I have discussed, there are many borrowers who truly can afford financing, but are just outside of the conforming guidelines we covered earlier in the chapter. You may have substantial income and assets, but damaged credit. Or perfect credit, but poor savings. Or great savings and income, but you wouldn't know it by looking at your tax returns. Borrowers outside of these guidelines are called *nonconforming borrowers*, and their loans are *nonconforming loans*.

Nonconforming loans can be held by an individual bank as a portfolio loan, or by a lender, private hard-money lender, or investor. Nonconforming loans can also be sold on the secondary market, but are rarely sold or guaranteed by Fannie, Freddie, or the government. This means that for any nonconforming loan, the lender is shouldering the risk: the lender will either keep the loan in their own portfolio, or will try to sell the loan directly to the secondary market. Because you do not meet the "traditional" lending profile, lenders will need reassurance that you will not default or walk away from your home, and you will have to prove your worth to receive a loan. I'm sure I don't need to remind you what that means: lenders will be extra cautious.

As a borrower, you will most likely need to work with a mortgage consultant to receive nonconforming financing. More nonconforming loan sources are available to brokers, and a broker will understand what additional documentation you will need to show a lender that you are a strong, although nonconforming, borrower, and that both you and your home are worth the lender's investment.

Many nonconforming loans are considered by the general public to be "creative" or "risky" to borrowers, but this is simply not accurate. Just because a loan is nonconforming doesn't mean it's a bad loan. It only means you are proving your worth to a lender in a different way, or that the loan has features not endorsed by Fannie or

Freddie. Many nonconforming loans use the same fixed rate, adjustable rate, interest-only, and combination structures we've already reviewed. Other loans—including the loans I'll review next (jumbo loans, Option ARMs, Alt-A, and subprime loans)—are strictly nonconforming. Of these loans, some are still offered today, some have disappeared altogether, and some may one day return. You may even currently have one of these loans yourself. It's hard at this point to determine what the lending market will do, but one thing is certain: there will always be a legitimate need for nonconforming loans. Many of these loans have value and purpose—when they are used correctly.

## Higher Costs and Prepayment Penalties

The drawback to nonconforming loans is their price. Nonconforming loans are riskier for a lender all the way around, so lenders make up for this risk by charging you more—either by charging higher interest rates or by requiring prepayment penalties.

---

DEFINITION  **Prepayment Penalties**

A prepayment penalty is a contract between you and your lender, where you agree not to pay off, sell, or refinance your home for a specific period of time (usually two to three years). If you need to break this contract, you are required to pay a lump sum, usually an amount equal to several months of interest or a percentage of the loan's balance. This could easily add up to several thousand dollars out of your pocket. Sometimes, you may be able to work with your lender to avoid this penalty. If you need to refinance *before* your prepayment penalty period is up, contact your original lender for refinancing options first. Some lenders may waive an existing prepayment penalty if they are given the business of refinancing your loan.

---

With nonconforming loans, prepayment penalties are very common, especially if your loan has an adjustable rate. Why? With most ARMs, a lender is offering you a lower than normal initial interest rate. While this lower interest rate is great for you, it doesn't allow the lender to make as much money on your loan, and it doesn't compensate for a loan's risk. If your loan is paid off, sold, or refinanced within the first few years of a loan, the lender will miss out on some of its profit. Great for you, bad for the lender. So a lender will "fix" the amount of time you are required to make payments on the loan. If the loan is paid off early—either by you, by someone buying your house, or by another lender who is refinancing your home—the lender will require that its profit be made up in the form of a prepayment penalty.

For a lender, prepayment penalties also help to make up for the risk associated with a nonconforming loan. If the lender is going to take a chance on you, it wants to know it's receiving something in return.

In almost all cases, including a prepayment penalty in a loan's terms means you will receive a better interest rate, but it will also tie you to your loan, at least until the prepayment penalty period is up, so pay careful attention to your mortgage documents to see if this penalty is part of the deal. If your loan has a prepayment penalty, it will appear in your Truth In Lending (TIL) Disclosure, which is one of documents you will receive when you are given an estimate or apply for a loan. It's usually nothing more than a small checkbox, so look carefully. I've included a sample of what you should look for in Figure 4.2, and you can also view a full TIL Disclosure (and how it can help you to understand your loan) in Appendix I in the back of this book.

If you don't want to be tied to your loan, and your loan includes a prepayment penalty, lenders will sometimes remove a prepayment penalty from your loan for a fee, to be paid in full at your closing. By paying this fee, you are providing the lender with some of their profit in advance, and in return, you receive the flexibility of being able to sell or refinance at a future date without additional costs.

INSURANCE:  The following insurance is required to obtain credit:
☐ Credit life insurance  ☐ Credit disability  ☑ Property insurance  ☐ Flood insurance
You may obtain the insurance from anyone you want that is acceptable to creditor
☐ If you purchase  ☑ property  ☐ flood insurance from creditor you will pay $  **1,100.00**  for a one year term.
SECURITY:  You are giving a security interest in:  **123 MAIN STREET, ANYTOWN FL 00000**
☑ The goods or property being purchased        ☐ Real property you already own.
FILING FEES: $        **200.00**
LATE CHARGE:  If a payment is more than    **15** days late, you will be charged    **5.000** % of the payment

✱PREPAYMENT:  If you pay off early, you  ☑ may  ☐ will not   have to pay a penalty.
                                          ☑ may  ☐ will not   be entitled to a refund of part of the finance charge.

*THE CHECKBOX*

---

**Figure 4.2: Check for a Prepayment Penalty** *Your prepayment penalty will be part of your Truth In Lending Disclosure, and is nothing more than a small checkbox.*

## Jumbo Loans

Loans can also be categorized as nonconforming simply based on the amount of the loan itself. Fannie and Freddie set limits for individual loan amounts, and loans above $417,000 are referred to as *jumbo loans*. Fannie and Freddie won't back jumbo loans, and do not offer to sell them to the secondary market. Instead, jumbos are usually held as portfolio loans, or are sold by the lender to private investors or other secondary market sources. Because a lender has to take on the risk of funding and selling your loan, a lender will usually charge a higher interest rate, typically at least 0.5 percent more.

In 2008, Fannie and Freddie temporarily increased the loan limits for conforming loans in an attempt to prevent additional foreclosures. As of this printing, loan limits for conforming loans have increased and range from $417,000 to $729,750 (depending on the county or state). What does this mean for you? A lot of loans that would once have been considered jumbo loans now qualify as conforming loans. For many people in many areas of the country, numbers like these are a shock. $729,750? Why would people in these loans need help? It's important to understand that while these prices seem high, housing prices are relative. Many areas of the country have very high costs of living, and what seems like an expensive home to you may actually be all that is available for a middle-class family in another market.

Why would changing Fannie and Freddie's limits help with foreclosures? Many high-cost areas were especially hard-hit by the real estate and lending collapse. By increasing the conforming loan limits, lenders can now finance or refinance higher loan amounts with the backing and support of Fannie and Freddie. The idea is that with this security, lenders will help more borrowers within high-cost areas.

But the key word here is "idea." Fannie and Freddie have raised the limits, but they can't force banks to openly lend these high amounts. In fact, in many cases lenders have tightened their own individual guidelines for high loan amounts and jumbo loan programs to protect themselves further against default. It's a pattern we in the lending world see again and again: the government opens the spigot to get a free flow of money moving to homeowners, but due to how lending works—and because there is still inherent risk to the lender—the lenders close the spigot right back up again with their own guidelines. You can't blame the lenders for doing this, as they are the ones who bear the loss if a home forecloses, and they also must incur the cost of the foreclosure itself, which is an expensive process.

As a consumer, you can still receive jumbo loan amounts by diligently proving your worth to a lender, by having good credit, and by having a large down payment. You'll just need to meet strict guidelines, and you'll have to document yourself as a borrower just like you would for a conventional loan.

In addition, the home or property will be carefully inspected as well; in the jumbo market, lenders will not lend more than 80 percent of a home's value, and will make sure any appraisal accurately reflects this amount. This means that with any jumbo loan, you will need at least 20 percent equity or a 20 percent down payment, no exceptions.

## Option ARM/Deferred-Interest Loans

Option ARMs—which go by many different names, including deferred-interest loans, pick-a-payment loans, and hybrid ARMs—are a unique concept: every month, you can select from any of four payment options for your mortgage. As the borrower, you are in control, and *you* decide what to pay each month. These loans were originally designed for the savvier homeowner or borrower who wanted to leverage their mortgage payments in order to save or invest. And when used correctly, these loans can be very beneficial, as was the case for Lisa and Mark, the homeowners whose story I told earlier in the chapter. Lisa and Mark were able to use an Option ARM responsibly to manage medical payments, to save money, and to pay down their loan.

When used incorrectly, however, Option ARMs can be dangerous—especially when borrowers use them to purchase expensive homes that are far beyond their means. Option ARMs allow for the *lowest payment* of any loan program, and during the boom, people quickly realized they could have a low affordable payment for a home that was twice as expensive as what they could afford with conventional financing. But what these borrowers didn't factor in were all of the equally supersized costs that come with a big expensive home, such as higher taxes, higher insurance, higher utilities, and higher upkeep. These costs, in addition to not understanding how to use the loan itself, got many borrowers into trouble.

## HOW YOUR OPTION ARM PAYMENT AMOUNTS ARE CALCULATED

### An Option ARM's Four Payment Options:

1. A deferred interest payment
   (The lowest payment, but your loan's balance will increase)
2. An interest-only payment
   (A lower payment, but your loan's balance will remain the same)
3. An amortized 30-year payment
   (Your loan's principal and interest are paid down)
4. An amortized 15-year payment
   (Your loan's principal and interest are paid down even faster)

You have four different payment options in an Option ARM each month—but how do you know how much you owe for the option you pick? Each month, depending on how much you paid the month before, your lender will recalculate your options based on two important numbers: your loan's balance and your loan's interest rate.

Let's say you have an Option ARM loan with a $200,000 balance. Your interest rate for the loan is an adjustable rate that changes every month, and this particular month, your interest rate is 7 percent. The loan also has a special predetermined interest rate of 4 percent that determines the minimum amount you *must* pay if you choose the deferred payment option. (This rate is disclosed to you in advance as part of your mortgage.)

### PAYMENT OPTION #1: DEFERRED INTEREST

A deferred interest payment allows you to pay only a *portion* of the interest you owe to a lender as your monthly payment. You aren't paying the lender their full profit, and you aren't paying anything toward the principal of your loan.

So what is your payment based on then? To determine your deferred payment, a lender first calculates your mortgage payment at the predetermined deferred interest rate. In this example, the predetermined interest rate is 4 percent. For a $200,000 balance, here is how your payment breaks down:

```
         Your payment at a 4% interest rate:
   ($163.94 Principal) + $666.67 Interest =
            $666.67 Monthly Payment
```

For your deferred interest payment, your lender will require you to pay $666.67 in interest. But there's more. Although a lender is charging you only 4 percent for this payment, your loan's *actual* interest rate is now 7 percent. At this interest rate, the lender really should be making $1,166.67 in interest this month, a difference of $500:

```
        Your payment at a 7% interest rate:
 ($163.94 Principal) + $1,166.67 Interest =
           $1,166.67 Monthly Payment


  $1,166.67 - $666.67 = $500 Lender Profit
```

Lenders do not want to give up this profit, so this $500 will be added to your loan's balance. Next month, instead of owing $200,000 on your loan, you will owe $200,500.

This process of deferring interest and adding it to your loan's balance is known as *negative amortization*. With negative amortization, there is a limit to the total amount of interest you can defer, which is usually 10 to 25 percent of the loan amount. (This is called a *negative amortization cap*.)

On a $200,000 loan, if your negative amortization cap is 25 percent, you would be able to defer a total of $50,000 in interest. If you deferred this full amount, your loan amount would increase to $250,000, and your loan would be "capped." Once this happens, your loan is recast, and you will have no longer have four payment options. You will be required to pay back the loan's balance (in this case, the $250,000) as a fixed- or adjustable rate loan, depending on the terms of your loan.

## PAYMENT OPTION #2: INTEREST-ONLY

With an Option ARM, lenders also offer an interest-only payment option. For this option, your lender calculates your payment using the 7 percent interest rate, for your loan's balance of $200,000. But with this option, you pay the interest only:

```
        Your payment at a 7% interest rate:
 ($163.94 Principal) + $1,166.67 Interest =
           $1,166.67 Monthly Payment
```

Your payment is $1,166.67, and it's all lender profit. Unlike the deferred-interest payment, nothing is added to your loan's balance, but your balance is not paid down either. Next month, you will still owe $200,000.

### PAYMENT OPTION #3: FULLY AMORTIZED 30-YEAR PAYMENT

Each month, you also have the option to pay *both* principal and interest, so you can begin to pay *down* your loan's balance. Your lender will amortize your payment over thirty years, which will yield you a payment just like a 30-year fixed rate loan. Your payment will be based on the 7 percent interest rate, and your loan's balance of $200,000:

```
$163.94 Principal + $1,166.67 Interest =
         $1,330.60 Monthly Payment
```

Your total payment is $1,330.60, and $163.94 goes toward paying down your loan's balance. Next month, you will owe $199,836.06 on your loan.

### PAYMENT OPTION #4: FULLY AMORTIZED 15-YEAR PAYMENT

You also have the option of paying at a 15-year amortized rate. This payment will be calculated just like it would be if you had a 15-year fixed rate loan. You will be paying more, but will also be applying more to the loan's principal:

```
$630.99 Principal + $1,166.67 Interest =
         $1,797.66 Monthly Payment
```

Your payment would increase to $1,797.66, but you would also be paying $630.99 towards your principal. Next month, you will owe $199,369.01 on your loan.

As you can see, an Option ARM loan provides a lot of options. But to be successful, it also requires *a lot* of consistency and self-control. Just as I advised with interest-only loans, if you choose an Option ARM you will need to plan and save so that what you save is *more* than what you defer. It really is that simple: If you choose to pay the deferred interest or interest-only payments, the money you save needs to be working for you elsewhere bringing in a return, or you need to be in a market where real estate values are appreciating. What you save (and what you make in returns from what you save) needs to be more than the amount you have deferred in interest, or you aren't saving anything at all.

If you choose to make the deferred payment and then *spend* the savings on something else, this loan cannot possibly work for you because you are creating even more debt by deferring interest.

Let's look at a simple example: let's say you have taken out a $200,000 loan on a $225,000 house. The first year, you defer *and* save $10,000 by not paying some of the loan's interest. But this $10,000 has been added to your loan, and your loan amount is now $210,000. If home markets are flat, or the money you have saved has not made a return, it's a wash. You haven't saved any more than you have tacked on, and you are right back where you started:

```
  $200,000  (original loan)
+  $10,000  (deferred interest)
-  $10,000  (money saved)
-----------------------------
  $200,000  (it's a wash)
```

But what if your home is in a moderate appreciating real estate market of 2 percent, and the $10,000 interest you defer is invested in a bank CD with a 2 percent annual return? Where would you be with the same loan?

```
  $200,000  (original loan)
+  $10,000  (deferred interest)
-  $10,108  (money saved @ 2%)
-   $4,500  (appreciating market)
─────────────────────────────────
  $195,392  (a $4,608 gain)
```

Even if you make only a moderate return on the money you save (in this case, 2 percent annually), and even if the local real estate market has low appreciation, with this loan and a good game plan, you can increase your financial stability and savings. Sometimes, these loans can be even more beneficial, as was the case with one of my clients, Rich.

---

CAREFUL PLANNING PAYS OFF

---

In early 2001, I met up with an old friend, Rich. Rich was a fairly detailed guy who was not afraid to ask questions. He invited me to his home for dinner one night, and after we caught up on old times, the talk soon turned to finance.

Rich's house was beautiful, with a secluded oversized lot with plenty of room for his two boys. Rich explained that he and his wife Jen already had a good amount of equity in the home, and since they had no plans to move, they wanted to know how they might make their home an even *better* investment. Rich had already read up on several loan programs, and had asked me over to discuss what options, if any, they had for better financing.

Rich pulled out stacks of research about his home, the area, the local real estate market, and his investments. It was obvious he was eager to learn as much as he could about utilizing their home as a savings vehicle, as well as a long-term asset. We went over standard 30-year fixed rate loans and several shorter-term loans, but Rich didn't perk up until I started to explain the Option ARM program. For the next hour, we meticulously reviewed every aspect of the loan: from the loan's four monthly payment options, to how the deferred interest and interest-only payments were structured, to the ARM indices that were used, and even the indices' levels throughout history.

By the end of the night, I had calculated what his various payments would be, and what long-term plans he would need to put in place for the loan to be beneficial. Later that week, after doing more research on his own on the program, Rich called with an "all systems go." Rich and Jen closed on the loan, armed with a detailed plan for the next five years.

Four years later, Rich called to let me know he was moving to Tennessee because of a company transfer he couldn't pass up. He also shared with me the success that had resulted from his home investment game plan. Rich had taken advantage of the deferred payment option, and between his home's appreciation and diligent saving and investing, he had saved $48,000 over the four years. Rich and his wife utilized the home and the loan as they should be used—as a savings vehicle. Rich's careful planning had paid off.

---

Loans like the Option ARM can be beneficial if you are a responsible borrower. Ideally, you need to be able to afford any of the four payment options for the loan. This will give you the most flexibility: do you save and invest, or do you pay down the principal and interest? Option ARMs are also a good solution if your income varies from month to month (for example, if you are self-employed, work on commission, or work seasonally), allowing you to make lower payments in months where your cash flow is tight, and higher payments in cash-full months.

Because Option ARMs are, just like the name says, adjustable rate loans, you also need to ask yourself the same questions you would with a regular ARM, plus a few more:

- What are your index, your margin, your initial interest rate, and your caps?

- How often does your rate adjust and how high can it go?
- Is there a prepayment penalty?
- What is your negative amortization, and how much can you defer in payments before your loan is recast?

In reality, most borrowers aren't as driven or meticulous as Rich. It can be easy to use this loan to get into a home you can't afford, or to get lazy and pay only the lowest payments, spending the monthly savings elsewhere and allowing your loan balance to creep higher and higher. Unfortunately, during the boom borrowers did exactly that. When the bubble burst, loan balances grew while home values declined, causing many lenders to pull these loans off the market.

## Alt-A and Subprime

Much of what went wrong during the boom has been blamed on two particular types of lending: Alt-A and subprime. To understand what these terms really mean, let's step back and take a broad view of the subject.

Within lending, there are basically three levels of borrowers. At the top are conforming borrowers, also referred to as "A" borrowers. Not only are they strong borrowers, but they can prove their worth just as Fannie and Freddie require them to. Right under A-rated is Alt-A. These are still good borrowers, but they can't provide documentation as Fannie or Freddie would like, so they have to prove their worth in an alternative, or "Alt," way. The last level are subprime borrowers who, because of characteristics such as poor credit or lack of income, are considered to be below usual lending standards. These borrowers have no choice but to try to prove their worth in any alternative way they can.

Subprime borrowers have one or more of the following characteristics:

- A credit score under 620
- Accounts in "open" collections

- Bankruptcies or foreclosures in the past seven years
- Late payments on any credit accounts
- Insufficient credit history
- Insufficient income or poor debt-to-income
- Insufficient income documentation
- Insufficient assets
- No down payment funds
- A poor rental or mortgage payment history

Because of these characteristics, and because Alt-A and subprime borrowers have to prove their worth to lenders in "alternative" ways, both Alt-A and subprime loans fall under the category of nonconforming loans, and, just like other nonconforming loans, Alt-A and subprime loans cost more. Conventional loans have the best rates and costs, followed by Alt-A loans, and subprime loans are at the bottom, with the poorest and most expensive rates and terms.

Because Alt-A and subprime borrowers usually can't provide documentation to lenders to prove their worth like a conforming borrower would be able to, Alt-A and subprime loans allow specific kinds of *alternative documentation*.

Some common alternative documentation programs include:

▸ **SIVA—Stated Income/Verified Assets:** Stated/Verified loan documentation requires you to verify your assets, but allows you to *state* your income. Keep in mind that "stating your income" means you can state what you want for your own income, but there are checks and balances in place to prevent you from saying you make an unreasonable amount. An underwriter will confirm that your income is in line with your profession, and your employment will be confirmed for the last two years, either by contacting your employer if you are a W-2 employee, or requiring a letter from a CPA if you are self-employed. Your debts and credit are also confirmed by the lender; from this, your debt-to-income (DTI) ratio is calculated. Funds needed for your down payment, closing costs, and financial reserves are usually required to be seasoned (to sit in your bank account) for at least sixty days and are verified either by bank statements or a verification of deposit from a bank representative.

▸ **SISA—Stated Income/Stated Assets:** Stated/Stated is pretty much what it sounds like—you are stating both your income and your assets—but it doesn't mean you are writing your own meal ticket. SISA documentation mirrors SIVA: your employment must be verified for two years, your DTI is calculated, and your debts are verified, even though your actual income and assets are not. Because this loan is a higher risk for a lender, higher interest rates are usually charged.

▸ **VISA—Verified Income/Stated Assets:** Verified/Stated documentation requires you to prove your income and employment, but allows you to state your assets. However, there is still flexibility in verifying your income: you can either provide your last two tax returns or two years' worth of W-2s and thirty days' worth of paycheck stubs, or a lender can perform a verification of employment to confirm your salary. If you are self-employed, your CPA will need to confirm in writing your actual reported income.

▸ **No Doc—No Documentation:** On a no doc loan, "no" really means no. No doc loans require no information or verification whatsoever for employment, income, or assets. Of course, to counter this, a lender will require a higher credit score, higher down payment, and higher interest rate. It's important to note that as of this writing, only select hard money lenders will consider a "no-doc" loan, and these lenders will charge you extremely high interest rates and fees.

From these four examples, you can see how easy it was for borrowers, brokers, and lenders to abuse alternative documentation guidelines during the boom. Even now, it's hard to believe some of these documentation types still exist, but they do—because lenders know there are still borrowers worth lending to who need this flexibility. Today, alternative documentation can be used responsibly when combined with compensating factors like good credit, assets, and reserves.

If you know that in the future you'll need to rely on alternative documentation to prove your income, assets, or employment, you should constructively work on the areas of your financial profile that will pique a lender's interest: strengthening all aspects of your credit, increasing your reserves, saving more, and spending less. I'll provide a clear plan for each of these areas in Part III of this book, and I also provide several credit and savings action plans on my website. Once you have the winning combination of good credit and a large down payment (usually 30 percent), a wide variety of nonconforming loan programs become available to you, including fixed rate, ARM, interest-only, and jumbo loans. Lenders are willing to take a chance on borrowers with strong credit and financial reserves, because these borrowers will generate a profit for them, and borrowers with good financial reserves are also less likely to default on a loan.

## ARE SUBPRIME LOANS BAD LOANS?

There is a common misconception that subprime lending was about bad loans. While it's true that there were several loan programs (which no longer exist today) that were targeted specifically toward subprime borrowers, the subprime crisis was really about irresponsible lending practices in general. Loans were suddenly made available to subprime borrowers, lenders became lax in their own guidelines, and loans were given freely with no proof of income. Lenders overlooked that borrowers had collections, bankruptcies, and foreclosures. Fees were paid to "take care of" credit issues. Documentation was stated rather than verified, "no money down" became a standard, and as long as you had a pulse, you could find a loan.

It's clear by now how different things are today. Subprime has an awful sound to it, but technically, it only means "below-prime." Today, many families are hurting from job loss, home loss, and the economy in general, and these conditions have forced many people into the "subprime" category. If this sounds like your situation, it doesn't mean you should write off the possibility of ever getting a loan. In many ways, my campaign is geared for people just like you, who need this extra help. Take faith that each and every one of the characteristics that make a borrower subprime can be worked on and improved. I'll show you how throughout this book, and in the meantime, there are still loan programs that can help you, including FHA programs, VA programs, and other community and specialty lending programs.

## FHA Programs

One avenue for assistance is the Federal Housing Administration (FHA). The FHA was established back in 1934 during the Great Depression to promote homeownership, and it's still an important source of affordable government-guaranteed financing today.

Affordable housing and affordable lending are real issues. FHA programs are designed for borrowers who are credit challenged, or who have little or no money for down payments and closing costs. From a borrower's point of view, the FHA operates very similarly to Fannie and Freddie. The FHA has its own set of guidelines, and if a lender's loan meets these guidelines, the FHA guarantees the loan.

For many borrowers searching for affordable financing, FHA loans are a welcome relief. Most FHA guidelines are very flexible, including affordable interest rates, no minimum credit score requirements, low 3.5 percent down payments (96.5% LTV), down payments that can come from relatives as a "gift," seller or third-party credits of up to 6 percent toward loan-related costs, non-occupant co-borrowers, no prepayment penalties, and many other allowances.

How is all of this possible? It all goes back to the fact that FHA loans are insured by the government. This may mean little to you as a borrower, but this means a lot to a lender. If a borrower defaults on an FHA loan, the government is responsible for a large part of the loan's balance.

This government guarantee is also very beneficial to both lenders and borrowers in the event of default or foreclosure. The FHA is very proactive in its efforts to avoid both circumstances, and offers many options to avoid foreclosure. The government doesn't want to have to

**Credit or Savings Issues? FHA Loans Can Help**

Even though the FHA has strict guidelines when it comes to proving you can afford your home (you will need to prove your income and meet specific debt-to-income requirements), FHA loans cater to borrowers with issues. Maybe you have poor credit, collections, or even a past foreclosure. Maybe you had a recent period when you were unemployed, or maybe you don't have a lot in savings due to job loss. Many of these issues would disqualify you from conventional financing. But if you can show there is a good reason for your issues, whatever those issues may be, an exception will most likely be granted and you'll be able to receive a loan. FHA is what I call the "story lender"—if your story makes sense, they will lend to you.

pay your loan, and so it doesn't want you to lose your home. To be able to guarantee loans in this manner, all FHA loans include an upfront 1.5 percent charge (which is added to a large FHA insurance fund) as well as mandatory mortgage insurance for *all* loans (regardless of the loan amount or LTV). And even though the FHA requires mortgage insurance, the mortgage insurance policy is discounted and is very affordable.

FHA loans sound too good to be true. Why isn't there a mad rush on these loans? Actually, there is—many borrowers are seeking out FHA loans, but there is a disconnect in the system. Unfortunately, some of the flexibility within FHA guidelines causes issues for many lenders, which then becomes a catch-22 for borrowers.

So what are the issues? First, all parties who are involved in selling an FHA loan, including lenders and brokers, are still held accountable by the FHA for the first twelve months of a loan. If a borrower defaults within this time frame and the FHA feels the lender or broker didn't do their job to truly qualify the borrower for the loan, *all* involved parties could be held liable for the loan, and the government insurance may *not* cover the default. And in the event of too many borrower defaults, a lender or broker could lose their FHA licensing. This means that even though FHA guidelines are flexible, lenders may, yet again, impose their *own* sets of guidelines to minimize the risk for them, even if this risk is only for a twelve-month period.

For example, you've just read that FHA loans have no credit score requirements, and they don't. But any given lender may impose their own credit score requirements—which supersede the FHA guidelines—making the actual FHA guideline of no credit score null and void. Lenders may also apply their own strict guidelines in many other areas, making a lender's requirements for FHA loans far different than the base FHA guidelines themselves.

Second, the FHA has very strict and expensive requirements for lenders and brokers to maintain FHA certification and approval, and also requires complex ongoing monitoring and compliance. Sometimes, these requirements make it difficult for a lender or broker to become or remain certified, which may make it more difficult for a borrower to find a source for FHA loans.

In the boom years, when other affordable loan programs were plentiful, many lenders did not offer FHA loans because they were viewed as "too much work" for the lender. Today, as the options for affordable financing dry up further, more and more lenders are deciding to get the certification needed to sell FHA programs. Throughout this book, I speak about the importance of having a mortgage consultant on your side, and with FHA loans it is no different. A competent consultant can ensure you do not miss out on all of the benefits FHA has to offer, and will help you to find a lender who imposes the least amount of individual restrictions on your loan. All in all, FHA loans can be of great help to many people and are a solid option for affordable financing.

## VA Programs

There are also affordable loan programs available for our country's veterans. The U.S. Department of Veterans Affairs (VA) provides, insures, and guarantees 100 percent financing for eligible veterans, without mortgage insurance or prepayment penalties. The VA can also provide high loan amounts to accommodate veterans in select high-cost areas of the country. VA loans benefit veterans as well as their spouses, and have similar loan qualifications, guidelines, and requirements as the FHA.

Just like with FHA loans, lenders and brokers who sell VA loans must be approved through the VA and uphold similar monitoring requirements to remain certified. Not surprisingly, VA lenders may also impose their own restrictions on top of VA guidelines, so borrowers should not only shop for a VA loan, but also for the best VA lender. Again, this is where good mortgage consultants are worth their weight in gold.

## Community and Specialty Loans

There are also several lending programs that fall into what is referred to as the "specialty" loan category. These loans conform to Fannie and Freddie or FHA guidelines, but cater to borrowers in special circumstances. Specialty programs include down payment assistance programs from the FHA, as well as community loan programs for teachers and for city and government employees, including police officers, firefighters, postal workers, and government staff.

The key to each and every specialty program is qualifying. There are many programs out there, but qualifying can be a challenge. Qualifying guidelines, which vary from city to city, include maximum home values (you won't be able to get a loan over a certain amount), income requirements and income limits (you can only make so much), and even restrictions regarding property location, making specialty financing a little harder to come by.

Community and specialty programs are available through many FHA lenders, and the good news is that with these programs, individual lenders don't add their own requirements—the program guidelines are strict enough.

Want to learn more about FHA, VA, specialty, or community programs? Would you like more information to see if you might qualify? Visit the reader's section of my website, or you can visit these agencies directly at www.fha.gov or www.va.gov.

• • •

I have always had a great desire to learn as much as I could about the finance industry, but I can confidently say that every time I think I've learned enough about financing, something else comes along. Loans and loan guidelines will forever be changing. The industry itself has changed so much over the years, and it will only continue to do so. Although the topic of home finance may continue to be intimidating, there is no better time to learn about it than now.

After reading this chapter, you should have a solid foundation and knowledge about loans, from how you can qualify for a loan, to the most common loan programs and how they can benefit you, to ways you can use loans to actually save some money, as well as options for affordable financing that you may not have known even existed. With this background, long-term realistic goals, and a plan for the future, you'll be able to make financing work for you.

## COMING UP

As you have seen, loans can be complicated. You might find you need someone to help you with your financing. It's easy to find a broker or consultant, but how do you find the right one? In the next chapter, I'll explain what you should look for, and expect, from any mortgage professional. And I'll also show you how you can find a mortgage consultant you can build a relationship with—and trust.

# 5

## Broker or Consultant

What to Expect from Your Mortgage Professional
and the Right Questions to Ask to Find
a Consultant for Life

Lending and loans can be complex and confusing for many borrowers. And right now, there are so many changes in lending itself that it's an even more troublesome marketplace if you need financing. For borrowers, it can be stressful, particularly if you don't have someone on your side you can trust through thick and thin, or someone you can rely on to guide you through the process.

Just as there is a need for good trainers or coaches in any field, I believe there will always be a need for consultants in home finance. You may have noticed that in several chapters and stories I refer to mortgage industry professionals as consultants, rather than as brokers. I personally use the title "consultant," because it truly is part of the mindset you need as a professional in the industry. Most individuals in the business are licensed as "mortgage brokers," and that's how they choose to label themselves, how they approach their clients, and how they are viewed by the public.

Brokers are focused on the business of selling loans, but this doesn't mean a broker will be focused on what's truly best for you or your home. A broker, by definition, is just a middleman. Instead, I choose to be a consultant, and not just a consultant, but a consultant for life. A consultant will always make time for you and will help you to understand your loan and any part of the lending process. A consultant will always keep you updated on what is happening with your loan and will make you feel involved. And a true consultant will advise you on making the best decisions and the right choices for you, and will always put your needs first.

## My Own Story

Over the years, I've been involved with many different clients and situations. I've become friends with borrowers and have worked with many of my clients for over a decade. I've gone out of my way to help clients, and have closed loans in hospitals, in a jail, and I've even had a closing on an airplane. I've also spent a lot of time helping people make choices that would enable them to one day own a home, regardless of whether there was any direct benefit to me. All of this is part of being a consultant.

Before entering the world of home finance, even I wasn't immune to being naïve about the "business of lending." I'd always had a keen interest in finance and considered myself to be good with numbers, but it wasn't until my own horrific home purchase that I opened my eyes to what could really happen in the industry. This single negative experience is the reason I decided to become a mortgage consultant, and is an important reminder of why I am the consultant I am today.

---

THE STORY THAT STARTED MY CAREER

---

Back in early 1994, I began the process of purchasing my first home and was thrilled to be fulfilling a personal goal of homeownership. I had been looking into building a new home, and I spent some time visiting communities and speaking with builders. I was a little nervous about making such a big decision, but it ended up being easy when a high school friend vouched for the builder I had chosen. I'd always put a high value on personal referrals, so as far as I was concerned, I was off to a good start. But I'd soon learn that sometimes going with your gut is the wiser move.

Not knowing much at the time about real estate or mortgages, I decided to use the builder's recommended mortgage company, which the builder personally had "great" experiences with. After meeting the mortgage broker and determining the pre-construction price for the home with the builder, I engaged in a 90% LTV contract. I was a bit hesitant about putting down a full 10 percent on the home: not only was it my first purchase, but since the home was pre-construction, I was also agreeing to a two-year building time frame. Two years? That alone was a little scary. But I defaulted back to my friend's recommendation and went forward. My home would soon be underway.

A few months went by, and I started to talk to the builder's mortgage broker about financing, but was told it was too early to start on my loan. A few more months went by, the permits came in, and construction started. I visited the site and kept personal progress reports on how construction was coming each week. From what I could tell, the builder seemed to be moving right along.

About a year into the process, I started to notice that construction was at a standstill, and I began to worry. Then construction stopped. When I approached the builder, he assured me everything was fine; construction for my home wasn't delayed, and everything was going according to schedule. But for some reason, I didn't quite believe him. Something was off. I asked him to detail the completion plan; it turned out my home would be finished in a month or two, at the most.

This also didn't seem right. My home was *this close* to being finished, and I *still* hadn't heard any more from the mortgage broker? I decided to give the broker a call myself. We scheduled a meeting, where we completed my loan application package and I signed on the dotted line. The broker quoted me a great interest rate and terms based on my credit rating, income, and assets. His estimate was solid, and I was happy. All I had to do then was wait for the builder to complete my home.

Unfortunately the builder didn't live up to his end of the bargain—

my home wasn't ready when he had promised—but eventually things were resolved. Finally, the actual closing was near. The week of my closing came and the broker's processing staff assured me that everything was set up and ready to go. But his staff couldn't give me specific answers: Was my loan locked? Could I get proof it was locked at the rate I was quoted? Was the loan cleared with the lender? Weren't these simple questions? Wasn't it the week of my closing? I had no solid answers and I couldn't get the broker to call me back. I just had to hope it all would work out.

The day of the closing came—5:00 p.m. on a Friday. The title company let me know early Friday morning what funds I needed to bring, and although the total fees were more than what was on my Good Faith Estimate, it wasn't enough to deter me from closing. Surely, the broker would clear everything up at the closing table. I arrived promptly at five, only to find that the broker was *not* attending the closing. I was furious and expecting answers. As I went over the final HUD settlement statement with the closing agent, it was clear why I needed more money for the closing—the broker fees had shot up $500 and there was no one there to explain why. I could only shake my head in disgust.

It turned out that the $500 was minor in comparison to what came next. My interest rate was 1.5 percent higher than quoted, and there were additional and unexpected fees from the builder as well. It was at that moment that I realized I had been taken by both the builder and the mortgage broker. I quickly calculated the difference in costs as I sat in silence. I had a choice to move forward, or walk away and possibly never see my 10 percent down payment again. I felt I had no choice but to close—so I did.

---

After this experience, I clearly felt taken advantage of. I also felt that I had been unprepared. Buying a home can be a difficult process, but this couldn't be how the system *really* worked . . . or could it? My broker had only cared about his own profit and the final sale. He wasn't looking out for my best interests (or really, any of my interests at all), he wasn't there to answer questions or to help me through the process, and he certainly wasn't a consultant. He wasn't even an ethical person. With stories like this one, it's easy to see how mortgage brokers have gotten a bad name.

Most people who have had a bad experience with buying a home or refinancing don't want anything more to do with the industry; they just want to put the experience behind them. But my experience with both the builder and the mortgage broker had the opposite effect on me. I wanted to understand the industry so I would never be put in the same position again. My experience showed me how many bad brokers could be out there, as well as how many homeowners could use guidance and help. With my interest in finance, I knew I could do a better job than most brokers could.

In early 1996, I closed on my first home, changed careers, and became a mortgage consultant. My own story is an example that no one can be too careful when it comes to one of life's biggest investments: a home.

## A Dime a Dozen

Since I started in the mortgage business, I have seen my share of good mortgage professionals, but the bad ones are a dime a dozen. In the past six years alone, I've had brokers come and go in my own company who never quite grasped the concept—and couldn't live up to the standard—of being a consultant. I've seen brokers at other firms make six-figure incomes by doing nothing other than shuffling papers and churning out borrowers. In the industry overall, service has been left by the wayside.

From managing over 100 brokers and consultants, I've also heard every story of success and rejection known to man when it comes to lending and loans. I've had to stand my ground with many lenders, realtors, and title companies to fight for a client's loan. I've had many successes due to my passion and knowledge of the business, and I've also learned the hard way more than once. And even though I've made mistakes over the years, I've made sure to take the time to learn from all of them. The finance industry has been kind to me and has yielded me a successful life because I have respected the industry and how I should act as a professional since day one.

## The Truth About Unqualified Brokers

Unqualified brokers are a reality in both the banking and lending industries. Your broker—who is making big decisions about your loan, your home, and your money—may not be qualified to do so. In fact, he or she may not even have formal training. Even if you choose to work with a bank instead of a broker, your lending representative may not have the knowledge or experience needed to advise you on your loan. How does this happen? Why is it allowed to happen? Even I have these same questions.

Mortgage brokers are *not* required by law to have a license to work for certain banks and mortgage brokerage firms. Commercial banks, most mortgage brokerage firms with a correspondent lending license, and mortgage lenders (which are the places you are most likely to go to apply for a loan) can all bypass licensing requirements for the brokers they employ. Within these business structures, brokers are also not legally required to take a course, pass an exam, or keep a license current. *Anyone* can be hired to sell you a loan.

Most of the time, unlicensed brokers are good sales people, but they may not have had any knowledge of the industry at all before they started selling loans. This isn't an exaggeration. Your mortgage broker could be selling insurance, cars, or homes one day, and selling mortgages to you the next. In addition, unlicensed brokers may not even receive training about loans or lending from the bank or lender they work for.

Of course, many banks and mortgage firms *do* require their brokers to be licensed. In my own business, I require every consultant to have a current license and to attend a minimum of several weeks of in-house training. How serious can finance professionals be if they don't take the time to learn the industry and become licensed?

But even a license is usually not enough to make a broker truly qualified to handle your finances. To receive a license in most states, a broker must take a class and pass a state exam. These classes can range from an intensive full month course to only a three-day cram course. In the best-case scenario, your broker has taken the time to learn the industry, attends a formal class several times a week for a month before the exam, and receives additional employer training. Worst case, your broker signs up for a three-day, all-day cram class followed quickly by a state exam, and before you know it, is sitting at a shiny new desk taking loan applications.

Licensed mortgage brokers are also required to take a continuing education exam every two years, but in many states the exam is an open-book test and can be completed online or by mail. It's up to the mortgage brokerage firm to make sure your loan is being handled properly by their representatives—the brokers. And within the industry, this type of setup allows many things to quickly fall through the cracks.

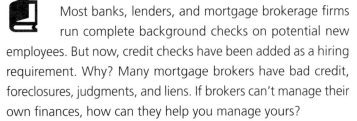

**MORE INFO  Background and Credit Checks**

Most banks, lenders, and mortgage brokerage firms run complete background checks on potential new employees. But now, credit checks have been added as a hiring requirement. Why? Many mortgage brokers have bad credit, foreclosures, judgments, and liens. If brokers can't manage their own finances, how can they help you manage yours?

It's easy to see that a complete overhaul and total reform within the lending industry is needed. The system is clearly broken, all the way to national and federal levels. And while the government is taking steps to fix these problems, it is going to be a very long process, and substantial reform will take quite some time.

What can you do in the meantime? Just because the industry is broken doesn't mean people have stopped needing loans. In fact, many people need loans now more than ever. As a borrower, how can you find the *right* person to help you find financing? In this chapter, I'll show you how applying for financing works, from your initial consultation, to choosing your interest rate, all the way to your loan's final approval. And I'll explain how a consultant should work together with you through this process, step by step.

I'll also help you to distinguish between a broker and a consultant, so you'll know if you are truly receiving the help you deserve with your loan. I'll outline where you can find reputable consultants, and I'll provide some questions you should ask any consultant to be sure they will put your needs first.

## Step by Step: The Lending Process and What You Should Expect from Your Lending Professional

So what can you expect—and what *should* you expect—when you work with any mortgage professional? Let's start with the lending process itself. It's your consultant's responsibility to handle all aspects of your loan, and to keep you informed with each step of the process, from start to finish.

The process for *any* loan should follow these ten steps:

### *Step 1: Your Initial Consultation*

Your mortgage consultant will meet with you to learn more about your specific needs for a loan. A good consultant will ask questions *and* listen to your answers:

- What are your goals with this loan?
- How does it fit into your long-term plans?
- Do you need help determining a long-term plan?
- What special challenges or circumstances do you have?

A consultant will also explain the lending process, provide a realistic view of the lending programs that are available, and answer any questions you may have.

## Step 2: Your Application

To find the right loan for either a purchase or a refinance, your consultant will need detailed information about you and your finances. Your consultant will help you in filling out a standard industry form called a *1003* (pronounced ten-oh-three), either via phone or in person. You can expect to provide details about anything and everything a lender may want to know, including your job and employment history, your finances, assets, debts and liabilities, your credit and credit history, any lawsuits, foreclosures or bankruptcies, your home or rental history, and of course your contact information, date of birth, and social security number.

At this point, your consultant is depending on you to accurately provide this information as best as you can. And although you won't be asked to provide documentation at this time, your answers are used to start the process of sourcing your loan (Step 4), so it's not in your best interest to tell any white lies or exclude any information from your application. If you do, it may hurt your chances for receiving a loan, and it will definitely delay the process and waste your consultant's time. Be honest in all of your answers. Remember, it's important for you to be able to trust your consultant; at the same time, your consultant must also be able to trust you.

## Step 3: Your Credit

After you complete your application, your consultant will run your credit. Your 1003 gives permission to run a *tri-merged credit report*, which is a special industry credit report that includes information about your credit from all three credit repositories (the national companies that gather and report credit).

Your consultant will use this report exclusively to evaluate your credit, and to determine what lending options might be available to you. Lenders will also rely heavily on this report to qualify you as a borrower. I'll explain more about how lenders will interpret what they see in your credit, what's in a tri-merged report, and how this may affect your loan (and your loan's approval) in Chapter 9.

---

MORE INFO **Shopping for a Mortgage Will *Not* Hurt Your Credit Score**

You may have heard that, when you are shopping for a mortgage, having your credit run too many times will lower your credit score. In fact, you may actually hear this from many brokers, who use this warning as a tactic to keep you from going somewhere else for your loan.

Let me set the record straight: running your credit when applying for a mortgage will *not* damage your credit score or credit history. Mortgage consultants, banks, and even the lender for your loan will all be running your credit multiple times throughout the course of applying for a loan. When you apply for a mortgage, the credit repositories know, expect, and allow multiple inquiries within a realistic time period, usually about one to two months. During this period, inquiries pertaining to your loan will not affect your credit in any way.

---

## Step 4: Sourcing Your Loan

Based on your initial consultation, your 1003, and your credit, your mortgage consultant will now be able to determine which loan programs will meet your needs and provide you with the best rates, terms, and options. As a liaison for many wholesale banks and lenders, a professional will also know immediately, based on your borrower profile, which loan programs you will qualify for (and which programs you won't).

If your consultant feels you might need an exception from a lender in order to be approved for financing, he or she can also run your application through a lender's automated underwriting system for an initial approval (and to double-check that you'll actually be able to qualify for the loan). Your consultant may even take the extra step to call the lender directly to discuss your loan, just to make sure the lender will view you as a good candidate for financing, and to be able to red flag any issues or concerns the lender may have. (If a lender has issues, it's definitely better to know about them sooner rather than later.) Your consultant will discuss any issues with you, and how you will be able to work around them, in advance, *before* you formally apply for the loan.

### Step 5: Your Good Faith Estimate and Truth In Lending Disclosure

After researching the best financing options, your mortgage consultant will provide you with all of the details on your Good Faith Estimate (GFE) and Truth In Lending Disclosure (TIL), which ensure you understand your loan and its costs (I've provided a detailed explanation of both your GFE and your TIL Disclosure in Appendix I). As required by law through the Real Estate Procedures Act (RESPA), these documents will show:

- Your interest rate and monthly payments
- If your interest rate can increase (and by how much)
- If your loan's balance can increase (and by how much)
- Whether there are prepayment penalties or lump sum balloon payments
- All of the costs for your loan, including estimated closing costs, and how your consultant will charge for services in yield spread premiums and origination fees

Both your GFE and TIL Disclosure are based solely on the information you have already supplied, and are estimates that basically say, "If you can document everything you've told your mortgage consultant, you will receive this loan, at these costs."

## Step 6: The Final Application Package

Once you are ready to proceed forward with your loan, your consultant will complete the "final application package," which includes your signed 1003, your GFE and TIL Disclosure, a servicing agreement (which explains if your loan can be sold), and a stack of other documents and disclosures—about twenty to forty total, depending on your loan. These signed documents mark the official (and legal) starting point for your loan.

WEBLINK Want to know what you can expect to sign beforehand? I provide examples of all of the documents that should be part of your initial loan package in the reader's section of my website.

## Step 7: Locking Your Loan's Interest Rate

Interest rates fluctuate constantly. The economy, the Fed, individual bank and lender policies, and even world events can affect interest rates on a daily, or sometimes even on an *hourly*, basis. Once you apply for a loan, it will be up to you to decide when you "lock in" your rate. Locking your rate means the lender *guarantees* you a specific interest rate if your loan is approved and closed within a specific period of time, no matter what happens in the market. You may choose to lock in a rate right away or you may wait—referred to as "floating a rate"—to see if interest rates get any better. How do you know when to lock your rate? Well, that's a million dollar question.

As I discussed in Chapter 3, you can keep tabs on interest rates by following the 10-Year Treasury note and by being generally aware of the federal funds rate and discount rate. If your loan has an adjustable rate, you will want to monitor your ARM's index. During the loan process, you'll also need to keep in close communication with your consultant to find out how your lender's own interest rates have adjusted in response to all of these variables. Keep in mind, a professional mortgage consultant will advise you, based on market conditions, when it might be a *good* time to lock your rate, but ultimately the final decision is up to you.

When you contact your consultant to lock your rate, your consultant will formally lock in your rate with the lender, and the clock for your loan starts. Rate locks typically last for thirty days, although lock periods can range anywhere from as little as ten days to as many as ninety days, depending on the program and lender. Usually, the shorter the lock period, the better the interest rate. This means from the day you lock your rate until the lock expires, your consultant has to 1) provide the lender with all the required documentation, 2) receive a final approval from the lender, and 3) close on your loan, which is all easier said than done.

In fact, if you are refinancing your loan, your consultant will have *even less* time. All refinances have a three-day period after you close on the loan when you can change your mind. If you decide the loan was a mistake, you can cancel the loan. Because of this, if you are refinancing, you will actually need to close three days before your lock's expiration date, so that three days later when your loan actually funds, your rate is still legally "locked."

## IF YOU NEED AN EXTENSION

If your loan runs into issues, and it looks like your lock will expire, some lenders will give you some breathing room by granting a *lock extension*. But don't be too flattered; lenders don't do this to be nice. Extensions usually cost money, anywhere from 0.125 to 0.25 percent of your total loan amount for a three- to fourteen-day extension.

If you've caused the need for the extension yourself, these fees will be charged to you and will become part of your closing costs. If your broker caused the issue (for example, by forgetting to submit a document to the lender, which does happen), this fee should be taken out of the broker's yield spread premium or origination fee. To prevent mistakes like this from happening, when you ask your consultant to lock your rate, make sure you ask to receive a confirmation of the lock *in writing*. A verbal approval from your consultant is not enough.

This written confirmation will include your interest rate, the details of your loan, when the loan was locked, and the lock's expiration date.

When you lock your loan, you can't change your mind. If rates go up that's great, because you are locked in at a lower rate. But if rates go down, well, you are still locked in, even if you beg and plead. Because of this, some borrowers prefer to wait to the very last minute before locking in their rate. In these cases, the very latest you can lock your rate is usually three days before your closing date. Every lender has slightly different guidelines for this, but three days is usually enough time to finish the final paperwork for your loan once the final interest rate is determined.

## PAYING POINTS TO LOWER YOUR RATE

If rates are high or you want to secure a lower interest rate, you can choose to pay for a lower rate, referred to as "paying points" or "paying discount points." Paying points gives you a lower rate (and lower payments), and at the same time, pays a lender for some profit in advance. And because all lenders like getting their money first, any lender will allow you to pay points. If you have a fixed rate loan, your interest rate will be lowered for the entire life of the loan. If you have an adjustable rate, paying points will lower a lender's margin (the fixed part of your interest rate, which is the lender's profit), which in turn lowers your total interest rate for the life of the loan.

If you are considering paying points, you need to make sure paying for a lower rate makes sense for how long you plan to stay in the home. Each point costs 1 percent of your total loan amount, and every point you pay typically lowers your interest rate anywhere from 0.125 to 0.5 percent. When paying points, you need to calculate your break even point. Will the amount you pay in points really save you money in the long term? Let's look at how you can find out.

Here's an example: On a $300,000 loan, let's say the lender's interest rate is 7 percent. At 7 percent, your mortgage payment is $1,995.91 a month. You decide to pay 1 point to lower your interest rate 0.25 percent. How much will it cost to lower your rate?

$$\$300,000 \text{ x } 1 \text{ pt. } (1.0\%) = \$3,000$$

For $3,000, your interest rate will drop from 7.0 to 6.75 percent. At 6.75 percent, your mortgage payment is now $1,945.79 a month. How much are you saving? Take your first mortgage payment at 7.0 percent, and then subtract your new payment at 6.75 percent:

$$\$1,995.91 - \$1,945.79 = \$50.12$$

Is saving $50.12 a month worth it? To know, you need to look at how long it will take at $50.12 a month to break even with the $3,000 you will be charged:

$$\$3,000 \div \$50.12 = 60 \text{ months } (5 \text{ years})$$

In this case, your break-even point is five years. If you are going to stay in your home longer than five years, paying points may be worth your while. If you plan on moving before five years, however, it would certainly not be worth your while. The value of paying points often depends on this break-even point, as well as exactly how much each point lowers your rate.

In this example, if paying 1 point lowered your rate by *0.5 percent* instead—for a final rate of 6.5 percent—you would be saving almost twice as much per month ($99.71) and it would only take 2.5 years to break even. This is clearly a much better deal, especially when you consider it will cost you $3,000 to do it. When paying points, you also need to factor in how you are going to pay for the points themselves. If you are purchasing a home, these fees would be out of your pocket,

> **⚠ A Note of Caution on Paying Points**
>
> Points are a very common and effective way to lower your interest rate. But paying points is also tied to a broker's profit, and if you don't know how to ask your broker about points (and if you don't know what to look for on your Good Faith Estimate), you may not receive the discount you have paid for. If you decide to pay points to lower your interest rate, you'll want to pay special attention to the next chapter, where I explain in detail how points and broker profit are related, and how you can avoid being overcharged to receive a lower interest rate.

due at closing. If you are refinancing, you could choose to pay for these fees at closing, or roll the costs into your refinance, depending on what you can afford.

 Still not sure if you should pay points? In the reader's section of my website, I provide worksheets and calculators that will help you to determine if paying points is right for you.

## Step 8: Documentation

While you are making decisions about your rate, your consultant will be very busy gathering the documentation your lender requires to approve your loan. These are the items I discussed in the last chapter: verification of your income, employment, assets, and more. Your consultant will work with you and ask for exactly what the lender needs, and in some cases, may even ask you to provide additional documentation to prove your strength and position as a borrower.

This documentation phase is usually the phase when, if you just *happened* to tell a small white lie on your loan application, the truth comes out. Your mortgage consultant will need to document the in-

**Paying In Advance**

Your homeowners insurance policy (which I'll be re-viewing shortly) and the fee for your appraisal should be the *only costs* you pay for prior to your closing. An appraisal typically runs between $300 and $500, and is based on the loan amount or sales price of the home. This payment should be made in the name of the appraiser or appraisal company, *not* the mortgage broker or mortgage company. Why is this fee re-quired in advance? Too often, the appraiser will do his or her job well, but the loan doesn't happen. This is not the appraisers' fault and is why the payment is usually COD.

formation you provided on your application, and if everything *can't* be documented, your loan can easily be denied. Remember that you are trying to convince the lender you are a great borrower. If your stories don't add up through documentation, your credibility drops, and your lender will easily move on to the next borrower. Providing a lender with accurate documentation is a key element in getting your loan approved.

During this period, your consultant will also manage other im-portant aspects of your loan, including ordering an appraisal to document the property's value, ordering a title search, and overseeing your homeowners insurance and real estate taxes.

## THE TITLE SEARCH

A *title search* is performed by the same title company or title attorney who will handle the closing of your loan. It lets the lender know if the property's title (a document that proves ownership) is free and clear of any liens (financial claims against the property) and any law-suits, or if there are any outstanding debts on the property that will need to be cleared up before you can close on your new loan.

When a title search comes back with no issues, your home's title is referred to as being "clear." But when issues are present, red flags go up for everyone involved with your loan. In rare cases, a lender may accept the issues as part of the loan, but usually a lender will require that the issues be resolved, or if the issues are significant enough, a lender may decide *not* to provide financing for the loan at all.

For example, let's say you were purchasing a home, and the title search revealed that the sellers haven't paid their real estate taxes on the home for several years. These taxes are out of your (and your lender's) control. Unless the sellers can pay the taxes in full, the lender will disqualify *your* loan, and you will need to search for another home.

## TITLE INSURANCE

Part of the title search also involves taking out a policy for *title insurance*. If during the title search any mistakes are made, something is overlooked, or there is any fraud connected to the title of the home, title insurance protects you, the borrower.

> For example, let's say you buy a home where the sellers had just put on a new roof. You move into your new house with a leak-free roof and couldn't be happier. A few years later, you decide to refinance the home and find out that there is a lien on your home from the roofer! This is not a good surprise, because it means the roofer has a legal "hold" on your property until the debt is paid. It turns out that the seller never finished paying the roofer, and the roofer placed a lien on the house right before you closed on your loan. The title search missed the lien, but because you have title insurance you are protected. At this point, the title company or title attorney steps in to make things right, and will work with the insurer to pay the roofer and satisfy any liens or claims made on the property, providing you with a clear title once more.

If you are purchasing a home, your title insurance will be a required one-time fee based on your actual loan amount (the exact cost varies from state to state). This amount will be listed on your Good Faith Estimate and your final HUD settlement statement, and is due in full at your closing.

If you are refinancing, you will still be required to have title insurance, but you may be able to save money on the policy. With a refinance, you will already have a title policy in place from when you first purchased your home. If this policy is under ten years old, you can request that the policy be *reissued*, and a reissued policy will cost anywhere from 10 to 25 percent *less* than if you took out a new title policy with your loan.

## HOMEOWNERS INSURANCE AND REAL ESTATE TAXES

Your consultant will also work with you regarding your *homeowners insurance* (also called *hazard insurance*) and your *real estate property taxes*. Lenders require homeowners insurance to protect the actual structure of the home itself; lenders want to know their investment is being protected, and will require proof that you have an insurance policy in place to do just that.

Your homeowner's insurance premium is primarily based on the replacement cost of your home, one of several values listed on your home's appraisal. If you are purchasing a home, you will need to purchase a full year's insurance policy prior to your closing. And if you are refinancing a home, you will need to provide documentation showing that a homeowners insurance policy is already in place. Your consultant will be able to guide you through this process, and will also advise you on your policy, to ensure that your insurance meets with a lender's approval.

For your real estate taxes, a lender will want to see a current tax bill for the home, which will be included as part of a lender's debt-to-income calculation. A lender wants to be sure you can afford the taxes *and* your mortgage payment as part of your total housing costs. If you are refinancing, a lender will also want to receive documentation that your previous taxes have been paid. Again, your consultant will work with you to make sure your lender receives all of the documentation that is required.

Now, if you are financing over 80 percent of your home's value, you can expect to work with your consultant even more regarding your home's insurance and taxes. When your loan is above 80% LTV, your loan will be structured to make sure your taxes and insurance are all paid automatically, and are saved in advance (again, to protect the lender). Your insurance premiums and real estate taxes will be estimated, divided up, and added to your monthly mortgage payments and to your closing costs, a process called *escrowing*. How escrowing works can be confusing, and understanding your escrow will usually require advice and explanation from your mortgage consultant. I've provided more information about escrows in Chapter 10, from how escrows work, to what they will cost, and how they will impact your taxes and insurance.

## Step 9: Clear to Close

In the lending industry, you would think the phrase "You're Approved" would be the words you want to hear. However, what you really want to hear is "You're Clear to Close." Once the lender accepts and is satisfied with everything your consultant has supplied, your loan is "clear" to close, and your consultant will call you with the good news. You are now one step away from the last and final step, your closing.

## Step 10: Your Closing

Finally, the day you have been waiting for! Because your closing is a legal transaction between you and a lender, your final closing will be completed by the title agent or title attorney who has been working with your lender and your consultant on your loan. Your mortgage consultant will work closely with the title company to advise you on the final closing date and time for your loan, and most times, your consultant will also attend the closing to be able to answer questions and explain the loan documents you will be signing.

Anywhere from a few days to several hours before your closing, you will be told the exact amount you need to bring for your final closing costs (in the form of a certified bank check), as well as any identification or paperwork that is required to close the loan.

If you are refinancing and are cashing out any of your home's equity, you'll also be told the final amount you will receive from the refinance after subtracting your final closing costs. These funds will be available to you three days *after* your closing: a lender will either send you a check, or will wire the funds to your bank account.

At your closing, you'll want to carefully inspect all of your loan's documents. Although you do have the legal right to inspect your final loan documents one business day prior to your closing, I will warn you, the entire lending process is often fast and frantic. As I mentioned in Chapter 3, your loan's final documents are sometimes not available until *minutes* before your closing and because of this, you'll want to bring your final Good Faith Estimate to your closing to compare it to your HUD settlement statement. If your consultant has done a good job, these documents will match up, your costs will be within $100 to $200 of what your consultant quoted, and you will painlessly close on your loan.

From start to finish, these ten steps usually take about a month or

---

CAUTION    **What if Your Closing *Isn't* so Painless?**

If you do run into issues with your loan or its costs (or even both), if you are purchasing a home, you may be able to ask for an *extension* of both your real estate contract and your loan's locked interest rate. If you are refinancing a home, you will be able to delay or even cancel the refinance entirely. I explain both of these options, as well as all of the things that could go wrong with your loan, in the next chapter.

less. If you are purchasing a home, the real estate sales contract and when your interest rate lock expires usually determine how fast things need to happen. And if you are refinancing, your interest rate lock will set the pace. Due to everything that needs to come together perfectly on your closing day, the entire process can be very fast, sometimes stressful, and certainly intense, but your home is worth it.

Once your loan has closed, your consultant's work is pretty much done. But if you ever have any questions about your loan in the future, or if you have questions about financing in general, a good consultant will always be available for you.

## Brokers vs. Consultants

Now that you have a better idea of what your mortgage professional needs to do to take a loan from its initial application to its final closing, the next question is: How do you know if he or she is doing a good job? When you apply for a loan, especially in the early stages of calling brokers and receiving estimates, it is usually up to *you* to discern whether a mortgage professional has your best interests at heart. So what should you look for, and what should you *look out* for? Let's look at how a broker and a consultant might handle many common situations:

▸ **A new client calls and asks, "What rates are available?"** A broker would immediately quote the *lowest* rate for the day, without knowing anything about the client or their financial situation.

Many mortgage brokers advertise interest rates in the newspaper, on the radio, or on television, but neglect to provide details on the rate's requirements. Just because a rate is advertised doesn't mean you qualify for the rate. It also doesn't mean the rate is part of a loan program you would even *want*. A rate of 4.5 percent could apply to a fixed rate loan, an ARM, an interest-only program, or any other loan the broker might offer. Look for the fine print. Instant rates are never a good sign. If a broker gives you rates without taking the time to learn about your situation or your long-term goals, you are *not* being provided with the service you deserve.

A consultant knows a loan's interest rate is just one part of a much bigger equation, and will never arbitrarily give a rate just to give a rate or to appease a client. Finances, financial background, job history, and credit scores all affect rates greatly. In fact, interest rates can range anywhere from 1 to 15 percent depending on the client situation. With such a range, why would anyone arbitrarily quote a rate? If you are hesitant about releasing personal information to a consultant early on, a consultant will be able to give you a range of rates, with brief descriptions of the loans that carry those rates and each loan's qualifications and guidelines.

▸ **A client asks, "Listen to this great deal my friend has! Can I get the same loan?"** A broker would most likely get frustrated and discredit the other financing. Many clients hear about a loan from a relative, colleague, or friend and decide this is the loan for them! A broker might stress the impossibilities of the loan in question, or may even imply that the client misunderstood the loan: "Come on, no loan like that exists!"

Why would a broker do this? Most of the time, it's for one of two reasons: the broker doesn't thoroughly understand or is unfamiliar with the competing loan, or the broker is lazy (or a combination of the two).

A consultant will start by getting as much information as possible on the loan to compare apples to apples. Do you have the same credit rating, down payment, or job history as the friend? How different or similar is this loan to your own loan? Why are you interested in the loan, and what other ways could the consultant help you to reach the same goals? A consultant will easily be able to explain, in detail, whether another loan program would or wouldn't work for you—and why.

▸ **A client asks, "I was quoted a much lower rate from another broker, but I'd like to go with you. Can you match the rate?"** A broker would definitely do whatever it would take to promise the rate and terms, but sooner or later, the rates would change. Many borrowers believe shopping for the best rate will get them the best loan, but it often just gets them broken promises. A broker may not tell the truth in order to get your business, and may come up with an unbelievable story close to closing to explain why the interest rate is higher, or why the loan's terms and conditions have changed. Techniques like this are very common, are usually unethical, and are sometimes even illegal. To help you protect yourself from brokers like these, I'll cover many of the shady techniques brokers use in the next chapter.

A consultant will openly entertain any competitive offer. Wholesale loans are usually priced at the same rate to all brokers, so to find out what the actual cost for the loan is, a consultant will ask to compare Good Faith Estimates and will have the professional resources to be able to check on the competition's loan rates and fees. And if a consultant *can't* match the rate, a true consultant will still be willing to advise a client on a loan, *even if* the client chooses to work with another broker or decides to work directly with a bank. Consultants are very aware of the perils within the industry and will try to protect you as best as they can.

▸  **A client asks, "What are these fees on my Good Faith Estimate?"** When asked this question, a broker might stumble. Many brokers aren't familiar with the exact makeup of these costs, especially fees from appraisers, insurers, and title companies. In addition, fees and charges are also ways for a broker to pad in extra money, and, many times, brokers will conveniently gloss over or downplay how they are compensated by the lender or by you. An important rule of thumb: if something is glossed over, it usually means there is something to hide.

A consultant will be able to detail all costs associated with the loan, and will not hesitate to explain how they are being paid. Every fee on your Good Faith Estimate (GFE) can and should be accounted for; there are *no* arbitrary or unknown costs on any GFE. And although the fees on a GFE are technically an estimate, I will stress again, they should be very close to the actual costs at closing.

As a borrower, your best defense is to compare GFEs. When requesting estimates, you'll want to be sure you are comparing the same loans, so be sure to compare your loan amount, interest rate, taxes, and insurance fees. You'll be looking for differences in lender's fees, underwriting fees, broker's fees, processing fees, origination fees, yield spread premiums, and any discount points you may be paying to reduce the cost of the loan.

You'll also be able to use your Truth In Lending Disclosure, which should accompany any GFE you receive, to compare costs between loan programs, and to compare loans between brokers and consultants.

---

MORE INFO **A Step-by-Step Guide to Your Loan's Costs**
In Appendix I, I've explained how you can use your Truth In Lending Disclosure to compare costs, and how the disclosure will also help you to understand your loan program better. In Appendix I, you'll also find a sample of a Good Faith Estimate and what exact costs to look for, and a few other samples of each of these forms on my website.

---

▶ **A client asks, "I have credit issues I need to fix, but I really need a loan. Can you help?"** Credit issues are the kiss of death for some brokers. They take time, and usually mean a loan is not guaranteed. And the one thing a broker doesn't want to spend is extra time, especially on a loan that may not happen. A broker would quickly review a client's credit issues to see if they could qualify for a loan. If they could, the broker would place the client into a loan as soon as possible, *even if* the loan had higher costs, higher rates, or wasn't right for the borrower. And if a client's credit issues were too bad, well, better luck elsewhere. A broker would be unlikely to spend time with the client, and would not be able to provide the client with a plan for the future.

A consultant will *always* look for the best possible financing for you, not just whatever financing is available, and will not be afraid to recommend waiting on financing if credit issues run too deep. Even without placing a loan, a consultant will always give a comprehensive game plan for fixing your credit and a strategy for qualifying for a loan in the future. Good credit or bad, a consultant will always be available to see if they can assist with any other needs or bigger goals.

▸ **A client asks, "I can't provide the documentation you asked for. Can I still get the loan?"** A broker might choose to do something fraudulent, including forging or creating false documents or changing recorded dates, in order to keep the client in the loan or locked into an interest rate. Cleverly resolving a "small issue" means the broker will not lose the loan *or* their commission. "Bending the rules" happens daily, but "breaking the rules" is illegal. (I'll explain more about these rules, and how brokers break them, in Chapter 6.)

A consultant will never jeopardize a relationship with any lender and will always aggressively look for alternative documents to satisfy a loan's conditions for approval. Remember, a consultant is a representative of a lender; it takes many years to build solid relationships, and in the business of lending the one thing you never want to tarnish is your name. A consultant values the relationship with their lenders as much as they value their relationship with you.

▸ **A client asks, "I know I closed on my loan months ago, but I have a few questions."** A broker would most likely be too busy for the client's call and will make minimal efforts to help because it would be deemed unprofitable at the time. The loan has closed, and the broker has been paid and moved on to other clients. The broker now has bigger fish to fry.

A consultant knows that relationships don't end at the closing of a loan, and will always make time for present and past clients. A consultant realizes that most clients will have questions before, during, and even after a loan has funded, and will always be available to answer any and all questions.

I could write an entire book devoted to the differences between a broker and a consultant. The truth is, anyone in the lending industry has the ability to choose: Am I a broker? Or am I a consultant? This choice is a very conscious decision, and how your broker or consultant views him- or herself will directly impact your loan.

## Finding the Right Consultant

It's pretty easy to see the difference between brokers and consultants, and how either might interact with you as a client. But how can you go about finding a consultant versus ending up with a broker? For many people, finding a professional consultant can be like searching for a needle in a haystack, but you can easily refine your search by following a few basic guidelines:

▸ **Check with the NAMB.** Established in 1973, the National Association of Mortgage Brokers (NAMB) represents the mortgage broker industry, with more than 25,000 members in all fifty states. Mortgage professionals who take their position seriously are often members of NAMB, and all NAMB members subscribe to a code of ethics and abide by the association's bylaws and professional lending practices. Visit NAMB's website at www.namb.org to search for local mortgage professionals in your area.

▸ **Ask for referrals.** Ask friends, neighbors, and coworkers if they would recommend their mortgage consultant. If they can't remember who handled their loan, it's a bad sign. Realtors often can make good recommendations, but be careful. Many real estate firms have their own in-house mortgage brokers, or have an exclusive "arrangement" with an outside mortgage brokerage firm. For every referral a realtor makes, he or she may be receiving some kind of perk or bonus. Remember that a referral is simply that—a referral. You still need to do your own homework. Research specific mortgage companies and mortgage consultants on the internet looking for reviews or complaints, and check with the Better Business Bureau and with your state's attorney general or Department of Banking and Finance.

▶ **Stay local.** Internet brokers may seem to have all the answers, but do they really know your area? Will they be able to meet with you and your family to understand your long-term goals? Will they be able to attend your closing with you? This is where local mortgage consultants excel and can provide you with the best service. By choosing a consultant in your area, you can meet face to face for every aspect of your loan. Your consultant will also be aware of local and state laws, taxes, and home values to be able to properly advise you on your loan.

▶ **Trust your instincts.** Is the broker reluctant to review your loan's terms? Did a broker "forget" to provide you with a Good Faith Estimate? Were costs or fees glossed over? All of these are red flags. Learn from my own experience—trust your gut.

Once you have a list of potential consultants, it's time to find out even more. As you speak with various consultants about your lending needs, ask questions. Look at this experience as if it were an interview and you were doing the hiring. There are four basic questions you should ask *any* mortgage consultant you are considering working with:

**1. "Do you consider yourself to be a broker or a consultant?"**
A true consultant will be very open to this question, and will respect the fact that you know the difference. A consultant will never make you feel like you are wasting time, won't rush you, and will encourage you to ask questions. A consultant will also acknowledge that you want the best for your loan, and that you know enough to ask questions. And last but not least, a true consultant will know exactly why you are asking this question. (They really will.)

**2. "How are you paid for my loan?"**
A consultant will never stumble on this question. In Chapter 3, we reviewed how any broker or consultant makes money: through yield

spread premiums and origination fees. Use this knowledge and ask. Consultants will disclose in detail how they will be compensated for their time and services.

### 3. "Can you explain paying discount points?"

As you have learned, discount points allow you to *lower* your interest rate. But what you will learn in the next chapter is that many brokers use discount points as a source of additional income. A consultant will always welcome this question and will be able to explain and demonstrate how discount points can be used, and will also openly advise you as to whether you should be considering discount points and whether they make sense for your loan.

### 4. "What is your take on current market conditions?"

This will be a key question in determining if an individual is just another broker or a true consultant. Why? A consultant will never sugarcoat anything, especially current conditions within the real estate market and lending industry. Even if you don't follow the market and the economy closely your consultant should, and *how* they answer this question can speak volumes.

Does the consultant take the time to explain how current rates are related to the economy? Does the consultant explain any new lending conditions that may be beneficial or detrimental to you and your loan? Does the consultant admit if economic conditions or your own circumstances may make financing difficult? Usually, if consultants answer with any detailed information other than "things are fine, we'll get you that loan," they most likely have a decent knowledge of the market. And if consultants are honest about current market conditions, they are more likely to be honest with you about your loan.

• • •

There's a lot to consider with financing in general, so it should be no surprise that there is an equal amount to consider when choosing a consultant. What I have detailed in this chapter should help you to find a professional who will be able to guide you through the world of lending. And though you now know what to expect and what to look for, you must also be able to use your own personal judgment. Take the time to look for a consultant in advance of when you need financing. Ask questions. Listen to your gut. Hold your consultant accountable for the job he or she is doing for you.

You can also protect and prepare yourself further by reading the next chapters, where I'll explain how you can spot and stop any issues you may encounter with your loan or your broker. Remember, it's your loan and your home on the line, but by taking the time now to learn and to find the right consultant, financing your home can actually be a very positive and rewarding experience.

# PART II

# Protecting Your Home

. . .

How to Protect Yourself From Predatory Practices, Default, and Foreclosure

The world of lending can be full of opportunity, and there are many professionals who will truly assist you with all aspects of financing a home. But although owning a home can be a positive and rewarding experience, there is also a dark side to lending and homeownership. Millions of homeowners are the victims of predatory lending, real estate scams, or their own troubled circumstances, and millions of homeowners are also facing default and foreclosure. What can you do to protect yourself and your family? And what can you do to safeguard your home, even if you've been a victim of lending pitfalls in the past?

In the next chapters, I'll show you how to recognize and avoid the most common lending and real estate scams, from high-cost loans to shady broker sales tactics, to real estate and foreclosure scams.

I'll also show you how you can protect your home, especially if you are faced with default or foreclosure. The possible loss of a home is a painful experience, and the number of individuals and families facing this reality grows daily. I will show you, step by step, what you can do now to prevent foreclosure. I'll explain why taking these steps is important, what you can expect from your lender, and what options you have to save your home, even if you feel like you have no options left. And if you have already lost your home, I'll help you to see that all hope is not lost. With a plan, a little help, patience, and some hard work, you can reestablish yourself, rebuild your life, and one day own a home again.

## 6

# Your Suit of Armor

Your Best Defense Against Predatory Lending,
Real Estate Scams, and Rescue Schemes

You'll often hear me say that knowledge is power. This is especially true within the lending and real estate industries, where scams and predatory practices are extremely real and can happen to just about anyone. But if you take the time to learn and understand how predatory lending, mortgage scams, and real estate schemes work, this knowledge will act just like a suit of armor, protecting not only you, but your credit, your finances, and your home.

Business scams and schemes are nothing new. Every industry has its share of scammers and swindlers, and while the mortgage and real estate industries are no different, too many homeowners are easily taken advantage of, and many end up paying a steep price.

Is your loan's interest rate so high that it makes paying your mortgage almost impossible? Did your lender or broker overcharge you to "secure" your loan? Did any part of your loan switch or did costs rise at the closing table? These are all signs of predatory lending. And even if you manage to obtain a loan safely, you still need to be careful if you ever want to sell or refinance. Predatory real estate scams, including scams claiming to quickly sell your home or rescue your home from foreclosure, are riddled with pitfalls and almost always result in the loss of your home.

After reading the first part of this book, you're already one step ahead of the game: you have a strong foundation and understanding for how lending and loans *should* work. You'll now be able to use this knowledge to help you to see when things are going wrong. In this chapter, I'll show you how you can identify—and stop—the most common scams and predatory situations involving your mortgage and your home.

To start, let's talk about who can be preyed upon: everyone and anyone. Regardless of your race, color, or creed, your education or income, you can easily become a victim if you are unaware of what *could* happen. Even financially savvy people are commonly duped. And although anyone can be victimized, research has proven that scammers do have targets they prefer: minorities and women. Just a short time ago during the boom years, minorities and women from all walks of life were charged much higher interest rates and received poorer loan terms than their Caucasian or male counterparts, even if they were equally qualified for a loan. How did scammers get away with this? Borrowers simply didn't know any better.

I like to compare scammers to great white sharks. Great whites are notorious for preying upon weaker and unsuspecting creatures. But when a great white senses its meal won't be as easy as it looks, or if it anticipates a confrontation, the shark won't exhaust its energy—it moves on. A scam artist will usually react the same way: if scammers feel you are on to them and will not be sold on some bogus notion, you become too much of a risk for *them*. In the end, your suit of armor (the knowledge you get from this book), will have given you the protection you need.

Let's begin building your armor by exploring where most scams usually start: with your loan. From high rates and costs to unethical and illegal ways to trick borrowers into paying more, many scams revolve around predatory lending.

**Predatory Lending**

Predatory lending can be so subtle and difficult to prove, it is often hard to legally define. As defined by the Mortgage Bankers Association, predatory lending involves intentionally placing consumers in loans with significantly worse terms and/or higher costs than loans offered to similarly qualified consumers in the same region, with the primary purpose of enriching the originator, and with little or no regard for the costs to the consumer.

## High-Rate, High-Cost Loans

High interest rates and costs are the first red flags to look for when it comes to predatory lending. A loan is considered to be predatory when the costs to you as a borrower have been inflated or have increased without good reason, resulting in you paying more for your loan—often much more—than you *should* be. One of the most common ways to be charged more for a loan is through a loan's interest rate: either through a high fixed rate, or if you have an adjustable rate mortgage, through a high margin (which makes your interest and mortgage payments higher and much riskier to you).

I want to clearly emphasize that having a high interest rate alone does not make your loan predatory. When you are charged a higher interest rate—but easily *qualify* for a lower and more affordable interest rate—this is when you head into predatory waters. As you learned in Chapter 4, your characteristics as a borrower (including your income, assets, and credit) all determine the loans you can qualify for and the interest rates you will receive. Generally, those with good income, assets, and credit will receive much better interest rates than those borrowers who have poor income, no assets, or have mismanaged their credit.

So if you qualify for a better rate, this means you should receive a better rate, right? Right—but this doesn't always happen. If you qualify for a better rate, but don't receive one, it's for one reason only: the broker wants to make a better profit.

One of the most common predatory practices during the boom years involved selling higher-rate subprime loans (or other similar high-cost loans) to those who easily qualified for lower-rate, conventional loans. For example, a borrower may have easily qualified for a 5.5 percent interest rate, but ended up with a 8.75 percent interest rate instead—a huge difference. Why did this happen? The subprime loan market and availability of credit created lazy and unscrupulous brokers who were looking for easy money at the expense of their clients. For many brokers, it was both easier and more profitable to get their clients approved for subprime loans, so it wasn't worth their time to have a loan approved under strict conventional lending guidelines.

> Here's how most of these scams transpire: A broker tells you conventional loans are extremely restrictive. They are usually fixed rate loans that lock you into a loan for a long time. They take away your options. Why would you want a loan like that? The broker also stresses that conventional lenders are very strict, so you may not even qualify for a conventional loan. But not to worry! The broker has another loan program you can easily qualify for, and with this loan you can pay less initially every month! Sure, the rates get higher later, but you can always refinance the loan again in a few years. Why risk not being approved—and miss out on buying a home—when you can get this other loan now, and also save money at the same time? It's a win-win decision.
>
> From the broker's sales pitch, you are eventually made to feel that the higher rate or higher cost loan is better for you or all you can qualify for, when in reality you may have easily qualified for a lower-rate program with lower costs.

Brokers who participate in this common scam simply have a complete disregard for their clients. Luckily, the highest-cost loans—subprime loans—are a thing of the past. But even today, there are still high interest rates and high-cost loans, and a broker may not put your needs first. Brokers may ignore a loan's costs, or put you into the wrong loan program altogether, just so they can make some extra profit. Some brokers may even encourage you to apply for a loan you don't even need. It happens all the time. A broker may insist you need to switch from your existing loan program to another, or encourage you to refinance *even if* there are no substantial financial benefits to you—because it will always have great financial benefits to them.

## Do Your Homework

How can you make sure your needs as a borrower come first? The first step is doing your homework. If you are actively shopping for a loan, know where you stand as a borrower. Can you qualify for conventional financing? (Take a minute to review the conventional guidelines from Chapter 4.) If you can, you should receive the best rates and terms, and they should not vary too much from lender to lender or broker to broker. Being aware of current interest rates and obtaining and comparing several Good Faith Estimates should give you the peace of mind that you are being charged a fair rate based on current market conditions. You can also use your Truth In Lending Disclosure to compare loans between lenders and brokers. Even if you are a nonconforming borrower, you still should be able to compare loan rates, fees, and programs, and the interest rates should not vary wildly. If one broker's quote is much higher than the rest, it's usually a bad apple.

If you are refinancing, you'll also want to carefully consider a loan's costs and benefits to you. People refinance for many reasons. You may want to pull equity from your home. You may want a lower interest rate or a lower monthly payment. You may want to switch from an adjustable rate to a fixed rate. Or you may be looking for better terms from another loan program. Just make sure there is a real and tangible benefit to you, and that the costs to refinance the loan don't outweigh the benefits you receive.

If you are unsure if you should refinance, I've provided a worksheet for you on the next page that will help you to determine if a refinance and its terms make sense for you. If you are encouraged to refinance without any of these benefits, or if your broker is encouraging you to refinance when it just doesn't make sense, it could very well be a form of predatory lending.

 If you'd like more help in analyzing if a refinance is your best decision, visit the reader's resource section of my website, where I provide additional worksheets and calculators that will help you to decide if a refinance is right for you.

## Rates and Points: Are You Getting What You Paid For?

How you ask your broker about interest rates will also help to ensure you are getting the best rate, and will help protect you from being overcharged for your loan. Many borrowers believe the interest rate for their loan is determined solely by the lender; this is actually far from the truth. Your broker, not the lender, will be the one to determine the *final* interest rate for your loan, and this can sometimes lead to trouble.

Every day—sometimes several times a day—lenders send brokers emails and faxes containing *wholesale rate sheets*, which are several pages of tables and charts outlining a lender's interest rates for that particular day. Loan programs aren't sold with only one interest rate; lenders offer a wide range of interest rates for each and every loan. Brokers pay special attention to these rate sheets, because in addition to listing the lender's interest rates, these rate sheets also outline a broker's potential profit. A lender's rate sheets show how interest rates will *directly* affect a broker's yield spread premium—how much a lender will pay a broker for selling the interest rate and the loan.

Let's take a look behind the scenes to see how this works. How much a lender will pay a broker is all based on a loan's *par rate*. A par rate is the bottom-line interest rate for a loan; think of a par rate as "level zero"—at a par rate, a lender pays a broker nothing. Interest

# Refinancing Worksheet

Should you refinance? The best way to decide is by making sure a re-finance makes *financial* sense, identifying your reasons for wanting to refinance, and calculating your break-even point.

**STEP ONE: ARE YOU REFINANCING FOR A GOOD REASON?**

| | YES | NO |
|---|---|---|
| Do you need to make your home more affordable? | ☐ | ☐ |
| Do you have an adjustable rate mortgage, and won't be able to afford the payment when the rate resets? | ☐ | ☐ |
| Do you need the stability of a fixed rate mortgage? | ☐ | ☐ |
| Do you want to change loans to pay more towards your loan's principal? | ☐ | ☐ |
| Do you need to consolidate other high-cost debt? | ☐ | ☐ |
| Do you need to tap your home's equity for an emergency? | ☐ | ☐ |

*If you've answered "yes" to any of these questions, a refinance may be a good idea. To see if you will also benefit financially, continue with Step 2.*

**STEP TWO: WILL A REFINANCE MAKE FINANCIAL SENSE?**

YOUR LOAN COSTS

| | | |
|---|---|---|
| Enter your current monthly mortgage payment | | $ |
| Subtract your estimated new monthly payment | − | $ |
| **Your savings each month** | **A** | $ |

YOUR CLOSING COSTS

| | | |
|---|---|---|
| Enter your total closing costs (including all fees and points) | | $ |
| Add your prepayment penalty (if applicable) | + | $ |
| **Total refinancing costs** | **B** | $ |

| | | |
|---|---|---|
| Divide your total refinancing costs **(B)** | **B** | $ |
| by your monthly savings **(A)** | **÷ A** | $ |

How long it will take to break even (in months):

*Do you plan to stay in your home for this long? If so, a refinance will financially benefit you.*

rates *higher* than the par rate pay a broker through yield spread premium. Interest rates *lower* than the par rate are better (lower) interest rates, and do not pay a broker anything at all. In fact, interest rates below the par rate will actually cost a broker money. Brokers will rightfully pass these costs on to you in the form of discount points (the same discount points we talked about in the last chapter). As a borrower, you are charged discount points to lower your rate, because your broker is being charged as well.

It's up to each lender, based on market conditions and their own costs, to determine what interest rates they will offer for a loan, a loan's par rate, how much they will pay brokers in yield spread premium, and how much they will charge brokers for below-par interest rates. It sounds more confusing than it is when you can look at the actual numbers yourself. But that's the problem—brokers don't share rate sheets with borrowers. These rate sheets are for a broker's eyes only.

Here's a very simplified example of a lender's rate sheet:

| RATE | YSP 15 DAY LOCK | YSP 30 DAY LOCK |
|---|---|---|
| 4.500 | 98.235 | 97.813 |
| 4.625 | 98.579 | 98.152 |
| 4.750 | 99.061 | 98.628 |
| 4.875 | 99.572 | 99.134 |
| 5.000 | 99.896 | 99.453 |
| 5.125 | **100.064** | 99.615 |
| 5.250 | 100.199 | 99.745 |
| 5.375 | 100.285 | 99.827 |
| 5.500 | 100.481 | **100.017** |
| 5.625 | 100.603 | 100.133 |
| 5.750 | 100.750 | 100.276 |
| 5.875 | 100.817 | 100.337 |
| 6.000 | 100.832 | 100.347 |
| 6.125 | 100.978 | 100.487 |
| 6.250 | 101.110 | 100.615 |

*PAR RATES*

**Figure 6.1: A Sample Rate Sheet for a 30-Year Fixed Rate Conventional Loan**
*Rates higher than the par rate (in black) will pay a broker through yield spread premium.*
*Rates lower than the par rate (in gray) will cost a broker; this cost is charged to you as discount points.*

The first column shows the interest rate, the second column shows what kind of yield spread premium the broker will earn with a 15-day rate lock, and the third column shows the yield spread premium with a 30-day rate lock. Why are there extra columns for the different rate locks? If you remember from the last chapter, the length of your loan's interest rate lock can affect your interest rate. If the rate is locked for a shorter period of time, it's less risky for a lender, and in return for this decreased risk, a lender offers slightly better interest rates. The longer the rate lock, the higher the offered interest rates. So when a broker looks at a rate sheet, they have to take the rate locks into consideration as well.

With all of the numbers on this chart, how do you know what to look at? We'll start by finding the par rates. Look at the second and third columns: par rates have a yield spread closest to 100 percent (100 percent represents the loan's bottom line). In this rate sheet, 5.125 and 5.5 percent are the par rates.

For this loan, the lender has decided to offer interest rates ranging from 4.5 to 6.25 percent. Your broker could make as much as 1.11 percent on your loan (through an interest rate of 6.25 percent with a 15-day lock), which would be paid to your broker by the lender after your closing. Or, your broker could charge you 2.187 discount points (which would become part of your loan's final closing costs) to secure the lowest interest rate of 4.5 percent with a 30-day rate lock.

As I mentioned, this is a pretty simplified example. Your final interest rate and your broker's final yield spread premium may also be subject to additional lender adjustments based on things like credit scores, prepayment penalties, loan value, and property type. From all of these variables, brokers will determine how much they will make from a loan, what final rates they will offer to the borrower, and how much they will charge you for a lower interest rate.

## When Points Become Predatory

By looking at the sample rate sheet, you can see how a lender charges a broker for lower interest rates—the lower the rate, the more a lender charges a broker. This also means the lower your rate, the more your broker will charge *you* in discount points.

As you learned in the last chapter, paying a point or even two discount points on a loan is common, and can even be beneficial and valuable to a borrower over the life of the loan—*if* the borrower truly receives the lower rate the points are paying for. Paying points becomes a problem—and becomes predatory—when brokers unethically use discount points as a way to increase *their* profit. Charging points becomes a scam when a broker charges you points but doesn't reduce your interest rate at all. This can happen one of two ways:

> **Scenario #1:** Your broker has great news. You can get the 6 percent interest rate you wanted, and it will only cost you 1 point—you will be charged 1 discount point by the broker. As the borrower, what you don't know is that you should have received this rate without paying a point. The rate didn't cost the broker anything; in fact, the rate paid the broker very well in yield spread premium (an amount they conveniently "forgot" to include on their Good Faith Estimate). The broker should have passed the 6 percent rate from the lender directly on to you. The charged discount point is nothing but broker profit.

> **Scenario #2:** You receive a Good Faith Estimate for a loan with an interest rate of 7 percent. Two weeks into the loan process, you decide you'd like to reduce the interest rate to 6.5 percent. Your broker explains it will cost you 2 points to do this. But this isn't true; for this particular loan, it will only cost the broker 1 point to reduce your interest rate by 0.5 percent. Where does the additional point go? To the broker, as profit.

An *ethical* broker will be honest with you about the interest rates a lender offers and how much lower rates will cost. They will also be honest about their compensation, and if an interest rate doesn't pay much or anything at all from the lender in yield spread premium, ethical brokers will explain how much they will charge you in origination fees to be paid fairly for their time. Ethical and honest brokers will have no problem laying these exact costs on the line, and they'll show their exact costs and profit on a Good Faith Estimate.

Ethical brokers will also be honest with you if yield spread premiums are in their favor. Let's say a lender offers all brokers higher-than-average yield spread premiums for a loan. An ethical broker will pass some of this windfall on to you, either by passing on a lower interest rate directly from the lender to you, without charging you points, or by applying some of their yield spread premium toward a lower interest rate (to make up for other lender charges). In essence, ethical brokers are paying for the lower rate with their own profit. Really? You bet. That's what any ethical broker will do.

But for every ethical broker out there, there are many *unethical* brokers who will put their own greed over their client's needs. Unethical brokers will not be honest about what interest rates a lender offers, charge you needlessly, or overcharge you for interest rates, and would never think of giving up any of their yield spread premium to lower your rate.

## How to Keep Brokers Honest

If you are paying points to lower your rate, how do you know you are getting the rate you've paid for? It's a frustrating dilemma for many borrowers, and rightfully so. There is only one way to combat against these techniques: when you ask for your Good Faith Estimates or inquire about interest rates—whether you are considering paying points or not—clearly ask for three things:

1. The interest rate
2. The interest rate with 1 discount point
3. The interest rate with 2 discount points

This will most likely keep brokers honest and will alert them that you understand how a lender pays a broker for selling the rate to you.

Here's an example of how this can play out:

**What You Ask:** You ask a broker what your interest rate will be, and what the rate would be if you paid 1 and 2 points.

**Broker A:** Broker A tells you your interest rate is 7 percent. With 1 point, your rate is 6.75 percent, and with 2 points your rate is 6.5 percent. As we learned in Chapter 5, each point you pay may reduce your rate anywhere from 0.125 to 0.5 percent. In this case, each point has reduced your rate 0.25 percent. So far, so good. You are able to confirm all of this on your Good Faith Estimate (GFE).

Your GFE also shows that the lender is paying the broker 2 percent in yield spread premium (YSP) at the 7 percent interest rate, and the amount of yield spread *decreases* with each point you, the borrower, pay: with 1 point, the broker is making 1.5 percent YSP, and with 2 points the broker is making 1 percent YSP. It's pretty clear your broker is being honest. The broker has supplied you with what you have asked for, and what is on your GFE makes sense: each point you pay reduces your rate by a fair amount, and the broker's yield spread decreases with each point they charge. It's a green light; it is safe to proceed.

**Broker B:** Broker B tells you your interest rate is 7 percent, but to get the 7 percent, the broker will need to charge 1 point. If you pay 2 points, you will receive an interest rate of 6.75 percent. Broker B has not told you what your interest rate would be with no points.

You look at the GFE, and you see that at 7 percent, Broker B is being paid 2 percent in yield spread premium from the lender. At the 6.75 percent rate, the broker is being paid *almost* the same amount: 1.875 percent YSP. Unlike Broker A, this broker's yield spread premium doesn't go down very much at all with each point, but it should—at lower rates, the lender is getting less profit in interest, and so will pay the broker less. Something may not be right, but it's hard to know, because Broker B hasn't provided you with all of the information you need. You need to question Broker B. The broker may try to avoid giving more details on the rates, or may try to justify the yield spread fees. If so, be very cautious. There may be a legitimate explanation, but usually the broker is trying to hide the true rates and costs.

When you ask a broker to quote you a rate, and a rate with points, you are clearly saying you want the numbers upfront and that you know the numbers need to make sense. You are speaking to brokers in their own language, and this technique helps to keep most brokers honest.

---

 **What About Banks?**

If you decide to work directly with a bank, do you also have to worry about being overcharged for rates or discount points by your bank's representative? No, you don't have to worry at all. A bank's representative does not "broker" loans like a mortgage broker does. Banks have guidelines and protocols in place for how a bank's interest rates, discount points, and fees are passed on to you. You may not be able to shop as easily for loans or rates as you would be able to with a broker, but with a bank, you don't have the additional worry about being charged unfairly for your loan.

---

## Predatory Fees

Loans are also considered to be predatory if there are unusually high lending or broker fees. Lending fees are an unavoidable part of any loan; you should expect lenders and brokers to charge for their services, and for any costs they incur during the lending process. And while every loan includes similar lending fees and costs (I've high-

Total Lending Fees Charged to You . . . . . . Up to 5 percent of your loan amount

    Lender Underwriting Fee . . . . . . . . . . $595 to $995

    Lender Inspection Fee . . . . . . . . . . . . Under $100

    Lender Tax Services Fee . . . . . . . . . . . Under $75

    Broker Origination Fee . . . . . . . . . . . . 2 to 3 percent of your loan amount

    Broker Processing Fee . . . . . . . . . . . . $375 to $795

    Credit Report . . . . . . . . . . . . . . . . . . $10 per borrower

    Appraisal . . . . . . . . . . . . . . . . . . . . $300 to $500

---

*Figure 6.2: Lender and Broker Fees* *For a full list of all fees, refer to Appendix I.*

lighted these fees for you in Figure 6.2), *excessive* fees can turn your loan into a questionable loan. There is an unspoken but very important rule within the lending industry: total lending fees over 5 percent of your loan amount are predatory. This means that on a $200,000 loan, you should not pay more than $10,000 to your lender and broker. The fees for your loan should always adhere to these two guidelines:

- Your broker's compensation (the yield spread premium and/or origination fees) should be *no more than 3 percent* of your total loan amount.

- The total fees for your loan (including all fees charged directly to you from your lender *and* your broker, including your broker's origination fee) should be *no more than 5 percent* of your total loan amount.

Again, all of these fees will appear on your Good Faith Estimate when you are shopping for loans, as well as on your HUD settlement statement, which is part of the final paperwork you sign at your loan's closing. (To see exactly where these fees appear on both your GFE and HUD, refer to Appendix I.)

Up until just recently, a broker's yield spread premium could be shown on a GFE either as a range or as a percentage, which made it very difficult for borrowers to understand exactly how much their brokers were being paid, and it contributed to many predatory practices. For example, reading that your broker could make anywhere from "1 to 3 percent" on a $325,000 loan is not as easy to understand as "your broker has made $9,750." Many brokers tried to hide how much they were making by downplaying the "percentage" of profit they might receive. Today, both yield spread premiums and origination fees are required by law to be calculated for you on your GFE as single, hard dollar amounts, so you can easily see, and double-check, the amount your broker will be making on your loan.

---

CAUTION  **When Brokers Ignore the Law**

Even though yield spread premium is required to be shown as an exact hard dollar amount on your Good Faith Estimate, many brokers will *still* show YSP as a range. Your broker may explain that since the interest rate is not locked, they are unable to show the exact yield spread premium they will receive from the lender. In other cases, some brokers will not show a hard dollar amount because they haven't decided which lender they will use, so they don't know how much yield spread they will receive. While these statements may have some truth to them, they don't help you as a consumer. And this doesn't mean your broker doesn't have to follow the law. No matter the circumstance, your broker is required to quote you their *exact* yield spread premium, just like they quote you an exact interest rate.

On your first GFE, your broker will quote you a real (not estimated) interest rate based on the best rates for that particular day. Your broker is also required to quote you a real (and fixed) yield spread premium based on this rate. If a broker tells you they can't because they don't know which lender they are using, the broker is just being lazy and deceitful. If a broker doesn't know what lender they are using, how can they even quote you an interest rate?

Once the interest rate for your loan is locked, if a broker's yield spread premium changes, a broker is also required to re-disclose their *new* yield spread premium to you on a new GFE. If your broker quotes you a range for yield spread premium on your GFE, protect yourself and ask for a hard dollar amount.

---

Once you understand all of the costs and fees that should appear on your GFE, bad estimates become easier to spot. I've included a "bad" broker estimate in Figure 6.3, so you can see how brokers try to trick buyers into paying more for their loan in broker profit. In this example, you've got two problems:

1. Your broker is charging you twice: once as a loan origination fee, and once as a mortgage broker fee. By charging you a total of $1,174 in origination and broker fees, your broker is already making 0.87 percent (almost a full point) on your loan.

2. Your broker also hasn't disclosed the yield spread premium, so you don't know how much the broker is making from the lender. This means there's no way to know if the origination and mort-gage broker fees are fair. If your broker is making 0 percent in YSP from the lender, your broker is being paid fairly. But if your broker is making 3 percent in YSP, your broker is making almost 4 percent total on your loan, and for a $134,900 loan, this is an unfair amount.

With all of this talk about a broker's profit, it's important to note that there are some loan programs that pay brokers very little, and there are even certain loans and interest rates that do not pay bro-kers any yield spread premium at all. In these cases, your broker will need to charge you an origination fee, but it doesn't mean it's okay for your broker to charge you *a lot* more. Again, just follow the rule of "no more than three." Add up any yield spread premium and the origina-

# GOOD FAITH ESTIMATE

| | |
|---|---|
| Applicants: **JACK BORROWER / JANE BORROWER** | Application No: |
| Property Addr: **123 MAIN STREET, ANYTOWN, FL 00000** | Date Prepared: **03/08/2009** |
| Prepared By: | Loan Program: |

The information provided below reflects estimates of the charges which you are likely to incur at the settlement of your loan. The fees listed are estimates - actual charges may be more or less. Your transaction may not involve a fee for every item listed. The numbers listed beside the estimates generally correspond to the numbered lines contained in the HUD-1 settlement statement which you will be receiving at settlement. The HUD-1 settlement statement will show you the actual cost for items paid at settlement.

\* **PFC** = Prepaid Finance Charge
**F** = FHA Allowable Closing Cost
**POC** = Paid Outside of Closing

| Total Loan Amount $ | 134,900 | Interest Rate: | 6.250 % | Term/Due In: | 360 / 360 | mths | | | |

| 800 | ITEMS PAYABLE IN CONNECTION WITH LOAN: | | | Amount | Paid By | * PFC / F / POC |
|---|---|---|---|---|---|---|
| 801 | Loan Origination Fee | Paid To Broker: | 0.500 % | 674.50 | Borrower | ✔ |
| 802 | Loan Discount | | | | | |
| 803 | Appraisal Fee | | | 400.00 | Borrower | ✔ |
| 804 | Credit Report | | | | | |
| 805 | Lender's Inspection Fee | | | | | |
| 808 | Mortgage Broker Fee | Paid To Broker: | | 500.00 | Borrower | ✔ |
| 809 | Tax Related Service Fee | | | | | |
| 810 | Processing Fee | Paid To Broker: | | 295.00 | Borrower | ✔ |
| 811 | Underwriting Fee | Paid To Lender: | | 495.00 | Borrower | ✔ |
| 812 | Wire Transfer Fee | | | | | |

*1. YOU ARE BEING CHARGED TWICE*

*2. THE BROKER HASN'T TOLD YOU THEIR YSP*

| | COMPENSATION TO BROKER (Not Paid Out of Loan Proceeds) : | | Amount | PFC |
|---|---|---|---|---|
| 816 | YIELD SPREAD 0%-3% | | $ | |

| 1100 | TITLE CHARGES: | | | Amount | Paid By | PFC / F / POC |
|---|---|---|---|---|---|---|
| 1101 | Closing/Escrow Fee: | Paid To Other: | TITLE COMPANY $ | 100.00 | Borrower | ✔ |
| 1105 | Document Preparation Fee | Paid To Other: ABSTRACT & TITLE SEARCH | | 85.00 | Borrower | ✔ |
| 1106 | Notary Fees | Paid To Other: TITLE EXAM | | 75.00 | Borrower | ✔ |
| 1107 | Attorney Fees | | | | | |
| 1108 | Title Insurance: | Paid To Other: | | 150.00 | Borrower | ✔ |
| 1109 | | Paid To ENDORSEMENTS | | 100.00 | Borrower | ✔ |
| 1110 | | Paid To WIRE AND COURIER FEES | | 40.00 | Borrower | ✔ |

| 1200 | GOVERNMENT RECORDING & TRANSFER CHARGES: | | | Amount | Paid By | PFC / F / POC |
|---|---|---|---|---|---|---|
| 1201 | Recording Fees: | Paid To Lender: | | 150.00 | Borrower | ✔ |
| 1202 | City/County Tax/Stamps: | | CITY/COUNTY TAX/STAMPS | 472.15 | Borrower | ✔ |
| 1203 | State Tax/Stamps: | Paid To Lender: | STATE TAX/STAMPS | 269.80 | Borrower | ✔ |

| 1300 | ADDITIONAL SETTLEMENT CHARGES: | | Amount | Paid By | PFC / F / POC |
|---|---|---|---|---|---|
| 1302 | Pest Inspection | $ | | | |

| | | Estimated Closing Costs | 3,806.45 | | |
|---|---|---|---|---|---|
| 900 | ITEMS REQUIRED BY LENDER TO BE PAID IN ADVANCE: | | Amount | Paid By | PFC / F / POC |
| 901 | Interest | Paid To Lender: for 5 days @ $ 23.5613 / day $ | 117.81 | Borrower | ✔ |
| 902 | Mtg Ins. Premium | | | | |
| 903 | Hazard Ins. Premium | | | | |
| 904 | | | | | |
| 905 | VA Funding Fee | | | | |

| 1000 | RESERVES DEPOSITED WITH LENDER: | | Amount | Paid By | PFC / F / POC |
|---|---|---|---|---|---|
| 1001 | Hazard Ins. Premium | mths @ $ / mth $ | | | |
| 1002 | Mtg Ins. Premium Reserves | mths @ $ / mth | | | |
| 1003 | School Tax | mths @ $ / mth | | | |
| 1004 | Taxes & Assessment Reserves | mths @ $ / mth | | | |
| 1005 | Flood Insurance Reserves | mths @ $ / mth | | | |
| | | mths @ $ / mth | | | |
| | | mths @ $ / mth | | | |

| | Estimated Prepaid Items/Reserves | 117.81 |
|---|---|---|
| TOTAL ESTIMATED SETTLEMENT CHARGES | | 3,924.26 |

| TOTAL ESTIMATED FUNDS NEEDED TO CLOSE: | | | | TOTAL ESTIMATED MONTHLY PAYMENT: | |
|---|---|---|---|---|---|
| Purchase Price (+) | 175,000.00 | Loan Amount (-) | 134,900.00 | Principal & Interest | 841.60 |
| Alterations (+) | | New First Mortgage(-) | | Other Financing (P & I) | |
| Land (+) | | Subordinate Financing (-) | | Hazard Insurance | |
| Refi (incl. debts to be paid off) (+) | | CC paid by Seller (-) | | Real Estate Taxes | |
| Est. Prepaid Items/Reserves (+) | 117.81 | Cash Deposit on sales contract (-) | 1,000.00 | Mortgage Insurance | |
| Est. Closing Costs (+) | 3,806.45 | | | Homeowner Assn. Dues | |
| New 2nd Mtg Closing Costs (+) | | | | Other | |
| PMI, MIP, Funding Fee (+) | | | | | |
| Discount (Borrower paid) (+) | | FHA Required Investment (-) | | | |
| FHA EEM Improvements (+) | | FHA MI Premium Refund (-) | | | |
| | | FHA 203k Rehabilitation Cost (-) | 0.00 | | |
| Total Estimated Funds needed to close | | | 43,024.26 | Total Monthly Payment | 841.60 |

☑ This Good Faith Estimate is being provided by _____ , a mortgage broker, and no lender has been obtained. These estimates are provided pursuant to the Real Estate Settlement Procedures Act of 1974, as amended (RESPA). Additional information can be found in the HUD Special Information Booklet, which is to be provided to you by your mortgage broker or lender, if your application is to purchase residential real property and the lender will take a first lien on the property. The undersigned acknowledges receipt of the booklet "Settlement Costs," and if applicable the Consumer Handbook on ARM Mortgages.

*Figure 6.3: A "Bad" Good Faith Estimate*

tion fees. As long as your loan is not extremely difficult or time consuming, the maximum your broker should receive from your loan is a total of 3 percent, based on your total loan amount. Legally, your broker can charge or receive more than this amount, but I consider anything above 3 percent to be predatory and *not* in your best interest.

## Bait and Switch

Most people have heard of the old "Bait and Switch" technique. Every industry seems to have its own form of this scam, and the lending industry isn't immune; bait and switch lending and sales schemes can happen easily in *any* lending market, good or bad. A broker may "bait" you with a loan or interest rate that's too good to be true. And once the broker knows you are hooked, they will switch your loan's terms or will charge you to "keep" the original loan rate and terms, all so they can make more profit.

> **How bait and switch works:** Let's say a client has put in an offer on a home and needs financing quickly, or the client needs to refinance immediately. A broker will quote the unsuspecting and unquestioning borrower a great rate, stating that the rate is locked and stable for thirty days. Knowing the client needs the loan right away, the broker proceeds with a flurry of activity: documents and information are needed from the client ASAP and paperwork quickly trades hands. The client is very involved in the process and feels that the broker is doing a good job. With all that is going on to get the loan approved on time, the client never thinks to ask for one important document: a written confirmation that the loan is locked. As far as the borrower is concerned, everything is going great. Then all heck breaks loose. The broker has done one of two things:
>
> **#1: The Rate Switch:** Two to three days before closing, the broker calls the client explaining there is a problem: the loan's

interest rate is now different from what was quoted and sup-posedly locked. The broker apologizes profusely, offering a vague and confusing explanation, but then conveniently has a *new* interest rate and payment handy, and convinces the borrower that the new rate is really not that bad.

The client can either approve this new rate (which "just happens" to pay the broker more) or pay the broker points to secure the original interest rate. The broker knows full well that the borrower more than likely will *not* walk away from the loan so close to closing, especially if financing was needed quickly, and nine times out of ten is able to convince the client to sign off on the new loan. The broker provides redisclosures for the loan, the client signs, and the loan closes at the higher rate or costs.

The borrower never realizes that all along the broker never had any intention of honoring the loan's quoted interest rate. The great rate was nothing other than bait.

**#2: The Last-Minute Program Switch:** Seven or ten days be-fore closing, the broker makes a call to the client with terrible news. An error has been made, and the loan program the client has been placed in is no longer available. The broker feels it's his duty to let the client know as soon as possible that there is a problem, and completely understands if the client needs to obtain financing somewhere else. However, the bro-ker does have one alternative program, and quickly explains the alternate loan's rate and terms.

All the while, the broker knows there is not enough time for the borrower to find other financing and still get the loan closed on time. The broker will follow up as much as possible with the client over the next few days, offering support as the client tries to find another loan somewhere else. In the end, the borrower is too frustrated and realizes other financing can't be found in time, and agrees to the loan with the new rate and terms.

Again, what the borrower doesn't know is that the program wasn't cancelled. The broker had "baited" the borrower with the first loan program, and had planned in advance to switch it out for a program that provided more broker profit.

I've had countless clients tell me how they, their family members, or friends have been the victims of bait and switch techniques. I hear "You won't believe what happened on my last loan" or "Let me tell you what happened to my sister" far too often. Unfortunately, there are countless bait and switch scams, and they happen all the time. Interest rates, loan programs, lending fees, broker fees—almost anything involving your loan can be switched at the last minute, and just like any lending scam, you can be assured the broker benefits directly by receiving more fees from either the lender or from you for the "new" last-minute rates or terms.

## When Lenders Play Bait and Switch

Bait and switch techniques can be pulled on borrowers by brokers, but they can also be pulled on the broker by the *lender*. This fact surprises most borrowers. A lender might lock a loan's rates and terms (with a confirmation in writing), but then without much warning—sometimes as little as a few weeks—the lender may cancel the lock, change the loan's requirements or qualifications, or even cancel the entire loan program, leaving brokers no choice but to try to sell a new loan to their own client. Even if a broker can prove to a client that it was the lender's decision, the lender's actions still make the broker look bad, and in the end, it's still the borrower who loses.

## Changes at the Closing Table

You've applied for your loan and have locked in your loan's program and interest rate with no scams in sight. You've been diligently monitoring your loan and your broker, you have a "clear to close" from the

---

**MORE INFO**

### How Ethical Brokers Handle a Lender's Bait and Switch

As much as I am warning you about bait and switch techniques, it is becoming increasingly common for brokers to be at the mercy of the lender. It's the lender's money, not the broker's, and it's the lender who decides how long to offer a loan program, when to change the program, and when to discontinue it. This can often happen right in the middle of your loan. A good consultant will be upfront with you and will be able to prove what happened, by showing you a memo or email from the lender about the loan program, or by setting up a conference call involving the lender's account representative to explain what has changed and why. And a good consultant will always try to place you in a new loan that is as close to the original loan as possible.

---

lender, and your closing date is near. Can you breathe easy? Not yet. Some of the most common lending scams happen right at the closing table. You could easily arrive at your closing expecting one loan, and receive another. In these cases, you can be sure your broker will be receiving something different too: more profit.

▶ **The fixed/adjustable switch.** By paying attention to your loan program as a whole, you can avoid being scammed. For example, do you know the details of your loan, or are you focused on the rate?

A broker may initially quote you a fixed interest rate. As your loan progresses, your broker may change your loan program but not disclose the new loan's terms, choosing to place the focus on "We'll get you that rate!" Many borrowers find themselves at the closing table with the rate they wanted, but a loan they do not: what started out as a fixed rate mortgage is now an adjustable rate, a completely different loan! The broker switched to an adjustable rate mortgage because it was an easy way to secure a lower rate or to secure more profit. Does the broker care that the rate will eventually go up, or that this wasn't the loan program you were quoted in the first place? Apparently not.

If your broker says they are able to get you an interest rate, they also need to show you this new rate, along with the full details of the loan program, in writing. Any time your loan changes, brokers are required by law to redisclose this information to you with a *new* Good Faith Estimate and Truth In Lending Disclosure, but many do not or wait until it is too late. As a borrower, it is your right and your responsibility to ask for these details in writing.

▸ **Other program swapping.** Brokers have also been known to swap out loan programs with similar terms to get borrowers to agree to loans that have better terms for the lender, and higher profit for the broker.

For example, take two loans. One is a 7-year ARM with an interest rate of 6.5 percent. The other is a 7-year balloon at 6.5 percent. Both of these loans will eventually "adjust," but there is a huge difference between them: the balloon loan will require payment of your loan in a few short years, *in full*. To thank the broker for placing this loan, the lender will pay the broker more in yield spread premium. Would you be able to spot a swap at your closing table? If you saw that the broker's yield spread premium had suddenly increased, would you know why?

As a borrower, you always want to make sure your loan's rates and terms match what you agreed to on your Good Faith Estimate and Truth In Lending Disclosure. If you have any questions at your closing, ask the title agent or title attorney to explain exactly what you are signing, as well as the terms and conditions of your loan.

▸ **Profitable prepayment penalties.** As I reviewed in Chapter 4, many nonconforming loans include a prepayment penalty. Nonconforming lenders like prepayment penalties because they ensure a borrower will pay a lender's profit, either by staying in the home and making mortgage payments, or by paying a lump sum penalty if the home is sold or refinanced within a predetermined period of time. For borrowers, a prepayment penalty usually means you will receive better rates or terms from the lender because they're getting paid more upfront. But for brokers—or more specifically, *dishonest* brokers—prepayment penalties are a way to make more profit.

Most borrowers don't know that prepayment penalties are more profitable for brokers. Lenders, who like the security the prepayment penalty provides, will pay brokers more yield spread premium if a prepayment penalty is part of a loan. And even the most savvy borrowers often do not realize that a broker can *add* a prepayment penalty to a loan themselves, even if one is not required by the lender. Yes, your broker—not the lender—may be the one to determine if your loan has a prepayment penalty, and, depending on the broker, you might never know it.

> **The Honest Broker:** Honest brokers will explain if a lender requires a prepayment penalty, and they will also explain how a prepayment penalty can be added and used as a tool to decrease your interest rate. An honest broker will work with you to determine if it would make sense to add a prepayment penalty to your loan.
>
> For example, if you are 100 percent certain you want to stay in your home for at least three years (and will be able to afford to do so), a three-year prepayment penalty could be used as a "no cost" way to lower your interest rate. You don't have intentions to move or refinance before the three years are up, so you won't have to worry about paying a penalty, and you receive a lower interest rate.
>
> **The Dishonest Broker:** Dishonest brokers may add a prepayment penalty regardless of whether it makes sense for you, just for the extra profit, and will claim the penalty is *required* by the lender. Very dishonest brokers may even add a prepayment penalty but not disclose it to you until your closing.

Brokers will use this tactic to appear more competitive when originally quoting your loan. For example, an honest broker may quote you a rate of 8 percent. A dishonest broker will quote you a rate of 7.5 percent, but will fail to tell you they were only able to secure this lower rate by tacking on a prepayment penalty. On your Truth In Lending Disclosure, they may "conveniently" forget to check off the box stating you have a prepayment penalty. The dishonest broker wants your business, and will do whatever it takes to close on the loan, leaving you with a surprise at the closing table.

If your loan carries a prepayment penalty, it should always be disclosed in advance, period. At your closing, a broker may claim the change was a last-minute lender requirement, and may ask you to sign a redisclosure for your loan on the spot. *Do not sign.*

No matter what your broker tells you, prepayment penalties are *never* last minute. Brokers will know from day one if a loan program includes a prepayment penalty—or if they are going to add one to obtain a lower rate.

Prior to your closing, review your Truth In Lending Disclosure carefully, and whether the prepayment penalty box is checked off or not, ask for confirmation. Does your loan carry a prepayment penalty or not?

---

 **When Prepayment Penalties Are Not Allowed**
Prepayment penalties cannot be added to certain loan programs. If your loan is a conventional loan (backed by Fannie and Freddie) or if your loan is a FHA or VA loan, prepayment penalties are not allowed. Prepayment penalties *can* be added to other loans, including bank portfolio loans, nonconforming loans, hard money loans, and home equity loans or lines of credit.

---

▶ **Additional or excessive fees, costs, or points.** Your interest rates, loan program, loan terms, or prepayment penalties aren't the only things that can change at the closing table. Lending fees, broker fees, points, processing fees, third party fees, and padded or miscellaneous charges can all mysteriously increase or appear when you review your final loan documents. Remember, with an honest broker, your final lending fees should be *no more than* $100 to $200 of your final Good Faith Estimate. If your final fees are a lot higher, it's most likely because your broker has not been honest, and there may be other hidden charges in your loan.

What should you do if your total lending costs appear predatory? What can you do if your broker profits have doubled? It is not too late, even if you are at the closing table—there is a way out.

## How to Stop the Scam

You may do everything right: you may have carefully selected your broker, you may understand the loans you qualify for, and you may obtain Good Faith Estimates. You may ask for your loan's interest rate with points, you may double check your total lending fees, and you may get everything in writing. Sometimes, no matter what you do—even if you do everything right—you may still encounter a predatory situation or scam.

---

WELL PREPARED . . . AND SCAM-FREE?

---

Tim came to my office as a referral from a past client. He had signed a real estate contract to purchase an existing home, and we spoke several times in depth on the phone about loan programs, interest rates, and his financial goals. He was one of my most prepared clients, even to this day. Tim made it perfectly clear that he was shopping around for the best rates, terms, and conditions and was working with several brokers and a bank. The day Tim came to see me, he was armed with several Good Faith Estimates and was leaning toward the lowest cost and most affordable option from another mortgage firm.

I respected Tim. He was a "see me—show me" type of client. At the end of our consultation, he made it clear that he was impressed with my office and my character, but had to go with the company offering the lowest cost, even though our rates and terms were very close. I let Tim know that, should something change, he was welcome to call me. He accepted, thanked me, and went on his way.

As Tim left my office that evening, I looked again at his real estate contract and logged the contract's expiration date in my computer's calendar with a reminder message six days prior. I just had a bad feeling.

Like clockwork, just four days before the contract's expiration date, Tim called me, sounding very stressed. From the conversation it was clear Tim had been a victim of a bait and switch. He told me that upon asking for a final written Good Faith Estimate from his broker, *both* his costs and his interest rate had increased. Tim was now looking for a miracle: his contract for the home was up in four days. Would I be able to close the loan in this time frame? Could he still get the same loan from my original quote?

Now, we all know how miracles work. They are rare and are never guaranteed. So I suggested Tim call his real estate agent to ask one important question: Could the agent negotiate a contract extension? Tim, even with all of his research, hadn't known this was an option. Tim was granted the fifteen day extension, and we closed on his loan with no problems—and with five days to spare.

---

Even the best of us can find ourselves in an unfortunate situation. You can even be very prepared, just like Tim, and still run into problems. Fortunately, as your closing date nears, if anything with your loan changes, or if something just doesn't sit right with you at the closing table, there are several things you can do:

▸ **Ask for a final disclosure three days before your closing.** By law, all changes to a loan must be disclosed to you before your scheduled closing date. This means that your broker should supply you with a final Good Faith Estimate *and* a final Truth In Lending Disclosure at least three days before your closing. If you haven't received your final GFE and TIL Disclosure by this three-day mark, call your broker and request that these be sent to you immediately.

Some brokers will ignore this three-day requirement and will later ask you to sign and backdate documents. If this happens, put down your pen and look for the door. If you are asked to backdate any changes on a disclosure, it should serve as further proof of a dishonest broker. No matter what your broker tells you, *do not* backdate *any* information or documentation for your loan during any part of the lending process.

▶  **Ask for a rate confirmation.** Did you receive a written confirmation that your rate was locked? If you didn't or forgot to ask, it is never too late to request a copy of the original confirmation. Even if it's only days before your closing, you will want to make sure you have a confirmation of your rate lock, in writing. This will prevent issues throughout your loan, will help you avoid surprises at the closing table, and, of course, is always good legal documentation if something goes wrong with your loan.

▶  **If you are purchasing a home, ask for a contract extension.** If you find yourself with a different interest rate, or your loan's terms are not what you expected or are unacceptable, stop the process. Do not go forward with the loan; instead, negotiate a *contract extension*.

When you purchase a new or existing home, you will sign a real estate contract. This contract has an expiration date, which requires you to obtain financing before the contract expires, usually in about thirty days (but sometimes this period is longer). When you ask for a contract extension, it's just what it sounds like—you will be granted an extension to work out any issues with your financing.

Depending on the seller and the circumstance, contract extensions can be granted for five, ten, or even fifteen days, sometimes more. You can easily use this time to work out things with your broker, or to find another broker entirely. If you are working with a real estate agent, the agent can negotiate this extension for you. Explain your circumstances clearly and ask for the agent to request the longest extension possible for you to secure a safe mortgage. Even the shortest of contract extensions can be used to correct issues or obtain new financing for your home.

---

DEFINITION **Who Decides if Your Contract Extension Will Be Granted?**

The seller, and the seller alone, will be the one to determine whether you will be given time to work out any issues with your loan. Most of the time, sellers will grant an extension because they don't want to lose out on the final sale of their home. But if you've already run into issues with a seller, if you've already had to ask for a contract extension, or if the seller has multiple offers (or higher offers) for the home, there is a chance the seller will deny your request and will let your contract expire for the home.

---

▸ **If you are refinancing, *stop* the process.** With any type of refinance, if something doesn't add up at the closing table, you are not obligated to proceed with the closing. No extension is needed. You can simply stop the process. Unlike a purchase, a refinance is based on *your* timeline, not a sales contract or what a lender wants. The decision to cancel or proceed forward with a refinance is your decision alone.

When you need to refinance, whether you are changing your interest rate, changing your loan program, or taking money out of your home, start the refinance process at least sixty days before you actually need to finalize the loan. This way, you will have plenty of time to look for other financing if you run into predatory practices or a dishonest broker. If you are cashing out any of your home's equity, sixty days will also give you enough time to address any issues with your appraisal or your home's value, which could affect how much money you receive, and could even determine if you are able to refinance at all.

▸    **If you are refinancing or are taking out a home equity loan or line of credit, use your right of rescission.** If you are purchasing a home, once you sign your loan's paperwork, there is no turning back, and the loan and the home are now legally yours. But if you are refinancing your home, or are taking out a home equity loan or line of credit, in most cases you will have three days *after* your loan closes (excluding Sundays and holidays) to change your mind. The Truth In Lending Act grants borrowers this *right of rescission*. During this three-day period, you can back out of the loan for any reason, no questions asked, and within twenty days, the lender must refund any fees you have paid on the loan.

While the right of rescission offers great protection to many borrowers, it doesn't apply to all loans; if you are refinancing, you must be living in the home as your primary residence (your right does not apply to investment properties or second homes), and the refinance must be with a *new* lender (it does not apply if you refinance with the lender who holds your original loan).

If you have taken out a home equity loan or line of credit, the rules are slightly different. If the home is your primary residence, you can cancel the entire loan or line of credit within the three day period. If you own but do not live in the home, you can only cancel the cash amount you have taken out, and not the loan or line of credit itself.

## A Warning About Financing on the Internet

The internet is an ever-growing resource for all subjects, and lending and mortgages are no exception. In fact, a single internet search just for the keyword "mortgage" produces literally millions of websites and hits. You'll notice throughout this book that I rarely make reference to internet-based lenders, companies, or brokers. This is because I *do not* recommend searching for your loan on the internet.

Purchasing or refinancing a home is one of life's biggest decisions, involving such important matters as your finances, your future finances, and your credit. If you choose to look for financing through the internet, be very careful who you give your personal information to. Do cross-reference research: Can you find a physical address for the company? Do you have a direct contact instead of a general sales number? Is the company or broker a member of any professional organizations? Do they have a good report from the Better Business Bureau?

One of the most common internet scams is the "tiny fee disclosure." An internet mortgage company will claim it can offer you a loan for very little cost. The company will claim it won't charge lending fees, origination fees, or even processing fees. You'll be offered the lowest rates possible, and you won't have to pay points to get the rate you want. Sounds great, doesn't it?

But if you look at the fine print, you will come across a line that reads "all loans are subject to additional fees" or "all loans are subject to a one-time company fee" or "rates, loan products, and fees are subject to change without notice"—which all are distinct warnings of what's to come. Usually this fine print is hard to find, but believe me, it is there. Unbelievably, tiny fine print is still technically considered to be a full disclosure. These companies may call their fees by different names, but rest assured you are still being charged, and may even be overcharged, for your loan.

Internet lenders are also notorious for charging advance fees, especially advance application fees. As you'll recall, there are only two items you should ever pay for in advance: your appraisal and your homeowners insurance policy (if required). Internet mortgage companies often advertise loan programs that are too good to be true, and may also intimidate you with the same sales techniques and predatory practices I have outlined in this chapter. The speed with which you can search for a loan on the internet may seem like it will save you time, but it will often cost you time…and money.

**What Is Mortgage Fraud?**

Mortgage fraud itself is a very broad category. If documents are forged, if income or asset verifications are falsified or are completed by ineligible parties, if last minute funds are added into checking or savings accounts, if an appraiser or third party influences a property's value, if documents are left blank or are backdated, if anything regarding the loan or the loan's approval is embellished, or if there are any "on the side" agreements or kickbacks, it's mortgage fraud, plain and simple.

## The "Little White Lies" of Mortgage Fraud

Believe it or not, most mainstream scams in lending happen quietly in the background, and are grouped under the title of "mortgage fraud."

Those who willingly participate in mortgage fraud all have one common goal: closing the deal. Brokers, lenders, appraisers, realtors, and title companies can all commit mortgage fraud to make sure they receive their profit on the loan. Mortgage fraud may be used to take advantage of borrowers in the ways I have described throughout this chapter, but it can also be used to secure loans for those who would otherwise be turned down for financing. Your broker may tell you the rules may need to be broken "just a little" to get you the loan you want, and you may tempted to look the other way for your own benefit. But as many people have found out the hard way, breaking the rules can easily have consequences down the line. If your broker tells a few white lies about your income, does this really mean you can afford the loan? If your home's value is artificially increased so you can take out money in a refinance, does it really pay off when you are now responsible for a much larger, and more expensive, loan?

The truth is, if a broker has no issue breaking the rules *for you*, it's also very likely your broker won't have an issue with breaking other rules that will hurt you, but will benefit them as a broker. You may think your broker is doing something to help you, but I would place a high bet that your broker's actions are really helping him or her. And even if all parties involved in a loan—lender, broker, seller, and buyer—all agree and find the manipulations harmless, someone always pays in the end. In the past few years, we've seen the effects of mortgage fraud hit our economy, our credit markets, and even global markets. So in effect, we've all paid for someone else's mortgage fraud.

If you believe you have been a victim of mortgage fraud, predatory lending practices, or a lending scam, there are many ways to get help. Contact at least one—and in some cases you may need to contact several—of the federal agencies I've listed for you here. You will also want to contact your state's Department of Banking and Finance and your state's attorney general. Mortgage fraud and lending scams are prosecutable. Many aspects of the mortgage lending system are broken. By registering your complaint, you will not only receive assistance yourself, you will help to fix the system and help others.

 Our government can't fix the system if it doesn't know what's wrong. Tell someone what has happened to you. In addition to the contact information I have provided in this chapter, you will find an expanded directory and links to additional federal, state, and local regulatory agencies on my website.

## The Scammer's Next Target: Your Home

Even after you have safely obtained financing, you are still a prime target for scammers. All homeowners need to be extremely cautious and protective of their homes, and this is especially true in today's market, where many homeowners are struggling and are faced with the very real possibility of losing their homes. Homeowners in distress are nothing but prime targets for scammers. If you are having difficulties in paying your mortgage or need to sell your home and are looking for help—you need to be very careful. You will want to be sure the help you receive is not the help of a scam artist.

# If You Need to File
# a Complaint or Get Help

## The Financial Institution Fraud Unit of the FBI

(202) 324-3000  |  www.fbi.gov

*Contact to report mortgage fraud, predatory lending, or any lending or real estate scams*

## The Federal Trade Commission

(877) 382-4357  |  www.ftc.gov

*Contact for complaints involving lenders, mortgage, and finance companies, as well as state credit unions*

## Office of Fair Housing and Equal Opportunity

(800) 669-9777  |  www.hud.gov/offices/fheo/

*Contact for complaints involving discrimination in mortgage lending or predatory lending practices*

## The Federal Reserve Board

(888) 851-1920  |  www.federalreserveconsumerhelp.gov

*Contact for issues involving truth in lending or discrimination*

## RESPA: The Real Estate Settlement Procedures Act

www.hud.gov/offices/hsg/sfh/res/respamor.cfm#UR

*Contact for complaints or information on disclosures, Good Faith Estimates, closing costs, or the servicing of your loan*

## Your State Attorney General

www.naag.org

*Contact for any complaints involving predatory lending, or fraudulent mortgage or real estate practices*

## Fannie Mae Mortgage Fraud Hotline

(800) 7 FANNIE  |  (800) 732-6643  |  www.fanniemae.com

*Contact for complaints or issues with any loan sponsored by Fannie Mae*

## Freddie Mac Mortgage Fraud Hotline

(800) 4Fraud8  |  (800) 437-2838  |  www.freddiemac.com

*Contact for complaints or issues with any loan sponsored by Freddie Mac*

## The FHA Resource Center

(800) 225-5342

*Contact for complaints or issues with any FHA loan*

## Department of Veterans Affairs

(800) 827-1000  |  (202) 273-5770  |  www.va.gov

*Contact for complaints involving loans guaranteed by the VA*

## Foreclosure Deed and Title Scams

Have you been late in paying your mortgage or have you missed any mortgage payments? If so, you've probably been bombarded by phone calls and emails, and your mailbox is surely full of letters and brochures from companies and individuals who claim to specialize in saving you from foreclosure. Unfortunately, many of these people will also prey on your vulnerability. These scammers will claim to want to help you, but they will only be looking to help themselves—by taking your home.

Although there are many variations of this scam, they all hinge on a few important legal documents. When you purchase a home, legal paperwork is filed describing the terms of the sale and the ownership of the property. Although these documents may vary slightly from state to state, they will most often include:

- *Your mortgage or a deed of trust, depending on your state law* (which documents the agreement with your lender)

- *A promissory note* (which defines your loan's terms—how you agree to pay back what you owe)

- *A warranty deed* (which defines your right to own and sell the property)

- *Your title* (which documents that you own the home)

These documents attach your name to the property and make the property yours and yours alone. Of these documents, scammers will focus on the two that define your ownership rights: your warranty deed and title. To scammers, these documents are gold.

While arranging to "help" you, scammers may ask you to sign and execute what is known as a *quitclaim deed*, and if they do, run like Forrest Gump. A quitclaim deed transfers, removes, or shares your ownership of a property. Quitclaim deeds are common legal documents, and when used properly are safe and secure. In fact, you may already have used a quitclaim deed yourself. For example, in the case of a divorce, a quitclaim deed can be used to transfer ownership of a home from one spouse to the other. These deeds can also be used to add someone to your title, providing for shared ownership of the home (as you might want to do when you get married). Quitclaims can also be used to completely remove one person from the title and add another.

Scammers use quitclaim deeds as an underhanded method to give themselves legal rights to your home. Once you add the scammers to your title, they will attempt to remove *you* from the title. If a scammer is on your title, they have as much right to the home as you do; their ownership is equal to yours. And if you are taken off the title completely, the scammers will have *complete* control and ownership of your property. You have not sold your home to the scammers, you've simply given it to them. In fact, you are still responsible for paying the mortgage for the home because the mortgage is still in your name, but you will be paying a mortgage for a home you no longer own.

You may be thinking that you would never sign over the ownership of your home. But scammers are tricky, and most homeowners don't understand the legalities about a home's deed and title. This might even be the first time you've read about how deeds and titles really work. If so, you are certainly not alone. This lack of knowledge is something scammers count on.

## "ASSIGNING" YOUR DEED AND TITLE

Let's say, for instance, that you need to sell your home. You might have a job transfer and need to sell quickly, or the need to sell may be urgent because you can no longer afford your home. But your local real estate market is flat—there are no buyers. Scammers see your home sitting on the market. They watch as you lower the price of your home and know you need to sell. Soon, you'll get a call from the scammers, saying they can arrange a quick sale of your home to an eager buyer; they may even tell you they already have a buyer lined up, ready to purchase your home. All you need to do is sign over, or *assign*, your deed and title.

The scammers explain that they can't sell your home without being named on the title, and if you assign the title, they will take full responsibility for selling your home. The scammers may even "allow" you to live in the home for free while the property is being sold. If your finances are tight, they might even give you a small amount of cash to help you pay your bills, and they will surely tell you to trust them.

Using the word "assign" makes the transfer sound harmless, but once you assign your title rights (which will be in the legal form of a quitclaim deed), you aren't just assigning the ability to sell the home; you're assigning *possession* of your home. Afterward, your home is no longer yours, no matter what you've been promised. You are still responsible for the mortgage and the repayment of the promissory note, but your title rights are gone. Your home is now the scammers'.

Even if the scammers have not removed you from the title, you may still be faced with loss. If you have any equity in your home (if you owe less than what your home is worth), a scammer will try to use being named on the title to fraudulently take out a second mortgage without your knowledge, stripping your home of its equity and making off with the cash. Also, if the scammers do sell your home as promised, they, not you alone, are now entitled to the profits because they are named on the title. For example, your home may be worth $225,000. You may owe $175,000 on your mortgage. To the scammer, there is up to $50,000 available, ripe for the taking. Even though this profit is also yours (as long as your name, too, appears on the title), you can be sure a scammer will commit whatever mortgage fraud is necessary to take as much of your profit as possible.

### The "Sale and Leaseback" Option

In another variation of this scheme, scammers will offer you a fantastic "sale and leaseback" option. Just assign your title to them, and they'll make the payments on your mortgage, while charging you a greatly reduced monthly rent so you can continue to live in the home. As soon as you get back on your feet, they promise they will sign the home's title back to you, charging you a small fee for their role in saving your home. You may even sign very official-looking paperwork saying this will happen. You can stay in your home, pay lower rent, and save money, all at the same time.

But again, as soon as you sign over the title, the home is no longer yours. The scammers won't pay your mortgage, but they'll still take rent from you, and do whatever they can to strip any equity from the house as well. You end up being left with no home and ruined credit from the unpaid mortgage.

During this process, many parts of the scam will feel real and very official. In fact, many scammers masquerade as fraudulent nonprofits or government organizations. They will play to your emotions and insist they are there to help, when they surely are not.

## The Straw Buyer

Sometimes scams are so elaborate and well thought out that there is no reason at all for you to suspect a scam. The Straw Buyer Scam starts with a homeowner who is in financial distress and is willing to entertain just about anything to sell their home. In collaboration, a group of "professionals," including a real estate agent, a mortgage finance representative, an appraiser, and a title company approach and convince a homeowner that they have a buyer who is interested in the home. This buyer will even pay above market value for the home, allowing the homeowner to make some additional profit, which of course will help with the homeowner's financial situation. The group of professionals can all work together to quickly complete the sale.

From the homeowner's perspective, there are so many different companies involved that it seems *impossible* that the offer could be a scam. Just like the other deed and title scams, a quitclaim deed is used to assign the home's title to a representative from the "professional group" who will act on the homeowner's behalf in selling the home to the new buyer.

Strangely, the homeowner never seems to meet this buyer, and the buyer never comes around to look at the actual home. This is because the buyer is what is known as a *straw buyer*—a completely fictitious person created from a stolen identity, or someone who is allowing their credit be used for the transaction, but has no intention of actually occupying the home. After much forgery and mortgage fraud by all members of the professional group, a loan is given to the straw borrower and the sale of the home is finalized. The home has been sold!

The original homeowner, who is elated, is told that all they have to do is wait a few days to receive the profits from the sale. Legally, when a home is sold, all profits are given to the homeowner immediately at the closing. But trace the scam back a few steps. Who was really the owner of the home at the time of the sale? The professional group's "representative." Ownership had been transferred to this representative through the quitclaim deed. The representative makes off with the profits and the scam is complete; the "professionals" become magicians and conveniently disappear.

### MORE INFO    How Do They Do It?

How do scammers convince so many homeowners to sign a quitclaim deed and sign over their titles? Many scammers are great sales people, and will be able to explain things in a way that makes sense. And some of their explanations may actually have some truth behind them, making it even harder for you to detect the scam. For example, scammers will tell you they legally need to be on your home's title to sell the home on your behalf. This statement is partly true. Only the owner of a home or a licensed real estate agent can legally sell a home—and receive profit from the sale. Scammers *could* help you sell your home without being on the title, but they wouldn't receive any profit for it. Scammers cleverly take this fact and twist it around for their own benefit.

## *How to Protect Yourself*

What can you do to avoid these real estate scams—and even new scams that may appear? The key to not becoming a victim lies in your home's title. A third party may act on your behalf. They may help you sell your home or they may help you work with your lender to avoid foreclosure. They may also help with your mortgage payments, or they may even help to arrange for better financing. But no matter the situation, they will *never* need your home's title to do so. By assigning your title, you are giving away your home—for free. But you cannot give away your mortgage, so you will still be legally responsible for your loan; you will have to pay a loan for a home you no longer own.

When you legally sell a home, you are no longer financially responsible for it. Your loan is paid off by the sale of your home. You will no longer own the home, but you will no longer have a mortgage either. This is the important difference. For any individual or organization to truly help you by "buying" your home, it must be a legal sale.

The bottom line is this: If you want to keep your home, keep the title in your own name. Do not sign any contracts or paperwork that will compromise your ownership. Simply keeping your title will protect you from most of the real estate fraud out there today.

 Have you heard about or been the victim of a mortgage or real estate scam? Help protect others. Log into the reader's section of my website and tell others about your experience. Together, we can help protect more people against predatory lending and mortgage and real estate scams.

## The Renters Eviction

So far, the scams I've explained in this chapter involve owning a home—from the loan for your home, to your actual home itself. But sometimes, real estate scams can impact where you live, whether you own it or not. Maybe you are renting, and are reading this book to learn more before you purchase a home. Or perhaps you are renting due to a previous foreclosure or financial difficulty. It's important to be aware that it is becoming more and more common for renters to become the victims of real estate scams, without even owning a home. How? It's actually very simple.

Many owners of rental property are not paying their mortgages, and instead are pocketing rental income and rolling the dice for when (or if) the lender comes calling. Some landlords are even skipping real estate tax payments and homeowners insurance, which are all reasons a lender can use to quickly foreclose on a property. So after dutifully paying your rent for months, you may find the home you live in is being foreclosed on, you've been served with an eviction notice, and you have nowhere to go.

This is a hard scam to keep track of, because it's hard for you to know if your landlord is paying the mortgage. But public record searches can help you to keep tabs on what is going on with the home you're renting or thinking of renting. Visit the website for your county or state's public records division, or take a trip to your county clerk's office. No matter where you live, and even if you do not have a computer, make sure you become very familiar with your area's public records (specifically property, deed, and real estate tax searches).

▶    First, you want to locate your county or state's property records site. You can usually find this site by searching for the name of your county and the words "property appraiser" or "tax assessor." On this site, you will want to search by the home's address to find the *legal owner* of the property. Keep in mind, this owner may *not* be your landlord, if your landlord is managing the property for someone else.

▶    Next, you'll want to search by the legal owner's name within your county and/or state's public records and tax collector's records. (Again, to find the right sites or place to conduct this search, do an internet search for the name of your county, plus the words "public records" or "tax collector.") If your state doesn't offer online services, or you have a hard time finding where to search, contact your local government to find out where you can get the information—remember, that's what they're there for! Usually, you'll find records about when the homeowner purchased the home, their mortgage, if they have refinanced, and when they have paid their real estate taxes. If you see the real estate taxes for the home are delinquent, or if you see liens are being placed on the property (which usually means the owner is not paying home-related bills), the home may soon be foreclosed on.

If you live in a state that uses a *mortgage* to document a homeowner's agreement with a lender (I've provided a chart of which states use mortgages in Appendix II), you may also see that a document called a *lis pendens* has been filed against the owner within public records. A lis pendens is legal notification that the lender has started the foreclosure process, and it's a sure sign that and anyone living in the home may soon be forced to leave.

If you live in a state that uses a *deed of trust* instead of a mortgage to document a homeowner's agreement with the lender (these states are also listed in Appendix II), you may be notified of an impending foreclosure by other methods: a certified letter, a sign on your front

---

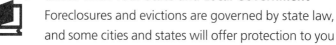

**Check With Your State and Local Government**

Foreclosures and evictions are governed by state law, and some cities and states will offer protection to you as a renter. If you are faced with a possible eviction, it's in your best interest to check with your local government representative as soon as possible to see what local or state laws will protect you. For example, in North Carolina and New York, most renters may remain in the rented property through the end of their leases, even if a foreclosure occurs. In California, renters have at least sixty days after a foreclosure to find a new home, and the city of Los Angeles prohibits renters from being evicted until a property is sold to a new owner. Your rights as a renter may buy you more time to find another place to live.

---

door, a sign on the front lawn, or even a notice in your local paper.

Finding out about an impending foreclosure can save you much sudden stress. If a lender forecloses on the home you are living in, and you don't know about it in advance, your first clue may be a sheriff appearing at your door with an eviction notice. Of course, this would be a stressful event for anyone. But by keeping tabs on what is happening with the home, you won't be caught off guard and will have the opportunity to look for other living arrangements in advance.

 New scams are hatched every day targeting owners and renters alike. As new scams unfold, I'll provide the details for you on my website. Another good resource is the U.S. Federal Trade commission, which provides complete information on predatory practices in many industries, including real estate and lending, along with important consumer tips. For more information, visit www.ftc.gov.

## The Scam Will Go On

Scams will unfortunately always be part of a free society and scammers will always try to improve their techniques and refine their targets. So it's always rewarding to see when scammers are caught in the act, as you'll see here in the story of Alvin and Sam.

| THE DYNAMIC DUO |
| --- |

I've encountered many characters throughout the years, but my favorites by far are Alvin and Sam. Alvin and Sam were a real estate agent and investment team whose clientele included distressed homeowners needing help selling their homes. Alvin and Sam had two specialties: taking ownership of a home's title and stripping profits from properties. The duo would convince some clients to sign over their titles while they searched for buyers. They would also convince a homeowner to sell for a greatly reduced price, find a buyer who was willing to pay more for the home, and the duo—not the previous homeowner—would pocket the difference. Other times, Alvin and Sam would act as real estate agents, and would charge the homeowner very high (and often predatory) real estate commissions for finalizing the sale.

In the brokerage and lending business, I am always cautious about excessive fees and shady practices, including predatory real estate practices. I'd heard about Alvin and Sam through the grapevine and could never quite figure out how they could get away with doing business as they did.

When I finally met the pair, it was because they had contacted my office looking for financing for a home owned by a gentleman named Mr. Diaz. They had a new buyer for Mr. Diaz's home, and this buyer needed a loan. Even though Alvin and Sam's reputation preceded them, I was curious. Just how did they manage to construct their deals? I had to take a look.

As I read the contracts, I saw that Mr. Diaz had agreed to sell his home for one price to Alvin and Sam as investors. Alvin and Sam were selling the home to the new buyer by assigning the real estate sales contract—but on this new contract, they had *increased* the sales price of the home. By changing the price on an assigned contract, the contract was now illegal. I wouldn't touch this deal, and I knew my lenders wouldn't either. Alvin and Sam would need to close on the home, and then sell it to the new buyer at the higher price, or they would need to be on the home's title to sell and receive any profits. Luckily for Mr. Diaz, he had not signed over his title.

When I explained this to Alvin and Sam, denial and ignorance took over. The duo swore up and down that what they were doing was completely legal. They could not imagine *why* my lenders would not accept the contract assignment for the new buyer, adding that another mortgage broker was closing similar deals for them all day long. I stood my ground through fifteen minutes of nonsense, and then told them that if they *did* have other brokers who knowingly closed loans that used this same type of contract assignment, then what these brokers were doing was fraudulent, period.

There was a dead silence. I had used the "f" word. Alvin and Sam assured me there were no fraudulent dealings among them. The conversation ended, and Alvin and Sam didn't call on my company again.

Several months later however, in a twist of fate, I did hear from Mr. Diaz, the homeowner from Alvin and Sam's deal. I was more than surprised. Mr. Diaz explained that he had heard my name early in the transaction, saw me recently on a local television news segment, and decided to call. I carefully explained why I was unable to help Alvin and Sam, and Mr. Diaz explained even more: Alvin and Sam had strung Mr. Diaz along for months, assuring him they would find a buyer for his home. Mr. Diaz grew more desperate as buyer after buyer were turned down for financing. Eventually, Alvin and Sam insisted the only solution Mr. Diaz had was to refinance his home, using Alvin and Sam's "affiliated" mortgage and title companies. By this time, Mr. Diaz realized Alvin and Sam were scammers, and were not trying to help him at all.

While waiting for Alvin and Sam's assistance in selling his home, Mr. Diaz had still been struggling to pay his mortgage, and was now on the brink of default and possible foreclosure. After many hours of consulting and counseling, I was able to help. I placed Mr. Diaz into a more affordable mortgage, and helped Mr. Diaz develop a better plan for his savings and spending so he wouldn't have to worry about losing his home again.

Not long afterward, I heard Alvin and Sam were in quite a bit of trouble. In addition to the mortgage and title companies they had acquired to facilitate their scams, they had also accumulated far too many properties as real estate investors, had no buyers, had angered most of their clients, and, best of all, were being investigated by the Florida Real Estate Commission (FREC) and other regulatory agencies. Arrests were made. Licenses were lost and hefty fines were paid. It was the end of the road for Alvin and Sam, and, all in all, I would say it was a very happy ending.

---

I want to point out that while Alvin and Sam posed as "real estate investors," buying, reselling, or investing in real estate are not bad practices in and of themselves. Many hardworking people make their living by legally flipping properties; by purchasing, repairing, and selling homes; and by investing in real estate to make long-term profits. I am not trying to give these professions a bad name. Unfortunately within both real estate and lending, there are just as many scammers as there are honest people. Scammers are unscrupulous, are out to make as much profit as possible, and will hurt you and others in the process. And in reality, not all scammers get what they deserve, and many scams do not have a happy ending.

With scammers, the best defense is a good offense. By knowing what to look for and by being aware of the possibility (and probability) of predatory lending practices, high rates and fees, or lending and real estate scams, you will be more prepared to protect yourself and your home.

If you are struggling financially, are having a tough time paying your mortgage, or are faced with foreclosure, you are even more vulnerable to predatory practices. You need help, but you may not know where to turn, and might unknowingly turn to a scammer to save your home. What scammers won't tell you is that there are steps you can take *yourself* to save your home. I'll be explaining these steps, and exactly what you can and should do to protect your home, in the very next chapter. From those who can no longer afford their homes, to those who are trapped in a mortgage, to those who need to sell their homes but can't due to market conditions, all homeowners in some way can benefit from reading more about defaults and foreclosure.

COMING UP

Are you struggling with the costs of your home or investment property? Are you afraid you might miss a mortgage payment? Have you already missed payments or are you in the process of a foreclosure? In the next chapter, I'll explain what happens from the minute you miss your first payment through the entire foreclosure process, and what you can do each step of the way to safeguard your home.

# 7

# Default and Foreclosure

## Part I: Before Foreclosure
*The Calm Before the Storm*

t's never easy to bring up the topic of foreclosure. Foreclosures have been around as long as real estate itself, yet it's still a difficult and emotional process. Each and every victim of foreclosure has their own story, their own set of circumstances. And today, defaults and foreclosures are all too common. With high mortgage payments, real estate values in distress, real estate taxes and insurance on the rise, lost jobs, and just everyday life getting in the way, it's easy to get behind. It starts with the first month's missed payment; then comes the second month's missed payment. And by the time you've missed your third month's payment, it's become a formal (and legal) pattern of *non-payment*, and you find yourself in the beginning stages of foreclosure.

You may feel trapped and alone. You may feel frustrated as you begin to consider the reality of losing your home. It's hard to know where to turn for advice or relief, and it's hard to know who to trust. Many brokers, in attempts to guide their clients, have made the foreclosure process even more uncomfortable and confusing than it already is. There are those in the lending industry who understand loans, but don't understand the legalities of a foreclosure. They may be afraid to admit they have very little knowledge of the process, so they pump themselves up, armed with bad information or complicated legal jargon, and as a result mislead or scare you, leaving you more frustrated than you already are.

Of course, there are also many brokers and industry experts who *will* be able to provide you with solid information you can use to save your home. But often, experts forget you don't know the industry like they do, and they forget that working with lenders, especially when you're trying to save your home, can often be confusing and intimidating. They may tell you *what* you can do—and it may be great information—but not how to go about it, and you may not understand the specifics. You may not know who to call, what to say, or even what to expect.

My approach to defaults and foreclosures has always been different. I emphasize that understanding *how* to get involved with your lender is the key to saving your home, and I'll show you, step by step, how to do it. From my years of working closely with every type of lender—from banks to wholesale and retail lenders—it's clear that lenders all have one very important thing in common: no lender wants to foreclose and take possession of your home. They really don't. Lenders want to remain lenders and they want to continue to receive payments. Understanding this fact will help you to stay in your home.

In our current market, foreclosure is a big unknown—even for lenders. Surprised? Most people are. Sure, lenders have a certain amount of foreclosure protocol and procedure in place, but the massive number of foreclosures lenders are faced with now and will be faced with in the near future is uncharted territory, even for them. Lenders are having to change their foreclosure guidelines, how they view defaults, and how they work with homeowners just like you. There is a window of opportunity you will have with any lender (which comes long before the legal ramifications of the foreclosure itself). Many homeowners miss this window, simply because they don't know what they should do, or when. I'm here to help you to open that window again.

It all starts with communicating with your lender. Like many homeowners, you may think hiding from your lender is the safest bet. Maybe you have missed mortgage payments, and your lender hasn't gotten around to contacting you, so you believe "no news is good news." What most people don't realize is that the opposite is actually true. The sooner you contact your lender, the more communication you have with your lender, the better your chances.

No matter what your situation is—if you are in any way worried about paying your mortgage or are struggling with your finances, if you are about to miss a payment, if you have already missed payments, or if your lender is already trying to reach you—start communicating with your lender immediately, and follow the steps as I've outlined for you here in this chapter. Lenders will look more favorably on you if you are truly proactive and are making an effort. There is so much that can be attempted in the beginning stages of foreclosure; there are so many steps you can try, and if you don't at least try, you will never know if you could have saved your home.

An important note: I can't promise miracles. I really wish I could. But what I *can* promise is that I will provide you with solid information, insider knowledge, and a plan of action for saving your home. Even so, my advice and instruction are only one part of the equation—your own attitude and efforts are just as important. You will need to be persistent, patient, and calm throughout the entire process, and you need to expect that you will hear the word "no" a lot. It will be frustrating. Don't give in. Don't give up. Although it will not be easy, this is your chance to keep your home, and you should give it your best effort.

## The Foreclosure Process

I use a lot of analogies when I speak about home finance, and analogies are just as helpful for the subject of foreclosure. The events that lead to foreclosure, and how you can protect your home against foreclosure itself, can be understood better by thinking of them in terms of a system that's used by the U.S. government. The government and military use a rating system called the Defense Readiness Condition, shortened to Defcon. This system uses levels, from Level 5 down to Level 1, to indicate how safe the country is, and how our armed forces need to prepare. Level 5 is in effect during peacetime. Level 1 is as bad as it gets. I'm going to use a similar system to describe how safe your home is, and what you should prepare for, in each stage of the foreclosure process.

It should always be your objective to remain in Defcon Level 5, where everything is peaceful, your mortgage payments are current, and your home is safe. But for many homeowners, staying in Level 5 is a struggle. It may be harder and harder each month to make your mortgage payments until one month, you just can't. You miss your first mortgage payment.

## Your First Missed Mortgage Payment

With your first missed payment, your home is referred to as being in *pre-foreclosure*. Pre-foreclosure is like a grace period; it is the window of time *before* your lender starts to take any formal legal action, but you are still one step closer to foreclosure.

| | |
|---|---|
| Level 5 | Your mortgage payments are current. Your home is safe. |
| Level 4 | **You miss your first mortgage payment.**<br>*Your lender attempts to contact you.* |
| Level 3 | You miss a second mortgage payment.<br>*Your lender sends a notice of default.* |
| Level 2 | You miss three or more mortgage payments.<br>*Your lender sends a notice of foreclosure.* |
| Level 1 | The foreclosure is final. Your home is sold at auction.<br>*You receive an eviction notice and must move from your home.* |

During this stage—Defcon Level 4—I often hear homeowners speak nonchalantly about missing a payment: "It's just the first missed payment" or "I have plenty of time before the lender contacts me." In reality, missing a payment should never be taken lightly. If you are late on your mortgage payment, the time to address the default and plan for future payments is now. Why? For several reasons:

▸ Once you miss a payment and are thirty days late, you are automatically considered to be in *default*. Being in default means you have not paid your mortgage as you have agreed to: by signing a mortgage and executing a promissory note, you have agreed to pay on a monthly basis until your loan is paid in full. If you miss just one payment, lenders can start foreclosure proceedings (the legal process of taking possession of a home) immediately. Most mortgages include a provision called an *acceleration clause*, which gives your lender the right to demand payment of your loan *in full* if you default.

Of course borrowers won't be able to pay the loan in full, and this non-payment can start the foreclosure process. And although most lenders won't take this action right away, it doesn't mean missing a payment isn't serious. It is. The minute you default, the foreclosure countdown starts.

▸ When you miss a payment, your account is also *past due*. Being past due means you haven't paid by your due date, and you will be charged a late fee as a penalty. Typically, late fees are about 5 percent of your total mortgage payment. So if your mortgage is $1,000 a month, you can expect to pay an additional $50, just for being late. To become current again on your loan, you will be expected to pay your missed payment, plus any late fees. Even if you make your next payment on time (or even if you make the next payment early), if you don't make up for the first missed payment and the late fees, you will still be considered past due *and* in default.

▸ Once you are thirty days late, your lender will report the missed payment to the credit repositories. Your credit will receive a strike, your credit score will drop (often by as much as 50 to 100 points), and the balance owed for the missed payment will be recorded in your credit report. As I'll explain in Chapter 9, your credit is becoming more and more important in general. Any strike on your credit, especially from a missed mortgage payment, is bad news and will definitely be noticed by anyone who might be considering approving you for credit in the future.

▶ If your real estate taxes or your homeowners insurance are required by your lender to be escrowed (paid monthly as part of your mortgage, and put aside for your next tax and insurance bills) and you miss a payment, you might not have enough in your escrow account when these bills are due. If this happens, your mortgage payments could rise, or you could be required to pay a lump sum to make up the difference.

For many, the first missed payment is usually the calm before the storm. Mortgage costs and late fees can easily snowball, and you are starting a trend that's hard to recover from without planning, assistance, and involvement from your lender. If you've missed a payment, it's time to ask yourself some serious questions:

- Do I have the ability to make my next mortgage payment?
- Do I have the financial means to make up the missed payment?

If you answer "no" to either of these questions, you most likely have a bigger issue to deal with than just the missed payment. Don't ignore it. Start planning and become proactive now.

## Start Communicating with Your Lender

Even if your lender hasn't contacted you at or before the thirty day past due mark, if you can't make up for the missed payment immediately or feel you might have trouble paying your mortgage in the future, call your lender and ask to speak with the *loss mitigation*

### When Lenders Won't Help...Until You Miss a Payment

I always encourage homeowners to be proactive and speak with their lenders *before* they miss a mortgage payment. However, some lenders have internal protocol in place that requires you to actually miss a payment (or even several payments) before they will work with you. With the passage of the federal government's Making Home Affordable program in 2009, the government is offering a financial incentive to lenders to work out solutions with homeowners before problems start, and this may change some lenders' internal procedures.

The Making Home Affordable program gives many homeowners the opportunity to refinance or modify their loans to allow for more affordable monthly payments. The program also helps those who are in adjustable rate, interest-only, or balloon loans who would like the stability of a fixed rate loan.

If in the past your lender has denied your request to discuss modifying your loan (or your mortgage payment) because you have managed to pay on time, if you are currently struggling with your mortgage or have recently missed mortgage payments, or if you have missed payments and have already tried to work with your lender but were unsuccessful, take the time now to see if you qualify for this program. For more information, visit www.makinghomeaffordable.gov, where you can also answer a few quick questions to see if you qualify. If you do, you'll want to contact your lender as soon as possible to start the process.

*department*. (Some lenders may refer to this department as the home retention department.) This department specializes in reducing a lender's financial loss; it's their job to save a lender both time and money, and one of the easiest ways to do this is to work out an arrangement with you where you *continue* to make mortgage payments, benefiting the lender, and you are able to keep your home, obviously benefiting you.

You aren't the only one who wants to avoid a foreclosure; your lender does, too, because everything regarding a foreclosure costs money. For a lender, the actual foreclosure is just the beginning of a long and expensive process. Not only does your lender incur the legal fees for the foreclosure itself, but there are also costs and time involved with selling or liquidating the property. Prepping the property for sale, real estate commissions, taxes, insurance—these expenses all come out of a lender's pocket.

To make matters worse, lenders are also faced with the decreased likelihood that they will ever recoup their entire financial investment (the amount they have loaned to you), because when a lender sells or liquidates a home, they usually accept far less than what the property is worth, just to avoid additional losses. In total, a foreclosure can cost lenders tens of thousands of dollars, sometimes as much as $50,000 to $75,000 or more. That's motivation enough for any lender to consider working out an arrangement with you.

## Make Sure You Reach the Loss Mitigation Department

I want to stress that it's very important that you reach someone in the loss mitigation department when you make this call; you do not want to leave the fate of your home in the hands of anyone else, especially your lender's regular customer service representatives. In fact, don't be surprised if the customer service department tells you that you have *no* options at all. Customer service representatives may only be able to advise you by using a repayment protocol script or a set of computer prompts. You may even be transferred to your lender's regular sales staff, who may try to talk to you about refinancing. Be firm in asking to speak with the loss mitigation department. A lender's loss mitigation representatives are the *only individuals* who are qualified to negotiate and provide you with the options you need to save your home.

When you first call your lender, you may have to supply several customer service representatives with your general information, but be very specific about your needs. Here's an example:

> Hello. My name is Mr. Smith and I'd like to speak with a representative in your loss mitigation department. I missed my last month's payment and I may not be able to make the next payment on time. I'd like to discuss the options I have with my mortgage. If you need any information or my account number, I'd be happy to provide it.

I do need to warn you: it can sometimes be a long battle before you reach the right department. Most homeowners start the process by calling the phone number listed on their mortgage statement. Keep in mind that this phone number may actually be for a mortgage servicer and not your lender. A mortgage servicer collects your mortgage payments on behalf of the bank, lender, or investor who holds your mortgage, and usually will not be able to make any decisions regarding your loan. But they should be able to assist you in tracking down who your lender is, and how to get in touch with them.

As you know from reading Chapter 3, your loan could have been sold, purchased, and sold again since your closing, requiring you to make many phone calls before you finally reach the lender or institution who currently owns your loan. And even after several rounds of the telephone game, it might take many *more* phone calls before you reach your lender's actual loss mitigation department.

Loss mitigation departments are extremely busy, and sometimes the contact information for a mitigation representative will *not* be given out freely. You may be asked to leave a message, you may be told someone will call you back, or you may be told you will be contacted via email. Speak with as many people as you need to until you reach a real "live" person, and when you do, confirm that whom you are speaking with has the authority to handle *your* loan—and be sure to take down their full name, their direct number or extension, and their email address. (I've provided a worksheet where you can start to

MORE INFO **Being Proactive and Being Honest**

When you speak with your lender, it's very important to discuss the reality of your situation openly. Don't be afraid to tell it like it is. By being proactive, you are telling your lender that you want to make the situation right, want to keep your home, and are sincere in wanting to negotiate a solution. On the lender's side, this takes away some of their uncertainty. If you don't contact your lender, they are left to guess: Are you going to continue to miss payments? Are you going to abandon the home? Are you simply in a rough spot? Your lender won't know unless you tell them. This is why communication is key.

Additionally, if you're the one who initiates communication, there will be no surprises for you. You won't have to wonder about what will happen. You won't have to be afraid to answer the phone or open the mailbox. And your lender won't have to resort to pressure tactics to make you pay, because they know they are already working with you.

gather this information in Appendix II.) This may seem like overkill, but trust me, it's not. There's nothing worse than needing to speak with your representative and having no way to reach them directly.

 WEBLINK Are you having a hard time reaching the right department? Visit the reader's resource section of my website, where I've provided up-to-date contact information for many lenders and for their loss mitigation departments.

## *The Loss Mitigation Representative*

By the time you've reached a loss mitigation representative, you have most likely explained your situation briefly to someone else. This representative has either reviewed the notes on your account or has been informed of your hardship. Even so, you will want to be very clear about the purpose of your call. Start your conversation by saying something like this:

> As you can see, I am currently past due on my mortgage and I realize I am in default. I am having trouble making my mortgage payments, and am hoping to be able to work out a forbearance plan or loan modification so I can begin paying on a timely basis again. I have reviewed my finances, and I do want to be part of the solution. I need your help in order to save my home.

This approach has a few key phrases that will help your cause. You have stated you are aware of your available options (specifically forbearances and loan modifications, which I'll review shortly) without demanding a single thing. And, even though you have made a knowledgeable request, you are asking for their help. In addition to making this statement, you also need to be prepared to provide specific and detailed information about your situation, because a loss mitigation representative will ask *many* questions.

What types of questions should you prepare to answer?

- Why have you missed your payment?
- When can you make the next payment?
- Do you feel you will miss future payments? Why?
- What kind of hardship are you experiencing?
- If you have lost your job, how are you actively seeking employment?
- Will you be starting another job soon? What will your income be?
- What is your current household income?
- Do you have any savings or equity in your home?

- Do you have any other assets?

- What other debts do you have?

- Have you missed other payments for your car, credit cards, etc.?

- How many payments have you missed? What were the amounts?

- Are you behind in your homeowners insurance or real estate taxes?

- Have any liens or judgments been placed against your home?

- Do you have a detailed budget for how you will afford your mortgage and other expenses in the future?

In addition, the loss mitigation representative may ask you to provide documentation regarding your income, assets, debts, and current loan. You should gather and have ready:

- Your original loan documents

- Your most recent mortgage statement

- Your income tax returns for the past two years

- Your current pay stubs or other proof of your income

- Your current bank statements

- Documentation and proof of any assets

- A list of your debts and any debts that are secured by your home

- Information regarding any liens placed against your property

- Statements for your homeowners insurance and real estate taxes

## YOUR HARDSHIP LETTER

A loss mitigation representative may also ask you to prepare a *hardship letter*. A hardship letter, also known as a *letter of explanation*, describes the events or circumstances that have led to your missed mortgage payments, why assistance from your lender is necessary, and a proposed plan of action for your home. In your hardship letter, be straightforward and honest, but don't write a book. You'll want to be as short and concise as possible; lenders have many hardship letters to read, so your actual letter should be no more than one to two pages.

There may be a single event or several events that have led to your current situation. Just make sure you are very clear in outlining what has happened, whether your hardship is temporary or permanent, and your intentions to work diligently with the lender.

Many different circumstances could easily lead to missed mortgage payments. Maybe you have lost your job or experienced a loss in income due to the economy or current markets. Maybe your business has shut down or failed. Or maybe you have been away or out of the country for an extended period of time due to your job, or are actively serving in the military.

Hardships can also be medical in nature. You may have been ill, in an accident, or hospitalized. You may be unable to work or faced with medical bills. Or there may be circumstances involving your spouse or co-borrower that have affected your ability to pay, including illness, death, separation, or divorce. There may *even* have been a natural disaster or unforeseen event that has resulted in unexpected expenses or significant damage to your home.

Of course, your missed payments could also be the result of poor planning, plain and simple. After paying other bills and expenses, you may not have had enough money left over to pay your mortgage. You may not have saved enough to cover your mortgage during a hardship or an emergency. Or you may not have been prepared financially for interest rate or payment increases.

Whatever the reason for your hardship, be truthful. Don't be dramatic or exaggerate. You'll also want to provide additional documentation to back up the facts in your letter (such as termination notices, new job contracts, medical bills, accident reports, divorce decrees, financial budgets, etc.). With so many people experiencing true hardship, lenders can easily sniff out fact from fiction, so resist any temptation you may have to embellish your story.

 WEBLINK Are you having a hard time writing your hardship letter? I've provided step by step instructions and a sample letter in Appendix II. On my website you'll also find additional sample letters, and templates to help you write your hardship letter.

## *Working It Out With Your Lender*

Once you have provided full details regarding your hardship, your finances, and your situation, the real work begins. A lender will now determine what options might work for them, and for you. This is referred to as a *loan workout*: a series of steps taken by a lender with a borrower to resolve the problem of delinquent loan payments. In the early stages of pre-foreclosure, lenders will often consider several different workouts, including forbearances, loan modifications, repayment plans, and reinstatements. In my professional opinion, any of these options—or even a combination of them—is an excellent starting point for recovery.

### FORBEARANCE PLANS

With a *forbearance plan*, also called a *forbearance agreement*, a lender sets a period of time (usually about a year or less) during which your mortgage payments are reduced or suspended. Depending on the lender, you might be required to pay only a portion of your mortgage each month, or you may not have to pay your mortgage at all.

Before you get too excited, you should understand that this does not mean your lender has forgiven your debt. You still have to make all of your loan payments, just at a later time. Think of a forbearance plan as putting your mortgage on a temporary hold—you are given time to work through your hardship (and work on your finances) and during this time, you won't have to worry about your home going into foreclosure.

Forbearances are usually granted due to job loss or sudden financial difficulty. As a homeowner, this means you will need to show your lender how you will be able to afford the mortgage *after* the forbearance period ends. Remember, granting a forbearance has to make financial sense for the lender; your lender will want to make sure that you can pay back what you have deferred or skipped, and that you will also be able to go back to paying your mortgage in full and on time. At the end of your forbearance period, your lender may choose

## The Importance of Being Very Specific

If you can't make your mortgage payments for several months or can no longer afford your payment at all, you may think this is the last thing you want to tell your lender. But in reality, this is *exactly* what your lender needs to know. Be as specific as possible, and counter what you *can't* do with what you *can*. Are you currently out of work, but have another job lined up and need just a few months to get back on your feet? Do you have a future source of income that will enable you to get caught up in three, six, or nine months? If you can't afford your current payment, can you show a detailed budget showing what you can and will afford? Being specific about what you can commit to will only increase your negotiating power. Remember, being vague about your situation will only make your lender nervous. Once they know the facts, lenders will be more likely to assist you.

to reinstate your original mortgage with a repayment plan—temporarily increasing your payment to make up for what you owe—or your lender may add what you owe to your loan's balance and proceed forward with a loan modification to change the structure of your loan.

## LOAN MODIFICATIONS

A *loan modification* permanently changes the structure of your loan to lower your payments, making your mortgage more affordable. A lender may lower your interest rate, change the length of your loan (the term), change the loan program itself (for example, from an adjustable to a fixed rate loan), or even reduce your total loan amount. In some cases, a lender may do all of the above. Your lender's goal is to keep you in the mortgage so you will continue to make payments without another default.

Loan modifications are granted frequently, but often require that you aggressively negotiate with your lender. A lender will require proof that you have the ability to pay the mortgage if your payments are changed, and that there is a valid reason to modify the loan to begin with. Again, this is where a good hardship letter, and supporting documentation, is very important.

## REPAYMENT PLANS

If you fall behind with your mortgage and are unable to make up any missed payments, but you *are* able to start making regular payments again, your lender may choose to institute a *repayment plan*.

With a repayment plan, also referred to as a *reamortization plan*, a portion of the past due amount is added to your mortgage payment each month until the debt is paid in full. Of course, this means your mortgage payments, at least for a while, will increase; just how much is added to each mortgage payment will be determined by the lender.

Again, you need to carefully consider what you will be able to budget and afford. Even though you *can* afford to start making payments again right away, you may not be able to make higher payments. Your lender will let you know in advance what kind of payment structure they are considering. You don't want to agree to a repayment plan if the initial payments are too high and unaffordable, or you'll end up right back where you started—in default and faced with a quick foreclosure. If this is the case, be very candid with your lender. Some lenders, in addition to a repayment plan, will also modify your loan to allow for more affordable monthly payments, *and* for the repayment of what is past due.

## REINSTATEMENT PLANS

When you miss a payment, it is always a lender's goal for you to become current on your mortgage as quickly as possible. If you are able to borrow funds, or if you know you will be able to eventually pay what you owe, your lender may consider a *reinstatement plan*. With a reinstatement, you promise to pay your lender a lump sum that includes the past due amount, plus any penalties and late fees imposed by the lender, by a certain date.

A lender knows that you don't have the money right now, or else you wouldn't have missed your payment in the first place. But lenders also know that given some time—and the right motivation—you might be able to take a loan from family or friends, sell some of your assets, or liquefy your stocks or other investments. In return for the lump payment, the lender reinstates your original loan as if nothing had happened.

A reinstatement can also be used in combination with other loss mitigation options, including a loan modification. Your lender may modify your loan, giving you new payments that are more affordable, and also require that you pay any missed payments and fees at a later date in one lump sum.

## Review Your Finances and Develop a Plan

Now that you understand some of your options, you need to take a look at your finances. Would a forbearance help you? What type of loan modification would you need? Could you pay what you owe later in one lump sum? Before you begin to negotiate with your lender, you'll want to do your homework. In Chapters 8 and 10, I'll show you how you can develop a budget for current and future expenses, and I also provide many tools on my website for budgeting and planning in general. Create a budget you can stick to, and then use this budget to determine what mortgage payment you can afford.

Next, you'll want to research interest rates, just like you did when you were shopping for your loan. Use the mortgage calculator on my website to determine how interest rates and loan terms will affect your monthly payment, and what combinations will yield you a payment you can afford. This way, if a lender speaks with you about modifying your loan's interest rate and term, you'll know what you will be able to commit to.

Here's an example: Let's say you have thoroughly reviewed your finances and have determined you can afford to pay a maximum of $900 a month for your mortgage. But you are still behind on many of your bills, and you could really use some additional breathing room. So you ask your lender for a forbearance for a set period of time to be followed by a loan modification, modifying your loan so your mortgage payments are around $900 a month.

During the forbearance period, you will apply what you would have been paying for your mortgage towards your other bills. And when you *do* start to make mortgage payments again, you'll know they are payments you can afford, because you have worked out the terms of your loan modification in advance.

With any type of loan workout, the more forthright you are with your lender about your current situation and future income, the more likely you are to receive a reworked payment schedule *you can afford*. If your finances are tight, the last thing you want to do is to negotiate an agreement with your lender and then not be able to live up to your end of it. This won't sit well with the lender, and will cause serious problems for you down the line (and by serious problems, I mean foreclosure). So again, be specific, and be truthful. If you need some time to get back on your feet, ask. If you can't afford something, do not say you can.

## While You Wait . . .

Even in good times, the loan workout process will most likely take at least several weeks and many, many conversations with the loss mitigation department. In some cases, negotiations with your lender could take many months, as lenders will often require you to submit documentation, complete their own loss mitigation applications, or simply provide more information. Be sure everything you send to your lender is very complete and thorough. A slight mistake or misstep in the process could delay the timing of your assistance significantly, and this can be a serious matter: if you are unable to make your mortgage payments during this period, some lenders may *continue* to report your mortgage as late—and this means that your credit score may drop further, despite your efforts to work something out with your lender.

No matter how long or frustrating the process is, remember, loss mitigation representatives are people too. They are usually overworked and stressed. Anything you can do to make their job easier will go a long way. And the easier it is to work with you, the more likely it is that your representative will want to help you to save your home.

While you are waiting to hear back from your lender, what other things can you do?

▸ **Make any mortgage payment you can, even if it is only a partial payment.** If you have the ability to do so, pay your lender whatever you can. Even a partial payment will prove to the lender again that you want to make the situation right. Partial payments are usually accepted on a case-by-case basis, so be sure to discuss this option with your loss mitigation representative. If you make partial payments without checking with your lender first, these payments may actually be returned to you; some lenders won't accept partial payments because they can be legally misconstrued as *acceptable* payment. If your payments are returned, set them aside in savings so they can be responsibly used to pay your mortgage after your lender has modified your loan.

As another sign of good faith, you can also attempt to send a separate check to specifically pay for any late fees you have incurred. Again, check with your loss mitigation representative first.

▸ **Request foreclosure counseling services.** There are many nonprofit organizations and certified counselors who will be able to assist you in understanding the legal steps of mortgage default and fore-closure, and many will be able to provide assistance in working with your lender's loss mitigation department. Government certified agencies and counselors will also be able to help you determine if there are any government foreclosure prevention programs, loans, or resources that can help you. National programs include:

**Hope Now Alliance and**
**The Homeownership Preservation Foundation**
(888) 995-HOPE | www.hopenow.com | www.995hope.org
*24/7 free foreclosure assistance*

**Certified H.U.D. Housing Counselors**
(800) 569-4287 | www.hud.gov
*Advice, state resources, and government-approved counseling*
*agencies near you*

**Neighborworks America**
(202) 220-2300 | www.nw.org
*Foreclosure information, resources, and counseling agencies near you*

▸    **Seek legal counsel or assistance.** Your lender will be considering loan workouts that work for them, but you also want to be sure the workout works for you, and that your own interests are protected. Many states and state bar associations offer a free or low-cost legal review of your situation and legal aid in securing a loan workout, as well as general foreclosure advice and legal representation.

    For low or no cost legal aid in your area, visit www.hud.gov. You can also find links to various legal resources, by state, in the reader's resources section of my website.

▸    **Keep detailed records.** Make sure to take notes on all conversations with your lender, including names of representatives, times, and dates. Keep copies of anything you fax, email, or mail, and keep a paper trail of any mortgage or late fee payments you make. And be sure to store everything in one place, so you can readily provide information when asked. You can use the worksheet I've provided in Appendix II to help keep track of your communication with your lender, and you can also print out an expanded version of this worksheet from my website.

When working with your lender toward saving your home, there is one rule you must always follow: you must put forth the effort. Remember, your lender did not force you to sign a mortgage. You may have been misled by an unscrupulous mortgage broker who didn't fully explain the details of your loan. You may be a victim of job loss or health issues. You may be unable to refinance your mortgage due to your home's value. Believe me, I understand. Just keep in mind that the reasons for your default are usually not the lender's fault, but the lender is still willing to help you. You may not get the answers you want immediately, but by putting forth the effort and being persistent, you can often save your home *and* put yourself in a much better financial position, no matter what your circumstance. This is exactly what one of my clients, Sam Snow, was able to do.

---

### SAM SNOW'S AVALANCHE

Sam Snow was a client I worked with in early 2003. He was a man who seemed to know exactly what he wanted out of his real estate investments, and he made it very clear that he never wanted to stay in a home longer than a few years. After a home appreciated in value, he would move on to the next home, tapping the first home's equity for the next home's down payment. Sam had a ten-year plan, and he was very set in his ways.

To make this plan happen, Sam had his eye on a few adjustable rate loans that had very low initial interest rates. The loan Sam was most interested in was called a 2/28 ARM; it had a low, fixed interest rate for two years, and after the two-year period was up, the interest rate would adjust each month. This particular loan had a very high margin, so once the loan adjusted, the interest rate (and payments) could potentially be very high. If Sam stayed in the home for more than two years, and if interest rates rose, he would be stuck with a monster of a payment.

Even with this possibility, Sam was adamant in requesting this loan— he wanted the lowest rate available and planned to sell right before the loan adjusted. It was risky. I warned Sam about the risks over and over, and I even pointed out a few holes in Sam's investment strategy. But there was no advising Sam Snow. Sam eventually got what he wanted: a 2/28 ARM with an interest rate of 4.375 percent fixed for the first two years, which was a very low rate at the time. Sam told me I did a great job for him and that I would see him again in two years.

In early 2005, Sam was back. This was at the height of the real estate boom, and Sam had doubled his profits from the home he purchased in 2003. He had also decided to purchase a bigger and more expensive home as his next two-year residence. Sam wanted another 2/28 adjustable rate mortgage that carried an interest rate of 4.75 percent.

This time around, I had to sit Sam down. Taking a chance with such a risky loan was going to get riskier: real estate values had to level off at some point, and the home inventory was beginning to pile up, which would make selling his next home even harder. I eventually got to the point where I refused to help Sam with his loan. Sam shrugged off my advice again and stuck to his plan, and went to another broker who was more than happy to help. As prepared as Sam felt he was when it came to mortgage payments, time periods, and his real estate strategies, I had a strong feeling I would soon see Sam again.

Sure enough, a little over two years later, Sam Snow did contact me again—only this time Sam was in a bind and wasn't sure what to do. He explained that he should have used more caution the last time around: the home he purchased in early 2005 was not getting any offers. His 2005 prices were suddenly overpriced by 2007 standards. I was able to do some research and quick math: Sam's area had been hit by the housing bubble, and there was also an inventory issue—there were far too many homes for sale in his area. To make matters worse, it was past Sam's magic two-year mark, and Sam's loan had already adjusted several times. His payment had already increased by $985 dollars and was increasing every month. Sam had planned to ride it out until the home sold, but it was quickly becoming very clear that this wasn't going to happen any time soon. Sam wasn't prepared for the avalanche.

Sam recognized his mistakes. He wanted to stay in his home but he simply couldn't afford it any longer. He had missed his most recent mortgage payment, was about to miss his second payment, and was technically in default. This time, Sam decided to take my advice. Sam needed to contact his lender immediately. I explained exactly how he should approach and work with his lender and added that I would be available should he need additional advice on any of the lender's proposals.

For several weeks, Sam called and updated me on his progress. Eventually, Sam was able to have his loan modified to a 30-year fixed rate loan at a 6 percent interest rate. The lender required that Sam become current with all late fees and penalties, and his missed payments were tacked on to his total loan amount, by being recalculated into his new payment. By late 2007, Sam was able to save his home, and his loan modification yielded him a more affordable payment, and a better financial position overall. Sam was happy, and, frankly, so was I.

---

Sam's motivation to keep his home kept him involved with his lender until there was a resolution, and even though Sam made poor decisions, he was able to show the lender how he would be responsible going forward. Sam's lender was a large, national lender who obviously had the flexibility and the desire to salvage the loan. And by doing so, the lender kept a client, continued to receive mortgage payments, and avoided foreclosure costs. Sam's story provides hope for many homeowners, and may easily provide some hope for you. Just remember, if Sam can do it, you may be able to as well.

## Your Second Missed Payment and Notice of Default

With your first month's missed payment, the foreclosure countdown starts. But what if you've already missed more than one payment? As unfortunate as it is to be caught in the initial stage of a mortgage default, it pales in comparison to what happens in the later stages of foreclosure. Once you've missed more than one payment, you will receive a notification of your default, and with continued missed payments, this will be followed by a notification of foreclosure, and, eventually, your home will be sold at auction.

This entire process can sometimes happen in as little as a few months, so you want to act while you still have time. How fast the clock is ticking is determined by state law; to get an idea of how much time you have, refer to Appendix II.

What can you expect with your second missed payment?

| | |
|---|---|
| Level 5 | Your mortgage payments are current. Your home is safe. |
| Level 4 | You miss your first mortgage payment.<br>*Your lender attempts to contact you.* |
| **Level 3** | **You miss a second mortgage payment.**<br>***Your lender sends a notice of default.*** |
| Level 2 | You miss three or more mortgage payments.<br>*Your lender sends a notice of foreclosure.* |
| Level 1 | The foreclosure is final. Your home is sold at auction.<br>*You receive an eviction notice and must move from your home.* |

▸   Once you miss your second mortgage payment, you are still considered to be in default. By now your lender should have made several attempts to contact you to make you aware of your delinquency. If they haven't, it doesn't mean they haven't noticed—it usually just means your lender is backlogged with other defaults and foreclosures.

▸ After your second missed payment is thirty days late, your credit will be marked with a second thirty-day past due strike. If you haven't paid your first missed payment, your previous thirty-day strike now becomes a sixty-day strike. The balance owed has doubled and by now your credit rating has plummeted by at least 100 to 150 points.

▸ If you escrow your real estate taxes and homeowners insurance, after two missed payments, you most likely won't have enough funds put aside to pay these bills when they are due—which means you will be faced with even higher mortgage payments to make up this difference.

If there isn't enough in your escrow account to pay your taxes, your lender will most likely pay the difference and add the cost to your mortgage payments. And if there isn't enough money in your escrow account to renew your existing homeowners insurance, a lender may take out their *own* insurance policy and charge you for it. This policy is monthly and expensive, and will protect the lender, not you as a homeowner. In Chapter 10, I'll cover what happens when a lender takes over your insurance, and how you can protect yourself and make the best decisions regarding your escrows.

▸ Generally, after your second missed payment, a lender will send you a formal *notice of default* (NOD), detailing the amount that is delinquent and how many days you will be given to "cure" the default before the lender proceeds forward with a foreclosure. In some states, lenders are required to reach you in person before they can file this notice; in other states, lenders are not required to even try to contact you at all! In either case, once this notice has been filed, you've moved from Defcon Level 4 to Level 3 and are one step closer to foreclosure.

Depending on state law, your notice of default may arrive one of several ways: a letter may be sent via certified mail, a notice may be posted on your home itself (usually on the front door), information about your default may be published in your local paper, or a lis pendens may be filed in public records.

> **MORE INFO** **I've Already Received a Notice of Default.**
> **Can I Still Save My Home?**
>
> While a notice of default is a formal—and legal—notification, it does not by itself prevent a homeowner from being able to save their home. A notice of default will not stop a lender from agreeing to a loan workout, and it should certainly not stop you from contacting your lender. If anything, it should let you know your lender is serious; a notice of default is required in many states to start the process of foreclosure, which is even more reason to contact the loss mitigation department right away.

A *lis pendens*, as I mentioned in the last chapter, is a recorded legal notice; it means that the lender has filed a complaint with the courts stating that you haven't paid your mortgage, and the lender is taking legal steps to initiate a foreclosure. Lis pendens means "lawsuit in progress." Filing the complaint means the lender has filed a lawsuit against you, so you should take this notice very seriously. If the lender wins the lawsuit, they will be awarded the foreclosure. Your lender will let you know that a lis pendens has been filed, and you can also search for these records online with your county or state's public records site. Once you are in county records, search by your name as it appears on your mortgage and title.

With all of these ways to be notified, how do you know which one your lender will use? It all goes back to state law. Individual states determine how you are notified, the steps that must be taken by both the borrower and the lender, how long the process takes, and whether the foreclosure process will be take place in or out of court.

 **WEBLINK** In Appendix II, I've provided a general overview of what you can expect in your state, and you can also learn more about your state's laws on my website.

## Other Foreclosure Solutions

In this and previous chapters, I've spent a lot of time discussing how you should work directly with your lender, whether you have missed a mortgage payment or are simply concerned about your mortgage in general. I strongly believe that your efforts should always be directed toward modifying your existing mortgage first. Some other foreclosure experts, however, suggest trying to refinance into a new loan once you find yourself in default.

### *Refinancing*

Can a refinance be used to help save your home? Technically, yes. If planned correctly (and if planned *well in advance*, long before you actually miss a payment and start heading down the road to foreclosure), a traditional refinance can be used to make your mortgage more affordable. But it's important to realize that this is usually a complicated solution and only works in certain situations.

First, you must be able to qualify for the refinance, and, honestly, most people who are experiencing any form of financial hardship will usually have a difficult time qualifying for most loans. Refinancing also costs money. Requesting a loan modification from your own lender will have the same end result as a refinance, but it usually will cost very little, sometimes as little as your own time and effort. In addition, your home also needs to "qualify" for the refinance. As you have learned, your new lender will carefully examine your home's value, as well as the condition of your local real estate market. If you are in a declining market, or if you currently owe much more than your home is worth, your options for refinancing are limited. And once you miss mortgage payments, your options for financing get worse:

▸   If you have missed mortgage payments, conventional lenders will usually not lend you their money. Lenders will look back over your credit history for a full twelve months, searching for late payments to determine if you are a candidate for a loan. If you have missed even one payment, your application will be denied.

▸ With missed mortgage payments, a mortgage broker may be able to provide you with a "band-aid" refinance or second mortgage, but these loans are far from ideal. Band-aid loans are typically *hard money loans* (also called hard equity loans) from a *hard money lender*. Hard money lenders will lend to you—even if you have missed mortgage payments and have been turned down by conventional lenders, but only at very high interest rates, accompanied by high fees and pre-payment penalties. Hard money lenders got their name by having these "hard" terms, and also by lending to borrowers who have a hard time getting financing elsewhere.

If you decide to take out a hard equity loan and then miss a payment, hard money lenders will *not* work with you on any type of loan workout, and will most likely begin foreclosure proceedings immediately. They *will not hesitate* to take your home, and because of this, hard money lenders should always be considered a lender of last resort.

So how do you know if you are dealing with this type of lender? Your broker should always tell you, but if he or she doesn't, there are several things you can easily look for. Hard money loans usually have interest rates of 10 percent or higher, will *not* be over 65 percent of your home's appraised value, and will include a prepayment penalty for at least one year. In addition, hard money lenders will usually charge a minimum of 2 additional points for your loan as a "lender fee," which will be payable upon closing. (This is in addition to any fees your broker may be charging you as well!) If you receive a Good Faith Estimate with most of these characteristics, you can be fairly sure the loan is a hard money loan. Just to be sure, ask.

## Foreclosure Help from the Government

Outside of working directly with your lender, the best opportunity for assistance lies with the government. The government is continuously instituting new guidelines and incentives for lenders to work with you to modify or refinance your existing loan. Earlier in this chapter, I talked about how the government's Making Home Affordable program may be able to help you, even if you have missed payments. In addition to this assistance, the government also provides foreclosure prevention if you have a government-insured loan.

If you currently have an FHA or VA loan, the government will go out of its way to help prevent foreclosure. As you learned in Chapters 3 and 4, FHA and VA loans are insured by the government, and in the case of default or foreclosure, the government is partially responsible. If you find that your lender is not willing to work with you regarding a loan workout, call the FHA and VA directly for assistance—they will be able to pull strings with your lender that you cannot:

**Federal Housing Administration**

(800) CALL-FHA  |  (800) 225-5342  |  www.fhasecure.gov

**Department of Veterans Affairs**

(877) 827-3702  |  www.va.gov

In addition, your local and state government may also be able to help. Many cities and states offer their own foreclosure prevention resources, counseling, assistance funds, and emergency grants for residents. For example, the city of West Palm Beach, Florida, helps those living within city limits by offering up to $10,000 in repayable emergency assistance for missed or upcoming mortgage payments. The state of Delaware offers low-interest loans to those who have fallen behind in their mortgage due to job loss, divorce, or disability.

Stay hopeful—there is more help available than you may realize. To find similar programs in your area, check with your city and state government representatives, or on your city and state websites, for foreclosure assistance programs that may be available to you. And check my website often; I'll be sure to outline any resources or opportunities that may be available to you.

Have you been helped by a city or state program? This is your chance to help others. Log in to the reader's section of my website, and send me a message with your name, the program name, your city, and your state. I'll be sure to post the information on my website and blog. With your help, together we can provide other homeowners with a similar opportunity, and you personally could help someone else to save their home.

# Default and Foreclosure

## Part II: Foreclosure

*The Eye of the Storm*

If you can look at your finances and develop a plan to get back on your feet, your lender will most likely listen and negotiate with you. But when you look at your finances, and you take a look several months down the road, you may see nothing but additional hardship. Or you may look ahead and see that your finances are likely to become even worse than they are now. If you see months and months of missed mortgage payments ahead, it may be time to take a hard look at the reality of your situation.

If you worked out a loan modification or repayment plan with your lender, would you still be able to afford the payments—or would you quickly slip back into default? Would a special forbearance be a solution—or would it just be a way to live mortgage-free for a few months? You may now be faced with making some difficult decisions regarding your home, and it may be time to ask yourself some tough questions. Take a minute—and take a step back—to look at the big picture. Read and answer these questions truthfully. No one but you will know the answers:

- Can I truly afford my home?
- Is there any way I can become current with my payments?
- Do I want to work out a new loan payment plan?
- Do I want to keep my home?

Sometimes, even when you want to keep your home you may not be able to. It's also possible that you may not *want* to keep your home, and that's okay. Your mortgage could be just one of many issues. Are you extended beyond belief with credit card debt or school loans? Are you behind with many of your other bills? Have your savings and retirement accounts been completely depleted?

As hard as it may be to admit, there may not be a way to save your home. You may have to shift your focus to saving what you can. It's at this point that you need to consider other options. Foreclosure isn't the only answer, though. There are other solutions, including a short sale, a deed in lieu, and bankruptcy, where you can cushion the blow of giving up your home. Let's take a look at what you should do next.

## First, Ask for Help

The first step, no matter what you do, is to ask for legal help. I recommended doing so at earlier stages, but once you decide it's time to give up your home, it becomes even more important. "Giving up your home" sounds simple, but in reality it can be complicated, and you will want to protect your own interests as much as possible. Before proceeding any further, you'll want to seek non-profit legal assistance or legal representation.

Having legal representation will help you in many ways. A lawyer or non-profit agency will be able to help in your final negotiations with your lender. There are several ways a lender can take possession of your home (which I'll explain next) that don't involve a formal foreclosure, and, in any of these, there are legal considerations, paperwork, and consequences to consider. You will want to make sure that whatever you work out with the lender not only satisfies the lender's requirements but also legally protects you, and ensures that you are no longer responsible for the home or your mortgage in any way.

If foreclosure is inevitable, you'll also need to seek legal counsel to fully comply with foreclosure proceedings. Foreclosure can often be confusing, and because procedures are different in every state, you will need someone to help guide you through the process. Visit my website for a list of non-profit agencies that can help you. You can also go back to the U.S. Department of Housing and Urban Development's website at www.hud.gov to search for legal help in your area, or you can search with your local or state bar associations at www.abanet.org.

If your finances are in very bad shape and foreclosure is just one of your concerns, you may also need to seek advice about the possibility of a bankruptcy. The two practices usually overlap, and many foreclosure attorneys will also be familiar with bankruptcy law and protection, which I'll discuss at the end of this chapter.

MORE INFO **Choosing the Right Attorney**

When you are faced with foreclosure, it's very important to set some time aside to find the right attorney. Use the following list of questions to narrow down your search to the most-qualified applicants:

- How long have you been practicing law?
- How long have you been practicing in my state and county?
- What percentage of your practice is dedicated to foreclosures?
- About how many foreclosure cases do you handle a year?
- How much do you charge per hour? (rates generally range from $100 to $300 per hour)
- Are you able to provide an estimate?
- How can I communicate with you? (email, telephone, in person)
- Are you available after hours?
- Do you have any references?

## A Short Sale

If you have tried to work things out with your lender and a loan work-out was denied or was not realistic, or you have determined you can no longer afford your home, ask your loss mitigation representative if they will consider a *short sale* of your home. Here's how a short sale works. Let's say you owe $230,000 on your home. However, in your local real estate market, you would be lucky to sell your home for $150,000—the market value is far less than your loan amount. A short sale is when your lender allows you to sell the property for less than what you owe—and accepts the proceeds of the sale as payment *in full*.

A short sale has other benefits, too, especially for your credit. Although any missed mortgage payments will damage your credit, a short sale itself will usually damage your credit less than a foreclosure. Generally, with a foreclosure, your credit score will drop by 250 to 300 points. But if your lender *agrees* to report that your short sale has paid your debt in full, the hit to your credit could be much less, sometimes as little as 50 to 80 points (on top of any decrease in your credit from missed payments).

Another benefit is that lenders will allow you to live in the home during the short sale process, *even if* you cannot make your mortgage payments. I personally know several homeowners who have been able to live in their homes for a full year or more, mortgage free, while their homes were on the market as short sales. How is this possible? A lender cannot evict you from a property they do not yet own (to evict you, a lender has to proceed forward with a foreclosure). Of course, it is also easier for a lender to sell a home that is maintained, so this arrangement benefits lenders as well.

Short sales are becoming more and more common as lenders weigh their options. Lenders know they will usually lose money in a foreclosure. By accepting a short sale, a lender will receive some money for the home and will also avoid the costs that come with taking possession of a home, such as prepping the home for sale, the cost of selling the home, and waiting to sell the home. If your lender

## When "As Is" Is Anything But

Keep in mind, a short sale contract needs to be structured correctly. Most lenders will accept a short sale "as is"—the sale is final, and you are released from both the burden of your home and your mortgage. Your loan is forgiven, in full. However in some cases, a lender may accept a short sale, but will try to recoup or hold you responsible for the difference between the sale price and the loan payoff. For example, say you owe your lender $200,000. Your lender accepts a $160,000 short sale. Depending on the structure of the short sale agreement, you could be left with a bill for the $40,000.

If the lender *does* forgive the debt, you'll also want to make sure you won't be taxed on it. Depending on your situation, Uncle Sam may view the forgiven debt as "income," which would be subject to capital gains tax. The Mortgage Forgiveness Debt Relief Act of 2007 exempts the majority of homeowners from this tax, but there are still IRS guidelines to follow. Overall, this is why it is vital to retain legal counsel (and even get advice from a tax specialist) before entering into any agreement with your lender. Be sure you fully understand your responsibilities— and always read the fine print.

agrees to proceed with a short sale, a real estate agent, who may be appointed by the lender, will be contracted to sell your home (sometimes a lender will allow you to select this realtor yourself). The final sale price for your home will be determined or approved by the lender.

Some lenders determine the final sales price and terms for the short sale *first*, based on recent sales in the area. Other lenders will see what offers come in and then decide what final sales price they will accept. This process varies from lender to lender and can often extend the short sale process from weeks to months, as lenders receive, review, and reject offers.

Keep in mind that when a lender finally does determine a price, it will usually be a *net* price. This is the amount a lender will expect for your home after any real estate commissions or fees related to the sale are paid, and is an important consideration if your lender allows you to hire your own real estate agent. For example, say your lender will accept $150,000 (net) as a short sale, but real estate commissions and other fees total $10,000. In this case, the final sales price would need to be at least $160,000.

With your home officially on the market, the real estate agent will work directly with your lender, receiving and submitting any offers that come through on the property. Ultimately your lender, not you, has the final say in accepting or rejecting a short sale offer. Of course, the success of a short sale relies on one very important detail: finding a buyer. In markets where inventory is high and too many homes are for sale, a lender may eventually decide *not* to wait for a sale. A lender may decide it is in their best financial interests to pursue a loan workout with you, or they may decide to proceed forward with foreclosure. This is why constant communication with your lender is still vital even at this stage of the game.

## A Deed in Lieu of Foreclosure

Another approach you can take with your lender is to ask for a *deed in lieu of foreclosure*. As you'll remember from the last chapter, your deed directly involves your ownership rights to your property. With a deed in lieu, you arrange to give your home back to the lender by transferring the deed, giving your lender title and full ownership of your home immediately.

In exchange for the deed, your lender agrees not to foreclose on the property. This is good news for you in many ways. First, a deed in lieu will relieve you of *all* responsibility. You will no longer own your home, but you won't be responsible for it either, and you will no longer be responsible for your mortgage or any past due mortgage payments or fees. The slate is wiped clean, and you will have a resolution sooner than if the lender proceeded forward with a fore-closure.

Second, if structured correctly, a deed in lieu of foreclosure can also be used to prevent additional damage to your credit, which by now has taken a significant hit from late and missed mortgage payments. Technically, a deed in lieu states that all indebtedness is released; you have made good on your mortgage by turning over your home. With some negotiation, your lender may agree to report to the credit agencies that your debt has been "paid in full," and this fact can sometimes be used by an aggressive credit attorney to repair and restore your credit much faster than would be possible with a foreclosure. This can make a deed in lieu an even better option for you.

How do you start the process for a deed in lieu? It all goes back to lender communication. Lenders usually will require that all other options be exhausted before considering a deed in lieu, including loan workouts and trying to sell your home at fair market value. And as with any decision a lender makes, your lender will also carefully analyze if a deed in lieu makes financial sense for them.

- For you, a deed in lieu makes the most sense when you have *little or no* equity in your home: when you hand over your home to your lender, you are also handing over your equity. The less equity you have, the less you have to lose.

- For the lender, the opposite is true. A lender will view a deed in lieu as a more favorable option if you have *more* equity in your home. They get your home, and the equity, and they can use this equity to offset the costs of selling your home after they take ownership.

Depending on how much you owe, and how much your home is worth, there may also be tax implications or even government regulation that comes into play. Just like with a short sale, you'll want to be sure you are not taxed on any forgiven debt. Deeds in lieu are also subject to higher government scrutiny: if your home's market value is much more than your loan amount, or you have a significant amount in equity in your home, the government could view a deed in lieu as predatory, and in these cases a lender will be more likely to consider a loan workout with you instead. When you add up protecting your credit, avoiding taxes, and considering your equity (if any), it's easy to see why it's important that both you *and* your legal counsel work together with your lender regarding this option.

---

MORE INFO

### How to Give Up Your Home AND Preserve Your Credit

You may be paying your mortgage to preserve your credit, but you know you can no longer afford your home. Will your lender still consider a short sale or deed in lieu? Not always, but some will. Many lenders will begin loan workout negotiations with you *before* you miss any payments, and, in these cases, you can come to an agreement for a short sale or deed in lieu (or any other solution your lender may offer) without missing a payment—and if your lender accepts the payments—without damaging your credit. This gives you great power. If you are also able to legally negotiate how your lender reports the short sale or deed in lieu sale on your credit, you may be able to give up your home with very little damage to your credit at all. Again, this is why it is a great idea to start communicating with your lender as soon as possible.

---

## Bankruptcy Protection

Your very last option involves bankruptcy protection. If you are faced with losing your home—and you also are experiencing extreme financial hardship—bankruptcy may be a way to save what you have left, and can sometimes be used to save your home. Although I still strongly suggest you do whatever you can to work together with your lender regarding your mortgage, you may want to begin to familiarize yourself with what bankruptcy means, the types of bankruptcy, and what bankruptcy options are available to you. A bankruptcy attorney can thoroughly explain and help you to understand the benefits of the most common forms of individual bankruptcy, which are known as Chapter 7 and Chapter 13. I'll provide a general overview for you here.

If you are having trouble paying your bills and your debts are mounting up, bankruptcy is a way to restructure or erase your debt. Many people think of bankruptcy as an easy way to press a reset button and start over. But bankruptcy is not a solve-all, and since the Bankruptcy Reform Act of 2005, the process of applying and being approved for bankruptcy protection has become more difficult.

Contrary to popular belief, bankruptcy does not mean that your debts will automatically be wiped clean. Depending on your individual circumstance—including variables like your income, assets, and total debt—you may be required to pay back some of your debt, including your mortgage.

Bankruptcy is sometimes used as a tactic to save your home, but it doesn't always work. A bankruptcy will always *stall* an impending foreclosure, but it might not help you to keep your home. This is an important distinction.

Here's a look at the process: once you file a petition for bankruptcy, you are granted an *automatic stay of relief*, which temporarily prevents your lender from foreclosing on your home. Although filing for either a Chapter 7 or Chapter 13 bankruptcy will protect your home against foreclosure and immediately stop foreclosure proceedings, it may only be a reprieve. In fact, a Chapter 7 bankruptcy filing may make it harder to keep your home in the long run.

## Chapter 7 Bankruptcy

Chapter 7 is a *liquidation bankruptcy*. It involves the complete liquidation of your property and assets to pay your creditors, it wipes out any remaining debts, and gives you a fresh start. How does this work? An assigned or court-appointed trustee gathers and sells all of your nonexempt assets. Nonexempt assets vary from state to state, but they usually include your bank accounts, stocks or bonds, tax refunds, vehicles, real estate, jewelry, collectibles, and other personal property. The trustee sells what they need to, and then uses the total funds to pay your creditors. If you don't have enough assets to pay your creditors in full, whatever debts remain are wiped clean.

How does your home factor into this equation? In most cases, you will *not* be able to keep your home in a Chapter 7 bankruptcy. Your home will either be sold to pay your creditors, or the judge will proceed forward with the foreclosure proceedings, turning your home back over to the lender.

But in some states, you *may* be allowed to keep your primary residence through Chapter 7 by signing a *reaffirmation agreement*. This agreement is a new contract between you and your lender reaffirming your debt and personal liability. Most lenders will only sign a reaffirmation agreement if you are current on your mortgage payments, and you don't have much equity in the home. (If you had equity in your home, the lender would want the equity turned over to them as repayment.) If, and only if, this agreement is approved by the court, you will be able to continue to make mortgage payments and continue to live in your home. In most cases, however, you should expect that you won't be able to keep your home if you file for Chapter 7.

Chapter 7 bankruptcies aren't for everyone: although Chapter 7 accounts for 70 percent of consumer bankruptcy filings, not everyone can qualify. In fact, if you make more than the median income in your state, your income alone will usually disqualify you. A Chapter 7 bankruptcy is best suited for people who don't have a steady source of income, have few assets, and cannot afford (and do not want to keep) their primary residence. If you want to keep your home, you'll usually want to consider a Chapter 13 filing instead.

## Chapter 13 Bankruptcy

A Chapter 13 bankruptcy is often referred to as a *reorganization bankruptcy*. To be considered for Chapter 13 protection, you must have a steady and reliable source of income. You will also be required to submit all of your financial records to the courts. These records include your income, assets, expenses, debts, and a plan to pay your creditors. This information will be processed and refined into a repayment plan, based on your individual circumstances and income.

In most cases, you can expect that for a period of three to five years, *all* of your income will go toward basic living expenses and re-paying your debts. Each month, you will be required to make predetermined payments to a court-appointed trustee, who then distributes the funds among your creditors and your lender. After the initial three to five year period ends, your remaining debt could be completely wiped out—or the payments could remain. It all depends on state laws, the individual, the creditors and the judge—many final details are determined on a case by case basis.

In any bankruptcy, you can expect for the courts to determine what you can and can't do, what is affordable, and what you should pay. But if you follow the court's rules, you can not only restructure your debt but also keep your home. If you meet the requirements for Chapter 13 and a bankruptcy is granted, all collection efforts will stop. You will no longer have to worry about future foreclosure proceedings. As long as the Chapter 13 bankruptcy is active and in place, and as long as you are making your payments, your home will be saved.

---

 MORE INFO · **The Accountability Bankruptcy**

I like to call Chapter 13 "The Accountability Bankruptcy." Many who file for Chapter 13 protection feel responsible for their debts, and when all else fails, they do the right thing by seeking protection, but also by owning up to what they owe. There is no shame in seeking refuge here.

---

Both forms of bankruptcy have their pros and cons. Bankruptcy laws have also changed over the years, so it goes without saying that you will always want to consult with an attorney to understand the process and consequences of filing either Chapter 7 or Chapter 13. Bankruptcies are serious business, so much so that they remain on your credit for up to ten years. Before proceeding, you also want to be sure you have truly exhausted all other viable avenues to save your home. Many people mistakenly believe that using bankruptcy to save their home is an easy fix. This couldn't be further from the truth. Bankruptcy is not easy. Bankruptcy is your *one last chance* to keep up with your payments. After bankruptcy, there are no other options. There are no second or third chances. Truly, bankruptcy should always be considered your final, and last, choice.

## Your Third Missed Payment and Notice of Foreclosure

If you are unable to work out an alternative to foreclosure with your lender, if you haven't responded back to your lender in time, or if you have decided you have no other option but to wait for the inevitable, you eventually will receive a *notice of foreclosure* (in some states this notice is called a notice of sale or a judgment of foreclosure).

---

| | |
|---|---|
| Level 5 | Your mortgage payments are current. Your home is safe. |
| Level 4 | You miss your first mortgage payment. *Your lender attempts to contact you.* |
| Level 3 | You miss a second mortgage payment. *Your lender sends a notice of default.* |
| **Level 2** | **You miss three or more mortgage payments.** ***Your lender sends a notice of foreclosure.*** |
| Level 1 | The foreclosure is final. Your home is sold at auction. *You receive an eviction notice and must move from your home.* |

---

I've included a sample of what this may look like in Figure 7.1. A notice of foreclosure is generally sent after your third missed mortgage payment, but it can be sent at any time. Some lenders may do so as

### NOTICE OF MORTGAGE FORECLOSURE SALE

THE RIGHT TO VERIFICATION OF THE DEBT AND IDENTITY OF THE ORIGINAL
CREDITOR WITHIN THE TIME PROVIDED BY LAW IS NOT AFFECTED BY THIS ACTION.

NOTICE IS HEREBY GIVEN: That default has occurred in the conditions
of the following described mortgage:

DATE OF MORTGAGE: December 1, 2005
ORIGINAL PRINCIPAL AMOUNT OF MORTGAGE:
Ninety-thousand and 00/100 dollars ($90,000.00)
MORTGAGOR(S): John Homeowner
MORTGAGEE: ABC Lending
DATE AND PLACE OF FILING: Filed January 19, 2009, Smith County Recorder;
Document No. A-12345
ASSIGNMENTS OF MORTGAGE: Mortgage Registration Systems,Inc.

LEGAL DESCRIPTION OF PROPERTY: ALL OF LOT TEN (10), IN BLOCK EIGHT (8), IN HERITAGE
VILLAGE, A PLANNED UNIT DEVELOPMENT, ACCORDING TO THE PLAT RECORDED IN PLAT
BOOK 55, PAGE 27. PARCEL ID#: 12-34-56-78-90-000-123

COUNTY IN WHICH PROPERTY IS LOCATED: Smith County
THE AMOUNT CLAIMED TO BE DUE ON THE MORTGAGE ON THE DATE OF THE NOTICE: Seventy-
two thousand, eight hundred sixty-eight and 65/100 dollars ($72,868.65).

THAT no action or proceeding has been instituted at law to recover the debt secured by said
mortgage, or any part thereof; that there has been compliance with all pre-foreclosure notice
and acceleration requirements of said mortgage, and/or applicable statutes;

PURSUANT, to the power of sale contained in said mortgage, the above described property
will be sold by the Sheriff of said county as follows:

*AUCTION DATE* →

**DATE AND TIME OF SALE: March 23, 2009 at 10:00 am**
PLACE OF SALE: Smith County Sheriff's Office, 123 Main Street, City and State

to pay the debt then secured by said mortgage and taxes, if any actually paid by the mortgagee,
on the premises and the costs and disbursements allowed by law. The time allowed by law for
redemption by said mortgagor(s), their personal representatives, or assigns is six (6) months
from the date of sale.

**THE TIME ALLOWED BY LAW FOR REDEMPTION BY THE MORTGAGOR, THE MORTGAGOR'S PERSONAL
REPRESENTATIVES OR ASSIGNS, MAY BE REDUCED TO FIVE WEEKS IF A JUDICIAL ORDER IS ENTERED UNDER
STATE STATUTES, SECTION 582.032, DETERMINING, AMONG OTHER THINGS, THAT THE MORTGAGED
PREMISES ARE IMPROVED WITH A RESIDENTIAL DWELLING OF LESS THAN FIVE UNITS, ARE NOT PROPERTY
USED IN AGRICULTURAL PRODUCTION, AND ARE ABANDONED.**

Dated: January 19, 2009
MORTGAGE REGISTRATION SYSTEMS, INC.    Mortgagee
SMITH & JOHNSON, P.A.    Attorneys for Mortgagee
98 1st Street  City, State 12345 (555) 555-5555
THIS IS A COMMUNICATION FROM A DEBT COLLECTOR.

*REDEMPTION PERIOD*

***Figure 7.1: Notice of Foreclosure*** *This is your notification that your lender has started formal foreclosure proceedings. This notice will also let you know how much time you have before your home will be sold at auction, and how long of a redemption period you may have.*

soon as they are able to by law; other times, you may not receive this notice for months, or even longer, simply because the lender is backlogged.

Like a notice of default, this notice may be delivered or posted one of many ways as dictated by state law (by certified mail, posted on the property, advertised, etc.), but no matter how you receive the news, it is not good news. A notice of foreclosure names you and your lender, describes your property and loan amount, and defines the date and time when your home will be sold at auction. This auction date, known as a *foreclosure sale*, *trustee sale*, or *sheriff's sale*, usually happens in thirty to ninety days.

At this point, you've reached Defcon Level 2 of the foreclosure process, and are one step away from losing your home. Even though it may not seem like it, the window of opportunity is still cracked open. You may have thirty to ninety additional days until the scheduled date of sale to try to work things out with your lender, or to pursue options such as a loan workout, short sale, deed in lieu, or bankruptcy protection. Thirty to ninety days may not seem like a lot of time, but, remember, it may have taken this same amount of time to reach this state of foreclosure. And there may be a way for you to gain some time.

## Ask Your Lender to "Produce the Note"

Some lenders, no matter how you have argued your case or proven your hardship (and your legitimate need for help), may be unwilling to consider anything other than foreclosure. If this happens to you, you can sometimes stall the foreclosure process—or give a lender an incentive to work out an alternative to foreclosure—by using a technique called "produce the note."

The "note" is your promissory note, the physical document that describes your mortgage and its terms, how much you owe, as well as who you owe it to. During the boom years, many mortgages were sold again and again, or split among multiple investors and packaged into various mortgage-backed securities. This means several lenders,

# The Last Stand
# to Save Your Home

Foreclosure can be a very confusing process. How do you know if you have truly exhausted your options? Take the time to review this list. If you missed any opportunities, try again. Once you have exhausted every option, you can move forward, knowing you have done everything you can.

- ☐ Are you able to borrow from a friend or relative?
- ☐ Do you have supplementary insurance, mortgage insurance, or disability insurance to help with your mortgage payments?
- ☐ Can you sell any assets?
- ☐ Have you liquidated stocks?
- ☐ Have you applied for government assistance?
- ☐ Have you researched state and local assistance?
- ☐ Are you able to refinance?
- ☐ Have you tried to sell the home on your own?
- ☐ Have you contacted your lender's loss mitigation department and…
    - ☐ Documented your hardship?
    - ☐ Requested a forbearance plan?
    - ☐ Requested a loan modification?
    - ☐ Discussed a repayment plan?
    - ☐ Asked for a reinstatement?
    - ☐ Suggested a short sale?
    - ☐ Requested a deed in lieu of foreclosure?
- ☐ Have you arranged for foreclosure or credit counseling?
- ☐ Have you consulted with a foreclosure attorney?
- ☐ Have you consulted with a bankruptcy attorney?
- ☐ Have you requested that your lender "produce the note"?

instead of just one, could actually hold your note.

In fact, your loan could be split up between so many lenders and investors that the physical note may be nearly impossible to find. And this is something that can benefit you. If your current lender is unable to produce the note, then legally they are unable to prove that they actually own the mortgage to your home, and they will be unable to foreclose on your home.

While this sounds like a loophole, a lost note is a very legitimate concern when you consider the consequences to you as a borrower. It all goes back to the very real possibility that more than one lender or investor may "own" your loan. When you receive your notice of foreclosure, there may be an attached document titled "Re-establishment of Note." This document admits that the lender cannot find the note. If a lender is permitted to foreclose on your home without showing they own the loan, another lender could easily come in at a later date and demand payment from you *for the same debt*, even if you no longer own the home.

With so many mortgages split into pieces, and so many mortgages owned by so many different lenders—and so many lenders wanting to be repaid on defaulted loans—this has actually happened to many homeowners. Consequently, a precedent has been set for how courts handle these cases. Today, more courts are siding with the homeowner. If the lender can't produce the note, they are usually out of luck.

The strategy for producing the note works basically like this:

- After receiving your notice of foreclosure, you file a request with the courts asking your lender to produce the original promissory note.

- If the lender does not respond within thirty days, you file another motion, and a judge will order your lender to produce the note.

- If the note still remains missing, the judge may hold a hearing to decide whether the lender will continue to be held responsible for proving that they actually own your mortgage.

If the outcome of the hearing is in your favor—if the judge determines that the lender does *not* have a legal claim to your property—the lender cannot foreclose on your home until the note is found, which could stretch the foreclosure process out anywhere from several months, to several years, to indefinitely. If you lose, you will at least have gained more time (and an extra reason to speak with your lender) regarding alternatives to foreclosure. Regardless of the outcome, you benefit.

 For detailed instructions and templates you can use to request the note from your lender, for legal forms you can file with your court, and for other legal resources and attorneys that can help with the process, visit the readers resources section of my website.

## Your Home Is Sold at Auction

At the time dictated in your notice of foreclosure, if you have not reached an agreement with your lender, your home will be sold. By the time your home goes up for auction, you've pretty much reached the end of the line: Defcon Level 1.

On the date of the foreclosure sale, your home will be sold in a public auction. Anyone can participate and bid on your home; in fact, bidding usually takes place right on the front steps of city hall. Your lender sets the starting bid, and the property eventually is sold to the highest bidder. If no one bids over the lender's price, your lender obtains your home by default (which happens the majority of the time). Your lender is then left with the task of trying to sell or liquidate the home to try to recoup their investment and their costs.

Usually, this sale is completely final. But depending on your state, the sale may be subject to a *redemption period*, which will be described on your notice of foreclosure. A redemption period is a period of time after your home is sold at auction during which you can reclaim your home. Keep in mind, the majority of states do not have a redemption period. Once your home is auctioned off, it's gone. But for the states that do offer redemption, you may have anywhere from ten days to two years to "buy" your home back, during which the new owner is legally required to sell it back to you.

During the redemption period, you can buy back your home from whomever purchased it at the foreclosure sale; however, you must pay for the home (at the price it sold for at auction), plus any court costs and interest, *in full*. This may sound unrealistic—and it usually is—but some people are able to buy back their home by borrowing money, by involving an investor, or, in cases where the redemption period is long, by eventually being able to qualify for a loan.

Even if you are able to buy back your home, you need to be careful. In certain states, if the proceeds from the auction don't cover what is owed to the lender (and your lender takes a loss on the home) the lender could be awarded a *deficiency judgment* for the difference. This is a court order stating that you are required to pay for the lender's loss. For example, let's say that when your home went to auction, the total amount owed to your lender was $200,000. Your home was purchased at auction for $125,000. You could buy your home back for $125,000—but you could also owe the lender the remaining $75,000.

Many lenders won't pursue deficiency judgments; they reason that if you're foreclosing on your home, it's very unlikely that you'll have any way to pay the judgment. But if you decide to buy back your property during the redemption period, this tells the lender that you *do* have some money they could come after, and the lender could have a change of heart. While the thought of buying your home back may sound comforting, not only is it unlikely, but it may have severe financial consequences of its own.

## Eviction and Moving Out of Your Home

Once your home has been sold, the title of the home will be transferred from you to the highest bidder. If you haven't already moved out of your home by this point, your status changes from owner to tenant and the new owner can file for an *eviction*—the legal process by

| Level 5 | Your mortgage payments are current. Your home is safe. |
|---|---|
| Level 4 | You miss your first mortgage payment. *Your lender attempts to contact you.* |
| Level 3 | You miss a second mortgage payment. *Your lender sends a notice of default.* |
| Level 2 | You miss three or more mortgage payments. *Your lender sends a notice of foreclosure.* |
| **Level 1** | **The foreclosure is final. Your home is sold at auction.** ***You receive an eviction notice and must move from your home.*** |

which a property owner physically removes a tenant or trespasser.

Once an eviction is executed, you'll usually only have twenty-four hours to move from the home. If you refuse to leave, a sheriff can forcibly remove you. The eviction process is not pretty, and an eviction judgment can also damage your credit further. Sometimes, you may be able to work out an arrangement with the new owner for extra time to move out, but the best idea is to plan to move from your home, leaving the home in good shape for the new owner, before your home's auction date.

## Every Case, and Every State, Are Different

The advice I have outlined in this chapter applies to everyone. However, the actual process and timeline for a foreclosure can vary widely, based on where you live and your individual circumstances. Foreclosures are governed by state law, and these laws may also vary within each state from county to county. To describe exactly what happens in each state and in each county obviously goes beyond the scope of this book, but it's very important information for you to have. You'll want to know not only what to expect, but what procedure to follow, how you will be notified, how long you will have to try save your home or prepare for foreclosure, how your home might be sold, and if you can buy it back.

In Appendix II, I provide general guidelines by state, and on my website, I provide many different resources, links, and explanations to help you to understand your own state's laws and procedures. Even with these resources, you'll most likely still need help. If you are faced with foreclosure, it's important to contact a local attorney who is very familiar with the laws that will apply directly to you. Take the time to learn about your state's laws, so you can protect yourself.

 Visit my website for a guide to your own state's laws regarding foreclosure. I also provide resources to help you find the right foreclosure attorney in your own area who can help you through the process.

. . .

Losing your home is truly a difficult experience, for both you and your family, but it's often possible to work out an arrangement with your lender that is best for you—whether this is saving your home, or lessening the effects of a foreclosure. If you have lost your home, either recently or in the past, you can't change what has happened. But in many ways, it can be an opportunity for you to start over. Learn from your experience, and make a vow to yourself, right now, that you will move forward. In the next chapter, and throughout the rest of this book, I'll discuss in depth how you can begin to build your life back up again, how you can improve your financial position, and how you can avoid having to face foreclosure again.

### COMING UP

Foreclosure can be the end, but it also can be a beginning. By planning carefully for your future, you can rebuild your life sooner than you think. In the next chapter, I'll show you what you can do and where to start. I'll help you to develop a plan to rebuild your credit, strengthen your finances, and plan for your next home.

# 8

# Starting Over

## A Three-Step Plan for Recovery

With every tragedy comes an opportunity for a new beginning. Recovering from a foreclosure—or a short sale, deed in lieu, or bankruptcy—will require time for you to regroup and rebuild. And while you have suffered a difficult loss, losing your home doesn't have to be the end of everything you once knew. Many books on foreclosure address starting over in a simple paragraph or two. I think you deserve more. In this chapter and in Part III of this book, on my website, and throughout my campaign, it's my personal goal to help not only those who are in danger of losing their homes, but those who have *already* lost their homes or experienced foreclosure. Like so many others, you are now faced with one question:

*What do you do now?*

Do you chalk up homeownership as a once-in-a-lifetime experience? Will you have to rent for the rest of your life? Do you even want to purchase again, after all of the stress you've just been through? It may seem overwhelming, but it's just a matter of taking one small step at a time. And your path to recovery begins with three simple steps:

Step 1: Work on your credit
Step 2: Budget and save
Step 3: Plan for your housing

These three basic steps will help you to slowly but surely rebuild your life, your credit, and your savings, so that one day you may own a home again. And although this won't happen overnight, even just one to two years of steady and diligent efforts on your part will make a huge difference.

## Step 1: Work on Your Credit

Your first step is to begin the process of repairing and improving your credit. Having good credit will improve your chances of owning a home in the future *and* have a direct impact on you today. When you have damaged credit, approvals often turn into denials and everything costs more, which is the last thing you need when you are trying to rebuild your life and your finances.

Before we discuss how you can work on your credit, let's first take a moment to understand how your credit has been impacted. No matter how valiantly you fought to save your home, your credit score and credit history will most likely be bruised and battered. Your *credit score* is a number, ranging from 300 to 850 points, that credit agencies use to indicate how well you manage your credit. And when this number drops below 660, it affects everything, from buying a home, to buying a car, to credit card interest rates and more.

It's a debate in the finance industry as to what impacts your credit score more—a foreclosure, a short sale, a deed in lieu, or a bankruptcy. The truth is, once you are faced with any of these options, you have most likely missed many mortgage payments and your credit has already taken a significant hit, anywhere from 100 to 300 points. Unless you worked out an arrangement with your lender *before* missing a mortgage payment, and unless you negotiated with your lender to preserve your credit (as you might be able to do with a short sale or deed in lieu), your credit most likely will have dropped by a total of 250 to 350 points or more—and in this range, any difference is simply splitting hairs. No matter what type of home loss you've experienced, your credit score most likely has bottomed out.

In addition to your credit score, your *credit history* may also be impacted, which will determine how quickly you can rebuild your credit overall, and how soon you may be able to own a home again. Your credit history is a report of everything that's happened with your credit, including details on past and present loans, credit card and store accounts, as well as your payment patterns through the years. Lenders and creditors pay just as much attention to your credit history as they do to your credit score; your credit history is used to gauge what you *might* do with your finances in the future. If you have experienced any type of home loss, you can be sure it will show up in your credit history in some form.

## Your Credit After Foreclosure or Bankruptcy

If you've experienced a foreclosure or a bankruptcy, it will be recorded in your credit history for as long as seven to ten years. Every time your credit is viewed, a record of your foreclosure or bankruptcy will be waiting to greet a creditor or a lender—which is not exactly the kind of first impression you want to make. Lenders will wonder if you will make the payments for your *next* home, and they'll need to see more of a positive credit history before they will even consider giving you a loan.

Because of this, you can expect to wait three to five years before you'll be able to receive decent financing for a home—and by decent financing, I mean financing that is affordable. You may be offered financing sooner, but keep in mind that most of the time these loans will be from a hard money lender, and, as you have learned, the interest rate and fees will be very high. The better long-term decision is to work hard at improving your credit to qualify for better rates and terms.

Most lenders have very specific guidelines in place regarding how soon they will lend to a borrower after a foreclosure or bankruptcy. In fact, these guidelines are actually set at a national level. Remember Fannie and Freddie? Fannie and Freddie's guidelines specify how much time must pass after a foreclosure or bankruptcy before you will be considered for a conforming loan, and most lenders use Fannie and Freddie's guidelines as a benchmark for their own loans. A waiting period of three to five years is considered to be the industry standard; that's usually enough time for lenders to see how hard you have been working on rebuilding your credit and, in turn, how responsible you might be with your next loan.

### Your Credit After a Short Sale or Deed in Lieu

Now, if you have worked out a short sale or deed in lieu of foreclosure with your lender, you may have a little more to work with. Depending on the lender (and your negotiations) a short sale or deed in lieu may or may not have been "officially" recorded in your credit history; it may be noted in your file with a description of the deficiency (the lender's loss), it may be listed as "the mortgage has been satisfied" (which means paid in full), or it may not even show up at all (which is great news for you).

If a short sale or deed in lieu *is* recorded, a future lender will review the facts on a case by case basis. How much of a loss did the previous lender take? Were you able to work out an agreement for the short sale or deed in lieu prior to missing any mortgage payments? A lender will also consider the fact that you *were able* to work something out with the previous lender, and that you didn't just walk away from the home. Lenders are often faced with homeowners who simply abandon their homes. To a lender, a short sale or deed in lieu shows that although you had trouble paying your mortgage, you took responsibility and tried to remedy the situation. All of these factors may help you to be approved for a loan sooner.

These same details may also help your credit score as well; many people find they are able to rebound and rebuild their credit faster after a short sale or deed in lieu (compared to a foreclosure or bankruptcy), sometimes significantly raising their credit score in as little as one year.

Across the board, I've found it usually takes a minimum of two years under the best circumstances before most lenders will consider financing a new loan. Look at this timeframe as a period for you to plan. Two years is not a long time, and the possibility of rebuilding your credit should give you hope.

## Building a New Credit History

How you use your credit from this point on will become part of your *new* credit history, and this new history has the power to impact and improve your credit score more than anything else. The most important thing you can do now is continue to use your credit (with established or newly secured credit cards) and to *always* pay on time, even if it may be very difficult to do so. You will also want to take some time to learn and understand more about credit in general. In the next chapter, I'll explain credit in great detail, including how credit works and why it is important, how you can view and interpret your credit report, how lenders and creditors evaluate credit, and the do's and don'ts for using credit, right down to the total number of credit cards you should carry.

In addition to this basic information, when you have suffered through a foreclosure or similar home loss, there are four important guidelines you will need to follow to improve your credit score:

### 1. Pay for new charges right away.

Continue to use your credit cards, but pay the new charges off immediately; this will begin to establish a good credit history. Granted, when I say "use your credit cards," I don't mean go on a spending spree. Plan ahead for the charges you make, make sure you will be able to pay for any new charges, and put aside funds for the payments early. By getting into this habit each and every month, you will be showing a responsible use of your credit. Whatever you do, *do not stop* using your credit. If you stop using your credit cards entirely, your credit history won't show how you are using your credit responsibly, it will just show that you aren't using your credit at all.

### 2.   Keep a low balance, or no balance.

If your credit cards already carry a balance, one of your goals will be to pay the balances down. Ideally, for each credit card, the card's balance should be no more than 20 percent of the card's limit. For example, if your credit card has a $1,000 credit limit, try to keep your balance around $200 or less. I know that early on this may be difficult, but this should be part of your long-term plan. Later in this chapter, and in Chapter 10, I'll show you how you can budget and save money to help you reach this goal, which in turn will lower your debt and strengthen your financial position overall.

### 3.   Watch your credit carefully.

When you are trying to rebuild your credit, you cannot afford to have *anything* damage your credit further. That's why you'll want to see if there are any details on your credit report right now that are incorrect and are dragging your credit down. Were your late or missed mortgage payments, home loss, or bankruptcy recorded correctly on your credit report? Have you checked? You would be surprised at how often there are errors in this process.

In the next chapter, I'll show you how you can review your credit report for errors like these, how to actively monitor your credit report going forward, and how you can correct any errors (no matter when the errors occur), which will help to improve your credit score immediately, and will allow you to rebuild your credit faster.

### 4.   Give your side of the story.

Your credit report contains a lot of information, including details on all of your accounts, your balances and payments, if you've been late making payments, and if any action has been taken against you because of unpaid bills. Your creditors continually report and update this information, which then tells other creditors how responsible you are in using your credit.

But this information is just one side of the story. You have the right to report your own information and to give *your* side of the story. Today, everyone views your credit, from potential employers to lenders and other creditors, and so you'll want to make sure it also includes your account of what happened.

You can request that a 100-word explanation appear with *any* event that is recorded in your credit history, including foreclosures, short sales, deeds in lieu, and bankruptcies. Do you have anything you would want a creditor, a future lender, or even a future employer to know about this period of time? Were you experiencing medical issues or extreme hardship? Had you lost your job, or were you unable to work? Take the opportunity to explain what happened. Anyone who reviews your credit will be able to read your explanation. Again, make sure to thoroughly read the next chapter, where I'll explain how to submit your explanation, and what you will need to do to keep it active within your credit file.

## Asking for Help: Credit Repair and Credit Counseling

What if losing your home was just one of many credit issues? Your credit could be damaged so severely that the road to stabilizing your credit could be a steep, uphill climb. Anyone can repair their credit on their own, but if you have badly damaged credit, you might benefit from the guidance of a professional.

There are many firms and organizations that can immediately help you with some of the biggest credit issues out there, with services ranging from full credit repair to personalized credit counseling. But you also need to be careful—you need to find the right firm to help you, and that may be easier said than done.

### CREDIT REPAIR

While credit repair sounds promising, just like anything else involving finance, the credit industry is littered with scams. A credit repair firm will be able to help you with legal paperwork and documentation, and its representatives will be more familiar than you are with credit law. But they will *not* be able to remove information from your credit just because the information is negative.

Many shady credit repair firms will claim they can make your foreclosure, bankruptcy, or credit issues disappear. However, if what is reported in your credit report is *accurate*—including negative information such as missed payments, liens, foreclosures, judgments, and bankruptcies—it won't just magically vanish, even if you have been promised otherwise. And such broken promises are no laughing matter when you consider the costs associated with credit repair: you may be charged anywhere from $50 to $2,000 or *more*, depending on your credit issues, the type of company you work with, and whether an attorney needs to be involved. This wide range of fees makes it very difficult for consumers to know if they are getting what they paid for, or if they are being scammed. To protect yourself, you'll want to do two things: 1) Do your research, and 2) Carefully review your contract.

Any credit repair firm you're considering should receive a good report from the Better Business Bureau. You'll also want to contact your state attorney general's office, at www.naag.org, or your Secretary of State's office to check on the firm's license, how long the business has been established, and if there are any complaints or pending investigations.

Once you meet with a credit repair firm and discuss your needs, you should be given a contract outlining what services will be performed. Don't accept a verbal summary—get the details in writing. Your contract should clearly define and include:

- What credit issues will be addressed
- What services will be provided
- How long it will take to reach the desired results
- The total costs and payment terms
- Full disclosures regarding your consumer rights

Don't feel pressured to sign. By law, you have *three* full business days to thoroughly review your contract. During this time, read the contract carefully; if it's not complete, if you don't like the terms, or if you simply change your mind, you can cancel the contract in full without penalty. If you are uncomfortable with the contract at all, don't chance it. Cancel the contract and look for another company.

Most importantly, if you are required to pay for any services upfront, be extremely cautious. Only 501(c) non-profit organizations are permitted to charge for any services in advance, and even then, any charges should be reasonable. Depending on the services you need, a non-profit's initial fees typically run from $50 to $200, and ongoing fees are usually around $50 a month.

The Credit Repair Organizations Act, passed in 1996, provides protection to you as a consumer: by law, companies providing credit repair *for a profit* must fulfill their promises to you first, *before* collecting payment. If you are working with a for-profit credit repair firm, pay for services as they are completed. If you are charged a set-up fee, this fee cannot be collected until your case is entered into their system and documented. If there are ongoing monthly fees, services must be provided for a full month before payment can be required.

You'll also want to be wary of high set-up fees or "special education" fees (which are padded fees a company may charge to "teach" you about credit); disreputable firms will charge you high fees at the start, and then do absolutely nothing to actually improve your credit. You could pay a huge sum for credit repair, and be right back where you started. Again, research any firm carefully to be sure you will receive the help you need.

## CREDIT COUNSELING

In addition to credit repair, there is also *credit counseling*. Credit counseling agencies are typically non-profit organizations that show you how to use your credit responsibly, and teach you how to get out of serious debt. You may have already had experience with a credit counselor as a requirement for bankruptcy, or maybe in an effort to save your home. Even after home loss, a credit counselor can provide solid guidance for managing your credit, your debt, and your finances in the future. Some credit counselors will also work directly with your creditors to work out payment plans.

Credit counseling is a highly competitive business, and, just like with credit repair, not all of the businesses are reputable. There are actually credit counseling agencies that will do your credit more harm than good. And although most reputable agencies are non-profits, the word "non-profit" is not a guarantee that a company is trustworthy—you still need to do your research.

Any credit counseling agency you choose should be accredited by a national organization such as the National Foundation for Credit Counseling (NFCC) or the Association of Independent Consumer Credit Counseling Agencies (AICCCA); they have member lists on their websites. The Department of Justice's website, www.usdoj.gov, also provides its own list of approved credit counseling agencies by state. And if you can't trust the Department of Justice, who can you trust?

With any type of credit repair or counseling, you will want to be as involved as possible. Make sure your information is kept confidential, ask for credentials, licenses, and training, find out about the timeframes and fees you can expect, and *always* get the details in writing. Remember, your credit is extremely fragile and extremely important. Repairing your credit *will* take time, so you will want to be sure your time is well spent. The last thing you want is to waste it with someone who is not helping you improve your credit. Work closely and be directly involved with any agency or firm you hire, and be sure to monitor your credit report throughout the entire process.

WEBLINK Overwhelmed by options? Visit my website for a list of prescreened and reputable credit attorneys and approved credit counseling agencies that can help you with your credit issues.

## Step 2: Budget, Save, and Pay Down Your Debt

If you are like most people, the problems with your mortgage have spilled over into other areas of your life. If you've only had trouble paying your mortgage, then your recovery might be easier. But it's more than likely you also have:

- Drained your savings and retirement accounts
- Lost the equity you had in your home
- Overextended or maxed out your credit card or store accounts

Does this sound like your situation? So many people today are faced with depleted savings and a mountain of debt, even if they haven't experienced home loss. Just like repairing your credit, rebuilding your savings starts with your personal commitment, a budget, and a few years of sacrifice.

Most people know they don't save enough, but they don't quite know what to do about it. Or, you may feel suffocated by the sound of the word "budget," and you may not want to give up the quality of life you are used to. But really, can budgeting your money be any harder than what you have already been through? If you've made it through a foreclosure or other home loss, you can get through anything, especially a budget. And by implementing a budget, you will not only be able to own a home again sooner, but you will also protect yourself from future financial hardship. If you haven't budgeted before, or you haven't budgeted *successfully* before, now is a great time to start.

MORE INFO **Don't Underestimate a Budget**

A budget is a powerful tool; it will allow you to measure income and expenses and plan for spending and saving. A budget will also help you to make intelligent choices about what you do with your money, and will outline ways you can make your money work harder for you.

## *Determine Your Total Income*

A budget, in its simplest sense, is about being aware: being aware of what you take in, and being aware of and planning for what you take out. I've included a worksheet in Appendix III that will help you to set up your budget. To start, you'll need to take some time to analyze your income, expenses, and spending patterns. First, you'll want to determine your total income. How much do you make every month? Are you receiving income from multiple sources? You will want to consider all sources of income, such as:

- Your salary
- Hourly wages
- Sales commissions
- Bonus pay
- Interest-bearing accounts
- Dividends
- Retirement or pensions
- Alimony
- Child support

Add up your total monthly income *after* taxes. If your income varies from month to month or is seasonal, you'll want to use a general average of your income for the purpose of your budget. Try to look back over at least four to six months to get a clear picture of how much you make on average, per month. If you anticipate making more or less in the near future, plan ahead and include these figures in your calculations.

## *Track and Analyze Your Expenses*

Next, you'll need to track at least two to three months of expenses. How much are you spending per month? In Appendix III, I've included an expense tracking worksheet. For the next two months, carry this worksheet around with you wherever you go; make a couple of copies if necessary. I've also included a version of this worksheet on my website that you can download and print.

Whenever you spend money, from paying bills, rent, or utilities, to the grocery checkout line, to buying your morning cup of coffee, write the amounts down, along with a description and date. Track everything you spend, down to the last penny. After two months of calculating and tracking, you should have a good idea of what you are spending, on average, every month.

If you have expenses that are paid on a bimonthly, quarterly, semi-annual, or annual basis that you might have missed, add them to your list. This might include expenses like your taxes, car maintenance and registration costs, insurance payments, and school expenses. If you spread these expenses out evenly over twelve months, how much would they cost?

After tracking all of your expenses, you'll need to refine your list further. For each expense, ask yourself if it is a fixed or a variable expense. *Fixed expenses* are expenses that repeat every month (or another set time period), and are necessary expenses that would be difficult to cut or decrease without advance planning, including:

- Your taxes (federal, state, and local)
- Your rent (or mortgage, if you are still in your home)
- Insurance (health, auto, life, etc.)
- Your utilities (electricity, gas, water)
- Auto costs
- Child support

*Variable expenses* are expenses you can easily change, increase, or decrease, including:

- Savings/retirement/emergency fund
- Paying down debt
- Medical expenses
- Gas and transportation costs
- Food/eating out

- Telephone/cell phone
- Cable/internet
- Clothing
- Entertainment
- Vacation

## Create and Follow Your Budget

Based on the figures you've gathered, compare your monthly income to your monthly expenses. Your expenses need to be equal to or less than your income, and if they aren't, you'll need to adjust your variable expenses first. How *should* you be spending your income? Evaluate your expenses, line by line. Which expenses are absolutely necessary? Which can you do without? Is there money that would be better spent padding your savings accounts or paying down your total debt? Don't design your budget based on what you are currently spending. Conform your spending *to* your new budget. Use the sample budget in Appendix III or the interactive budgets on my website to customize a plan that works for your needs.

Use your budget each month to track your actual spending and how these costs fit into your budget. You'll find you may need to shift and adjust the amount you are allowed to spend from one category to another until you find the right balance. Your goal at this point is to pay your bills, save as much as possible, and pay down your debt. You

---

MORE INFO **Don't Forget Your Savings**

When many people budget, they are tempted to skip adding enough into their savings. But budgeting for your savings is extremely important. By purposefully planning what you contribute to your savings, you'll not only rebuild the savings you have lost, but you will start to build up the down payment and reserves you will need if you purchase a home in the future.

---

MORE INFO

**Your Budget Breakdown:**

How should you be spending your money? Many budgets depend on your own personal circumstances: What area of the country do you live in? Are the costs of living high? Do you have children and are you married? You may need to adjust these numbers for your own life, but a good rule of thumb to follow is:

*Percentage of Your Total Income*

| | |
|---|---|
| Housing and living expenses | 20% – 35% |
| Food | 15% – 20% |
| Transportation | 5% – 20% |
| Debt and credit card bills | 5% – 10% |
| Savings and emergency fund | 5% – 10% |

may need to make sacrifices and give up some things for a while to reach these goals, but once you have adequate savings and lower debt you can easily loosen the reins and relax your budget.

## CREATE AN EMERGENCY FUND

Your budget should also include putting money into an emergency fund. Ideally (and notice I did say ideally) your emergency fund should cover six months of your most basic living expenses, including your rent or mortgage, utilities, insurances, food, and transportation. Start small, and use a six-month reserve as your final goal.

Also, be sure to keep your reserves in a safe place. Many banks offer no-penalty Certificates of Deposit (CDs), which are perfect for an emergency fund. No-penalty CDs earn interest, and also allow you to access and withdraw funds at any time without penalty, just like a checking or savings account. But unlike a regular checking or savings account, withdrawing the money takes a little bit of time and effort, so with this arrangement, you won't be tempted to use your emergency reserves for anything other than a true emergency.

When you first start working on your budget, you may become frustrated. You may feel that you just don't make enough and that saving money may be close to impossible. Rebuilding your finances is certainly hard and difficult work, and your personal circumstances may make it even harder. Don't give in to your frustration. Stay positive—there are many creative ways to save money.

In Chapter 10, I'll show you many ways you can save and be smarter with your money, both now and in the future, from large unavoidable expenses including taxes and insurance, down to everyday spending habits. Read these chapters carefully and take them to heart. There are also many books available on budgeting and financial planning, so I suggest spending more time at the library or the bookstore. I've even provided a list of recommended books for you on my website. (Notice I didn't suggest buying anything, because you really do need to budget *everything*.) With some patience, and some practice, your budget will do the one thing you need it to do most: speed up your recovery.

 In addition to the worksheets I have supplied in this book, I provide many additional resources on my website for budgeting and saving in general, including step-by-step interactive budgeting tools and worksheets, budgeting tips, and many everyday ways to save more and spend less.

## Step 3: Plan for Your Housing

The last step to your recovery is to plan for your housing. If you would like to own a home again, you'll need to show you have the ability to pay for a future mortgage, and you will need to prove to lenders that you have reestablished yourself. The good news is, by following the first two steps of your recovery plan, you'll be addressing both of these needs. By following Step 1 (by working on your credit), you'll be showing lenders that you are responsible. And by following Step 2 (by budgeting, saving, and paying down your debt), you'll increase your savings and reserves to show you have the necessary funds for a down payment, and that you will be able to responsibly pay a mortgage each month.

*How* you pay your bills will also determine how soon you'll be able to own a home again. Lenders will want to see a track record of full and timely payments. Late payments of *any kind* are the kiss of death—they will clearly tell any lender that you are habitually late in making payments regardless of your circumstance. So no matter what you do, don't be thirty days past due with any bill, credit account, or installment loan. And most importantly, never be late on a rent payment after a foreclosure, bankruptcy, or any other type of home loss.

I stress your rent payment because most likely you will be renting for some time, though hopefully for no more than two or three years. Being late on a rent payment is just as bad as being late on a mortgage payment; even though you don't own the home, these payments carry the same weight to a potential lender. When the time comes to finance your next home, your lender will carefully scrutinize your twelve-month rental history. If you've been late, *even just one time*, it will be a red flag for any lender, and usually you will be denied for the loan. As far as a lender is concerned, if you are late on your rent, why wouldn't you also be late in paying your mortgage? So make sure your rent payments are always on time.

## Getting a Step Ahead With a Lease-Purchase

Renting after owning your own home can be a big adjustment, and you may miss living in your *own* home. But there are a few possible alternatives to conventional homeownership as we know it, and you may have more options for housing than you think. With so much housing inventory, it's very possible you will find a homeowner who is willing to give you a chance to own again in the form of a lease-purchase option.

A *lease-purchase*, also known as a *lease-to-own* or *rent-to-own*, is a lease contract that includes the option to purchase the home later at a predetermined, agreed-upon price. A lease-purchase contract usually lasts three years; at any time during this period, you can choose to purchase the home.

For many people, a lease-purchase option is the perfect solution, and can be beneficial in many ways. To start, you have the opportunity to search now for the home you would like to live in permanently, but *without* the obligation of the purchase itself. You can almost think of a lease-purchase as test-driving a home. And if you do decide to purchase the home, you will have had the entire contract period to rebuild your credit and your savings, so you can more successfully apply for financing.

In addition, a lease-purchase is a smarter use of your money: every month, a portion of your rent payment, known as *rent premium*, is applied toward the sale price of the home, essentially paying down the price of the home as you pay your rent. Instead of your rent money working for someone else, your rent money is working harder for you. And while a lease-purchase option requires that you pay an *option fee* at signing (which is a fee ranging from 1 to 5 percent of the home's purchase price), this fee is applied toward the purchase price as well. For example, let's say the lease-purchase price of a home is $200,000, and your option fee is 2 percent, or $4,000. After paying the option fee, the purchase price lowers to $196,000. In effect, the option fee immediately becomes equity in your future home. That's a pretty good deal.

Lease-purchases can be a good option for the owner of the home as well. Lease-purchases often "secure the sale"—it's more likely you will follow through with the purchase of the home after paying the option fee and several years of rent premium. At the end of the contract, if you are unable or choose *not* to purchase the home, the owner doesn't lose anything: the option fee and rent payments are retained by the owner as income, and the home can now be sold to someone else. With this mutual benefit, lease-purchases can be a great win-win for everyone.

If you find a homeowner who is willing to lease their home with the option to purchase—and it is a home you could see yourself in for at least five years—it's time to negotiate. You'll want to negotiate an

**MORE INFO** **Continue to Be Cautious**

While lease-purchases are a viable option, there are a few things to be cautious of. Do your research: Could the homeowner be in default or in the process of foreclosure themselves? Are there any liens on the property that would not allow the home to be sold to you at a later date? (Remember, a lender will not lend their money for a home with judgments or impending lawsuits.)

Also, make sure your contract does not *obligate* you to purchase at the end of your lease term—you may discover something about the property you don't like, you may change your mind, or you may not be approved for financing within the contract period. You want the *option* to purchase, not the obligation.

Your contract could also disqualify you from a future option to purchase if you are late with your rent payment (even just once) so be sure to read your contract carefully. If you are unsure of anything you are signing, or if you have questions, it's always a smart decision to contact a real estate attorney.

affordable rent payment (which, by the way, should fit within your budget), as well as the rent premium amount (how much of your rent is applied to the purchase price each month—usually around $200 to $300), the option fee, and the home's final purchase price.

Sometimes, you may find that owners who list their homes for rent are open to discussing a lease-purchase option with you directly. Or you may have better luck with a rent-to-own real estate office. If you choose to work with a real estate office, just be very cautious of any fees, particularly upfront fees. A reputable rent-to-own realty firm makes their money by charging the homeowner, not you.

In the event that the opportunity for leasing or renting-to-own does not present itself, there are a few other options that may be available. A relative or close friend could co-sign for a mortgage. You could rent to own from a family member. And the government or even your local community could help you out. As I mentioned in Chapter 4, the Federal Housing Administration offers several loan programs that will allow for damaged credit, gift funds, co-signers, and even grant options. When you apply for these programs, your credit will be evaluated as a whole, and you'll also be able to provide a letter of explanation for any derogatory marks or negative events within your credit history, including foreclosures, bankruptcies, short sales, and deeds in lieu. Depending on your own situation, you may be approved for financing sooner than you think.

· · ·

Sometimes, the biggest fear in starting over is the fear of the unknown. In reality, starting over can easily be the beginning of much better things to come. You now have a plan, you know where you can look for help, and you know what to expect. Your choice now is whether to move forward. Make today the first day you start working on your credit, developing a budget, and planning for the future. With a little work, you will eventually travel far along the road of recovery. And one day, this road will lead to your new home.

*"A pessimist sees the difficulty in every opportunity; an optimist sees the opportunity in every difficulty."* — WINSTON CHURCHILL

# PART III

# Improving Your Financial Future

· · ·

How to Take Control of Your Credit,
Your Finances, and Your Future

R ight now, we are all faced with uncertainty. In our current economy, you may feel as though you have lost control of so
much—of your finances, your home, maybe even your life. You
know where you would like to be: safe in your own home, with a secure financial future. The question is, how do you get there?

In the following chapters, I'll show you how the basic principles
of credit, planning, budgeting, and saving will help you to regain control and achieve your homeownership goals. I'll explain how credit
works, from how important your credit score has become, to the real
meaning behind your credit report, to how everyday decisions impact your credit and your finances. And I'll also outline steps you can

take immediately to improve or restore your credit, and your financial and self-worth.

You'll also see how you can make better decisions about how you spend and save, from large expenses that come with owning a home, including taxes and insurance, down to the everyday costs of living. And more importantly, you'll see how simply changing your frame of mind towards money will enable all of this to happen.

And finally, I'll share more about my personal mission to help you. No matter if you currently own your home or are rebuilding to one day own again, this book can be a new beginning, and an opportunity to help yourself. I'll explain more about my campaign, what you can find on my website, and how you have the opportunity to receive direct assistance for a better future—one that includes owning your own home.

# 9

## Your Credit

Why Your Credit Is More Important
Now Than Ever

L ike many people, you may have a general sense that your credit is important, or that having good credit is something to strive for. But the fact is, in today's market, your credit is more important than ever. Not only will your credit determine your ability to purchase or refinance a home, it will also affect the loan programs you can qualify for and ultimately how much this financing will cost. And it doesn't stop there.

Most companies, weary of what's happened in the real estate and lending markets, are relying more and more on credit to help safeguard their businesses. Retailers, credit card companies, insurance companies, landlords, and businesses in general are all scrutinizing your credit, measuring how responsible you are with your finances, and whether they should (or should not) do business with you. Even employers are reviewing your credit as part of the hiring process, and they may routinely check your credit throughout your employment, just to see how responsible and trustworthy you are.

In our society, your worth is defined by your credit. And as a result, the credit report has become one of the most-viewed and in-demand documents in modern times, so much so that the task of compiling and reporting credit information has become a multi-billion-dollar business of its own.

Credit hasn't always been this complicated; it actually started from a very simple concept: convenience. Back in the early days of credit, going all the way back to the eighteenth century, goods were purchased "on account" to be paid in full at a later date or through multiple smaller payments (which, unbelievably, were usually interest-free). Merchants decided if they would grant credit on a case-by-case basis, according to a person's reputation, or the merchant's own personal experience with a customer.

Over time, as credit caught on and more people purchased on credit, businesses found that offering credit allowed them to do *more* business, enabling consumers to purchase more expensive items—or more items—than they would have been able to before. Businesses quickly saw that more credit meant more *profit*. As more and more businesses began to accept and extend credit, it was clear a system was needed to evaluate credit applicants. Businesses needed to know if a person was worth giving credit to without having to do all of the research themselves. And this is how the credit rating system that we know today was born.

## The Big Three of Credit

Today, the process of rating and reporting credit revolves around massive amounts of information that is gathered, analyzed, stored, and sold by *credit repositories* (also known as credit bureaus, credit reporting agencies, or consumer reporting agencies).

The repositories collect information about your credit activities, and then provide this information to businesses or individuals who need to know if you are *creditworthy*—if you are able to meet your financial obligations, and if you are able to repay your debt. In return for this service, all companies that lend money or grant credit, including banks, lenders, finance companies, retailers, department stores, utilities, and billing agencies, agree to supply new and updated information about you, your account, and your payments right back to the credit repositories. Think of credit reporting as a giant, continuous cycle of information: creditors need up-to-date information supplied by credit repositories to approve or grant credit, and the credit repositories need information from creditors so they can provide accurate information and truly do their job.

In the U.S., there are three major consumer credit repositories: Equifax, Experian, and TransUnion. The "big three" of credit are such large and impressive organizations that many believe they have some kind of legal authority, government affiliation, or Big Brother power for reporting credit. And while credit reporting agencies *are* subject to regulations and oversight by the Federal Trade Commission, they have *no* special authority, and they aren't taking orders from the government. The big three are private companies that just happen to be in the business of supplying information about credit for a profit—a big profit.

For the most part, how the repositories decide to collect, report, and score credit information is determined by each repository itself. And creditors can choose how they work with the repositories too; they may report information to all three repositories, or just one. Repositories charge creditors a subscription fee to report and access credit, so many times who creditors decide to report to is determined by the cost of the subscription itself.

Each of the three credit repositories work separately and in direct competition with each other, providing both you and your creditors with three independent versions of your credit report, and three different credit scores.

## Understanding Your Credit Report

Although the repositories all gather and report slightly different information, credit reports themselves are pretty standardized. The information detailed in your credit report will always fall into one of six general categories:

1. **Identifying Information.** Your identifying information includes your name, date of birth, social security number, current and previous addresses, current and previous employers, and any aliases you may use or have used in the past. This section of your credit report helps to ensure that what is reported about you is, well, actually about you! Without this information, details about Joe Smith from California could easily be mixed in with information about another Joe Smith from California or even Joe Smith from New York.

The repositories track identifying information through your social security number, and through any updated information they receive from your creditors. It may seem like this information would be easy to track, but it's actually far from a fail-safe system. Think of how many times you've received a bill where your name is spelled wrong, your address is incorrect, or your personal information is outdated. This incorrect information can easily make its way from your creditors straight on to your credit report, which also makes it very likely that *other* information on your credit report could be wrong too. The credit repositories don't check all of the information that's provided, they only *report* it, which means things can easily slip through the cracks.

---

CAUTION **Mistakes May Be a Sign of Bigger Trouble**

If there are mistakes in your identifying information, it may be a sign that your credit identity has been stolen. This is one of many reasons why you should always monitor your credit carefully, something I'll review in detail later in this chapter.

---

2. **Account Information.** The largest part of your credit report will be your account information. For every account, both past and present, your credit report will detail the creditor's name; the account number; a description of the account; the date the account was

opened; if the account was closed (and why); the account's terms and credit limits; your monthly balances or required payments; the highest balance; any outstanding balance; and a complete payment history shown month by month, detailing when you have paid on time, and when you have been late. Even if an account is inactive, closed, or paid in full, it may remain as part of your account information and part of your credit history for up to ten years.

This is the area of your credit report where potential creditors and lenders will spend most of their time. They'll want to see what types of debt you currently have, and if you have a history of responsibly managing your credit and paying what you owe. From reviewing your account information, your creditors will be able to answer two important questions: 1) Are you creditworthy? and 2) What is your credit depth?

> **Creditworthiness:** Are you able to pay creditors back, and is it likely that you *will* pay them back?

> **Credit Depth:** Do you have an established history of both borrowing and paying creditors back?

Credit worthiness and depth are deeply intertwined. You need an established credit history (your credit depth) to prove how "worthy" you are. And as more creditors view you as worthy, they'll grant you *more* credit, and you'll be able to use this increased credit to build a stronger history of responsibly borrowing and paying creditors back.

**3. Public Records.** The credit repositories also gather information from federal, state, and county court records, including details of any judgments, liens, notices of default, foreclosures, or bankruptcies—which, as you know, will greatly impact your ability to receive credit or a loan. Even details about divorce, wage garnishment, or un-paid child support may appear. As long as the information is directly related to your financial obligations, it can show up on your credit report.

### How Long Does Information Stay on Your Credit Report?

Good or bad, the information in your credit report will stay with you for many years to come. By law, credit repositories are required to remove most negative information from your account after seven years. If information remains on your credit report past the time lines I've listed in this table, it's within your authority (and it's your responsibility) to have the information removed.

Accounts in good standing ................................. 10-plus years
Late or missed payments ................................... 7 years
Collections ....................................................... 7 years
Judgments ....................................................... 7 years
Foreclosures .................................................... 7 years
Bankruptcies ................................................... 10 years
Paid tax liens .................................................. 7 years
Unpaid tax liens ............................................... 15 years
Credit inquiries ............................................... 2 years

**4. Collections.** If you've been very late in paying your bills (or if you haven't paid some bills at all) a creditor may turn your account over to a collection agency. Once this happens, a notice of collection will immediately be listed on your account.

Of course, anyone who is reviewing your credit report doesn't want to see that you've been seriously delinquent with any account. As far as a creditor is concerned, if it happened once, it could easily happen again. Collections lower your credit score, and remain on your credit report even *after* you pay what is owed, which means you will have to work hard to show potential creditors that you'll be responsible with your credit in the future. Just like with a foreclosure or bankruptcy, you will need to rebuild your credit. If you have any collections, you can follow the advice I have outlined in Chapter 8, as well as the section "The Ten-Step Plan to Improve Your Credit" at the end of this chapter.

**5. Inquiries.** Every time your credit is requested, it is recorded as a *credit inquiry*. This section of your credit report details the name of each company that has requested your credit files, their address, and the date of the inquiry. Credit inquiries are grouped into two categories:

- **Inquiries shared only with you:** These inquiries *do not* impact your credit score, and include requests from employers, potential investors, current creditors, promotional offers, and your own requests to check your credit. These inquiries will only be visible to you on your credit report; no other creditor will be able to see them.

- **Inquiries shared with others:** These inquiries *do* impact your credit score, and include requests by companies where you have applied for credit or financing. These inquiries will be visible to anyone who views your credit report.

Credit inquiries may seem harmless, but to potential creditors (and to the credit repositories) too many inquiries may mean you are desperate for credit, or that you may soon have *more* available credit—and potentially increased debt—in the near future. If you have too many inquiries within a short period, your request for credit or a loan could be denied, and your credit score could drop by a few points per inquiry. In the case of multiple inquiries, this could add up. Because of this, you'll want to limit inquiries into your credit, and you'll also want to monitor your credit report to determine if any inquiries are inaccurate or were made without your consent.

**6. Your Credit Score.** When most people see their credit report, they tend to zero in on their credit score, and rightfully so. Your credit score is a very important number: it instantly sums up months or even years of your credit history in just three digits. Lenders, businesses, and em-

**MORE INFO** **Who's Allowed to Access Your Credit Report?**

With so much personal and private information on your credit report, knowing who has access to this information is very important. Only those who have your direct permission to run your credit, or those who have a *valid* business reason to review your credit, are permitted to access your credit file. If someone has checked your credit without your knowledge or without good reason, they are in violation of the Fair Credit Reporting Act, which could result in a year in prison and a fine of up to $5,000—*payable to you*—which should be a great incentive for you to check your credit inquiries often. Legitimate credit inquiries include:

- Lenders and mortgage professionals
- Businesses where you have applied for credit
- Businesses that have already granted you credit
- Insurers who are writing a new policy or renewing a policy
- Potential or current landlords
- Potential or current employers
- Hospitals and health care providers
- Government agencies
- Inquiries governed by court order or subpoenas
- You, at your own request (in writing)

ployers all make decisions based on an individual's credit score alone: over 75 percent of mortgage lenders and over 90 percent of credit card lenders use credit scores when making their final lending decisions, which makes a credit score one small number with *a lot* of power.

## How Credit Scores Are Determined

When most people talk about their credit score, they're usually referring to their *FICO score*, a credit scoring model developed by the

Fair Isaac Corporation. Developed in the 1950s, the FICO scoring model has been used to rate millions of credit scores, and has proven the test of time in accurately conveying a person's credit history and credit worthiness.

FICO credit scores can range from 300 to 850 possible points. The higher the score, the better the credit. In the U.S., the average credit score is between 580 to 650 points, and only 20 percent of Americans have a credit score above 720. (If you are within this top 20 percent, give yourself a pat on the back and keep up the good work—but keep reading.)

While a credit score is a simple number, how it is determined is part of a much bigger and more complicated equation. Your credit score is a direct product of everything contained within your credit report. Statistical models, scoring tables, and various equations are all used to translate this information into a score. And although *all* of the information in your credit report contributes to your credit score, some information is more important than others.

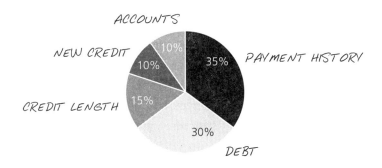

*Figure 9.1: What Makes Up Your FICO Credit Score?*

35%   Your payment history: How often do you pay on time?

30%   Your debt: What are your credit limits, how much debt do you have, and how is your debt distributed?

15%   Credit length: How long have you been using credit?

10%   New credit: How many inquiries and new accounts do you have?

10%   Account type: What kinds of accounts do you have?

In addition to the FICO scoring model, each of the three credit repositories also uses its *own* statistical models and scoring systems to process credit information. Think of a scoring model as a filter to process information; with different filters, you'll have different results. This is why, when a business or lender runs your credit, you'll often receive different—and often widely varying—credit scores.

| REPOSITORY | CREDIT SCORING MODEL |
|---|---|
| Equifax | Beacon Score |
| Experian | Fair Isaac Score |
| TransUnion | Empirica Score |

FICO, the Beacon Score, Fair Isaac Score, and Empirica Score are the most recognized scoring models, but there are literally hundreds of scoring models that are used in the credit industry. New scoring models, industry-specific scoring models, and customized scoring models are being developed all the time. Why the variety? Well, different scoring models are often used for different situations. For example, one model may be used by auto financers, another by insurers, and another by healthcare providers. And although these models may be very useful to specific industries, it makes things *very* confusing for consumers.

As a borrower, you could receive one credit score from your lender, and a completely different score when you apply for a car loan. And when you check your credit yourself, you'll receive a different credit score from each credit repository. One person could literally have dozens of different credit scores, and it makes it very difficult to know how good, or bad, your credit score really is.

For example, FICO's scoring range is from 300 to 850 points. But other scoring models range from 501 to 990 points. Saying you have a 720 credit score may mean you have excellent credit, *or* it may mean your credit is below-average, depending on the scoring model. That's a huge difference.

Every few years, this topic rears its ugly head within the credit industry, sparking discussion about a one-score system to prevent the confusion that results from multiple scoring models. Currently, there is an effort among the credit repositories to make the VantageScore the final scoring system, but only time will tell if this change will happen. For now, to help consumers accurately gauge their credit score, the repositories qualify their scores further. Your credit score may be accompanied by a grade from A to F, the repository may show you a percentile rank, or your credit may be shown on a scale from "bad" to "great" or from "high risk" to "super prime."

While I always recommend that you carefully review what is listed in *all three* credit reports (I'll explain how you can receive a free copy of your reports later in this chapter), when it comes to your actual credit score, you'll want to pay the most attention to the FICO scoring model. FICO scores are used by lenders and most businesses, and your FICO score will give you the best sense of your true credit rating, and where you stand as a potential borrower.

---

MORE INFO **No Matter What the Repositories Say, Stick with FICO**

As you become more familiar with credit, you'll notice how the "big three" will each claim that their own scoring models (which are advertised on their websites) are now being used by lenders instead of the FICO score. Is this true? No. Only the FICO scoring model is used by mortgage lenders, and, currently, out of the three repositories, only Equifax provides FICO scores to consumers (for a fee). You can also pay to have your FICO scores run online, which may run as much $15 to $20 per report.

The smarter idea is to get your FICO scores for free: If you are currently applying for a loan, your mortgage consultant will be able to supply you with a copy of your credit report that will show your FICO score from all *three* repositories. And free is a price that can't be beat. If your consultant hasn't provided you with a copy of your credit report, be sure to ask.

## Your Credit Score Through the Eyes of a Lender

When lenders review your credit, they'll be looking at a customized version of your credit report called a *tri-merged credit report*. This report includes information from each of the three repositories, filtered through the FICO credit scoring model. Since each repository collects different information, a lender will receive three sets of information, and three different FICO credit scores. Of these scores, lenders will use the middle value, referred to as your *middle score*, as your final credit score. (The lowest and highest scores are discarded.) Here's an example:

## 685/705/722

### The lender uses 705 for the loan.

Why are the scores so different? It all goes back to the information that's used to calculate the score, and the fact that the three repositories all gather different information.

Here's a real-world example: Let's say you opened a credit account with a furniture store and purchased a living room set on credit for $1,500. A few months later, you were late in making one of your payments. The furniture store reports this information to one repository, which now reports you have a late payment. The fact that you have $1,500 in new debt, plus a late payment, collectively *lowers* your credit score.

But since the furniture store only reports to *one* of the repositories (and not all three), the other two repositories have no idea that you even made the purchase, let alone that you were late in making a payment. According to these repositories, you don't even have the account, so they'll give you a *higher* credit score.

With all of the different information that the repositories *could* collect, it's easy to see how you could have very different credit scores. You should always expect that your three FICO scores will vary, and sometimes widely.

## *How a Lender Grades Your Credit*

Although the credit repositories will tell you if *they* think your credit is good or bad, what matters most is how your lender views your credit. Most lenders grade your credit as follows:

> A score above 720 is considered *Excellent*
> A score between 700 to 719 is considered *Good*
> A score between 660 to 699 is *Acceptable*
> A score between 620 to 659 is *Low*
> A score between 580 to 619 is *Poor*
> A score between 300 to 579 is *Bad*

If only one person is applying for a loan, a lender will use the individual's middle credit score to determine what type of financing they might qualify for. But if two people are applying jointly for a loan, each person's credit will be run independently, their middle scores will be determined, and the *lower* of the two middle scores will be used for the loan. This is an important fact to keep in mind when you are shopping for a mortgage, because this lower credit score will limit the loans you can qualify for—if you can even qualify for a loan at all! Let's take a look at a husband and wife's credit. Here is how their scores appear on the tri-merged credit report:

```
Husband's Scores: 560/575/588
    Wife's Scores: 725/732/744
The lender uses 575 for the couple's loan.
```

This couple's 575 credit score is poor, and will be too low to qualify for any type of affordable financing in today's market. However, if the wife could qualify for the loan on her own (based on her income, assets, savings, and debt), with a 732 credit score the couple could easily receive very good financing.

## How Lenders Have Changed Their Credit Requirements

It used to be that a credit score of 620 would open doors for you with many lenders. But that's no longer the case: shortly after the housing boom came to an end, lenders started to change their credit score requirements. In today's post-boom finance market, a *minimum* score of 660 is required to qualify for most affordable conventional loans. In the world of credit, the change from 620 to 660—a difference of 40 points—is significant, and it directly affects the ability of many hard-working people to obtain decent financing. Currently, if your credit score is below 660, financing will be more expensive, or you may be turned down for a loan entirely. Your best bet is to concentrate your efforts on securing an FHA or specialty loan program, or wait on financing until you have improved your credit score.

If you have a high credit score, it will help when you apply for a loan, but I want to emphasize once again that even a high credit score does not *guarantee* that you'll receive a loan. Whether your loan is approved or denied is decided by a lender's underwriter, who determines on a case-by-case basis if a borrower is qualified, if the risk is worth taking, and if the loan is favorable for the lender.

One of the ways a lender will determine this risk is by scrutinizing your credit report many times over. This includes:

- How do you manage your debt?
- What payment patterns do you have?
- What kind of debt do you have?
- How much debt could you have?
- Are your credit patterns relatively stable, or are they erratic?

If anything about your credit report doesn't sit right with an underwriter, you could be turned down for financing. For example: A loan program may require a 660 credit score. You meet all of the written requirements, including the 660 credit score. But the underwriter doesn't like your spending patterns, and denies the loan. It happens every day.

## How Everyday Decisions Impact Your Credit . . . and Your Loan

Even when you understand what's in your credit report, how your credit score is calculated, and how lenders view your credit, it is still sometimes difficult to see how everyday decisions will impact your credit.

Most credit issues today are caused by an inability to *stop* using credit. Charging too much, making late payments, and not paying down balances responsibly will obviously all hurt your credit. And habits like this don't only damage your credit. They also end up being a deal-breaker just when you need your credit the most: when you are in the process of purchasing or refinancing your home.

When you apply for a loan, your credit score, credit history, overall debt, assets, and income are all carefully examined many times before and during the loan approval process. Lenders like consistency, and if anything changes, a *single* change can immediately become a monumental obstacle and can jeopardize your loan's approval. Most times, these changes occur in your credit. A change could be a purchase, a missed payment, or even opening a new account. In most cases, a small purchase on an existing credit account will not matter to a lender. But the addition of a new car payment ten days before closing on a loan, or charging a card close to its limit during the loan approval process—well, that's a different story.

For example, you may always pay your bills on time. But one month, you forget to mail your mortgage payment, and your credit is hit with a 30-day late. Even though you have a record of on-time payments, a single 30-day late on your credit report can set your credit score back by 50 or more points—and in the lending industry, this reduction could take you from an excellent borrower (with a credit score of 720) to an average borrower (with a credit score of 670) in seconds.

Or maybe you have neglected to tell your loan consultant about the new fishing boat you just purchased that has a payment of $1,100 a month. Overnight, your credit will change—and most likely, your credit score will drop. Your new debt, and your new credit score, has also set off multiple red flags with your lender. Your lender will need to determine if you can afford your new *total* debt: you may think you can afford your new mortgage and your boat, but your lender may not agree, and could decide to loan you *less*. In addition, since your credit score has changed, you may no longer qualify for your loan, or your lender could decide to charge you more for your loan because you are seen as more of a risk.

All of this could happen just because of a boat? Yes. Simply put, a new large debt is as risky as it comes. All lenders want minimal risk, and they never want to see dramatic changes in your credit habits anywhere close to the day they must write their big check for you.

---

### THE 85-POINT NOSEDIVE

Jay and Laurie were first-time homebuyers and had spent a lot of time talking with banks, consultants, and brokers, looking for the best loan. They were a young couple, and had very good credit—they each had several active credit card and gas card accounts and had maintained enough of an on-time payment history to establish good credit depth. Jay and Laurie were considered "A" borrowers, and even though this was their first home purchase, they had many lenders fighting for their business. They had very good job histories, a twelve-month perfect rental history, and money in savings from their wedding to use as a 15 percent down payment. As an added benefit, Jay and Laurie both had small retirement accounts with solid balances, which made them even better borrowers in the eyes of a lender.

Because of their borrower profiles, I was able to place Jay and Laurie into a good loan quickly. Jay and Laurie signed their loan application, and after only a week their loan was underway: the application had been submitted to the lender, the lender had been supplied with all of the required documentation, the appraisal for the property was ordered, the required homeowners insurance was paid, and their loan's interest rate was locked and secured. We just needed to allow the lender some time to process the loan, and soon Jay and Laurie would be in their new home. I left them with instructions to sit tight, detailing what to do (and what not to do) prior to their closing date. It would be smooth sailing—or so I thought.

The week of their closing, I received a call from the lender's underwriter. There was a problem. A *big* problem. The underwriter explained that, in keeping with final stages of quality control, they had run Jay and Laurie's credit one last time prior to closing. It turned out that Jay and Laurie had gone on a shopping spree to decorate their new home, charging new furniture and appliances. On top of that, because their credit was so good, one store had given them a new $8,000 credit limit, which they had almost maxed out. In the eyes of the lender—and the credit repositories—the shopping spree was a triple hit: they had maxed out their available credit, they had a new credit card, and they now carried much higher debt. And as if this debt weren't enough, Jay and Laurie had also purchased a very expensive new car. I was devastated. I knew we were in trouble and I braced myself for the worst news of all: *Their middle credit scores had dropped 72 and 85 points.*

Jay and Laurie no longer qualified for their loan, and the only solution was a new loan with a higher interest rate. Were the purchases truly too hard to pass up? Couldn't they have waited? Of course they could have. But Jay and Laurie didn't realize the power of their own credit, and they unfortunately learned the hard way.

Jay and Laurie didn't fully understand—or fully believe—how their new purchases would impact their credit, and they also didn't realize their lender would be watching their credit throughout the entire loan process. I spend a lot of time working with my clients on the consequences of credit. I really don't enjoy being the bearer of bad news: credit issues are *never* missed or conveniently overlooked by lenders. If you have good credit, it should never be taken for granted. And you should always be extremely cautious about how you use your credit before, during, and after you apply for any kind of financing.

## How Bad Credit Will Cost You More

When you apply for financing for a home, having bad or even mediocre credit means higher interest rates, more money out of your pocket, and lending surcharges. Even homeowners insurance premiums and mortgage insurance will cost more, because from the insurer's perspective, bad credit means there is a higher chance you might file a claim. And even if you don't own a home, poor credit will follow you. Car insurance rates run 20 to 50 percent more. Automotive loans cost more. And individual credit cards may carry an interest rate two to three times higher than standard rates. These are all great reasons to work on improving your credit.

Having bad credit doesn't mean you are a bad person. It's easy to have issues impact your credit: job loss, medical problems, divorce, and simply trying to make ends meet or balancing what you can and cannot pay will easily affect your credit. Even those who once had good credit have been hurt by the housing and lending crash, missing payments on mortgages, car loans, credit cards, and more.

The good news is that anyone can actively work on and improve their credit, and usually it will only take your time and patience. Let's get started.

## The Ten-Step Plan to Improve Your Credit

Think it's too hard to improve your credit? You'll be surprised. Clearing up many common issues can give you a higher credit score in as little as thirty to ninety days. Whether you have good credit or bad, anyone can benefit from following these ten steps:

### Step 1: Complete a Clean Sweep of Your Credit

Start by thoroughly reviewing a copy of your credit report from each of the three repositories. Be sure to check recent information, but also check back as far as each report goes, making sure *all* of the information in your report is accurate.

### Your Free Credit Report

By federal law, consumers are entitled to a free credit report from all three repositories one time each year. You can access your reports by visiting www.annualcreditre-port.com or by calling (877) 322-8228. These services are authorized and monitored by the Federal Trade Commission, and were developed specifically for the purpose of providing consumers with a copy of their credit. Take advantage of this service—the credit report itself is provided for free. If you'd like for your report to include your credit score (as most people do) you will be charged a small fee, usually $5 to $7 per report.

You can also order a copy of your credit report and your credit score directly from each repository for a one-time fee, which generally runs $15 or less per report:

www.equifax.com | (800) 685-5000
www.experian.com | (889) 397-3742
www.transunion.com | (866) 887-2673

If you have recently been denied credit, you are also entitled to receive a *free* copy of your credit report for up to thirty days after the initial rejection. You can request this copy by contacting the credit repositories directly, and by supplying them with a copy of your rejection letter. Any time you are denied credit, you can—and should—request a copy of your credit report.

---

▶ **Check your identifying information:** Are there any misspellings or inaccuracies? Does your credit report list any addresses where you haven't lived? Is there any other information you don't recognize? Remember, you are checking for mistakes, but you also want to be sure that your identity hasn't been stolen, and that another individual's information hasn't made its way onto your credit report.

▸ **Check your account information:** For each account, are the account numbers, dates, balances, limits, and terms all correct? Are there any accounts that are not yours, or is there any account activity you don't recognize? If you have paid your bills on time, are any of your accounts showing as late or delinquent? And if you *have* been late or have missed payments, is the reported information correct? There's a big difference between being late by thirty, sixty, and ninety or more days, both in how your credit score is calculated, and in how potential creditors and lenders will rate your file, so be sure this information is correct, even if the information is from the past, and even if it may mean additional work to check your own records.

▸ **Check your public records information:** Are your public record listings correct? More importantly, should they still be listed on your report? Check back again to the chart on page 298 to see when information is legally required to be removed from your credit report. You want to make sure any negative information doesn't stay on a minute longer than it has to (to remove it, see Step 2). Although by law this information must be removed after the designated time period, there is no law stating the information must remain on your report for the entire time period. In fact, there is no law that states this information must appear on your credit report at all! You may be able to have some items removed sooner, simply by making the request to have it removed yourself.

▸ **Clear up any outstanding accounts or derogatory remarks:** Did you forget to send in a payment? Are any of your accounts marked "not paid as agreed" or "charged-off"? A *charge off* in your credit file means that the creditor doesn't expect to collect the debt, and has written the debt off as a loss. This usually happens after three to six months of nonpayment, but it doesn't mean you no longer owe the amount, and it doesn't mean a creditor won't continue to try to collect it either.

If any of these terms appear in your credit report, take action as soon as possible to rectify the issues with your creditors. Pay what is owed or work out a payment plan and then note it in your credit report, which I'll explain how to do in Step 3. If disputes or derogatory remarks are reported incorrectly, get the information corrected or removed as soon as possible. To do this, see Step 2.

---

MORE INFO

### When to Let Sleeping Dogs Lie

I always advocate being responsible for your debt, but there is one case where being responsible and taking care of your debt will actually harm your credit. If you have any old collection accounts or charge-offs (accounts that are at least two to three years old), paying them off will actually *lower* your credit score. Why? Because suddenly, the account is active again, and part of your new credit history. Even though you are paying off the debt, the scoring models will be reminded that the debt was there in the first place, and your score will drop.

If you are not applying for financing anytime soon, take the time now to pay off the charges, and then work on improving your credit score, so that when you *do* need your credit, your score has improved. If you have already applied for financing, wait to see if the lender will require you to pay off the account. If they make an exception and you aren't required to bring the account current, you can wait until after your loan has closed to pay the collection and rebuild your credit score.

---

## Step 2: File Disputes as Needed

Don't be surprised if there are a lot of mistakes on your credit report. The big three of credit may do a great job of collecting information, but they don't do the best job of making sure the information is accurate. This is actually *your* job. If you find any incorrect information, you will need to file a dispute.

Many people feel like they won't be able to handle a dispute themselves, or that they need legal representation. There is no need to feel this way. Remember, the credit repositories are private companies, and they have an obligation *to you* as a consumer to report accurate information. All three credit repositories are required, by both federal and state law, to remove any inaccurate information from your credit report. And once this information is removed, it cannot be put back on. Any issue on your credit report can be disputed: from small issues (for instance, a closed account that is reporting as open) to larger issues, from missed payments that were paid on time to collections that are incorrect or not yours. Even facts about a foreclosure or bankruptcy can be disputed if they are reported incorrectly. So if you find information that's not right, what should you do?

▸ **First, contact the repositories:** To file a dispute, you'll need to contact the credit repository directly. If the issue appears on all three of your credit reports, you will need to contact and file three separate disputes. However, if the issue only appears on one report, don't contact the other two repositories, even as a preventative measure. Remember, the credit repositories all collect *different* information. Disputing information that isn't wrong on a report only opens up the potential for new errors to be introduced somewhere else.

Contacting the repositories is easy: you can actually file disputes online. Each repository has its own web-based system where you can submit the dispute, check for status updates, and receive a final resolution. You can also file a dispute by mail: the repositories' websites provide information for how to file a dispute in writing, including special dispute forms and mailing addresses for dispute documentation.

 If you're not sure where to look on the repository's websites, I've made things easier for you by gathering all of this information in one place. Visit the reader's section of my website, where you'll also find direct links to each repository's dispute department.

▶   **Next, contact your creditor:** In addition to contacting the repositories, you will also need to contact your creditor to correct the error, either via phone or in writing. The repositories aren't acting on your behalf when they contact your creditors; they are only investigating and verifying if your dispute is accurate. Don't put the fate of your credit in the hands of the repositories. You'll want to be sure you receive a resolution with the creditor yourself, and that this information has been corrected in their own records and files.

Some errors are small, and your creditor will have no problem updating your records. But larger errors—a missed payment that was actually paid on time, for example—might require more effort and proof. If you don't get anywhere at first, ask for a supervisor or send your request to a higher department. Once you have resolved the issue, request that the information be accurately reported back to the repository, and that you are sent a confirmation in writing when this is complete.

---

 **Put It in Writing**

In all of your correspondence (both with the credit repositories and with your creditors), be prepared to provide paperwork or documentation to show that an error is, in fact, an error. A verbal explanation usually won't correct anything: put it in writing and back it up with facts, send correspondence via certified mail, and keep a copy of all correspondence for your records.

---

If the credit repositories do not hear back from your creditors within thirty to forty-five days of when you originally submitted your dispute, by law the information is required to be removed. If the repository is unable to reach the creditor or is unable to thoroughly research the dispute, the information is *also* required to be removed.

Once the information has been corrected, you may want others to know about it. If you request it, your corrected credit report will be supplied to anyone who has reviewed your credit within the past six months, and to employers who have reviewed your credit within the past two years, free of charge.

### Step 3: File a 100-Word Explanation

There may also be information on your credit report that is negative but correct. In these cases, you won't be able to remove the information, but you are able to explain why the information is appearing in your report. For *any* event or information that appears in your credit report, you may provide a 100-word explanation to tell your side of the story, or to explain why you were unable to work out a solution with a particular creditor.

You will need to file this explanation with each repository that is reporting the information, and you will also want to check your credit report twice a year (as I recommend in Step 5) to make sure this explanation is accurate and visible to anyone who views your report. Some repositories will leave these explanations on your report indefinitely or until you request they be removed; others will require you to update or renew the explanation every six months.

 Are you unsure of what to write, or where to send your explanation? I provide samples of various explanations and disputes, and how this information should be submitted to the repositories, on my website.

### Step 4: Request a Score Improvement Analysis and a Rapid Credit Rescore

There may be times when you need to improve your credit score quickly (for example, when you are applying for a loan), or you may just want to see what you should work on that will improve your credit the most. In both cases, you can benefit from what's known in the industry as a *score improvement analysis*.

Mortgage consultants, credit counselors, credit attorneys, and other lending professionals all have access to industry programs that will analyze approximately how much your score will increase by correcting errors, paying off accounts, paying down accounts, closing accounts, or resolving other credit issues. A score improvement analysis is a great tool and will easily provide you with a plan of action for which areas of your credit report you should work on first to improve your score the fastest, and what you can work on to improve your score the most.

Once you follow this plan and have taken measures to improve your credit (which might include paying missed payments, paying down high balances, or working out other issues with your creditors), you can also request what is known as a *rapid credit rescore* from your mortgage consultant. In a rapid credit rescore, the credit repositories quickly rescore your credit, which can increase your credit score in as little as twenty-four to seventy-two hours. Yes, it's really that fast. Rapid credit rescores may only be requested by a mortgage consultant or lender (you cannot contact the repositories yourself about this service), and they usually cost anywhere from $10 to $30.

Score improvement analysis and rapid credit rescoring are frequently used as part of the lending process. For example, your credit score could be too low to qualify for a loan program, or your low score could be costing you money. Many times, making even small improvements to your credit can make a big difference.

Let's take a look at Jack and his friend Jill, who both were interested in the same Fannie Mae conventional loan:

> Jack and Jill are both interested in a conventional loan program by Fannie Mae. In this program, borrowers who have a credit score under 680 are charged higher lending fees. Jack is purchasing a $300,000 home with 20 percent down. He has a 670 credit score, and his loan fees total $3,000.
>
> Jill is also purchasing a $300,000 home with 20 percent down. But Jill has a credit score of 680—*just 10 points higher.*

Her loan fees total only $1,800.

Jack works with his mortgage consultant to quickly improve and rescore his credit. By improving his credit by only 10 points, Jack saves $1,200.

## Step 5: View Your Credit Report Yourself at Least Twice a Year

Get in the habit of running your credit report twice a year, especially if a major issue has been resolved, if any major purchases have been made, or if large debts have been paid off. The credit repositories are constantly updating your credit report. Just because you resolve issues and errors doesn't mean *new* issues won't appear in your report in the future. By reviewing all three reports at least twice a year, you will also:

- Be able to catch errors and correct them immediately, preserving your credit score

- Become more familiar with what's in your report, making it easier to spot issues in the future

- Receive your actual credit score from all three repositories. (When someone else runs your credit, they often supply you with only one of these scores.)

- Have a good overview of your loans, credit accounts, and total debt, all in one place

If you are purchasing or refinancing a home or have plans to own a home in the future, I always recommend that you check your own credit a minimum of ninety to 120 days before your closing date. If there are any issues, this will give you enough time to resolve them *before* you proceed with your loan.

You should also check your credit before you apply for other loans (such as student loans) or before you sign up for new credit card accounts. Feel free to pull your own credit report as much as you feel you should: when you request to review your own credit for *any* reason, it is not considered to be an official credit inquiry, and it will not impact your credit score in any way.

## Step 6: Always Pay Your Bills on Time

I don't want you to part with your money any more than you do, but if you have credit issues (and even if you don't), you don't want to be even one day late on your payments. Remember, 35 percent of your credit score is based on your payment history. Any payments that are thirty days past due can set your credit back substantially, so make paying on time a priority.

Better yet, pay your bills early. If you habitually pay during your grace period (the period of time after your due date where you can still make your payment and not be considered late), even though the payment isn't officially late, your account will be noted as a *slow pay*, which will *also* affect your credit. Because of this, you'll always want to make your payments so they arrive *before* the statement due date. Doing so is actually a proven technique to raise your credit score.

## Step 7: Use Credit and Credit Cards the Right Way

You may think using your credit cards means to "charge-it," but there are actually ways you can use your credit to improve your options for financing *and* your credit score.

▶ **Use your cards regularly.** Creditors and lenders want to see that you can manage credit responsibly. As I mentioned in the last chapter, lenders would prefer to see cards that are used regularly and paid down regularly, than cards with no balance or even no credit cards at all. In fact, even if you don't carry a balance, you should use each of your credit cards at least three times a year (paying off new charges) to keep the accounts active and beneficial to your credit history. Most lenders will look for each credit card to have a credit activity of at least twenty-four months. This lets a lender know you have a longer history of making responsible payments, making it more likely you will responsibly pay your mortgage as well.

▸ **Avoid carrying a balance.** Use your cards to build your credit or for the convenience of a payment, but try not carry a balance. I know that for many people, this is difficult. You might need to carry balances on your credit cards just to make ends meet, but you can still work at paying balances down by working on budgeting and spending. Take a minute to refer again to Chapter 8 for my advice on budgeting, and be sure to read through Chapter 10 for many ways you can cut costs and save money. Pay off your credit cards as consistently as you can, with the goal of carrying no more than 20 percent of the card's total credit limit as a balance. If you have balances on several credit cards, try to distribute the balances by paying down higher balances first.

▸ **If you have to carry a balance, keep it under 50 percent of the card's limit.** Credit cards that carry balances over 50 percent of the card's credit limit will cause your credit score to drop, *even if* you make your payments on time and *even if* your credit limit is low. Even on credit cards with very low limits? Yes. The credit scoring models look at the *ratio* of your balance to your spending limit. For example, let's say you have two credit accounts: one with a $200 limit and a $190 balance, and one with a $5,000 limit and a $4,750 balance.

$$95\% \rightarrow \frac{\$190}{\$200} \qquad \frac{\$4{,}750}{\$5{,}000} \nwarrow 95\%$$

Each card is at 95 percent of its spending limit. Believe it or not, you'll be penalized the *same* way for each card. The closer you get to owing 100 percent of your credit limit, the more your score is lowered.

What does this mean for you? It's better to have several credit cards with small balances than one card that is close to being maxed out. Many people will carry a high balance on a credit card because it has a low interest rate compared to their other credit cards, not realizing that they are hurting their credit score in the process.

▸ **Pay at least the minimum payment.** Always make as big of a payment as you can, but at the very least, pay the minimum payment each month. This is a required amount; not paying at least the minimum payment is not making a full payment. And as you know, when you don't make a payment, your payment is considered late and your credit score drops.

## Step 8: After You Establish Credit Accounts, Limit the Cards You Carry

There is a lot of conflicting advice within the personal finance industry when it comes to credit cards, especially about the amount of credit cards you should carry. You may hear that it's okay to have as many credit cards as you want, but you really *do* want to limit the number of credit cards you carry. There is also a difference between using credit cards you have had for a long time (which establishes a credit history) and opening up new accounts at every new department store. So what cards should you avoid, and what cards should you keep?

▸ **Avoid department store cards**. To a lender, too many cards means the potential for even more debt, which increases a lender's risk. And to the credit repositories, too many department store credit cards are frowned upon, because they are given to anyone, even to people who shouldn't be granted credit. In fact, opening a department store credit card may actually *lower* your credit score by as much as 20 points! The repositories view applying for department store credit cards as an impulse decision, or a fast fix to get more credit, and they'll dock you for it—even if opening the account was a planned decision on your part. As a consumer, you must always balance between your own needs for having access to credit, how a lender views credit, and how the credit cards you have affect your credit score.

▸ **Keep four to six long-term credit cards.** Ideally, every person should have four credit cards, each with at least a one thousand dollar limit. If you can't stick to four, up to six cards is fine too. If you don't have at least four credit cards, you'll want to open additional accounts, using the new cards every few months and consistently making payments to establish your use of credit.

All of your credit cards should be long-term cards, so when you are deciding what accounts to open, choose cards you know you will use regularly, and will want to keep for many years to come. Having and using four credit cards will establish a good payment history and credit depth, and can allow for a better distribution of your total debt.

▸ **Don't jump to cancel your cards.** If you have too many credit cards, you will want to carefully consider which cards you cancel, or if you should cancel them at all. While canceling cards (and decreasing your possible debt) will make a lender happy, in most cases, the credit scoring models will take notice and will actually *decrease* your credit score. Here's why: credit scoring models like ratios. When the scoring models look at how much you owe (which accounts for 30 percent of your credit score) they compare this to how much you *could* owe—your credit limits.

For example, let's say you carry a total credit balance of $4,000. You have six credit cards, and between these six cards, you have $15,000 in available credit. Let's pretend you cancel two of the credit cards, and you now have $10,000 in available credit.

How much of your available credit is used?

$$26\% \rightarrow \frac{\$4,000}{\$15,000} \qquad \frac{\$4,000}{\$10,000} \leftarrow 40\%$$

To the credit scoring models, you now look like you are using *much more* of your total available credit, and your credit score will be docked.

Because of this, if you do decide to cancel credit cards, cancel accounts that are new with a short credit history *before* you cancel any mature or long-standing accounts. When you cancel your cards, you must cancel in writing, stating that the cancellation is to be noted in your file as "closed at the customer's request." And last but not least, try not to cancel any more than two cards per year to have the least impact on your credit score.

## Step 9: Guard Your Credit Inquiries

If you do apply for new accounts, do so with caution: when you apply for credit of any kind, these applications are listed as an inquiry, along with any other inquiries that may be happening within your credit file. If you have four or more inquiries within a two-month period, everyone will take notice: the credit repositories, who will lower your score, and lenders, who will think you are scrambling for money.

There are only two exceptions to this rule: inquiries that are made when you apply for a mortgage (which may come from the lender, a mortgage broker firm, or a credit reporting firm) or credit inquiries made by you.

If inquiries appear on your account that you didn't authorize, you can file a dispute or call the creditor asking for proof that you gave permission to run your credit. Even if the company does have a legitimate reason for running your credit, many times, big companies just don't have the time to provide this documentation, and the creditor will remove the inquiry from your report, which will increase your credit score.

## Step 10: Keep Your Cards From Being Cancelled

With a decline in the availability of credit, many credit card companies are actively canceling cards that have not been used recently or have been dormant for long periods of time. You may think you have enough credit, only to open your mailbox one day to find that one of your credit card accounts has been closed. The door to open credit has been slammed shut. Not only have you lost access to the credit, but as you've learned, your credit score may drop, because you now have less available credit. If you are carrying any debt, this means your debt-to-credit ratios could change—along with your credit score.

Can you prevent your credit cards from being cancelled? Yes, by using every one of your credit cards at least once every two to three months. Make a small charge on each card, and pay the charges off to keep the cards active.

If you have already received a notification that a credit card has been cancelled, you'll want to see how the cancellation has been reported on your credit report. Check that the account has been reported as "paid in full," and that it has been "closed at the customer's request." If the account still shows a balance, or if the card has been noted as "closed at the *creditor's* request," contact the credit card company. You'll want to resolve any balance, and/or ask that the card be reported as "closed at the *customer's* request," which will have less impact on your credit score and be viewed more favorably by future creditors. If the creditor refuses, you can always file a dispute (and a 100-word explanation), to be noted in your credit report.

· · ·

Taking control of your credit is not difficult, and it is important for everyone, no matter where you live, what you do, or if you have good credit or bad. Having good credit will mean more opportunity, whether this opportunity is in the form of a home, a car, or even a job. You'll receive lower interest rates for anything you finance, and as a result, you will be able to save more money. And more money and good credit are two things everyone can benefit from, and are the two items you need to achieve your goals for owning a home, or for securing your financial future. Take the time to take control of your credit. The results are worth it.

## COMING UP

Now that you have a better handle on your credit, it's time to look at your finances. In the next chapter, I'll show you how you can make smart decisions with your money, and how changing your relationship with money will allow you to save more, spend less, and regain your financial security.

# 10

# The Bigger Costs of Living

Taxes, Insurance, and Everything in Between

*How to Make the Most of What You Can't Change,*
*and How to Change What You Can*

W ho doesn't want better finances? Who wouldn't like to save more money? We all would, of course. Having financial security and stability is important to just about everyone. Being able to save money has always been part of financing and owning a home, but within our current lending markets, saving money is even more important. Saving more to have more of a down payment will allow you to receive better loan terms and interest rates. It will also keep your lending options open if you don't fit conventional lending standards, or if you have anything other than absolutely perfect credit. As the saying goes, money talks—and in lending, it certainly does.

Being able to save and budget money is also extremely important if you are struggling to pay your mortgage, or if you have high or adjusting mortgage costs that you need to find the money to pay for. And as I discussed in Chapter 8, if you are recovering from any type of home loss or a bankruptcy, regaining control of your finances is an essential part of your recovery.

Even beyond the subject of homeownership, saving money and

spending wisely is crucial in any economy. Everyone can benefit from improving their finances and preparing for the times ahead. And today, almost everyone is looking for more ways to save money and make ends meet. It seems every newspaper article and news story of late contains staggering statistics of job loss, home loss, and good people who have very few options left. We all need ways to save more, or at least keep the money we have left.

I know it's hard to avoid the negativity that's out there about the state of our economy. I am not claiming there is an easy recovery in sight, and I'm certainly not claiming there is an easy solution. But negative thinking isn't the answer. We've been in situations just as bad—and recovered from them—before. Let's take a look at what's happened just in our recent history:

- From 1973 to 1974 the price of oil quadrupled, sending the U.S. into an energy crisis. The crisis peaked again in 1979.

- In 1978 and 1979 the average interest rate was between 11.5 and 13.3 percent. In December 1980 the prime rate hit an all-time high of 21.5 percent.

- The Savings and Loan Crisis of the 1980s involved over 3,800 financial institutions and left taxpayers with a bill of $126.4 billion.

- The 1990s dot-com crash was responsible for the loss of over $5 trillion in market value, and wiped out the savings of many middle-class Americans.

What's my point here? You will get through this. We have before. A majority of homeowners are in serious trouble. But focusing on the negative isn't a form of assistance and, in my opinion, it just doesn't help. Be aware of the challenges you face, but don't dwell on them. Every time you encounter an obstacle, stop yourself. Count to five. Ten if you need it. And instead, concentrate on what you *can* do to help yourself, and to start making improvements.

In this chapter, you'll see how you can make smarter decisions about how you spend and save money. You'll learn how simply changing your thinking on many financial issues, from some of the biggest costs of homeownership all the way down to the smallest financial decisions you make every day, will make a significant difference. I'll give you insider advice on expenses like real estate taxes, homeowners insurance, and escrows that will allow you to be proactive, plan ahead, *and* save money. And I'll also help you develop a plan for how to control and improve your finances overall, and where you can go for extra help if you need it.

Let's start with how you can begin to take action in regard to some of the bigger costs that come with owning a home: taxes and insurance.

## Hey, Mr. Taxman

Taxes. Everyone pays them and everyone complains about them. All states have real estate taxes, so no matter where you live, if you choose to own a home, you will always pay taxes. But there *are* ways to be smarter about your tax bill. If you are thinking about making a purchase or refinancing any time in the near future, it's time to start thinking about taxes. And if you currently own a home and are paying property taxes, there may be ways you can decrease your tax bill immediately.

Just how are real estate taxes determined? Although every area of the country levies taxes differently, property taxes always involve two important values: market value and assessed value. *Market value* is how much your home is worth (or could sell for) in a current real estate market; this amount is usually determined by your local government's property appraiser or tax assessor. The market value is then used to determine your *assessed value*, the actual value your local government uses to tax your home.

Assessed value can be calculated many different ways: sometimes a tax credit is deducted from a home's market value; other times, the assessed value may be a straight percentage or a complex calculation based on market value. Either way, this is the number you really want to pay attention to, because it determines how much you pay yearly in taxes.

For example, let's assume that in your area the assessed value is 60 percent of market value. Your county's real estate tax rate is 2 percent. What would taxes be for a $200,000 home?

```
$200,000 x 60% = $120,000 assessed value
$120,000 x 2% = $2,400 in taxes
```

In addition to understanding how you are being taxed, you also need to consider how *often* your taxes might change. In many areas, your home's market and assessed values are reevaluated every year, so every year your taxes can change. In other areas, your home's value may only be assessed every few years (for example, every three or six years), or when there are structural improvements made to the property. And in some areas, your taxes really won't change much at all for the entire time you own the home.

For example, in California, after you purchase a home, your taxes are "capped" and will not rise more than 2 percent a year, even if your home's value increases. And if your home's value *decreases*, you can appeal for lower taxes (which I'll explain shortly)—so if your taxes do change, they'll be changing for the better. The taxes really won't change much at all until you *sell* the home. After the sale, the home's sales price is used to recalculate the taxes for the new owner.

Understanding how your taxes are calculated may seem insignificant. The government is going to charge taxes as they see fit, right? Well, this is true, but there are ways you can lessen your tax burden. Most homeowners are simply unaware that options even exist.

▸ **Challenge or appeal your assessment.** Depending on how often your taxes are calculated, you might be paying too much in taxes. For

**Research Your Tax Information**

Depending on where you live, your property taxes may be determined by your county, your city, or your town. This information is all available online; you can find out how your home is assessed and taxed through your local government's property appraiser, tax assessor, or tax commissioner's website. Or you can always research how and when your home will be taxed in the future by reviewing your previous years' tax statements.

example, what if where you live, home values are normally evaluated every three years? This might mean that the last time your home's value was assessed was during the height of the real estate boom. Since then, home values have dropped. Today, your home could be worth significantly less, while you are *still* paying taxes based on the previous, high value.

There could also be a mistake in how the appraiser has valued your home. For example, the square footage, number of rooms, lot size, or improvements to your property might have been noted incorrectly. Your home could also have issues (leaks, an old roof, disrepair) that an assessor wouldn't know about. Issues like these that would normally *hurt* your chances of selling a home can often *help* you in decreasing your home's assessed value, and in lowering your taxes—making this the one and only time you'll be happy if your home has any serious issues.

It's also possible that your home has been assessed at a higher value than other homes right in your own neighborhood without a valid reason. Compare your home's market value to recent real estate sales in your area. Does your value reflect recent sales? You can also review online property tax records to compare your home to similar homes in your neighborhood. Are your values and taxes in line with your neighbors'? You won't know until you check.

---

MORE INFO **When Identical Homes Have Different Taxes**

If you live in an area like California, where taxes aren't reevaluated until there is a sale or an appeal, home prices within a given area could vary greatly. Your home could be identical in every way to your neighbor's, but if you purchased your home recently and your neighbor has owned his home for thirty years, you and your neighbor will have dramatically different assessed values, and dramatically different taxes.

---

If you find an error or if your home has been assessed incorrectly, don't be surprised—it is estimated that over *40 percent* of property tax appraisals contain errors of some kind. Your local tax assessor won't be looking out for mistakes, because higher assessed values mean more revenue for your local government. But a higher assessment means higher taxes for you, so you want to be aware and be proactive.

As a homeowner, you have the right to file an appeal to challenge how your home has been assessed; forms and instructions for filing will be on your local tax assessor's website. Check in advance for how your local area handles appeals. There are usually hard deadlines in place for filing, and you typically are only able to appeal your current tax bill within a specific period of time. Be smart and check ahead.

When you appeal, you'll need to document your case carefully. Providing a recent, professional appraisal of your property will help to substantiate your claims. The good news? Three out of four people who have legitimate appeals are successful and walk away with lower taxes.

▸ **Check for discounts.** Most areas offer property tax adjustments for senior citizens, veterans, the disabled, and low-income homeowners. These programs are widely available, but they're usually not taken advantage of. In fact, in some cities, only 40 percent of eligible homeowners have actually applied for these programs. The remaining 60 percent are still paying too much in taxes.

Many areas also grant *homestead exemptions*. With an exemption, homeowners receive a fixed tax credit, which is applied to the home's assessed value. The result? Lower real estate taxes. And while this exemption doesn't apply to investment homes or second homes (you must live in the home as your primary residence), it can offer great tax relief for residents. Again, check with your local tax assessor for the programs that are available in your area, and be sure to check back every year for any new programs or updates.

▸ **Deduct your property taxes.** Even if you aren't able to reduce your property taxes, you can at least use what you pay to lower your income taxes. In most cases, your property taxes may be used as a deduction on both your federal and state income taxes. Be sure to consult with an accountant regarding these deductions, as federal and state laws are sometimes complex and frequently change.

---

 MORE INFO **When Home Values Drop and Taxes Go Up**

Even with recent declines in home values, many homeowners are still faced with higher-than-expected taxes as local governments are forced to increase tax rates—and tax bills—to cope with shortages in revenue. Declining home values, costs associated with local foreclosures, and the current economy have left many cities without proper funding and "in the red." This makes it even *more* important for you to proactively check your tax bill, appeal any mistakes or inaccurate assessments, and investigate any tax discounts that may be available to you.

---

## Budgeting and Planning for Real Estate Taxes

When you are thinking about purchasing or refinancing a home, understanding how your home will be taxed will also allow you to shop smarter, plan, and avoid any tax shocks down the road. If your area's property taxes adjust yearly, you will need to budget and save in the expectation that your taxes will most likely go up every year. If your taxes adjust every few years, you can still plan in advance, so when your taxes do finally increase, you aren't faced with a tax bill you can no longer afford. In fact, you may even decide to *put off* the purchase of a home or wait on remodeling your current home if you know your taxes will increase because of it.

When you finance a home, the *type* of home you purchase can also have an impact on how you budget for property taxes:

▸ **Are you purchasing an existing home?** When you purchase an existing home, it's very likely you will be paying higher taxes than the previous owner. No matter how your local area determines your property taxes, taxes are *always* adjusted when there is a sale. And more often than not, this means higher taxes for you.

> Mr. Jones is selling his home, which he purchased back in 1998. Back then, his home's assessed value was $70,000. In Mr. Jones's area, any increases in taxes are capped until a home is sold. Because of this, Mr. Jones's taxes have been low for years, which couldn't make Mr. Jones happier.
>
> Mr. Jones is selling his home to you. He tells you how much he has been paying in taxes, and you are thrilled about the low rate. But with the sale of the home, the local government reevaluates how much the home is worth in today's market. Surprise! Mr. Jones's home assessed at $175,000. Your taxes will be based on this new, higher value (a significant increase in taxes).

▸ **Are you purchasing a new home?** When you purchase a home through a builder, your first year of real estate taxes will be based on *unimproved property* tax rates. This means you are being taxed only on the undeveloped vacant property. What does this mean financially?

Your tax bill for the first year will be a lot lower, but your taxes will increase significantly the next year.

To estimate what your *final* property taxes will be, ask the builder for the first year's *unimproved tax estimate*. You can also check your county's public tax records, or ask someone in your county's property appraiser or tax assessor's department for this information. Take the unimproved tax estimate and multiply the amount by two. If you live in California, Florida, Massachusetts, New Jersey, or New York, multiply by three. This number should be a fair estimate of what your property taxes will be after the first year.

Now, enter this amount into your budget. Can you still afford the home? If so, great! If not, you may want to consider a less expensive home. With a new home, you can lessen your tax burden by changing the two things that will affect your home's future taxes: the lot size and the square footage of the home. Simply selecting a different lot, or a smaller home model, will help to decrease your future tax bill.

▸ **Are you purchasing a home that is less than a year old?** You find a home that is perfect for you and your family, and the realtor or homeowner tells you what the taxes are. Or maybe you are searching for homes online, and the yearly tax bill for the home you're looking at is part of the home's property listing. Are these taxes based on the *unimproved property* tax rate, or are they the *actual* property taxes for the home? When a home is under one year old, you'll need to check.

Again, you can easily find this information online within your area's property tax records. Search by the home's address to view the current tax bill (which will also detail the tax rate); many times, you will also be able to view the estimated tax bill for the upcoming year. You may find that the taxes are too high. If they are, take the time (before you look for any other homes) to determine what price of home you *should* be looking for. Many tax assessors' websites offer an online property tax calculator, which will estimate your taxes, based on a home's sales price. Try a few home prices to see how they affect your yearly taxes, and use this information to determine what price of home you can afford.

▸ **Are you refinancing your home?** When you refinance your home, be aware that your home's value—and your taxes—might increase. Even though refinancing doesn't involve a sale, it could trigger a reevaluation of your property, and if you have recently made any structural improvements to the property (for example, if you have added a room or an outside patio), your taxes may go up.

This is a great opportunity to plan in advance. If you want to refinance but are also considering remodeling in the near future, refinance *first* to avoid the possibility of higher taxes. If you have already made improvements to your property, you can still plan ahead by making sure you consider higher taxes as part of the *total costs* of your refinance.

How can you determine what your new taxes might be? When you apply for a refinance, your home will be appraised, and your home's new appraisal will reflect any change in market value (including any increases in value from remodeling or improvements). You can use this new market value to estimate your assessed value, and, in turn, the possible change to your taxes. If the taxes go up by so much that the refinance wouldn't be beneficial, you can decide not to refinance, and keep your old loan.

## The Cost of Escrowing Real Estate Taxes

Another important consideration for real estate taxes is whether you will be required to escrow. If you finance or refinance more than 80 percent of your home, your taxes will be *escrowed*, which means you will be paying for your taxes in advance with each month's mortgage payment. This helps to protect the lender by making sure the taxes will be paid on time and in full; the lender wants to avoid the possibility that you may not pay your taxes, which would result in a tax lien being placed on your home.

How does escrowing work? An *escrow account* is an account in your name, set up by the lender. The lender reviews a home's current tax bill and uses it as an estimate for the home's next tax bill; this estimate is then divided by twelve and added to each of your monthly mort-

**What Is a Tax Lien?**

If you don't pay your property taxes, your local government will put a tax lien on your home, which gives your county or city a legal claim to your property until the taxes are paid in full. If your taxes remain unpaid for a certain amount of time (the exact amount of time varies from state to state), your home can actually be foreclosed upon by your *local government*—not your lender. For a lender, this is serious business, because when this happens, the tax lien will be paid first, leaving whatever money is left over from the foreclosure sale to pay back the lender. Of course lenders want to avoid this risk, so they will require you to escrow your taxes as a way to protect their own investment in your home.

gage payments. Every month when you pay your mortgage, this extra amount for your taxes is automatically deposited into the escrow account, so when the taxes are due there is enough money to pay your tax bill in full. In many ways, you could think of escrowing as a forced savings plan.

For example, let's say your tax bill is $2,400. Your mortgage payment is $900 a month. So each month, $200 is added to your mortgage payment to prepay for your taxes:

```
$2,400 tax bill ÷ 12 = $200 per month
$900 mortgage + $200 escrow = $1,100 payment
```

## ESCROWING WHEN YOU PURCHASE A HOME

If you are purchasing a home, you may be required to add *more* money to your escrow account in addition to prepaying for your taxes each month. Here's why: when you close on a home, a lender still has work to do; the mortgage must be recorded, and legal paperwork needs to be filed. To allow time for this process, there is often a delay between the date of your closing and when your first mortgage payment is due—usually about thirty to forty-five days.

For example, if you close on a home in January, your first actual mortgage payment may not be due until March. This is a great break for you. But for the lender, this means there are two months' worth of missing escrow payments. Your escrow payments have been calculated based on you making twelve full payments per calendar year. Since you'll be missing two that year, a lender may require that you pay those two months' worth of taxes (plus an additional month or two of payments as a cushion) in full at your closing. This way, the lender makes sure your escrow account will have enough money to cover all your taxes later on. This is called "paying into your reserves."

## ESCROWING WHEN YOU REFINANCE YOUR HOME

Now, if you are refinancing your home, the amount you are required to pay into reserves could be much more, depending on when you refinance and when your home's taxes are due. Lenders pay careful attention to your tax due date; the closer you get to the date, the more you will be required to pay into reserves to cover the tax bill. Here's how this works:

> Let's say in your area, taxes are due in November. You decide to refinance in September. Your lender looks ahead and sees that the entire tax bill is due soon, so the lender will require that you deposit enough into your escrow account at your closing to cover the bill in full.
>
> However, if you can *wait* to refinance until December, the situation is entirely different. The taxes have already been paid, and your lender will only require that you deposit one to two months' worth of payments into the escrow account as reserves for the following year's tax bill.

My advice? If you are required to escrow, one to two months before real estate taxes are due is the *worst* time to refinance. One to two months after taxes are due is the *best* time. If you can't avoid refinancing right before taxes are due, and you are having a tough time coming up with the full amount required for your reserves, the best option is to roll all of your new escrow costs right into your refinance amount, which is what most people do, and what most mortgage consultants will recommend.

What if you were already required to escrow on your *existing* loan? Can't the lender you are refinancing with just use the funds that are in your current escrow account? Unfortunately, no. Even though you are financing the same home, it's a different loan, and a different escrow contract. Escrows aren't transferable between loans or between lenders; the rule is one escrow account per loan, which means your new lender will require a *new* escrow account and *their own* escrow reserves. You will still be required to prepay into the new escrow account each month, and you will still be required to come up with the necessary reserves at closing (which will be calculated as if you didn't have an existing escrow account at all). Once your refinance has closed and funded, your old escrow account will be closed and any funds in it will be returned to you within thirty days.

---

**MORE INFO   Escrow Accounts and Rising Taxes**

If your taxes rise from one year to the next, there still may not be enough in your escrow account to pay your new tax bill in full. If this happens, your lender will pay the difference, and then send you a bill. Either you'll be required to pay for the difference in full or the difference will be divided and added to your monthly mortgage payments. Your regular monthly escrow payments will *also* be recalculated and will increase, based on your new, higher tax bill.

A rule of thumb when escrowing: whenever your taxes increase, your mortgage payments will increase as well.

---

Can you tell your lender you don't want to escrow? Yes, if you finance *less* than 80 percent of your home (if your down payment is more than 20 percent, or if you have more than 20 percent equity in your home). If this is the case, you aren't required to escrow taxes at all. Now, some lenders may charge you a small fee or make a small adjustment to your interest rate if you choose not to escrow, but these fees can usually be waived (if you question the fees and point them out to the lender or broker). But even if they aren't, the cost of the fee is very minor in comparison to the costs associated with an escrow.

How could an escrow cost you money if it's for the same amount you would have to pay in taxes later? Because if your money's not being held in escrow, it could be earning interest for you elsewhere: in a CD, in an interest-bearing savings account, or in another investment account. And unlike with an escrow, you will have access to this money at all times. All in all, if you can avoid having to escrow, it means your money can be working harder for you.

## Homeowners Insurance: Taking Control to Control Costs

Taxes aren't the only thing you may be required to escrow. If you finance more than 80 percent of your home, you will also be required to escrow your homeowners insurance. As I discussed in Chapter 5, homeowners insurance protects both you and your lender; without insurance everyone's investment is at risk. So if you own a home, you should *always* have insurance. But sometimes, even homeowners who aren't required to escrow insurance choose to do so. It's more convenient to have someone else handle paying and renewing the insurance, and it's one less thing to worry about when everything is rolled into one mortgage payment. Right?

Wrong. As a professional, I always recommend *not* escrowing insurance if you are able. If you aren't actively monitoring what is happening with both your insurance rates and renewals when you escrow, your lender is in charge. And that's almost never good news for you: if you forget to renew your insurance and your insurance is cancelled, lenders will take out their *own* insurance policy with an insurance company of their choice—which means your policy coverage will most likely change, your insurance premium may increase (usually by twice as much), and your estimated monthly escrow payments will increase to cover the higher costs. Once a lender takes over, everything is more expensive.

Sometimes, though, taking control of your insurance is about more than saving money. We can all learn from what happened to Joey D., who escrowed his insurance and allowed his lender to take control.

---

MY INSURANCE WILL COVER IT . . . OR WILL IT?

---

A client of mine, Joey D., recently had fine wood floors installed in his home. He was thrilled—he had been able to purchase the flooring from a friend and got a great deal, and his buddy even installed the flooring. And although the project was time-consuming, preparing his house for the new flooring wasn't as bad as he thought it would be. The process was painless, and the floor was beautiful. For weeks, all Joey D. could talk about were his new floors.

About five months after the flooring was installed, I received a panicked call from Joey D. When he was out of town for a weekend, Joey D.'s air conditioning unit had sprung a leak, flooding his entire downstairs. The water had puddled, sat around, and ruined about 70 percent of the flooring. When the buddy who installed the floor came over to inspect the damage, he could only break the bad news: the entire floor would have to be replaced. Not only was the wood flooring destroyed, but this particular flooring had been discontinued. The price of replacement flooring and installation? $3,550.

Joey D. contacted his insurance company immediately to report a claim, expecting some significant compensation to apply toward the cost of the new floor. But when he finally spoke with the insurance representative, Joey D. was informed that he was out of luck. It turned out that a few months back, Joey D. had forgotten to renew his insurance policy. When his lender called to find out what was going on with the insurance,

Joey D. decided to accept the lender's offer of *lender-placed insurance*. And as it turned out, the lender had taken out a new policy from a different insurance provider. To file a claim, Joey would need to contact this new insurance company instead.

But Joey D. was in for a shock. When he called the new insurance company, he was informed that, although he *did* have lender-placed insurance, the policy did *not* allow claims other than catastrophe replacement. And a leaky AC and ruined floors—while very upsetting to Joey D.—were not catastrophic by anyone's definition. This policy clearly protected the lender, but offered no additional protection for the homeowner or the homeowner's property.

Joey D. was furious. This was never explained to him when he agreed to the lender's offer to place the insurance, but when he reviewed the actual policy he realized his fate was sealed. He was unable to make a claim for the floor and, when all was said and done, learning the hard way cost Joey D. over $3,500.

If you can't avoid escrowing your homeowners insurance, is there anything you can do to protect your own interests as a homeowner? Yes, you can still avoid many of the pitfalls of escrowing by taking charge of as much as you can:

▸ **Shop early to control costs.** If you are purchasing or refinancing a home, shop for your own insurance coverage prior to your closing date. As long as the policy you choose includes 100 percent replacement costs (which protects the lender completely), your lender should accept the policy.

▸ **Check that your insurance actually covers what you need it to.** Shopping for your own insurance will save you money, but money isn't always the most important consideration when you are shopping for insurance. Basic and more inexpensive policies usually don't cover personal property (such as wood floors like Joey D.'s, furniture, and clothing). Many times, you will need to expand a homeowners insurance policy if you would like this coverage.

▸ **Prepare for the costs of escrowing.** If you are purchasing a home, you will need to pay for your first year's insurance policy in full, in advance. After this policy is in place, the requirements for escrowing your insurance are the same as they are for your taxes: you will be required to pay a certain amount at closing for insurance reserves, and you will also be prepaying for *next* year's insurance policy as part of your monthly mortgage payments. Your lender will determine the reserve amount, and how much is added to each mortgage payment, based on the cost of your current policy.

If you are refinancing your home, the process is a little different, as you'll already have an insurance policy in place for your home. Your lender will require proof of your current insurance and will ask that your insurance company send over a copy of the *declarations page*, which is a one- to two-page summary of your coverage. A new escrow account will be set up, and you will be required to pay into reserves.

Just like when you escrow real estate taxes, the closer you are to your insurance renewal date, the more you will need to pay into reserves. If you aren't able to pay this amount in full at your closing, you may also be able to roll the costs into your refinance. If you had an escrow account already in place with your previous lender, this account will be closed out, and any money in it will be returned to you within thirty days.

▸ **Memorize your insurance renewal date.** Put it on your calendar, tattoo it on your arm—whatever you need to do. But make sure that you—not your lender—determine what happens at your renewal. As crazy as it sounds, your insurance company may *not* contact you with your renewal rates, even though you are the one who took out the policy. When insurance is escrowed, renewals are sometimes only sent to the lender.

To avoid any problems, contact the insurance company directly for your new policy rates at least one month before your renewal date. This will give you enough time to look for a new policy if your renewal rates are too high or you want to switch your coverage. Once you decide on how you are handling your insurance renewal, any insurance company will be able to provide the lender with the information they need.

▸ **Consider the costs of replacing lender-placed insurance.** What if you missed your insurance renewal date and have lender-placed insurance like Joey D.? Can you change it—and should you change it? It depends. Does the policy offer the protection you need (for example, liability or personal property coverage)? Are the costs reasonable? If your answer is "no," don't feel like you are stuck. Lender-placed insurance is usually a monthly policy, which means you can easily change the policy from one month to the next without penalty.

When you change your insurance, you will first need to purchase a new policy, and insurance companies will require that you pay up to your renewal date in full. Any money that is in your escrow account (which is currently being used to pay for the lender-placed insurance) may be used for this purchase, but if there isn't enough in the account to pay for the policy in full, you'll be required to make up the difference.

Once a lender has proof that a new policy is in effect, they will cancel the lender-placed insurance and things will go back to how they should be: you'll continue to make your escrow payments every month, and you'll have a policy in place that you've selected and that protects you.

Escrowing in general can be confusing, even for those within the industry. And because escrows and reserve amounts are unique from one loan to another, they are usually handled on a case-by-case basis. A good mortgage consultant will help you to understand if your taxes or insurance need to be escrowed, what your monthly escrow payments will be, and what reserve amounts are required (and why).

WEBLINK To help you learn more about escrows, I've provided a few case studies on my website. These studies will help to reinforce how the escrow process works, what costs you can expect, and how you can plan ahead and be prepared.

## Coping With Bigger Expenses and Everyday Costs

You should now feel more prepared when it comes to your taxes and insurance, and hopefully you've also found a few ways in the previous pages to control costs and save money. While taxes and insurance are certainly big costs, I know they aren't the only expenses you're faced with. You may be juggling your finances, your mortgage payments, and other living expenses. And even if you have a good job and are able to pay your bills today, financial security is not guaranteed. Everyone can benefit by making smarter decisions about how they view, manage, and save money. No matter what your situation is, it's never too late to work on your finances.

Here are four steps you can take right now—and every day going forward—to improve both your finances and your future.

### *Step 1: Take Control of Your Checkbook*

The first step is the most important one: changing how you view your relationship with money. To do this, we're going to start with a very basic concept: a checkbook. Sound too simple? Have you ever been surprised when you received your bank statement? Have you ever bounced a check? Do you know how much money is in your accounts right now?

Keeping your checkbook balanced is not about entering numbers into a calculator; it's about being in control. And when you force yourself to balance your checkbook—to really look at and know exactly what's going on with your money—you will also force yourself to become accountable for the choices you make in regards to spending and saving.

Take a simple deposit. When you make a deposit, you've essentially added to your personal worth. You are now faced with choices: What do I do with this money? Do I pay bills? Do I save it? Can I even *afford* to save it? These questions, and many more, should always be at the back of your mind every time you add money to your account.

You should also be asking yourself similar questions whenever you *subtract* money from your account. People often convince themselves they don't have choices about what they do with their money, but that just isn't true—you always have a choice. Sometimes you just need to look at the options that are right in front of you. Let's look at a few examples:

### "I don't have enough money to pay my bills."

You look at your checkbook and see you won't have enough to pay your bills. Although it looks like you don't have a choice, stop and think: What choices do you have? You can choose to get a different job, or a second job. You can choose to get a roommate, rent out a room in your home, or move somewhere more affordable. You can choose to reevaluate your bills and potentially change the amount you owe: Do you really need cable? Are there ways you could be using less electricity? You can also choose to ask for help.

Even if you can't make a change to help pay your bills right away, realizing you have a choice is an important first step. And this first step should make you feel empowered.

### "I don't have the money in my account. I'll just charge it."

You may be charging things as a necessity, or as a way to manage your finances. But unfortunately, every time you make a charge without paying it off immediately, you are actually choosing to contribute to your debt—and to pay more for each purchase, once you add in interest charges. Every time you make a purchase, ask yourself: Do you need this? Are you able to choose savings and security instead?

At first it will take some effort on your part to step back and realize that whatever you decide to do with your checkbook, deposits, and withdrawals—essentially, with your money—is your choice, and it really is in your control. And one of the best ways to begin to take control of your checkbook is by implementing a budget.

In Chapter 8, I outlined how you can review and analyze your income and your expenses to create a detailed budget. I've included a budgeting worksheet in Appendix III, and I provide many budgeting resources on my website. Even if you feel you are in good control of your finances, a budget is a good way to look at the bigger financial picture—and in the process, you'll usually discover ways you can save more and increase your financial security further. And if you *need* to get in control of your finances, or are struggling financially, a budget is the best place to start.

**MORE INFO** **Your Checkbook and Your Budget**
Your checkbook and your budget go hand in hand. Review Chapter 8 again, and, if you haven't already, take the time to set up your budget. Together, these tools will help you to spend less, start saving, and regain control of your finances.

Changing your habits can be a long process. There are entire books devoted to changing spending and saving habits, but no book (including this one) can force you to make the right choices. It's probably safe to say you've spent and saved money the same way for years. Don't expect an instant turnaround. Set small goals for yourself; give yourself room to fumble, but also the power to step up and try again.

I credit my mother for teaching me the value of balancing a checkbook when I was young. My first checkbook was a royal blue vinyl register with a $25 balance. At the time, I didn't recognize that her lesson was about much more than adding and subtracting dollars and cents. It was a lesson about realizing that I had choices, and that I was in control of my money, not the other way around. It is something I will never forget, and something I myself practice every day.

## Step 2: Start Saving by Spending Less

Once you start thinking differently about your choices and your relationship with money, you'll also begin to see many ways that you can *save* more money. This is exactly what happened with my friend Dave, who found himself worried about his mortgage, his taxes, and his debt.

---

THE ONE-YEAR EXPERIMENT

---

Dave is a great guy. He is married to a wonderful woman named Sara and they have an eight-year-old son, Dylan. To everyone else, Dave's life looks perfect. He has a nice home and a great family life. But for years, beneath the surface, Dave was always stressed out; he never seemed to be able to catch up on his debt. With taxes rising in the area, Dave was beginning to worry if he could afford his home. His bills were out of control, and he was getting deeper into debt. So one day, Dave came to me and asked for help.

We embarked on what I call the "One-Year Experiment." I helped Dave work out a budget and develop a plan for his total debt. At the end of the year, Dave had painlessly saved over $7,200 and was able to pay off two of his credit cards. In fact, Dave was so successful in saving money, he continues to use the same budget to this very day.

---

How did he do it? Dave was able to save by carefully monitoring his expenses and examining where he could cut or reduce costs, and by making the choice to think outside of the box for ways he could make things cost less. And as a result of his efforts, with more money in savings and less total debt, Dave was able to gain financial security.

I'll explain a few of the areas where Dave cut his expenses, but you don't need to do exactly what I have outlined here. Everyone has different circumstances, costs, and incomes, and there isn't one set budget or plan that will work for everyone. But you can use these ideas to think about areas in your own life where you can cut costs. Take a step back and take a hard look at your life. Are you spending out of habit, or because you truly need to? Could you be creative about how you trim costs? You may be surprised by the answer and what you *are* able to do.

## YOUR LAWN

If you currently own a home, you most likely have a yard you need to maintain. And if you live in a warmer climate, as I do, this maintenance is a year-round expense. I know many people who have a yard service, even when it doesn't make financial sense. Between lawn care, pest control, and fertilization, it can add up fast. You could say that these costs are an unavoidable part of owning a home, but there are ways you can take control to cut your costs.

The average cost for cutting a lawn is $25.00. If your lawn is cut three times per month, you'll spend $75.00, and if you need to maintain your lawn year-round, your costs total $900.00.

Even if you purchase a lawn mower ($269.00), a trimmer ($99.96), and an edger ($49.95), your total cost is only $418.91. To be fair, let's also include $69.71 in gas for the entire year and $50.00 for oil and miscellaneous parts.

This brings the grand total to $538.62. Even with all of these costs, what are you saving?

```
    $900.00 (lawn service)
  - $538.62 (lawn equipment)
  _____

    $361.38 Savings (year #1)
```

In the first year you would save approximately $361.38. The second year, since you already own the equipment, you would save more:

```
    $900.00 (lawn service)
  - $119.71 (gas, oil, parts & tax)
  ─────────────────────────────────
    $780.29 Savings (year #2 & on...)
```

By making an initial investment in equipment, and by doing things yourself, you save $780.29 a year.

Sometimes, one of the easiest ways to trim expenses is simply by making the choice to do things yourself. To this day, I still maintain my own lawn; I get a therapeutic value out of lawn and landscaping maintenance. By viewing this maintenance a little differently, what once was a chore can become time spent with family, time outside in the fresh air, time bonding with your spouse, exercise—you may even feel the Zen I feel when you are finished.

What if you don't have a yard, or what if you are physically unable to do the work? Making changes in your life to improve your financial position isn't just about your lawn; it's about anything you could handle yourself. Ask yourself: What do I really need to pay for and what can I do myself? What can I give up for a while? Once you start thinking differently, it's easy to do.

## GOURMET ITEMS

Are you still buying items every day that you may not need? Are you watching your accounts drain down while you sip on a double latte? Everyone complains about how overpriced they are, but have you ever done the math? At $3.25, three lattes a week add up to $507.00 a year. That's a lotta latte. A latte is just one example of a gourmet item—if you take any gourmet item out of your budget, or even reduce how much you spend on gourmet items on a regular basis, you'll see an immediate impact on your yearly savings.

- A bottle of wine a week costs $10.95. That's $47.45 a month, and $569.40 a year.

- A nice cigar a week costs $10.50 per cigar. That's $45.50 a month, and $546.00 a year.

- A pack of cigarettes costs about $9.00. Two packs per week cost $18.00. That's $78.00 a month and $936.00 a year.

- A small gourmet coffee a day costs $3.25 and $22.75 for the week. That's $98.58 a month, and $1,183.00 a year.

These are just a few examples of common gourmet items. I am certain you can come up with many more. I have advised many people on budgeting and saving, and most know they need to save, but there are things they feel they just can't do without. This is where changing your frame of mind is extremely beneficial. You don't have to do without certain expenses or gourmet items *completely*; simply cutting back on what you spend is a smart choice.

For the examples I have listed, you could easily choose to make your coffee at home, or enjoy one glass of wine instead of two. Usually, once you start cutting back, you realize it's not so difficult after all. And in the process, you have saved money, and paid down other debt.

## EATING OUT

How often do you eat out, and how much do you spend when you do? Most people are shocked when they actually add up these numbers. One of my clients didn't believe how much he and his wife had been spending on dinner, until they saw the figure themselves.

A few times a week, Mike and Tonia would go out to eat. Nothing extravagant. Between meals, drinks, and a tip, their bill usually was about $30.00. Going out to eat was easy because of their busy

MORE INFO **Progress in Just 30 Days**

This easy plan helps many of my clients, and if you can make a firm commitment to yourself for thirty days, it may help you. For thirty days pay bills and necessities only. Skip the extras, such as clothing, movies, coffee, and toys. Any time you want to make a purchase, or any time you even think about making a purchase, write it down on a list with the date, item, and price. At the end of the thirty days, give yourself a small reward and pull up a comfortable chair to tally your list.

Usually, by the end of the month the list is very long. You will quickly see how much you would have spent on unnecessary items—and that's usually enough to shock yourself into some better spending habits. You'll also see that you have managed very well without making the purchases. I have a few clients who follow this plan a few times a year when they feel their spending needs a quick reality check. It's a useful tool, one that is no-cost and can be used often.

---

schedules, and it also helped them to unwind after work. But the yearly total for this convenience put things in a much different light:

```
$30 a meal x 3 times a week = $90
$90 a week x 52 weeks = $4,680 a year
```

For Mike and Tonia, this number was a shock. $4,680? What they were spending in meals could easily cover their mortgage payments for four months. By planning ahead and deciding to prepare more of their meals at home, they now are spending one third of what they used to.

## ENTERTAINMENT

Entertainment is one of the keys to a satisfying life, but is spending money on entertainment truly a necessity? Our society plays a major role in making sure all forms of entertainment are readily available—for a price. How many times have you heard yourself complaining about how much Goobers cost at the movies, or the admission price at any theme park, or even the price of a DVD? Again, there are many ways you can cut back, and there is plenty of free or inexpensive entertainment. If you start thinking differently, you can also open your eyes to a lot of experiences you are missing.

Most county and state parks have a minimal entrance fee and they offer so much: outdoor activities, exercise, time with your family. Explore nearby hiking trails. Take a walk around your neighborhood. Invite your neighbors over for coffee. Attend free festivals and music events. Just spend time in your own backyard. What does it cost you? Very little, if anything at all.

## TAKE SMALL STEPS IF YOU NEED TO

For many people, making sweeping changes to their spending habits can be discouraging. But even the smallest change in your habits can make a profound difference. If you feel overwhelmed at first, or your habits are very hard to break, start small. Here are a few easy ways to get started:

▶ **Pay in order.** Every month when you pay your bills, pay your savings, debts, and necessities first. Whatever is left over can be used for everyday spending. If you pay your bills at the *end* of the month, you're likely to spend more daily, and you'll be more likely to come up short when your bills are due.

▶ **Go automatic.** You can save every month automatically. Set up your main checking account to make a small deposit into your savings account, a CD, or an investment account automatically. Start small, with a weekly or monthly amount you think you won't miss. Even $10 is a start: by saving just $10 weekly, you will save $520 a year. Once you get used to the amount that you've been saving, increase either the amount or frequency.

▸ **Go "green" or prepaid.** An easy way to spend less is to pay with cash for everything but your bills. The convenience of credit cards has certainly contributed to our bad spending habits: it's easy to spend money when you know you have the choice to pay for it later and when it won't instantly drain your bank account. Decide on your week's budget in advance and leave your credit cards at home (excluding one single credit card for emergencies only).

Don't want to carry cash? Visa, Mastercard, and American Express all offer reloadable prepaid cards, where you can add money to the cards each week as part of your budget. These cards are a great option because they also allow you to track your spending online. Paying this way will force you to keep your spending within set limits, and you won't be able to spend more than what you have, which will help you to decide at any particular moment if you can truly afford something—instead of making a purchase and regretting it later.

▸ **Freeze your credit.** If you have bigger issues and tend to purchase on impulse, you can always put a temporary freeze on your credit cards; if you try to spend, you'll be denied. Of course, it's also in your power to unfreeze your accounts, but placing a freeze on your account ensures you won't be able to make any immediate purchases. This way, you'll be more likely to think it through, and make the best decision.

To place a freeze on any of your accounts, call your credit card company directly. You can also freeze your entire credit report by calling the three credit repositories. Freezing your report will not allow you to open any additional credit cards or store accounts, or apply for loans, until you authorize removing the lock from your credit file.

Although freezing your credit sounds like a great idea, it should only be used as a temporary solution. As you learned in the last chap-

# More Ways to Save

Even after eliminating all of your unnecessary spending, you may still have a very difficult time making ends meet. For many people, the examples I have listed throughout this chapter—and even in this list—may seem like luxuries. But when you are struggling, every penny does make a difference, and except in the most dire of circumstances, there are always more ways you can save.

- ☐ Take in a roommate
- ☐ Carpool or use public transportation
- ☐ Make your own coffee and meals
- ☐ Stock up on "buy one, get one free" groceries
- ☐ Buy generic food, personal products, and medicine
- ☐ Buy all food and supplies in bulk, with friends and neighbors if necessary
- ☐ Avoid paying for ready-made and prepackaged items
- ☐ Buy used, not new
- ☐ Enroll your home in an energy-management program
- ☐ Conserve electricity: regulate your thermostat, turn off ceiling fans, and unplug appliances you don't use
- ☐ Remove unneeded services from your telephone service
- ☐ Disconnect your land line and rely on your cell phone
- ☐ Compare gasoline prices, and use the lowest octane possible
- ☐ Sell your car and purchase a less expensive model
- ☐ Modify your health or auto insurance coverage, shop for less expensive insurance, or increase your insurance deductibles
- ☐ Make sure your banking is 100 percent no cost, no fee
- ☐ Ask your creditors for extensions
- ☐ Cancel unnecessary subscriptions for magazines and newspapers
- ☐ Trade DVDs and books with your friends and neighbors
- ☐ Visit your local library
- ☐ Trade services with your friends and neighbors

ter, your credit score is impacted by your credit history. When your credit accounts aren't used for a while, your credit score could drop, since there's no responsible use of credit to report. Eventually, after you have a plan in place for your spending, you will want to thaw your accounts and begin using them responsibly again.

There are an infinite number of ways you can plan ahead, reduce costs, and save money based on your own life and circumstances. Are there ways you have been able to budget and save successfully? Tell me about it on my website. Even the simplest ideas could easily help someone else to manage their finances and save more.

 Do you have budgeting tips or techniques that have worked for you? Do you have ideas for other ways to save money? In the reader's section of my website, you can share your ideas with others and find more ways to save in today's economy.

## Step 3: Pay Down Your Debt and Start an Emergency Fund

Once you are able to cut expenses and start saving, you'll want to allocate your new funds to two important areas: paying down your debt and building an emergency fund. Debt can create a continuous and dangerous downward spiral: Debt lowers your credit rating, which increases the cost of borrowing on credit. As the cost of paying back this debt increases, you'll find yourself *even deeper* in debt. But by simultaneously decreasing your spending and paying down your debt, you will be able to break this cycle.

So where should you start? As I explained in Chapter 9, you'll want to pay down your credit card balances so that the balance on each card is no more than 50 percent of the credit limit. Keeping your cards under this 50 percent mark will help protect your credit score. Work on reducing your credit card debt card by card, starting with your highest balance and highest-interest rate cards. You may also want to move balances from one credit card to another (depending on the cards' interest rates), to keep under this 50 percent mark.

At the same time, you'll also want to contribute to your emergency fund. In Chapter 8, I reviewed a few of the basics behind budgeting and planning for an emergency. I understand that when you have debt and bills to pay, emergency reserves may not seem as important. But as much as you need to pay down your debt, you also need to protect yourself should you have a further loss in income. Try for small and steady efforts. Put a small amount aside each month, with the goal of saving up for three to six months' worth of living expenses, including your housing, utilities, insurance, food, and transportation.

## Step 4: Keep Your Savings Safe

When you do save money, you want to make sure it's safe, and that it is also earning additional money *for* you. All of your money should be invested in a bank, savings and loan, or credit union that is insured by the Federal Deposit Insurance Corporation (FDIC). With protection from the FDIC, if the bank goes under or experiences problems, your accounts are insured by the government.

As of this printing, individual accounts are protected up to $250,000, joint accounts are protected up to $250,000 per owner, and individual retirement accounts are protected up to $250,000. Keep in mind, these insurance limits are *per* account. If your total savings exceed these FDIC limits, you'll need to divide up your assets among several different accounts to keep all of your money safe.

You'll also want to make sure your money is invested in a checking account, savings account, or CD that earns interest. Even if the return rate is small, the profit for you is effortless. Each bank's programs are different, and there may be restrictions for how much money you can withdraw or access at any given time (especially for accounts with higher rates), so pay special attention not only to the rate of return an account offers but to the account terms and penalties as well.

## Ask for Help

Once you have tried everything you possibly can, you may still need help. You are not alone—so many people need help today, and there are many ways you can receive assistance. Inquire about your state and local social services. You may be eligible for unemployment benefits, welfare, food stamps, help with child care, or Medicaid. And although this may not be enough to live on, it might help to make ends meet. Some states also offer job placement assistance, emergency one-time grants for temporary housing, help with utility costs, and emergency cash assistance.

Start by searching online for your state and local government websites, or search by your state name and the keyword "social services." If the information is hard to find, it doesn't mean it is not there. Call and speak with government representatives so they can direct you to the appropriate department or website. Remember, the government's job is to work for you. Ask for assistance in locating the information you need.

There are also many organizations and churches that are doing everything they can to help. And there are also individuals, myself included, who are trying to make a difference as well. When you ask for help, continue to put forth the effort yourself and be sure that what you ask for is what you truly need. When you are honest and earnest in your requests for help, the more help you'll usually receive.

---

A HOLIDAY LESSON

---

December 2007 was a time in my life when I started reading everything I could get my hands on regarding the housing crash and the many families in need. Right around the holidays, I started following a special series in my hometown newspaper highlighting local families in need of assistance. Many had serious financial issues or were dealing with other extreme circumstances. About thirty individuals and families were featured at a time, and each listing included a short story about their situation, a short wish list, and how you could donate to help. I found myself reading these wishes each and every week. Most were requesting assistance with housing, medical supplies, or hospital bills, and I found myself deeply compelled to help. Our local community reached out, and it was reported that each and every one of the thirty individuals and families had received assistance.

After a few weeks, new individuals and families appeared in the paper with their own wish lists. But this time, I was disappointed. About 80 percent of the people weren't asking for things that they really needed, they were just asking for expensive luxury items: iPods, XBoxes, video games, and even tickets to Disney World. I was simply at a loss for words. Buried within this new group of people were two shining stars: they asked only for jobs, assistance with gas to travel to work, and linens or clothing. They were truly trying to make ends meet, and they didn't know what else to do but to ask for help.

A few weeks later, the paper reported that there was a tremendous outpouring of assistance for these two people, more than in any other week, and in any other year. In fact, the level of assistance was unprecedented. The lesson? Respect what your true needs are, and help will come.

## COMING UP

In this chapter, I've shown you many ways you can help yourself. In the next chapter, I'll share more about how *Saving Your American Dream* might be able to help you even more. I'll explain my campaign, the resources you'll find on my website, and how you can use this book to tell me your story and to apply for assistance.

# 11

# Our Campaign

## A New Beginning

S o you've made it! You've reached the end of the book. But really, this book is just the beginning.

I hope that I've been able to help you to understand more
about the world of home finance, how you can protect yourself and
your home, and how to plan for your future. It's been my goal to provide all the information you need in one place—and to provide information that would allow anyone to help themselves. Hopefully,
my personal stories and experiences have given you some insight;
maybe they've made my advice a little more interesting, and maybe
they've even reassured you that you are not alone. I have one last story
to share with you, and it's a story that will help to explain my campaign and my purpose for this book even more.

A few years ago, my wife and I watched a television show about a
group of lucky lottery winners. I have to admit, I am fascinated by
the lottery, and over the years, I've seen my share of shows on the lottery and how its winners live the high life. I've also seen a few sensa-
tionalized programs on how other lottery winners haven't been so

lucky and have quickly squandered their millions.

But this program was different. Although most of the lottery winners had won large jackpots ranging from $1 million up to $25 million, they weren't thinking only of themselves: they were all doing something inherently *good* with the wealth they received. They donated to charities, lived modestly, and helped in their local communities. For a full hour, the show focused not just on lottery winners, but on lottery winners who were trying to make a difference. It was inspiring.

At the end of the program was a story about a billionaire businessman from Japan who owned homes around the globe, including several homes in Hawaii. The homes were beautiful, in exotic locations, and were lavish in every detail. But somewhere along the way, this businessman realized that the homes were only empty structures unless there was someone there to enjoy them. So he created an opportunity—what you might call a small lottery of his own. He offered the use of several of his Hawaiian homes to local, lower-income families for a ten-year period, without the worry of a mortgage, taxes, or insurance. This generous man was simply looking to make a difference, and to change a few people's lives.

One of the families he helped was featured on the show. They were overwhelmingly thankful and had plans to make the best of their good fortune. Not only did they have a place to live, but they would be able to save money over the following ten years, which would provide for a more secure future. The single gift of a home changed their lives immediately and would also continue to benefit them in many ways for years to come.

This program had a profound impact on me, and it has always remained in the back of my mind. Sometimes, the biggest gift is in what you can give to others.

## A Campaign to Help: Tell Us Your Story

As my wife and I began our work on *Saving Your American Dream* in 2007, we felt we needed to find a way to make a similar impact as this

Japanese businessman—to truly change someone's life. At the same time, we saw the urgent need around us and knew that we needed to help as many people as possible. Our solution was to write this book for you. By reading this book, we hope that we have provided you, and many others, with a solid foundation to make positive decisions regarding your home (or your future home) and your finances.

As you've read through the book, I'm sure you've noticed that I often refer you to the reader's section of my website, where you'll find expanded book content, resources, links, interactive worksheets, templates, case studies, and much more. I'll also be using my website to keep you informed. As the industry and our economy change day by day, I'll use my website and blog to explain what these changes mean, how these changes may impact homeownership in general—and most importantly, how they may impact you. If you haven't been there already, you can log on at www.savingyouramericandream.com.

And although what I've provided on the website and in this book is a way to help many, it's not the end of the story. This book can help you even more.

On the inside back cover, you'll find a peel-off label that reveals a unique access code. This code will allow you to register your book online, where you will also be able to write to me directly for help. If you don't have online access, you can also use the form I've provided at the back of the book. I want you to tell me your story: tell me about you, your life, your home. Tell me how I can help you.

I'm certainly not a billionaire like the Japanese businessman whose story inspired me, but I am a businessman who is willing to take my knowledge and know-how and use it to give back to others. Profits from this book, plus financial resources from various partnerships, sponsors, and endowments, make up a fund that is being used to directly help readers who need it the most. In fact, just by purchasing this book, you have helped to make a difference, either for yourself or for someone else.

From the stories I receive, I'll be selecting individuals and families to help one-on-one. For some, I'll help by making their mortgage payments for a while to provide some relief. For others, I'll provide the funding, advice, or action that's needed to help prevent or stop foreclosure. For others still, I'll provide financial assistance and planning to help with down payments, with rent, or with lease-to-own purchases. The options for assistance are as unlimited as the stories I receive. I'll personally read every story, and whether you are struggling to pay your mortgage, have recently lost your job, or have already lost your home, you'll have the same opportunity to ask for assistance. Even if you are managing to stay current on your mortgage, I know you may still need some help. It doesn't matter what your situation is, and it doesn't matter where you live—but it does require a long-term commitment from you.

For those I help, I'll need to know that you are ready to make a positive change in your own life, and that you are as committed to helping yourself as I am to helping you. I'll work with you to develop a long-term plan for your finances, your home, and your future. I'll expect you to reach certain milestones, and to receive ongoing financial counseling and education. I believe in giving responsibly, and providing this assistance is just one of many ways you will be able to reach your goals. Together, we can turn your life around. Just follow the steps on my website or at the back of this book to submit your story. Then tell your friends about it. Share this idea with others. Although I can't help everyone, my goal is to help as many people as possible. And with your help to get the word out, we can make that happen. The concept behind our campaign is simple: the more people who read our book, the more people we can help.

As more people register online and our online community grows, we can make even more of an impact. You'll have access to other financial aid, legal help, counselors, and non-profit organizations who all can provide immediate assistance. You'll be able to talk to others in your own area through community message boards, or join the discussion on my blog. And maybe together, we can all help each other out.

In the end, it all comes down to making a difference. Both writing this book and developing our campaign has been a long and intensive process. My wife and I have both worked hard, knowing that if we could use our talents for the greater good, our efforts would be worth it.

If we can make a difference for even one person, we are richer for it. That's our goal for this book—and for saving your American dream.

# Appendix I

## Understanding Your Loan Documents

- ► Good Faith Estimate

- ► Truth In Lending Disclosure

- ► HUD-1 Settlement Statement

- ► Amortization Schedule

# Good Faith Estimate

No matter if you work with a bank or a broker, every loan begins with a Good Faith Estimate (GFE). A GFE details all of the costs associated with a loan, from the interest rate and monthly payments down to the loan's final closing costs, with charges itemized for you line by line.

Although Good Faith Estimates come in several different formats, all of the information is organized and numbered to correspond with charges on your HUD settlement statement (see page 382 in this appendix). Overall, GFEs are broken up into eight sections:

## Section 1: General Information

Your name, the property address, the loan amount, the interest rate, and the term will all be listed at the top of your Good Faith Estimate. You'll also want to look for the area that describes the type of loan program (fixed rate, adjustable, balloon, interest-only, jumbo, etc.), so you can accurately compare one quote to another.

## Section 2: Items Payable in Connection With Loan (800s)

This section includes fees charged by a lender and/or mortgage broker. Although these costs will vary from one loan to another, you can usually expect to see some (if not all) of the following charges:

### LEGITIMATE LENDING FEES AND CHARGES

▸　**Loan Origination Fee (801):** If a broker needs to charge you for placing and securing your loan, this amount will be listed as an origination fee. Sometimes, this charge will show up under the line item "Mortgage Broker Fee" (808). An origination fee will be shown as both a percentage and a hard dollar amount, and should always be compared to the yield spread premium (listed on line 813). As long as these two fees aren't more than 2 to 3 percent of your loan amount,

# GOOD FAITH ESTIMATE    *LOAN PROGRAM*

Applicants: **JACK BORROWER / JANE BORROWER**
Property Addr: **123 MAIN STREET, ANYTOWN, FL 00000**
Prepared By:

**1**

Application No: **JACK & JANE PURCHASE**
Date Prepared: 04/08/2006
Loan Program: **30 YEAR FIXED**

The information provided below reflects estimates of the charges which you are likely to incur at the settlement of your loan. The fees listed are estimates - actual charges may be more or less. Your transaction may not involve a fee for every item listed. The numbers listed beside the estimates generally correspond to the numbered lines contained in the HUD-1 settlement statement which you will be receiving at settlement. The HUD-1 settlement statement will show you the actual cost for items paid at settlement.

\* PFC = Prepaid Finance Charge
F = FHA Allowable Closing Cost
POC = Paid Outside of Closing

Total Loan Amount $  **134,900**   Interest Rate: **6.375** %   Term/Due In: **360 / 360** mths

| 800 | ITEMS PAYABLE IN CONNECTION WITH LOAN: | | Amount | Paid By | * PFC / F / POC |
|---|---|---|---|---|---|
| 801 | Loan Origination Fee | *NO ORIGINATION FEE* $ | $0 | | |
| 802 | Loan Discount | | | | |
| 803 | Appraisal Fee | Paid To Other: APPRAISAL CO.  **2** | 400.00 | Borrower | |
| 804 | Credit Report | | | | |
| 805 | Lender's Inspection Fee | | | | |
| 808 | Mortgage Broker Fee | | | | |
| 809 | Tax Related Service Fee | | | | |
| 810 | Processing Fee | Paid To Broker: | 495.00 | Borrower | ✓ |
| 811 | Underwriting Fee | Paid To Lender: | 595.00 | Borrower | ✓ |
| 812 | Wire Transfer Fee | | | | |

## *BROKER'S COMPENSATION*

| COMPENSATION TO BROKER (Not Paid Out of Loan Proceeds) : | | Amount | PFC |
|---|---|---|---|
| 813 | YIELD SPREAD PREMIUM PAID BY LENDER | 2.000 % $  **2,698.00** | |

| 1100 | TITLE CHARGES: | | Amount | Paid By | PFC / F / POC |
|---|---|---|---|---|---|
| 1101 | Closing/Escrow Fee: | Paid To Other:  TITLE COMPANY $ | 200.00 | Borrower | ✓ |
| 1105 | Document Preparation Fee | Paid To Other: ABSTRACT & TITLE SEARCH | 125.00 | Borrower | ✓ |
| 1106 | Notary Fees | Paid To Other: TITLE EXAM | 125.00 | Borrower | ✓ |
| 1107 | Attorney Fees | **3** | | | |
| 1108 | Title Insurance: | Paid To Other: | 300.00 | Borrower | ✓ |
| 1109 | | Paid To ENDORSEMENTS | 120.00 | Borrower | ✓ |
| 1110 | | Paid To WIRE AND COURIER FEES | 50.00 | Borrower | ✓ |

| 1200 | GOVERNMENT RECORDING & TRANSFER CHARGES: | | Amount | Paid By | PFC / F / POC |
|---|---|---|---|---|---|
| 1201 | Recording Fees: | Paid To Lender: $ | 200.00 | Borrower | ✓ |
| 1202 | City/County Tax/Stamps: | CITY/COUNTY TAX/STAMPS  **4** | 472.15 | Borrower | ✓ |
| 1203 | State Tax/Stamps: | Paid To Lender: STATE TAX/STAMPS | 269.80 | Borrower | ✓ |

| 1300 | ADDITIONAL SETTLEMENT CHARGES: | | Amount | Paid By | PFC / F / POC |
|---|---|---|---|---|---|
| 1302 | Pest Inspection | **5** $ | | | |

Estimated Closing Costs    3,351.95

| 900 | ITEMS REQUIRED BY LENDER TO BE PAID IN ADVANCE: | | Amount | Paid By | PFC / F / POC |
|---|---|---|---|---|---|
| 901 | Interest | Paid To Lender:  for **25** days @ $ **23.5613** / day $ | 589.03 | Borrower | ✓ |
| 902 | Mtg Ins. Premium | | | | |
| 903 | Hazard Ins. Premium | **6** | 1,100.00 | | ✓ |
| 904 | | | | | |
| 905 | VA Funding Fee | | | | |

| 1000 | RESERVES DEPOSITED WITH LENDER: | | Amount | Paid By | PFC / F / POC |
|---|---|---|---|---|---|
| 1001 | Hazard Ins. Premium Reserves | mths @ $ | / mth $ | | |
| 1002 | Mtg Ins. Premium Reserves | mths @ $ | / mth | | |
| 1003 | School Tax | mths @ $  **7** | / mth | | |
| 1004 | Taxes & Assessment Reserves | mths @ $ | / mth | | |
| 1005 | Flood Insurance Reserves | mths @ $ | / mth | | |
| | | mths @ $ | / mth | | |
| | | mths @ $ | / mth | | |

Estimated Prepaid Items/Reserves    589.03

TOTAL ESTIMATED SETTLEMENT CHARGES    3,940.98

| TOTAL ESTIMATED FUNDS NEEDED TO CLOSE: | | | TOTAL ESTIMATED MONTHLY PAYMENT: | |
|---|---|---|---|---|
| Purchase Price (+) | 175,000.00 | Loan Amount (-)  **8**  134,900.00 | Principal & Interest | 841.60 |
| Alterations (+) | | New First Mortgage(-) | Other Financing (P & I) | |
| Land (+) | | Subordinate Financing (-) | Hazard Insurance | |
| Refi (incl. debts to be paid off) (+) | | CC paid by Seller (-) | Real Estate Taxes | |
| Est. Prepaid Items/Reserves (+) | 589.03 | Cash Deposit on sales contract (-)  1,000.00 | Mortgage Insurance | |
| Est. Closing Costs (+) | 3,351.95 | | Homeowner Assn. Dues | |
| New 2nd Mtg Closing Costs (+) | | *DUE AT* | Other | *MORTGAGE* |
| PMI, MIP, Funding Fee (+) | | FHA Required Investment (-)  *CLOSING* | | *PAYMENT* |
| Discount (Borrower paid) (+) | | FHA MI Premium Refund (-) | | |
| FHA EEM Improvements (+) | | FHA 203k Rehabilitation Cost (+)  0.00 | | |
| **Total Estimated Funds needed to close** | | **43,040.98** | Total Monthly Payment | **841.60** |

☑ This Good Faith Estimate is being provided by _____, a mortgage broker, and no lender has been obtained. **These estimates are provided pursuant to the Real Estate Settlement Procedures Act of 1974, as amended (RESPA). Additional information can be found in the HUD Special Information Booklet, which is to be provided to you by your mortgage broker or lender, if your application is to purchase residential real property and the lender will take a first lien on the property.** The undersigned acknowledges receipt of the booklet "Settlement Costs," and if applicable the Consumer Handbook on ARM Mortgages.

*A Sample Good Faith Estimate*

your broker is charging you fairly for the loan.

▸   **Loan Discount (802):** If you choose to pay discount points to lower your interest rate, these charges will be shown as a *loan discount*. Discount points are usually between 0.125 to 2 percent of your loan amount, and will be shown on your Good Faith Estimate as both a percentage and a hard dollar amount.

▸   **Appraisal Fee (803):** For any loan, a home's market value will be evaluated and documented by a professional appraiser. The cost of an appraisal can be anywhere from $300 to $500, based on the loan amount or sales price of the home. By law, your lender is required to provide you with a copy of your appraisal. If you haven't received one, you can request a copy directly from your lender.

▸   **Credit Report (804):** To evaluate your credit, your broker will order a tri-merged credit report, which usually costs about $10 per borrower. By law, brokers are prohibited from upcharging and making any profit from this service. If you're being charged more than this, it's not because the report cost more—it's because your broker wanted to *earn* more. Question the amount or ask that it be removed.

▸   **Lender's Inspection Fee (805):** If you are building a home, or are buying a home that's under construction, some lenders will want to inspect the home prior to closing to make sure the construction has been completed. Inspections are conducted by either the lender or a third-party inspector of the lender's choosing, and are usually under $100.

▸   **Tax Services Fee (809):** Some lenders hire a third-party service to monitor and/or handle the payment of your real estate taxes. Fees for this are usually less than $75, and are based on your loan amount.

▸   **Processing Fee (810):** If your broker works for a mortgage company, a mortgage processor will usually assist your broker in overseeing your loan, collecting documentation, and coordinating with third parties. Processing fees typically range from $375 to $795, but are sometimes negotiable. And although these fees are called "processing" fees, they should *also* cover the "cost of doing business," including credit reports, couriers, overnight shipments, document storage, etc. This means if you are being charged a processing fee, you shouldn't be nickel-and-dimed or double-charged for these services elsewhere on your GFE.

▸ **Underwriting Fee (811):** Lenders also charge to review, evaluate, and process your loan. Depending on the lender, underwriting fees may be anywhere from $595 to $995, and are usually *not* negotiable.

▸ **Yield Spread Premium (813):** If your broker is being paid directly by the lender, it will be listed on your Good Faith Estimate as a yield spread premium. This should always be clearly marked as both a percentage and a hard dollar amount, *even if* your broker is making $0 on your loan. Again, as a rule of thumb, the yield spread premium and origination fee should add up to no more than 2 to 3 percent of your loan amount.

## JUNK FEES

Does your GFE contain other lender or broker charges? If so, carefully evaluate each charge to make sure it's legitimate. Have you asked your broker what the charges are for? Are other brokers charging the same fees, and are the fees consistent? Sometimes, Good Faith Estimates are filled with unnecessary fees that do nothing more than pad the lender or broker's profits.

Common junk fees include:

• Administrative fees
• Application fees
• Appraisal review fees
• Courier fees

- Document preparation fees
- Miscellaneous broker fees
- Miscellaneous lender fees
- Review fees
- Sign-up fees

If these or other junk fees appear on your GFE, what should you do? Negotiate—ask that the fees be removed, or go to another bank or broker.

### Section 3: Title Charges (1100s)

Charges from a title company or title attorney are a necessary part of any loan. These costs cover your loan's actual closing, and allow for funds to be dispersed. If you are purchasing a home, you and the seller can usually negotiate who pays for these charges; if you are refinancing, all title charges are your responsibility.

Title charges are based on the loan amount and/or sales price of the home, and usually include:

▸ **Closing/Escrow fees (1101) or Attorney fees (1107):** You will be charged by the title company or title attorney for facilitating the closing, preparing your closing documents, and conducting the closing itself.

▸ **Document preparation fees (1105):** These fees cover preparing the deed and transferring ownership from one party to another.

▸ **Title insurance (1108):** Your lender will require that you purchase title insurance, which will protect both you and the lender if future issues occur (fraud, liens, judgments, etc.) involving your title and ownership rights to the home.

▸ **Other fees, including:** notary fees, title search fees, title exam fees, endorsement fees, and wire transfer fees.

## Section 4: Government Recording and Transfer Charges (1200s)

Your local and state government will require that your loan be recorded and taxed. These fees vary by area and include recording fees (if you are purchasing), reconveyance fees (if you are refinancing), city or county tax/stamps, and state tax/stamps.

## Section 5: Additional Settlement Charges (1300s)

Additional settlement charges include any third-party charges that are not related to lending or title fees. These charges commonly include pest inspections, surveys, and off-site documentation storage.

## Section 6: Items Required to Be Paid in Advance (900s)

Your lender will sometimes require certain costs to be paid in full, in advance. These charges will be listed on your Good Faith Estimate, and usually include:

▶ **Prepaid Interest (901):** Even though your first mortgage payment usually isn't due until one to two months *after* your closing date, a lender wants to make sure they make up for these few months of missed profit in advance. Lenders will pro-rate and charge you interest for this period of time, to be paid in full at your closing.

▶ **Homeowners/Hazard Insurance (903):** All lenders will require that your homeowners insurance policy be paid in full, in advance of your closing. Occasionally, depending on the lender and the insurance company, you may be able to pay for this policy at your closing (as part of your total closing costs). Generally, the cost of your insurance is based on your home's replacement cost, one of the values listed on your appraisal.

If you are refinancing and already have homeowners insurance, you will need to show your lender that a policy is already in place, in advance of your closing.

▶ **Flood Certification/Insurance:** Your lender will want proof that your home isn't in a flood zone or, if it is, you'll be required to pay for flood insurance in advance of your closing. I also want to point out that flood insurance is a *separate* policy; it will *not* be part of your homeowners insurance. On average, flood insurance costs about $500 a year.

## Section 7: Reserves Deposited With the Lender (1000s)

If you are required to escrow, your Good Faith Estimate will itemize how much you will need to pay each month for homeowners insurance, flood insurance, mortgage insurance, and real estate taxes as part of your total mortgage payment, and how much you will be required to pay into your escrow reserves at your loan's closing.

## Section 8: Total Estimated Funds Needed to Close

The last section of your Good Faith Estimate shows the total out-of-pocket costs for your loan, including your final closing costs, the items you are required to pay in advance, your escrow reserves (if required), and your down payment (if you are making a purchase rather than refinancing). This section of your GFE also breaks down what your loan will cost on a monthly basis, including any escrowed amounts for your homeowners insurance, taxes, or mortgage insurance that are being included in your mortgage payment.

### When Should You Sign?

Although every Good Faith Estimate is printed with a signature panel, you are *not* required to sign a GFE until you are ready to proceed forward with your loan. After you sign, if your loan changes at all—for example, if you change loan programs, if you lock in a different rate, or if fees and costs change—you should receive a new Good Faith Estimate. Even though this new GFE is a redisclosure, read it *all* again carefully before signing. If you agree with the changes, you'll be required to sign the new GFE. If you don't like the changes, simply don't sign.

# Truth In Lending Disclosure

While your Good Faith Estimate provides a lot of detail about how much your lender, broker, and others will charge you for your loan, it doesn't cover the specific costs of the loan itself. That's the job of your Truth In Lending Disclosure Statement (TIL). Your Good Faith Estimate should always be accompanied by this disclosure, which provides more detail about your loan and the big picture costs associated with financing, including how much financing will cost over the *life* of the loan.

All in all, Truth In Lending Disclosures are the best way to compare costs between different loans, and between the different Good Faith Estimates you receive from various banks and brokers.

A Truth In Lending Disclosure is broken down into seven main areas:

## 1. Annual Percentage Rate (APR)

Comparing interest rates from one loan to another is easy, but what happens when you start factoring in other charges like origination fees, discount points, prepaid interest, and mortgage insurance? If brokers are all offering different combinations of rates and charges, how do you know which loan you should choose? This is where a loan's annual percentage rate comes in.

Not to be confused with your loan's *interest rate*, the annual percentage rate on your Truth In Lending Disclosure summarizes the true cost of your loan, by taking the other costs of financing into consideration. This gives you a reliable way to compare costs across different loan programs.

Because of how the APR is calculated, it will always be higher than your loan's interest rate. This isn't something to worry about. A loan's APR is just a summary of your loan's total costs—it doesn't change your loan or your loan's interest rate in any way.

# TRUTH-IN-LENDING DISCLOSURE STATEMENT
### (THIS IS NEITHER A CONTRACT NOR A COMMITMENT TO LEND)

Applicants:      **JACK BORROWER / JANE BORROWER**          Prepared By:

Property Address: **123 MAIN STREET**

                  **ANYTOWN, FL 00000**

Application No:   **JACK & JANE PURCHASE**          Date Prepared: **04/08/2006**

| ANNUAL PERCENTAGE RATE | FINANCE CHARGE | AMOUNT FINANCED | TOTAL OF PAYMENTS |
|---|---|---|---|
| The cost of your credit as a yearly rate | The dollar amount the credit will cost you | The amount of credit provided to you or on your behalf | The amount you will have paid after making all payments as scheduled |
| **1**    * 6.616 % | **2** $ * 172,017.40 | **3** $ * 130,959.02 | **4** $ * 302,976.42 |

☐ REQUIRED DEPOSIT:  The annual percentage rate does not take into account your required deposit

PAYMENTS:  Your payment schedule will be:

| No. of Pmts | Amount of Payments ** | Payments Due | No. of Pmts | Amount of Payments ** | Payments Due | No. of Pmts | Amount of Payments ** | Payments Due | No. of Pmts | Amount of Payments ** | Payments Due |
|---|---|---|---|---|---|---|---|---|---|---|---|
| | | Monthly Beginning: | | | Monthly Beginning: | | | Monthly Beginning: | | | Monthly Beginning: |
| 359 | 841.60 | 06/01/2008 | | | | | | | | | |
| 1 | 842.02 | 05/01/2038 | | | | | | | | | |

**5**

☐ DEMAND FEATURE:  This obligation has a demand feature.

☐ VARIABLE RATE FEATURE:  This loan contains a variable rate feature.  A variable rate disclosure has been provided earlier.

**6** *THE DETAILS OF YOUR LOAN WILL BE LISTED HERE*

CREDIT LIFE/CREDIT DISABILITY:  Credit life insurance and credit disability insurance are not required to obtain credit, and will not be provided unless you sign and agree to pay the additional cost.

| Type | Premium | Signature | |
|---|---|---|---|
| Credit Life | **N/A** | I want credit life insurance. | Signature: |
| Credit Disability | **N/A** | I want credit disability insurance. | Signature: |
| Credit Life and Disability | **N/A** | I want credit life and disability insurance. | Signature: |

INSURANCE:  The following insurance is required to obtain credit:

☐ Credit life insurance ☐ Credit disability ☑ Property insurance ☐ Flood insurance

You may obtain the insurance from anyone you want that is acceptable to creditor

☑ If you purchase ☑ property ☐ flood insurance from creditor you will pay $ **1,100.00** for a one year term.

SECURITY:  You are giving a security interest in: **123 MAIN STREET, ANYTOWN FL 00000**

☑ The goods or property being purchased ☐ Real property you already own. **7**

FILING FEES: $ **200.00**

LATE CHARGE:  If a payment is more than **15** days late, you will be charged **5.000** % of the payment

PREPAYMENT:  If you pay off early, you ☐ may ☑ will not have to pay a penalty.

                            ☐ may ☑ will not be entitled to a refund of part of the finance charge.

ASSUMPTION: Someone buying your property

☐ may ☐ may, subject to conditions ☑ may not assume the remainder of your loan on the original terms.

See your contract documents for any additional information about nonpayment, default, any required repayment in full before the scheduled date and prepayment refunds and penalties ☑ * means an estimate ☑ all dates and numerical disclosures except the late payment disclosures are estimates.

* * NOTE: The Payments shown above include reserve deposits for Mortgage Insurance (if applicable), but exclude Property Taxes and Insurance.

THE UNDERSIGNED ACKNOWLEDGES RECEIVING A COMPLETED COPY OF THIS DISCLOSURE.

| Applicant **JACK BORROWER** | Date | Applicant **JANE BORROWER** | Date |
|---|---|---|---|
| Applicant | Date | Applicant | Date |
| Lender | Date | | |

*A Sample Truth In Lending Disclosure*

## 2. Finance Charge

Your loan's finance charge summarizes *all* of the profit a lender will receive for your loan, including the interest payments you'll make over the life of the loan and any prepaid finance charges you'll pay at your loan's closing.

## 3. Amount Financed

The *amount financed* is how much you are actually financing, and it provides another way for you to compare one loan to another. But isn't the amount you are financing your loan amount? Well, almost. The amount financed takes into consideration what you are paying to a lender in advance (prepaid finance charges, discount points, etc.), which are *subtracted* from your loan amount. The amount financed also includes any charges you may be *adding* to your loan amount to finance (for example, if you are refinancing and decide to roll your closing costs into your loan).

The exact amounts that can be added or subtracted are part of a much bigger equation, but you can generally break the amount financed down like this:

```
      Loan Amount
  +   Additional Financing
  -   Prepaid Charges
      ─────────────────────────
      Amount Financed
```

## 4. Total of Payments

How much will financing cost you? If you pay the minimum required principal and interest payment each month, the "total of payments" box shows how much you have *really* paid for your home, by adding the amount financed (box 3) to the finance charge (box 2). This is the point when the true cost of financing hits home for many people, as this number is usually a very *large* and very *expensive* number.

Keep in mind, this total is just for your loan—it doesn't include payments for real estate taxes or homeowners insurance, even if these charges are escrowed as part of your monthly mortgage payment.

## 5. Payment Schedule

This area of your Truth In Lending Disclosure breaks down how much you'll be paying in principal, interest, and mortgage insurance each month; the total number of payments you will make; and when payments are due. If you have a fixed rate mortgage, your payment schedule will be very simple, as you can see in the example I've provided. But if your loan has any variables (including an adjustable rate, an initial fixed rate, a balloon payoff, or an interest-only fixed period) you'll want to pay special attention to this section, as it will show the range of payments you should plan for.

## 6. Demand and Variable Rate Features

In the middle of your Truth In Lending Disclosure are two small but very important check boxes: one for a demand feature, and the other for a variable rate.

### DEMAND FEATURE

A *demand feature* is a clause within your loan documents that allows the lender to "demand" that your loan be paid in full at any time, for *any* reason. For example, if you have a very low interest rate on your loan and interest rates are now much higher (meaning your lender could make even *more* on the same loan amount), the lender could demand that your loan be paid in full immediately, so they can make more money by lending that money to someone else. Most state laws regulate when (or even if) this feature can be added to a loan and luckily, most loans today do not have a true demand feature.

However, many brokers mistakenly check this box, confusing a demand feature with two other common clauses in a loan:

▸ **Acceleration Clause:** If you have violated conditions of your loan (for example, if you default or stop making payments entirely), the lender can demand full payment of the loan immediately.

▸ **Due-on-Sale Clause:** When the home is sold or transferred to another party, the balance of the loan is due in full; your loan cannot be assigned to the new buyer.

If the demand feature box is checked, make sure it's checked for the right reason. Acceleration and due-on-sale clauses are acceptable; demand features are not.

### VARIABLE RATE FEATURE

The second box is for a *variable rate feature*. If you have anything other than a fixed rate loan, your loan has a variable rate. In addition to checking off this box, your broker should also describe your loan in the area underneath. For example, if you have an adjustable rate mortgage, the description should detail your initial interest rate, how long the initial rate lasts, your margin, how often your interest rate adjusts, and all of your caps. If your loan balloons, if your payments are interest-only for a set period of time, or if the loan's balance can be deferred, it should all be spelled out for you here.

## 7. Other Loan Conditions

Grouped at the bottom of your Truth In Lending Disclosure are other conditions of your loan, including:

▸ **Insurance:** Does your loan require homeowners or flood insurance? This area of your TIL Disclosure reminds you that you can purchase your own insurance, and tells you how much your lender will charge if you accept lender-placed insurance.

▶ **Filing Fees:** This is the estimated cost of recording your mortgage or deed of trust, which will also be shown on your Good Faith Estimate on line 1201.

▶ **Late Charge:** If you are late in paying your mortgage, your TIL disclosure lets you know in advance how much you will be charged in late fees.

▶ **Prepayment Penalty:** If your loan is a nonconforming loan, it might carry a prepayment penalty. The box on the first line indicates whether your loan has a prepayment penalty. If you *do* decide to pay your loan off early, the box on the second line lets you know if what you've already paid to the lender in finance charges will be refunded to you, or not.

▶ **Assumption:** An assumable loan is a loan that can be passed on to a third party with no change in interest rate or conditions. Today, only FHA, VA, or owner-financed loans may be assumed.

---

MORE INFO **When Should You Sign?**

Banks and brokers should provide your Truth In Lending Disclosure at the same time they provide your Good Faith Estimate. Like your Good Faith Estimate, you'll be required to sign your TIL disclosure *only* when you are ready to proceed forward with your loan.

---

# HUD-1 Settlement Statement

At your closing, all of the costs and charges you've already become familiar with on your Good Faith Estimate will now be detailed on your final HUD-1 settlement statement. This statement, also known as your *closing statement*, is prepared by your title company or title attorney, and details the final costs and charges for your loan, as well as how money will be dispersed from one party to another. Your HUD will be just one of many loan documents you sign at your closing, but it's the only document that lists *all* of your loan's final costs.

As a borrower, you'll want to make sure that these costs are correct by comparing your HUD to your *final* Good Faith Estimate (you should receive your final GFE at least three days before your closing). You'll be paying attention to items in the left column, which detail the borrower's costs and charges. The right column shows the seller's charges (and how much is due to the seller) if the closing involves the purchase of a home.

You'll want to check:

**1.  Loan and Identifying Information:** Is the type of loan correct? Are your name, address, and the property address correct?

**2.  Sales Price and Loan Amount:** Check your sales price and/or loan amount against Section 8 (the last section) of your final Good Faith Estimate. These numbers should match up exactly. If they don't, be extremely cautious. If your loan amount changes—even by a small amount—it should always be redisclosed to you *before* your closing.

**3.  Items Payable in Connection With Loan (800s):** These charges should match up to your Good Faith Estimate—especially the fees that are being paid to your broker. If you are being charged more than what's on your GFE, stop and find out why. If you're not satisfied with either the charge or the broker's answer, and are purchasing, you can ask for an extension. If you are refinancing, you have no obligation to proceed forward with the loan.

**A. Settlement Statement**

**U.S. Department of Housing and Urban Development**

OMB Approval No. 2502-0265

**B. Type of Loan**

| 1. ☐ FHA | 2. ☐ FmHA | 3. ☑ Conv. Unins. | 6. File Number: 12-345AB | 7. Loan Number: 987654 | 8. Mortgage Insurance Case Number: |
|---|---|---|---|---|---|
| 4. ☐ VA | 5. ☐ Conv. Ins. | | | | |

**C. Note:** This form is furnished to give you a statement of actual settlement costs. Amounts paid to and by the settlement agent are shown. Items marked "(p.o.c.)" were paid outside the closing; they are shown here for informational purposes and are not included in the totals.

| D. Name & Address of Borrower: | E. Name & Address of Seller: | F. Name & Address of Lender: |
|---|---|---|
| JACK BORROWER **1** <br> JANE BORROWER <br> 348 OLD HOME DRIVE <br> ANYTOWN, FL 00000 | THE SELLER <br> 76 MAIN STREET <br> ANYTOWN, FL 00000 | YOUR LENDER <br> LENDER ADDRESS <br> ANYTOWN, FL 00000 |

| G. Property Location: | H. Settlement Agent: YOUR TITLE COMPANY | |
|---|---|---|
| 123 NEW HOME DRIVE <br> ANYTOWN, FL 00000 | Place of Settlement: <br> TITLE COMPANY ADDRESS <br> ANYTOWN, FL 00000 | I. Settlement Date: <br> MAY 08, 2006 |

| J. Summary of Borrower's Transaction | | K. Summary of Seller's Transaction | |
|---|---|---|---|
| **100. Gross Amount Due From Borrower** | | **400. Gross Amount Due To Seller** | |
| 101. Contract sales price | 175,000.00 | 401. Contract sales price | |
| 102. Personal property | | 402. Personal property | |
| 103. Settlement charges to borrower (line 1400) | 3,983.48 | 403. | |
| 104. *SALES PRICE* | | 404. | |
| 105. | | 405. | |
| **Adjustments for items paid by seller in advance** | | **Adjustments for items paid by seller in advance** | |
| 106. City/town taxes to | | 406. City/town taxes to | |
| 107. County taxes to | | 407. County taxes to | |
| 108. Assessments 5/08/06 to 09/30/06 | 49.92 | 408. Assessments 5/08/06 to 09/30/06 | |
| 109. | | 409. | |
| 110. | | 410. | |
| 111. **2** | | 411. | |
| 112. | | 412. | |
| **120. Gross Amount Due From Borrower** | 179,033.40 | **420. Gross Amount Due To Seller** | |
| **200. Amounts Paid By Or In Behalf Of Borrower** | | **500. Reductions In Amount Due To Seller** | |
| 201. Deposit or earnest money | 1,000.00 | 501. Excess deposit (see instructions) | |
| 202. Principal amount of new loan(s) | 134,900.00 | 502. Settlement charges to seller (line 1400) | |
| 203. Existing loan(s) taken subject to | | 503. Existing loan(s) taken subject to | |
| 204. | | 504. Payoff of first mortgage loan | |
| 205. *YOUR LOAN AMOUNT* | | 505. Payoff of second mortgage loan | |
| 206. | | 506. | |
| 207. | | 507. | |
| 208. | | 508. | |
| 209. | | 509. | |
| **Adjustments for items unpaid by seller** | | **Adjustments for items unpaid by seller** | |
| 210. City/town taxes to | | 510. City/town taxes to | |
| 211. County taxes 01/01/06 to 05/08/06 | 403.54 | 511. County taxes to | |
| 212. Assessments to | | 512. Assessments to | |
| 213. | | 513. | |
| 214. | | 514. | |
| 215. | | 515. | |
| 216. | | 516. | |
| 217. | | 517. | |
| 218. | | 518. | |
| 219. | | 519. | |
| **220. Total Paid By/For Borrower** | 136,303.54 | **520. Total Reduction Amount Due Seller** | |
| **300. Cash At Settlement From/To Borrower** | | **600. Cash At Settlement To/From Seller** | |
| 301. Gross Amount due from borrower (line 120) | 179,033.40 | 601. Gross amount due to seller (line 420) | |
| 302. Less amounts paid by/for borrower (line 220) | ( 136,303.54 ) | 602. Less reductions in amt. due seller (line 520) | ( ) |
| **303. Cash ☑ From ☐ To Borrower** | 42,729.86 | *TOTAL CLOSING COSTS* | |

Section 5 of the Real Estate Settlement Procedures Act (RESPA) requires the following: • HUD must develop a Special Information Booklet to help persons borrowing money to finance the purchase of residential real estate to better understand the nature and costs of real estate settlement services; • Each lender must provide the booklet to all applicants from whom it receives or for whom it prepares a written application to borrow money to finance the purchase of residential real estate; • Lenders must prepare and distribute with the Booklet a Good Faith Estimate of the settlement costs that the borrower is likely to incur in connection with the settlement. These disclosures are mandatory.

Section 4(a) of RESPA mandates that HUD develop and prescribe this standard form to be used at the time of loan settlement to provide full disclosure of all charges imposed upon the borrower and seller. These are third party disclosures that are designed to provide the borrower with pertinent information during the settlement process in order to be a better shopper.

The Public Reporting Burden for this collection of information is estimated to average one hour per response, including the time for reviewing instructions, searching existing data sources, gathering and maintaining the data needed, and completing and reviewing the collection of information.

This agency may not collect this information, and you are not required to complete this form, unless it displays a currently valid OMB control number.

The information requested does not lend itself to confidentiality.

*A Sample HUD-1 Settlement Statement (Front)*

**L. Settlement Charges**

| | | | Paid From Borrowers Funds at Settlement | Paid From Seller's Funds at Settlement |
|---|---|---|---|---|
| **700. Total Sales/Broker's Commission based on price $** @ % = | | | | |
| Division of Commission (line 700) as follows: | | | | |
| 701. $ to | | | | |
| 702. $ to | | | | |
| 703. Commission paid at Settlement | | | | |
| 704. | | | | |
| **800. Items Payable In Connection With Loan** | | | | |
| 801. Loan Origination Fee ⟨$0⟩ *NO ORIGINATION FEE* | | | | |
| 802. Loan Discount % | | *BROKER'S* | | |
| 803. Appraisal Fee 400.00 to Appraisal Company | | | 400.00 | |
| 804. Credit Report to | | *COMPENSATION* | | |
| 805. Lender's Inspection Fee | | | | |
| 806. Mortgage Insurance Application Fee to | | *3* | | |
| 807. Assumption Fee | | | | |
| 808. Underwriting Fee to Your Lender | | | 595.00 | |
| 809. Processing Fee to Your Mortgage Firm | | | 495.00 | |
| 810. Yield Spread Premium paid by Lender to Your Mortgage Company | ⟨2,698.00 POC⟩ | | | |
| 811. | | | | |
| **900. Items Required By Lender To Be Paid In Advance** | | | | |
| 901. Interest from 05/08/06 to 06/01/06 @$ 23.5613 /day | | *4* | 565.47 | |
| 902. Mortgage Insurance Premium for months to | | | | |
| 903. Hazard Insurance Premium for 1 years to Your Insurance Company | | | | |
| 904. years to 1,100.00 POC | | | | |
| 905. | | | | |
| **1000. Reserves Deposited With Lender** | | | | |
| 1001. Hazard insurance months@$ per month | | *5* | | |
| 1002. Mortgage insurance months@$ per month | | | | |
| 1003. City property taxes months@$ per month | | | | |
| 1004. County property taxes months@$ per month | | | | |
| 1005. Annual assessments months@$ per month | | | | |
| 1006. months@$ per month | | | | |
| 1007. months@$ per month | | | | |
| 1008. months@$ per month | | | | |
| **1100. Title Charges** | | | | |
| 1101. Settlement or closing fee to Your Title Company | | *6* | 150.00 | |
| 1102. Abstract or title search to Your Title Company | | | 125.00 | |
| 1103. Title examination to Your Title Company | | | 125.00 | |
| 1104. Title insurance binder to | | | | |
| 1105. Document preparation to | | | | |
| 1106. Notary fees to | | | | |
| 1107. Attorney's fees to | | | | |
| (includes above items numbers: ) | | | | |
| 1108. Title insurance to Your Title Company | | | 150.00 | |
| (includes above items numbers: ) | | | | |
| 1109. Lender's coverage $ 134,900.00 ($150.00) | | | | |
| 1110. Owner's coverage $ | | | | |
| 1111. Endorsements paid to Your Title Company | | | 116.06 | |
| 1112. Wire and Courier fees paid to Your Title Company | | | 80.00 | |
| 1113. | | | | |
| **1200. Government Recording and Transfer Charges** | | | | |
| 1201. Recording fees: Deed $ 18.50 ; Mortgage $ 171.50 ; Releases $ | | *7* | 190.00 | |
| 1202. City/county tax/stamps: Deed $ ; Mortgage $ 269.80 | | | 269.80 | |
| 1203. State tax/stamps: Deed $ ; Mortgage $ 472.15 | | | 472.15 | |
| 1204. | | | | |
| 1205. | | | | |
| **1300. Additional Settlement Charges** | | | | |
| 1301. Survey to Survey Company | | *8* | 250.00 | |
| 1302. Pest inspection to | | | | |
| 1303. | | | | |
| 1304. | | | | |
| 1305. | | | | |
| **1400. Total Settlement Charges (enter on lines 103, Section J and 502, Section K)** | | *9* | ⟨3983.48⟩ | |

*THIS TOTAL SHOULD BE
NO MORE THAN
$100–$200
OVER YOUR GFE*

*A Sample HUD-1 Settlement Statement* (Back)

**4.  Items Required to Be Paid in Advance (900s):** If your loan closes a few days before or after it was originally supposed to, you'll find that the prepaid interest charges may be slightly more or less than what is shown on your final GFE. Small changes here are okay: your lender will prorate how much they are charging you in prepaid interest by the day. All other prepaid charges (including mortgage insurance and homeowners insurance) should match those on your GFE.

**5.  Reserves Deposited With Lender (1000s):** Again, match these fees with the ones on your Good Faith Estimate. As long as you've received a final GFE a few days prior to closing, there should be no surprises.

**6.  Title Charges (1100s):** Because final title charges come from a third party (the title company or title agent), you may see small differences in the final fees, or the fees may be worded or grouped differently than they are on your final GFE. Total the fees on both your GFE and your HUD. As long as the total charges are close, you are set. If the title company is charging dramatically more than what is listed on your GFE, you have the power to negotiate with the title agent right at the closing table.

**7.  Government Recording and Transfer Charges (1200s):** All recording fees and transfer charges should either match up exactly or be extremely close to your final GFE. What's extremely close? Final charges should be within $10 to $50 of those listed on your GFE.

**8.  Additional Settlement Charges (1300s):** If there are any charges from third parties, these charges should all have been billed or determined well in advance (and in enough time to make it onto your final GFE). All third-party charges will be itemized and should match those on your final Good Faith Estimate.

**9.  Your Total Settlement Charges (1400):** Match up line 1400 to the line "Total Estimated Settlement Charges" on your final GFE. If your bank or broker has done their job well, your final settlement charges should be no more than $100 to $200 above your GFE.

# Amortization Schedule

An amortization schedule shows how much you'll be paying in principal and interest (and how these amounts change each month) over the life of your loan. At the beginning of a loan, more of your payment goes towards paying the lender in interest. As you get further into your loan, more of your payment goes toward the principal (which pays down your balance faster).

On a $200,000 mortgage, with a fixed interest rate of 6 percent for 30 years, your monthly payment is $1,199.10. At the end of this loan, you will have paid $200,000.00 in principal and $231,676.38 in interest for a total cost of $431,676.38.

| Payment | Principal | Interest | Balance | Payment | Principal | Interest | Balance |
|---------|-----------|----------|---------|---------|-----------|----------|---------|
| 1 | $199.10 | $1,000.00 | $199,800.90 | 45 | $247.96 | $951.14 | $189,980.41 |
| 2 | $200.10 | $999.00 | $199,600.80 | 46 | $249.20 | $949.90 | $189,731.21 |
| 3 | $201.10 | $998.00 | $199,399.71 | 47 | $250.45 | $948.66 | $189,480.76 |
| 4 | $202.10 | $997.00 | $199,197.60 | 48 | $251.70 | $947.40 | $189,229.06 |
| 5 | $203.11 | $995.99 | $198,994.49 | 49 | $252.96 | $946.15 | $188,976.11 |
| 6 | $204.13 | $994.97 | $198,790.36 | 50 | $254.22 | $944.88 | $188,721.89 |
| 7 | $205.15 | $993.95 | $198,585.21 | 51 | $255.49 | $943.61 | $188,466.40 |
| 8 | $206.17 | $992.93 | $198,379.04 | 52 | $256.77 | $942.33 | $188,209.63 |
| 9 | $207.21 | $991.90 | $198,171.83 | 53 | $258.05 | $941.05 | $187,951.57 |
| 10 | $208.24 | $990.86 | $197,963.59 | 54 | $259.34 | $939.76 | $187,692.23 |
| 11 | $209.28 | $989.82 | $197,754.31 | 55 | $260.64 | $938.46 | $187,431.59 |
| 12 | $210.33 | $988.77 | $197,543.98 | 56 | $261.94 | $937.16 | $187,169.65 |
| 13 | $211.38 | $987.72 | $197,332.60 | 57 | $263.25 | $935.85 | $186,906.40 |
| 14 | $212.44 | $986.66 | $197,120.16 | 58 | $264.57 | $934.53 | $186,641.83 |
| 15 | $213.50 | $985.60 | $196,906.66 | 59 | $265.89 | $933.21 | $186,375.94 |
| 16 | $214.57 | $984.53 | $196,692.09 | 60 | $267.22 | $931.88 | $186,108.71 |
| 17 | $215.64 | $983.46 | $196,476.45 | 61 | $268.56 | $930.54 | $185,840.16 |
| 18 | $216.72 | $982.38 | $196,259.73 | 62 | $269.90 | $929.20 | $185,570.26 |
| 19 | $217.80 | $981.30 | $196,041.93 | 63 | $271.25 | $927.85 | $185,299.01 |
| 20 | $218.89 | $980.21 | $195,823.04 | 64 | $272.61 | $926.50 | $185,026.40 |
| 21 | $219.99 | $979.12 | $195,603.05 | 65 | $273.97 | $925.13 | $184,752.43 |
| 22 | $221.09 | $978.02 | $195,381.96 | 66 | $275.34 | $923.76 | $184,477.09 |
| 23 | $222.19 | $976.91 | $195,159.77 | 67 | $276.72 | $922.39 | $184,200.38 |
| 24 | $223.30 | $975.80 | $194,936.47 | 68 | $278.10 | $921.00 | $183,922.28 |
| 25 | $224.42 | $974.68 | $194,712.05 | 69 | $279.49 | $919.61 | $183,642.79 |
| 26 | $225.54 | $973.56 | $194,486.51 | 70 | $280.89 | $918.21 | $183,361.90 |
| 27 | $226.67 | $972.43 | $194,259.84 | 71 | $282.29 | $916.81 | $183,079.61 |
| 28 | $227.80 | $971.30 | $194,032.04 | 72 | $283.70 | $915.40 | $182,795.91 |
| 29 | $228.94 | $970.16 | $193,803.10 | 73 | $285.12 | $913.98 | $182,510.78 |
| 30 | $230.09 | $969.02 | $193,573.01 | 74 | $286.55 | $912.55 | $182,224.24 |
| 31 | $231.24 | $967.87 | $193,341.78 | 75 | $287.98 | $911.12 | $181,936.26 |
| 32 | $232.39 | $966.71 | $193,109.39 | 76 | $289.42 | $909.68 | $181,646.84 |
| 33 | $233.55 | $965.55 | $192,875.83 | 77 | $290.87 | $908.23 | $181,355.97 |
| 34 | $234.72 | $964.38 | $192,641.11 | 78 | $292.32 | $906.78 | $181,063.65 |
| 35 | $235.90 | $963.21 | $192,405.22 | 79 | $293.78 | $905.32 | $180,769.87 |
| 36 | $237.07 | $962.03 | $192,168.14 | 80 | $295.25 | $903.85 | $180,474.62 |
| 37 | $238.26 | $960.84 | $191,929.88 | 81 | $296.73 | $902.37 | $180,177.89 |
| 38 | $239.45 | $959.65 | $191,690.43 | 82 | $298.21 | $900.89 | $179,879.68 |
| 39 | $240.65 | $958.45 | $191,449.78 | 83 | $299.70 | $899.40 | $179,579.97 |
| 40 | $241.85 | $957.25 | $191,207.93 | 84 | $301.20 | $897.90 | $179,278.77 |
| 41 | $243.06 | $956.04 | $190,964.87 | 85 | $302.71 | $896.39 | $178,976.06 |
| 42 | $244.28 | $954.82 | $190,720.59 | 86 | $304.22 | $894.88 | $178,671.84 |
| 43 | $245.50 | $953.60 | $190,475.09 | 87 | $305.74 | $893.36 | $178,366.10 |
| 44 | $246.73 | $952.38 | $190,228.37 | 88 | $307.27 | $891.83 | $178,058.83 |

| Payment | Principal | Interest | Balance | Payment | Principal | Interest | Balance |
|---------|-----------|----------|---------|---------|-----------|----------|---------|
| 89 | $308.81 | $890.29 | $177,750.02 | 157 | $433.49 | $765.61 | $152,688.70 |
| 90 | $310.35 | $888.75 | $177,439.67 | 158 | $435.66 | $763.44 | $152,253.04 |
| 91 | $311.90 | $887.20 | $177,127.77 | 159 | $437.84 | $761.27 | $151,815.21 |
| 92 | $313.46 | $885.64 | $176,814.31 | 160 | $440.03 | $759.08 | $151,375.18 |
| 93 | $315.03 | $884.07 | $176,499.28 | 161 | $442.23 | $756.88 | $150,932.96 |
| 94 | $316.60 | $882.50 | $176,182.67 | 162 | $444.44 | $754.66 | $150,488.52 |
| 95 | $318.19 | $880.91 | $175,864.49 | 163 | $446.66 | $752.44 | $150,041.86 |
| 96 | $319.78 | $879.32 | $175,544.71 | 164 | $448.89 | $750.21 | $149,592.97 |
| 97 | $321.38 | $877.72 | $175,223.33 | 165 | $451.14 | $747.96 | $149,141.83 |
| 98 | $322.98 | $876.12 | $174,900.35 | 166 | $453.39 | $745.71 | $148,688.44 |
| 99 | $324.60 | $874.50 | $174,575.75 | 167 | $455.66 | $743.44 | $148,232.78 |
| 100 | $326.22 | $872.88 | $174,249.52 | 168 | $457.94 | $741.16 | $147,774.85 |
| 101 | $327.85 | $871.25 | $173,921.67 | 169 | $460.23 | $738.87 | $147,314.62 |
| 102 | $329.49 | $869.61 | $173,592.18 | 170 | $462.53 | $736.57 | $146,852.09 |
| 103 | $331.14 | $867.96 | $173,261.04 | 171 | $464.84 | $734.26 | $146,387.25 |
| 104 | $332.80 | $866.31 | $172,928.24 | 172 | $467.16 | $731.94 | $145,920.09 |
| 105 | $334.46 | $864.64 | $172,593.78 | 173 | $469.50 | $729.60 | $145,450.58 |
| 106 | $336.13 | $862.97 | $172,257.65 | 174 | $471.85 | $727.25 | $144,978.74 |
| 107 | $337.81 | $861.29 | $171,919.84 | 175 | $474.21 | $724.89 | $144,504.53 |
| 108 | $339.50 | $859.60 | $171,580.34 | 176 | $476.58 | $722.52 | $144,027.95 |
| 109 | $341.20 | $857.90 | $171,239.14 | 177 | $478.96 | $720.14 | $143,548.99 |
| 110 | $342.91 | $856.20 | $170,896.23 | 178 | $481.36 | $717.74 | $143,067.63 |
| 111 | $344.62 | $854.48 | $170,551.61 | 179 | $483.76 | $715.34 | $142,583.87 |
| 112 | $346.34 | $852.76 | $170,205.27 | 180 | $486.18 | $712.92 | $142,097.69 |
| 113 | $348.07 | $851.03 | $169,857.19 | 181 | $488.61 | $710.49 | $141,609.08 |
| 114 | $349.82 | $849.29 | $169,507.38 | 182 | $491.06 | $708.05 | $141,118.02 |
| 115 | $351.56 | $847.54 | $169,155.81 | 183 | $493.51 | $705.59 | $140,624.51 |
| 116 | $353.32 | $845.78 | $168,802.49 | 184 | $495.98 | $703.12 | $140,128.53 |
| 117 | $355.09 | $844.01 | $168,447.40 | 185 | $498.46 | $700.64 | $139,630.07 |
| 118 | $356.86 | $842.24 | $168,090.54 | 186 | $500.95 | $698.15 | $139,129.12 |
| 119 | $358.65 | $840.45 | $167,731.89 | 187 | $503.46 | $695.65 | $138,625.67 |
| 120 | $360.44 | $838.66 | $167,371.45 | 188 | $505.97 | $693.13 | $138,119.69 |
| 121 | $362.24 | $836.86 | $167,009.21 | 189 | $508.50 | $690.60 | $137,611.19 |
| 122 | $364.06 | $835.05 | $166,645.15 | 190 | $511.05 | $688.06 | $137,100.15 |
| 123 | $365.88 | $833.23 | $166,279.28 | 191 | $513.60 | $685.50 | $136,586.55 |
| 124 | $367.70 | $831.40 | $165,911.57 | 192 | $516.17 | $682.93 | $136,070.38 |
| 125 | $369.54 | $829.56 | $165,542.03 | 193 | $518.75 | $680.35 | $135,551.63 |
| 126 | $371.39 | $827.71 | $165,170.64 | 194 | $521.34 | $677.76 | $135,030.29 |
| 127 | $373.25 | $825.85 | $164,797.39 | 195 | $523.95 | $675.15 | $134,506.34 |
| 128 | $375.11 | $823.99 | $164,422.28 | 196 | $526.57 | $672.53 | $133,979.77 |
| 129 | $376.99 | $822.11 | $164,045.29 | 197 | $529.20 | $669.90 | $133,450.56 |
| 130 | $378.87 | $820.23 | $163,666.41 | 198 | $531.85 | $667.25 | $132,918.72 |
| 131 | $380.77 | $818.33 | $163,285.64 | 199 | $534.51 | $664.59 | $132,384.21 |
| 132 | $382.67 | $816.43 | $162,902.97 | 200 | $537.18 | $661.92 | $131,847.03 |
| 133 | $384.59 | $814.51 | $162,518.38 | 201 | $539.87 | $659.24 | $131,307.16 |
| 134 | $386.51 | $812.59 | $162,131.87 | 202 | $542.57 | $656.54 | $130,764.60 |
| 135 | $388.44 | $810.66 | $161,743.43 | 203 | $545.28 | $653.82 | $130,219.32 |
| 136 | $390.38 | $808.72 | $161,353.05 | 204 | $548.00 | $651.10 | $129,671.31 |
| 137 | $392.34 | $806.77 | $160,960.71 | 205 | $550.74 | $648.36 | $129,120.57 |
| 138 | $394.30 | $804.80 | $160,566.41 | 206 | $553.50 | $645.60 | $128,567.07 |
| 139 | $396.27 | $802.83 | $160,170.15 | 207 | $556.27 | $642.84 | $128,010.81 |
| 140 | $398.25 | $800.85 | $159,771.90 | 208 | $559.05 | $640.05 | $127,451.76 |
| 141 | $400.24 | $798.86 | $159,371.65 | 209 | $561.84 | $637.26 | $126,889.92 |
| 142 | $402.24 | $796.86 | $158,969.41 | 210 | $564.65 | $634.45 | $126,325.27 |
| 143 | $404.25 | $794.85 | $158,565.16 | 211 | $567.47 | $631.63 | $125,757.79 |
| 144 | $406.28 | $792.83 | $158,158.88 | 212 | $570.31 | $628.79 | $125,187.48 |
| 145 | $408.31 | $790.79 | $157,750.58 | 213 | $573.16 | $625.94 | $124,614.32 |
| 146 | $410.35 | $788.75 | $157,340.23 | 214 | $576.03 | $623.07 | $124,038.29 |
| 147 | $412.40 | $786.70 | $156,927.83 | 215 | $578.91 | $620.19 | $123,459.38 |
| 148 | $414.46 | $784.64 | $156,513.37 | 216 | $581.80 | $617.30 | $122,877.57 |
| 149 | $416.53 | $782.57 | $156,096.83 | 217 | $584.71 | $614.39 | $122,292.86 |
| 150 | $418.62 | $780.48 | $155,678.21 | 218 | $587.64 | $611.46 | $121,705.22 |
| 151 | $420.71 | $778.39 | $155,257.50 | 219 | $590.57 | $608.53 | $121,114.65 |
| 152 | $422.81 | $776.29 | $154,834.69 | 220 | $593.53 | $605.57 | $120,521.12 |
| 153 | $424.93 | $774.17 | $154,409.76 | 221 | $596.50 | $602.61 | $119,924.62 |
| 154 | $427.05 | $772.05 | $153,982.71 | 222 | $599.48 | $599.62 | $119,325.15 |
| 155 | $429.19 | $769.91 | $153,553.52 | 223 | $602.48 | $596.63 | $118,722.67 |
| 156 | $431.33 | $767.77 | $153,122.19 | 224 | $605.49 | $593.61 | $118,117.18 |

| Payment | Principal | Interest | Balance | Payment | Principal | Interest | Balance |
|---------|-----------|----------|---------|---------|-----------|----------|---------|
| 225 | $608.52 | $590.59 | $117,508.67 | 293 | $854.21 | $344.89 | $68,124.42 |
| 226 | $611.56 | $587.54 | $116,897.11 | 294 | $858.48 | $340.62 | $67,265.94 |
| 227 | $614.62 | $584.49 | $116,282.49 | 295 | $862.77 | $336.33 | $66,403.17 |
| 228 | $617.69 | $581.41 | $115,664.81 | 296 | $867.09 | $332.02 | $65,536.09 |
| 229 | $620.78 | $578.32 | $115,044.03 | 297 | $871.42 | $327.68 | $64,664.67 |
| 230 | $623.88 | $575.22 | $114,420.15 | 298 | $875.78 | $323.32 | $63,788.89 |
| 231 | $627.00 | $572.10 | $113,793.15 | 299 | $880.16 | $318.94 | $62,908.73 |
| 232 | $630.14 | $568.97 | $113,163.01 | 300 | $884.56 | $314.54 | $62,024.17 |
| 233 | $633.29 | $565.82 | $112,529.73 | 301 | $888.98 | $310.12 | $61,135.19 |
| 234 | $636.45 | $562.65 | $111,893.27 | 302 | $893.43 | $305.68 | $60,241.77 |
| 235 | $639.63 | $559.47 | $111,253.64 | 303 | $897.89 | $301.21 | $59,343.88 |
| 236 | $642.83 | $556.27 | $110,610.81 | 304 | $902.38 | $296.72 | $58,441.50 |
| 237 | $646.05 | $553.05 | $109,964.76 | 305 | $906.89 | $292.21 | $57,534.60 |
| 238 | $649.28 | $549.82 | $109,315.48 | 306 | $911.43 | $287.67 | $56,623.17 |
| 239 | $652.52 | $546.58 | $108,662.96 | 307 | $915.99 | $283.12 | $55,707.19 |
| 240 | $655.79 | $543.31 | $108,007.17 | 308 | $920.57 | $278.54 | $54,786.62 |
| 241 | $659.07 | $540.04 | $107,348.11 | 309 | $925.17 | $273.93 | $53,861.46 |
| 242 | $662.36 | $536.74 | $106,685.75 | 310 | $929.79 | $269.31 | $52,931.66 |
| 243 | $665.67 | $533.43 | $106,020.07 | 311 | $934.44 | $264.66 | $51,997.22 |
| 244 | $669.00 | $530.10 | $105,351.07 | 312 | $939.11 | $259.99 | $51,058.10 |
| 245 | $672.35 | $526.76 | $104,678.73 | 313 | $943.81 | $255.29 | $50,114.29 |
| 246 | $675.71 | $523.39 | $104,003.02 | 314 | $948.53 | $250.57 | $49,165.76 |
| 247 | $679.09 | $520.02 | $103,323.93 | 315 | $953.27 | $245.83 | $48,212.49 |
| 248 | $682.48 | $516.62 | $102,641.45 | 316 | $958.04 | $241.06 | $47,254.45 |
| 249 | $685.89 | $513.21 | $101,955.56 | 317 | $962.83 | $236.27 | $46,291.62 |
| 250 | $689.32 | $509.78 | $101,266.24 | 318 | $967.64 | $231.46 | $45,323.98 |
| 251 | $692.77 | $506.33 | $100,573.47 | 319 | $972.48 | $226.62 | $44,351.50 |
| 252 | $696.23 | $502.87 | $99,877.23 | 320 | $977.34 | $221.76 | $43,374.16 |
| 253 | $699.71 | $499.39 | $99,177.52 | 321 | $982.23 | $216.87 | $42,391.93 |
| 254 | $703.21 | $495.89 | $98,474.30 | 322 | $987.14 | $211.96 | $41,404.78 |
| 255 | $706.73 | $492.37 | $97,767.57 | 323 | $992.08 | $207.02 | $40,412.71 |
| 256 | $710.26 | $488.84 | $97,057.31 | 324 | $997.04 | $202.06 | $39,415.67 |
| 257 | $713.81 | $485.29 | $96,343.50 | 325 | $1,002.02 | $197.08 | $38,413.65 |
| 258 | $717.38 | $481.72 | $95,626.11 | 326 | $1,007.03 | $192.07 | $37,406.61 |
| 259 | $720.97 | $478.13 | $94,905.14 | 327 | $1,012.07 | $187.03 | $36,394.55 |
| 260 | $724.58 | $474.53 | $94,180.57 | 328 | $1,017.13 | $181.97 | $35,377.42 |
| 261 | $728.20 | $470.90 | $93,452.37 | 329 | $1,022.21 | $176.89 | $34,355.20 |
| 262 | $731.84 | $467.26 | $92,720.53 | 330 | $1,027.33 | $171.78 | $33,327.88 |
| 263 | $735.50 | $463.60 | $91,985.03 | 331 | $1,032.46 | $166.64 | $32,295.42 |
| 264 | $739.18 | $459.93 | $91,245.86 | 332 | $1,037.62 | $161.48 | $31,257.79 |
| 265 | $742.87 | $456.23 | $90,502.98 | 333 | $1,042.81 | $156.29 | $30,214.98 |
| 266 | $746.59 | $452.51 | $89,756.40 | 334 | $1,048.03 | $151.07 | $29,166.96 |
| 267 | $750.32 | $448.78 | $89,006.08 | 335 | $1,053.27 | $145.83 | $28,113.69 |
| 268 | $754.07 | $445.03 | $88,252.01 | 336 | $1,058.53 | $140.57 | $27,055.16 |
| 269 | $757.84 | $441.26 | $87,494.17 | 337 | $1,063.83 | $135.28 | $25,991.33 |
| 270 | $761.63 | $437.47 | $86,732.54 | 338 | $1,069.14 | $129.96 | $24,922.19 |
| 271 | $765.44 | $433.66 | $85,967.10 | 339 | $1,074.49 | $124.61 | $23,847.70 |
| 272 | $769.27 | $429.84 | $85,197.83 | 340 | $1,079.86 | $119.24 | $22,767.83 |
| 273 | $773.11 | $425.99 | $84,424.72 | 341 | $1,085.26 | $113.84 | $21,682.57 |
| 274 | $776.98 | $422.12 | $83,647.74 | 342 | $1,090.69 | $108.41 | $20,591.88 |
| 275 | $780.86 | $418.24 | $82,866.88 | 343 | $1,096.14 | $102.96 | $19,495.74 |
| 276 | $784.77 | $414.33 | $82,082.12 | 344 | $1,101.62 | $97.48 | $18,394.12 |
| 277 | $788.69 | $410.41 | $81,293.42 | 345 | $1,107.13 | $91.97 | $17,286.99 |
| 278 | $792.63 | $406.47 | $80,500.79 | 346 | $1,112.67 | $86.43 | $16,174.32 |
| 279 | $796.60 | $402.50 | $79,704.19 | 347 | $1,118.23 | $80.87 | $15,056.09 |
| 280 | $800.58 | $398.52 | $78,903.61 | 348 | $1,123.82 | $75.28 | $13,932.27 |
| 281 | $804.58 | $394.52 | $78,099.03 | 349 | $1,129.44 | $69.66 | $12,802.83 |
| 282 | $808.61 | $390.50 | $77,290.42 | 350 | $1,135.09 | $64.01 | $11,667.75 |
| 283 | $812.65 | $386.45 | $76,477.78 | 351 | $1,140.76 | $58.34 | $10,526.98 |
| 284 | $816.71 | $382.39 | $75,661.06 | 352 | $1,146.47 | $52.63 | $9,380.52 |
| 285 | $820.80 | $378.31 | $74,840.27 | 353 | $1,152.20 | $46.90 | $8,228.32 |
| 286 | $824.90 | $374.20 | $74,015.37 | 354 | $1,157.96 | $41.14 | $7,070.36 |
| 287 | $829.02 | $370.08 | $73,186.34 | 355 | $1,163.75 | $35.35 | $5,906.61 |
| 288 | $833.17 | $365.93 | $72,353.17 | 356 | $1,169.57 | $29.53 | $4,737.04 |
| 289 | $837.34 | $361.77 | $71,515.84 | 357 | $1,175.42 | $23.69 | $3,561.63 |
| 290 | $841.52 | $357.58 | $70,674.32 | 358 | $1,181.29 | $17.81 | $2,380.33 |
| 291 | $845.73 | $353.37 | $69,828.59 | 359 | $1,187.20 | $11.90 | $1,193.14 |
| 292 | $849.96 | $349.14 | $68,978.63 | 360 | $1,193.14 | $5.97 | $0.00 |

# Appendix II

## Foreclosure Resources

- Lender Discussion Worksheet
- Writing a Hardship Letter
- Foreclosure Procedures By State

# Lender Discussion Worksheet

When you speak with your lender, it's important to have everything about your loan in one place. Use this worksheet to record your loan's information, the lender's contact information, and all communications you have with your loss mitigation representative. Need more space? A downloadable version of this worksheet is also available on my website.

**LOAN INFORMATION:**

Account Number

Monthly Payment

Date of Last Payment

Number of Months Behind

Amount Past Due

Loan Balance/Payoff

Market Value of Home

**LENDER CONTACT INFORMATION:**

Name of Lender

Phone Number

Loss Mitigation Department Phone Number

Loss Mitigation Representative

    Name

    Phone Number

    Fax Number

    Email

    Preferred Contact Method

**DATE CONTACTED**                    /        /

Notes:

**DATE CONTACTED**                    /        /

Notes:

**DATE CONTACTED**                    /        /

Notes:

# Writing a Hardship Letter

The purpose of your hardship letter is to clearly show your lender two important facts: that what you are requesting is necessary, and that the plan you propose will work.

When writing a hardship letter, *do*:

1.  Provide information about your loan, including:
    *   Your name and the names of any co-borrowers
    *   The property address
    *   The loan number
    *   Your phone number

2.  State the reason for your letter, including the type of loan work-out you're looking for and your end goal—if you want to keep your home, or if you've decided you can no longer afford your home.

3.  Explain the details of your hardship, and why you've been unable to pay your mortgage.

4.  Describe how your hardship has affected your total income (give facts), and whether this loss of income is temporary or permanent.

5.  Be specific in what you *are* able to pay or do, and prove to your lender that you'll be able to follow through with these plans.

6.  Provide supporting documentation to back up your hardship *and* your plan.

7.  Include any other information that your loss mitigation representative has requested.

John Smith
Loss Mitigation Specialist
Mortgage Company
Address, City, State and Zip
Month/Date/Year

RE: Borrower name/Any co-borrowers
Property address
Loan account number: 00987654321

Dear Ms. Smith:

Thank you very much for your time on the phone today. As we discussed, I am writing this letter to ask for your assistance in working out a loan modification. I've carefully reviewed my finances, and believe that by modifying my mortgage to $900 a month, I will be able to start making payments again immediately. As you know, I'm a long-time homeowner and have lived in my neighborhood for over ten years. I'm extremely committed to staying in my home, and am very motivated to work out a solution with your help.

For the past five years, I had been employed as a Human Resources Manager, and I had great job security. Unfortunately, my company closed unexpectedly in January. Since then, I've used my savings to pay my mortgage. I've recently found stable employment as an office manager, but due to the economy and the job market, my new salary is lower and my income has dropped by almost 30 percent. I've also been struggling to manage some unexpected costs for medical insurance. I have a pre-existing heart condition and need to maintain insurance, so right now I am paying for insurance through COBRA. With my previous employer, my medical insurance cost $160 a month; this same coverage now costs $325 a month. Between the loss of income and the increased insurance, it's been much more difficult to make ends meet, and as a result I missed my last mortgage payment.

*Sample Letter for a Loan Modification*    (Continued on next page)

I understand that my mortgage is my responsibility, and I've already taken many steps to make sure I will be able to continue to make payments on my home: I have new employment, I've created a full budget and have cut my expenses, I've taken extra work assignments, and I've rented out a room in my home to add to my income. As you can see from the attached budget, my total income is $4,200 a month, and I've been able to reduce my expenses from $2,000 to $1,600. By modifying my mortgage to $900 a month, I am certain I will be able to start making my payments again, and I'll also be able to make up for my missed payment.

With this letter, I've also included documentation about my hardship, including information about my previous company's closing, a letter from my new employer about my position and my salary, and a copy of my COBRA insurance statement. I've also provided copies of my recent pay stubs, the lease my roommate has signed, and my full budget, showing how reduced payments at $900 would be realistic, and would allow me to avoid any issues with paying my mortgage in the future.

Again, I want to thank you for your help, and for the time you've taken to work with me so far. I know you can understand that staying in my home is very important to me, and I'm continuing to make efforts on my end to improve my finances to make sure I do not default again. If you have any questions, or if you have suggestions for other ways we can work out a solution, I can be reached at 555-555-1234.

Sincerely,
Jane Homeowner

---

*Sample Letter for a Loan Modification (Continued)*

When writing a hardship letter, ***don't:***

1.  Write too long of a letter or give unnecessary information.

2.  Exaggerate the facts, or focus on the need for sympathy.

3.  Stress what you can't do or what you can't pay. Focus on what you *can* do instead.

4.  Focus too much on what's already happened, and not enough on your solution.

5.  Rely on someone else's words or a form letter.

---

 **The Power of Your Own Words**

The sample letter I provide for you here in addition to others on my website will help to guide you through the process, but it's still important for you to explain your situation in your own words. Lenders receive far too many "form letters" from homeowners experiencing hardship. By using your *own* writing style and explanations, your hardship letter will make more of an impact, and will keep the attention of your loss mitigation representative. Don't worry about making your letter perfect. Just do your best to make it count.

---

# Foreclosure Procedures by State

While every state has its own procedures, what happens during a fore-closure is largely determined by how your agreement with your lender was written, and if you have a mortgage or a deed of trust (some states use only one or the other). If you have a mortgage, your lender will usually follow the procedures for a *judicial foreclosure*: an attorney will file a complaint with the courts to initiate a lawsuit, a lis pendens will be recorded, and your case will be handled by your local court system.

If you have a deed of trust, lenders are able to bypass the court system and will proceed with a *non-judicial foreclosure*. Non-judicial foreclosures involve three parties: you, your lender, and a trustee—an unbiased third party who acts on the lender's behalf. The trustee is usually required to notify you about your missed payments; if you don't respond, the trustee will follow out-of-court procedures determined by state law to start the foreclosure.

Again, state laws change frequently, so you'll always want to check your state's statutes (you'll find links and resources that explain how foreclosures are handled in every state on my website), and you'll want a good foreclosure attorney or non-profit agency on your side to help guide you through the process.

| STATE | MORTGAGE OR DEED OF TRUST | JUDICIAL • OR NON-JUDICIAL ○ | | FIRST STEP | TIMING (IN MONTHS) | DEFICIENCY JUDGMENT POSSIBLE | WHO HANDLES SALE | REDEMPTION PERIOD (IN DAYS) |
|---|---|---|---|---|---|---|---|---|
| Alabama | M/D | • | ○ | NOD/NOS | 1/3 | Yes | Trustee | 365 |
| Alaska | M/D | • | ○ | Notice of Default | 3/4 | Yes* | Trustee | 365* |
| Arizona | M/D | • | ○ | LP/NOS | 3/4 | Varies | Trustee | 30–180 |
| Arkansas | M/D | • | ○ | Notice of Default | 4/5 | Yes† | Trustee | 365* |
| California | D | • | ○ | Notice of Default | 4/4 | Yes* | Trustee | 365* |
| Colorado | M/D | • | ○ | Notice of Default | 2/5 | Yes | Trustee | None |
| Connecticut | M | • | | Complaint/LP | 5/6 | Yes | Court | By case |

| STATE | MORTGAGE OR DEED OF TRUST | JUDICIAL • OR NON-JUDICIAL ○ | FIRST STEP | TIMING (IN MONTHS) | DEFICIENCY JUDGMENT POSSIBLE | WHO HANDLES SALE | REDEMPTION PERIOD (IN DAYS) |
|---|---|---|---|---|---|---|---|
| Delaware | M | • | Complaint/LP | 3/7 | No | Sheriff | None |
| D.C. | D | ○ | Notice of Default | 2/4 | Yes | Trustee | None |
| Florida | M | • | Complaint/LP | 5/5 | Yes | Court | None |
| Georgia | M/D | • ○ | Complaint/NOS | 2/2 | Yes | Trustee | None |
| Hawaii | M/D | • ○ | Compliant / LP | 3/4 | Yes | Trustee | None |
| Idaho | M/D | • ○ | Notice of Default | 5/6 | Yes | Trustee | 365 |
| Illinois | M | • | Complaint/LP | 7/10 | Varies | Court | 90 |
| Indiana | M | • | Complaint/LP | 5/7 | Yes | Sheriff | None |
| Iowa | M/D | • ○ | Complaint/LP | 5/6 | No | Sheriff | 20 |
| Kansas | M | • | Complaint/LP | 4/4 | Yes | Sheriff | 365 |
| Kentucky | M | • | Complaint/LP | 6/5 | Yes | Court | 365 |
| Louisiana | M | • | Complaint/LP | 2/6 | Yes | Sheriff | None |
| Maine | M | • | Notice of Default | 6/10 | Yes | Court | 90 |
| Maryland | M/D | • | Complaint/LP | 2/2 | Yes | Court | By case |
| Massachusetts | M | • | Complaint/LP | 3/4 | No | Court | None |
| Michigan | M/D | • ○ | Notice of Sale | 2/2 | Varies | Sheriff | 30–365 |
| Minnesota | M/D | • ○ | Notice of Default | 2/3 | Yes | Sheriff | 180–365 |
| Mississippi | M/D | • ○ | Notice of Default | 2/3 | No | Trustee | None |
| Missouri | M/D | • ○ | Complaint/NOS | 2/2 | No | Trustee | 365 |
| Montana | M/D | • ○ | Complaint/NOS | 5/5 | Yes* | Trustee | None |
| Nebraska | M | • ○ | Complaint/NOD | 5/6 | No | Sheriff | None |
| Nevada | M/D | • ○ | Notice of Default | 4/4 | Yes | Trustee | None |
| New Hampshire | M/D | ○ | Notice of Default | 2/3 | Yes | Trustee | None |
| New Jersey | M | • | Complaint/LP | 3/10 | Yes | Sheriff | 10 |
| New Mexico | M | • | Complaint/LP | 4/6 | Yes | Court | 30–270 |
| New York | M/D | • | Complaint/LP | 4/8 | Yes | Court | None |
| North Carolina | M/D | • ○ | Notice of Hearing | 2/4 | Varies | Sheriff | None |
| North Dakota | M | • | Complaint/LP | 3/5 | Yes | Sheriff | 180–365 |
| Ohio | M | • | Complaint/LP | 5/7 | Yes | Sheriff | None |
| Oklahoma | M/D | • ○ | Complaint/LP | 4/7 | Yes | Sheriff | None |

| STATE | MORTGAGE OR DEED OF TRUST | JUDICIAL • | NON-JUDICIAL ○ | FIRST STEP | TIMING (IN MONTHS) | DEFICIENCY JUDGMENT POSSIBLE | WHO HANDLES SALE | REDEMPTION PERIOD (IN DAYS) |
|---|---|---|---|---|---|---|---|---|
| Oregon | M/D | • | ○ | Notice of Default | 5/5 | Yes* | Trustee | 180* |
| Pennsylvania | M | • | | Complaint/LP | 3/9 | Yes | Sheriff | None |
| Rhode Island | M/D | • | ○ | Notice of Default | 2/3 | Yes | Trustee | None |
| South Carolina | M | • | | Complaint/LP | 6/6 | Yes | Court | None |
| South Dakota | M/D | • | ○ | Complaint/LP | 6/9 | Varies | Sheriff | 30–365 |
| Tennessee | M/D | | ○ | Notice of Sale | 2/2 | Yes | Trustee | 730 |
| Texas | M/D | • | ○ | Demand Letter | 2/2 | Yes | Trustee | None |
| Utah | M/D | • | | Complaint/NOD | 4/5 | Yes | Trustee | By case |
| Vermont | M/D | • | | Complaint/LP | 7/10 | Yes | Court | 180–365 |
| Virginia | M/D | • | ○ | Complaint/NOD | 2/2 | Yes | Trustee | None |
| Washington | M/D | • | ○ | Complaint/NOD | 4/5 | Yes* | Trustee | None |
| West Virginia | M/D | • | ○ | Notice of Default | 2/2 | No | Trustee | None |
| Wisconsin | M/D | • | ○ | Complaint/LP | 4/10 | Yes | Sheriff | 180–365 |
| Wyoming | M/D | • | ○ | Complaint/NOS | 2/3 | Yes | Sheriff | 90–365 |

*Judicial foreclosure only    †Non-judicial foreclosures only

**Mortgage or Deed of Trust:** Does your state use mortgages, deeds of trust, or both?

**Judicial or Non-Judicial:** Are foreclosures in your state judicial or non-judicial, or does your state allow both?

**First Step:** What first step is a lender or trustee required to take? Depending on your state, your lender may follow one of the following procedures:

- *Complaint/Lis Pendens (Complaint/LP):* A lender will file a complaint or a petition with the court. In judicial foreclosures, this complaint will be recorded as a lis pendens.

- *Notice of Default (NOD):* A lender will file a notice of default to document your missed payments. Depending on your state, this notice could be sent to you via certified mail, posted on your home, filed with the court, or published in your local newspaper.

- *Notice of Hearing:* A lender will request a hearing with the courts. At the hearing, the clerk of the court will decide whether the lender has the right to foreclose. If the clerk authorizes the foreclosure, the lender will set a sale date, notify you in writing, and follow the procedures for a notice of sale.

- *Notice of Sale (NOS):* A lender will file a notice of sale to let you know that your home will soon be sold at auction. Just like a notice of default, this notice could be sent to you via certified mail, posted on your home, filed with the court, or published in your local newspaper.

**Timing:** How long will the foreclosure process take? What is the legal minimum amount of time required by your state (the first number), and what is the probable amount of time you can expect (the second number)?

**Deficiency Judgment Possible:** If the foreclosure sale isn't enough to cover your mortgage, is it possible for a lender to file a judgment against you for the difference?

**Who Handles Sale:** Is the auction and sale of your home conducted by the court, a trustee, or the sheriff?

**Redemption Period:** Are you allowed to buy back your home after it is sold at auction? If so, how long do you have?

# Appendix III

## Planning Worksheets

- Home Cost Planning Worksheet

- Expense Tracking Worksheet

- Monthly Budget

# Home Cost Planning Worksheet

How much will a home really cost? When you're thinking about buying a home, whether for your primary residence or as an investment property, you'll need to consider the home's *true* costs, and what these costs will be in both best- and worst-case scenarios:

| | BEST CASE | WORST CASE |
|---|---|---|
| **MONTHLY COSTS** | | |
| Fixed rate mortgage | | |
| Adjustable-rate mortgage | | |
|     Payment at lowest interest rate | | |
|     Payment at highest interest rate | | |
| Homeownership costs | | |
|     Real estate taxes | | |
|     Homeowners insurance | | |
|     Homeowners association dues | | |
|     Homeowners assessments[1] | | |
| Utilities | | |
|     Electric/gas | | |
|     Water/sewer | | |
|     Telephone | | |
|     Cable | | |
|     Internet | | |
| Maintenance | | |
|     Home remodeling and repair | | |
|     Home maintenance | | |
|     Yard maintenance | | |
|     Emergency funds | | |
| Investment property costs | | |
|     Rental insurance | | |
|     Rental upkeep | | |
| | | |
| **TOTAL MONTHLY COSTS** | $ | $ |
| X 12 MONTHS | | |
| **TOTAL YEARLY COSTS** | $ | $ |

| | BEST CASE | WORST CASE |
|---|---|---|
| **ONE-TIME LOAN COSTS** | | |
| Down payment | | |
| Lender-required cash reserves | | |
| Closing costs[2] | | |
|     Discount points | | |
|     Lender and broker costs | | |
|     Title costs | | |
|     Government fees and taxes | | |
|     Third party costs | | |
|     Escrow reserves | | |
| **TOTAL LOAN COSTS** | $ | $ |

| | BEST CASE | WORST CASE |
|---|---|---|
| **INVESTMENT PROPERTY COSTS** | | |
| Preparation for rent | | |
| Preparation for sale | | |
| . Real estate rental commissions | | |
| Real estate sale commissions | | |
| **TOTAL RENTING AND SELLING COSTS** | $ | $ |

[1] *If you live in a community with a homeowners association, you may be charged an assessment to pay for community expenses or improvements that are not covered by your regular association dues.*

[2] *These costs will be on your Good Faith Estimate.*

# Expense Tracking Worksheet

To track your expenses, enter the date, a description, the amount, and whether the expense is fixed (a repeating expense that's hard to change) or variable (easily increased or decreased). If you need more space, you can also download an 8.5x11 version of this worksheet from my website.

| DATE | DESCRIPTION | AMOUNT | FIXED | VARIABLE |
|------|-------------|--------|-------|----------|
| JAN 1 | MORNING COFFEE | $2.00 | | X |
| | | | | |
| | | | | |
| | | | | |
| | | | | |
| | | | | |
| | | | | |
| | | | | |
| | | | | |
| | | | | |
| | | | | |
| | | | | |
| | | | | |
| | | | | |
| | | | | |
| | | | | |
| | | | | |
| | | | | |
| | | | | |
| | | | | |
| | | | | |
| | | | | |
| | | | | |
| | | | | |
| | | | | |
| | | | | |

# Monthly Budget

Each month, track your actual expenses and compare them to the amounts you have budgeted. Then, refine your budget (or your spending) as needed. Need some help? I've provided sample budgets and an interactive version of this worksheet on my website.

| DESCRIPTION | BUDGETED | ACTUAL | DIFFERENCE |
|---|---|---|---|
| **INCOME** | | | |
| Salary | | | |
| Hourly wages | | | |
| Sales commissions | | | |
| Bonus pay | | | |
| Interest | | | |
| Retirement | | | |
| Pension | | | |
| Alimony | | | |
| Child support | | | |
| | | | |
| **FIXED EXPENSES** | | | |
| Federal taxes | | | |
| State taxes | | | |
| Local taxes | | | |
| Mortgage or rent | | | |
| Insurance *(divide by 12 if annual)* | | | |
|     Homeowners insurance | | | |
|     Health insurance | | | |
|     Auto insurance | | | |
|     Life insurance | | | |
| Utilities | | | |
|     Electricity | | | |
|     Gas | | | |
|     Water | | | |
| Car payment | | | |
| Child support | | | |

| DESCRIPTION | BUDGETED | ACTUAL | DIFFERENCE |
|---|---|---|---|
| **VARIABLE EXPENSES** | | | |
| Savings | | | |
| Retirement | | | |
| Emergency fund | | | |
| Debts | | | |
|     Creditor/credit card #1 | | | |
|     Creditor/credit card #2 | | | |
|     Creditor/credit card #3 | | | |
|     Creditor/credit card #4 | | | |
| Medical and dental | | | |
|     Deductibles | | | |
|     Out-of-pocket costs | | | |
|     Prescription medications | | | |
| Transportation | | | |
|     Gas | | | |
|     Auto upkeep | | | |
|     Bus or subway | | | |
|     Airfare | | | |
|     Other | | | |
| Food | | | |
|     Groceries | | | |
|     Eating out | | | |
|     School lunches | | | |
| Phone/cable/computer | | | |
|     Telephone | | | |
|     Cell phone | | | |
|     Cable | | | |
|     Internet | | | |
| Kids | | | |
|     Childcare | | | |
|     Clothing | | | |
|     Supplies | | | |
|     Babysitting | | | |
|     Child allowances | | | |
|     Other | | | |

| DESCRIPTION | BUDGETED | ACTUAL | DIFFERENCE |
|---|---|---|---|
| **VARIABLE EXPENSES (CONTINUED)** | | | |
| Pets | | | |
|     Pet food | | | |
|     Pet supplies | | | |
|     Vet costs | | | |
| Personal care | | | |
|     Clothing | | | |
|     Haircuts | | | |
|     Laundry | | | |
|     Dry cleaning | | | |
|     Other | | | |
| Entertainment | | | |
|     CDs and DVDs | | | |
|     Movies, plays, concerts | | | |
|     Sports | | | |
|     Vacations | | | |
|     Gifts or cards (holidays) | | | |
|     Other | | | |
| Subscriptions/dues | | | |
|     Newspaper subscriptions | | | |
|     Magazine subscriptions | | | |
|     Club dues | | | |
|     Other | | | |
| Other expenses | | | |
|     Miscellaneous #1 | | | |
|     Miscellaneous #2 | | | |
|     Miscellaneous #3 | | | |
| | | | |
| | | | |
| | | | |
| | | | |
| | | | |
| | | | |
| | | | |

# Tell Us Your Story

## Application

Do you need help with your mortgage, your home, or your finances? Tell us your story and how we can help you! There are two ways to submit your story: register online at www.savingyouramerican-dream.com, or complete and mail this form to the address provided below. Here are some general guidelines, and a little more about what you can expect from the process.

### YOUR ACCESS CODE

To send in your story, you'll need your access code, which is located on the inside back cover of this book. Keep in mind that your access code is a unique number and can be used for one person only. (Do not purchase this book if the access code is missing or has already been revealed.) After you've registered and submitted your story, be sure to hold on to your book and access code! You'll need it again later if your story is chosen.

With your access code, you can also take advantage of all of the reader resources on the website. If you register your book by mail and would like online access, just visit the website, click on the sign in tab, and follow the steps on your screen. After confirming some basic information, you'll receive an email confirmation for complete access to the site.

## YOUR APPLICATION AND STORY

We'll personally read and evaluate each and every story we receive. If your story is selected for further consideration, we'll contact you to set up a time where we can get to know you a little better. You'll be required to complete a more in-depth application and to provide financial, credit, and background information. We'll be using all of this information, along with your original application and story, to determine what assistance we may be able to provide.

## IF YOU ARE SELECTED

If you are selected to receive any type of financial assistance, we'll work with you one-on-one to determine how we are able to help you, and what assistance would benefit both your short- and long-term goals. We'll set up a plan and outline an agreement for the goals and milestones you'll be working toward. Remember, you'll be required to meet certain expectations to continue to receive assistance; but don't worry, we'll be working closely with you throughout the entire process to make sure that you succeed.

# Part 1: Tell Us More About You

All information is confidential.

Today's date: _____

_____
Full name

_____
Address

_____
City

_____
State                                          Zip

_____
Home phone                          Work phone

_____
Cell phone

_____
Email address

What's the best way to contact you? _____

Gender: ☐ Male   ☐ Female

Date of birth: _____ Age: _____

Ethnicity: _____

Marital Status:

☐ Single  ☐ Engaged  ☐ Married  ☐ Partnership  ☐ Separated

☐ Divorced  ☐ Widowed  ☐ Other _____

Do you currently:
- ☐ Own your home
- ☐ Rent a home
- ☐ Rent an apartment
- ☐ Live with a friend or relative
- ☐ Other: _____

I am working:
- ☐ Full time
- ☐ Part time
- ☐ Out of work for _____ months
- ☐ Disabled
- ☐ Other: _____

What is your occupation? _____

What is the name of your employer(s)?

_____

Employer contact names and phone numbers:

_____

_____

What's the total income for your household? _____

Do you have any children living at home with you?     ☐ Yes  ☐ No

If so, what are their ages? _____

Does anyone else live with you in your home?     ☐ Yes  ☐ No

If so, tell us more about them: _____

# Part 2: Tell Us About Where You Live

**2A. IF YOU OWN YOUR HOME:**

*(If you don't own a home, skip ahead to Section 2B.)*

What type of home do you live in?

☐ Single family    ☐ Attached home    ☐ Townhome    ☐ Condo

☐ Other: _____

How long have you owned your home? _____

What names are on your mortgage?

_____

What names are on your home's title?

_____


**YOUR MORTGAGE PAYMENT:**

How much is your mortgage payment? _____

Are your real estate taxes, homeowners insurance or mortgage insurance included in this payment?   ☐ Yes   ☐ No

If **yes**, please list the amounts you pay each month:

_____ Mortgage              _____ Homeowners insurance

_____ Real estate taxes     _____ Mortgage insurance

If **no**, how much do you pay each year (total) for your:

Taxes _____ Homeowners insurance _____

Are you current on your taxes and insurance?   ☐ Yes   ☐ No

## MISSED PAYMENTS:

Are you current on your mortgage payments?  ☐ Yes  ☐ No

If **no**, how many mortgage payments have you missed? _____

Has your lender contacted you about your missed payments?
☐ Yes  ☐ No  ☐ Not Sure

Has your lender sent you a notice of foreclosure, notice of sale, or judgment of sale?  ☐ Yes  ☐ No  ☐ Not Sure

If **yes**, what date is your home scheduled to be sold at auction?

_____

## OTHER FINANCING:

Do you have a second mortgage or other financing on your home? (Including home equity loans, personal loans, etc.)  ☐ Yes  ☐ No

If so, what are these payments? _____

Are you current with these payments?  ☐ Yes  ☐ No

## YOUR HOME'S VALUE:

How much do you currently owe on your home? _____
Use your most recent mortgage statement or contact your lender for this amount.

What is the current market value of your home?

_____

Please provide an estimate of your home's market value from zillow.com. If you have a recent appraisal, please provide the value from the appraisal as well.

This value is from:  ☐ Zillow  ☐ Appraisal  Appraisal date _____

Do you own any other properties?  ☐ Yes  ☐ No

If so, how many? _____

What are they used for?_____

_____

Have you ever lost a home to foreclosure?     ☐ Yes  ☐ No

Do you want to save your current home?     ☐ Yes  ☐ No

If **no**, please explain your plans for your home:

_____

_____

### 2B. IF YOU DON'T OWN A HOME:

Are you currently renting?  ☐ Yes  ☐ No

If **yes**, what is your current rent payment? _____

If **no**, please describe your living arrangements and any financial

obligations you have for where you are living:

_____

_____

_____

Have you ever owned a home before?  ☐ Yes  ☐ No

Have you ever lost a home to foreclosure?  ☐ Yes  ☐ No

Do you want to own a home?  ☐ Yes  ☐ No

# Part 3: Tell Us Your Story

On a separate sheet of paper, tell us more about you, your current situation, and what kind of help you need. Please keep your story to one to two pages maximum. If you'd like to submit a photo or other materials, feel free to do so, but they aren't required.

Are pictures or other materials included?  ☐ Yes  ☐ No

If you have included any photos or other information, please do not send original copies or any materials that you need returned.

# Part 4: Final Information

What is your book's access code? _____

Where did you purchase your copy of *Saving Your American Dream*?

_____

Please complete and mail this application and your story to:
Saving Your American Dream
P.O. Box 213488
West Palm Beach, FL 33421-3488

Saving Your American Dream is an organization committed to helping individuals and families affected by the housing and lending crisis, regardless of their current situations. Please keep in mind that the process for assistance may take some time and is ongoing. And as much as we wish we could, we are unable to assist everyone. If you are faced with immediate or extreme financial difficulty, we encourage you to pursue alternatives and other assistance. We also encourage you to visit our website, where we have provided additional resources and links to those in your local community who may be able to provide immediate or emergency assistance or relief.

By signing below, I agree and warrant that I have completed this application honestly and accurately. I understand that Saving Your American Dream is choosing to provide assistance to readers at its own discretion and does not have any obligation to me. If my story is selected for additional consideration, I understand that I'll be required to complete and sign applications and release forms, and to provide credit and background information. If I am selected to receive financial assistance, I understand that the amount, type, and timing of the assistance will be decided solely by Saving Your American Dream.

I affirm and agree that I am not relying on this opportunity in making decisions about my home, mortgage, or finances. By signing this application, I understand and agree that Saving Your American Dream is not responsible for any claims, actions, damages, liabilities, losses, costs and expenses, including attorney's fees without limitation, that arise from or relate to my personal situation or this application.

_____

Signature

_____

Printed name

_____

Date

# Index

# About the Author

With a career in real estate and lending that spans more than fourteen years, Jason Biro has helped more than 2,000 individuals and families fulfill the dream of owning a home. After years as a mortgage consultant and partner of a residential lending firm, Jason founded Saving Your American Dream as a way to help local communities, and to provide counseling and assistance to those impacted by the housing and lending crisis.